W. D. (William Douglas) Parish

List of Carthusians, 1800-1879

W. D. (William Douglas) Parish
List of Carthusians, 1800-1879
ISBN/EAN: 9783337060428
Printed in Europe, USA, Canada, Australia, Japan
Cover: Foto ©ninafisch / pixelio.de

More available books at **www.hansebooks.com**

LIST

OF

CARTHUSIANS,

1800 TO 1879.

EDITED BY

W. D. PARISH,

Chancellor of Chichester Cathedral, Vicar of Selmeston with Alciston, Sussex.

LEWES: FARNCOMBE AND CO.

1879.

TO

MY SCHOOLFELLOWS,

WHOSE AFFECTION

HAS ADDED SO MUCH TO THE HAPPINESS

OF MY LIFE,

I DEDICATE THIS WORK,

IN THE HOPE THAT IT MAY TEND TO REVIVE

MANY OLD FRIENDSHIPS,

AND UNITE MORE CLOSELY

ALL CARTHUSIANS.

W. D. P.

*N.B.—The Mark * indicates a Gown Boy.*

LIST

OF

CARTHUSIANS,

1800 to 1879.

The Dates following the Names indicate the year of entering and leaving the School.

A.

ABBOTT, Vernon Montague, 1824, b. 1816. Solicitor.

ABDY, Anthony John, 1868-71. Son of J. T. Abdy, late Regius Professor of Civil Law, Cambridge. Of Great Baddow, Chelmsford, b. 1856. Lieut. R.A.

ABDY, Neville James, 1868. Brother of the above, b. 1857. Scholar Trin. Hall, Cam. d. 1878.

ABRAHAM, Lionel Augustus, 1876. Son of Rev. T. E. Abraham, Rector of Risby, Suffolk, b. 1865.

ABRAHAM, Thomas Palmer, 1859-66. Brother of the above, b. 1847. Trin. Hall, Cam. Law Tripos. Called to the Bar; subsequently ordained. Curate of Pakenham.

ACKLAND, Thomas Gilbank, 1801-7, b. 1789. St. John's Coll. Cam. Vicar of St. Mildred's, Bread Street, d. 1844.

ACKLOM.* Harold George, 1865-70. Son of Rev. J. Acklom, b. 1854, d.

ACLAND, Alfred Dyke, 1873. Son of Dr. Acland, Regius Professor of Physic, Oxford.

B

List of Carthusians.

ACLAND,* Herbert Dyke, 1866-72. Brother of the above, *b.* 1855. Ch. Ch. Oxf. *d.* 1877, in Ceylon.

ACOCKS, George John, 1867-68, *b.* 1854.

ACRET, William Henry, 1828, *b.* 1813. Queens Coll. Cam. Holy Orders, *d.*

ADAM, Francis Joseph, 1805-6, *b.* 1791.

ADAMS, Francis Bryant, 1878. Son of F. B. Adams, of The Elms, Croydon.

ADAMS, James Henry, 1817, *b.* 1805.

ADDISON, Thomas Batty, 1802-3. Son of John Addison, of Preston, *b.* 1788. Barrister. Recorder of Preston.

ADDISON, William Dering, 1871. Son of C. G. Addison, *b.* 1859. Merchant's Office, Hamburg.

ADYE, Stephen Bawtree, 1816. Son of Major R. W. Adye, R.A., *b.* 1803. Caius Coll. Cam. 98th Regt. Drowned in fording a river at the Cape of Good Hope, 1832.

AGASSIZ, Arthur, 1810-13, *b.* 1797. Merchant, *d.*

AGASSIZ, Lewis Stanislaus, 1822, *b.* 1812.

AGASSIZ, Robert, 1811-13, *b.* 1800. Trin. Coll. Cam. Formerly Curate of St. Dunstan's-in-the-West.

AINGER, Stewart Delemain, 1875. Son of Rev. Dr. Ainger, Rector of Rothbury, *b.* 1861.

AINGER, Walter Henry, 1876. Brother of the above, *b.* 1864.

AINSLIE, Charles Philip, 1820, *b.* 1808. Colonel of 1st Royal Dragoons. General, 1877.

AINSLIE, Edward Francis, 1874-76. Son of E. Ainslie. E. I. Civil Service.

AINSLIE, Gilbert, 1802-11. Son of Henry Ainslie, M.D. (Senior Wrangler), *b.* 1793. Master of Pemb. Coll. Cam. 9th Wrangler, *d.* 1870.

AINSLIE, Gilbert Hamilton, 1873. Son of Montague Ainslie, of Grizedale, Lanc. *b.* 1859. Civil Engineer.

AINSLIE, Montague (of Grizedale, Lanc.), 1802-7. Son of Henry Ainslie, M.D., *b.* 1792. E. I. Civil Service, Bengal, 1810-35; J.P. and D.L. for Lancashire.

AINSWORTH, Thomas, 1809. Trin. Coll. Cam.

ALCOCK,* George, 1857-62. Son of Ed. Vigors Alcock, of Ballynoe, Co. Carlow, *b.* 1843. Gold Medal. Orator, &c. Scholar B.N.C., Oxf. 1st Class Mods. 3rd Class Lit. Hum. Sub-Warden of St. Columba's College, 1872.

ALDERSON (Sir) Edward Hall (Knt.), 1800-1. Son of Robt. Alderson, Recorder of Norwich, *b.* 1787. Caius Coll. Cam. Senior Wrangler, Smith's Prizeman, Chancellor's Medalist. Appointed Justice of the Court of Common Pleas 1830, and Baron of the Exchequer 1834. Knighted on his elevation to the Bench, *d.* 1857.

ALDERSON, James, 1817. Brother of the above, *b.* 1805, *d.* 1823.

ALDERSON, Robert Jervis Coke, 1816. Brother of the above, *b.* 1802. Ex. Coll. Oxf. Rector of S. Matthew's, Ipswich; and afterwards Rector of Wetherden, Suffolk, *d.* 1868.

ALDRICH, John Cobbold, 1821, *b.* 1807. Linc. Coll. Oxf. Perpet. Curate of St. Lawrence, Ipswich, *d.* 1874.

ALEXANDER, Henry, 1821. Son of Dr. Alexander, a distinguished oculist, *b.* 1810. Medical Student; died young.

ALEXANDER, Richard Chandler, 1822. Son of R. H. Alexander, of Corsham, Wilts, *b.* 1809. Wad. Coll. Ox. M.D., F.R.C.P., an eminent Botanist, changed his name to Prior. J.P. for Somersetshire.

ALEXANDER, Robert (C.B.), 1827. Son of late Robert Alexander, Madras Civil Service, and cousin of late Lord Cranworth, *b.* 1813. Indian Civil Service. Retired, 1859.

ALEXANDER, William Daws, 1823, *b.* 1812.

ALISON, Randal Frederick, 1876-79. Son of Sir Archibald Alison, Bart.

ALLAN, Charles George, 1863. Son of John Allan, of Calcutta, *b.* 1849. Merchant. (Chiselhurst).

ALLAN, Joseph William, 1811, *b.* 1800. Trin. Coll. Cam. Solicitor (Old Jewry).

ALLAN, Thomas Robinson, 1811-17, *b.* 1799. Gold Medal. Trin. Coll. Cam. Barrister,

ALLEN,* Alfred Bird, 1845-53, *b.* 1834. 24th Bengal Native Infantry, Assistant Commissary.

ALLEN,* Francis William Thomas, 1806-8, *b.* 1794.

ALLEN,* George John, 1821-27. Son of Dr. J. Allen, Bishop of Ely, *b.* 1810. Orator. Trin. Coll. Cam. Master of Dulwich College.

ALLEN,* James, 1816. Son Rev. D. B. Allen, Rector of Burton Pembrokeshire, *b.* 1802. Orator. Trin. Coll. Cam. Vicar of Castlemartin, Dean of St. David's, 1878.

ALLEN, John, 1827. Son of John Allen, of Bath, *b.* 1813. B.N.C., Oxf. Holy Orders.

ALLEN, John Henry Thomas, 1823. Son of John Henry Allen, *b.* 1809. B.N.C., Oxf. Holy Orders.

ALLEN, Robert, 1827, *b.* 1816. Corpus Coll. Cam. *d.* 1846.

ALLEN, William, 1817. Brother of James Allen, *b.* 1800. Jesus Coll. Oxf. Rector of Besherston and St. Bride's, *d.* 1872.

ALLEN, William Joseph, 1821. Son of the Bishop of Ely, *b.* 1812. India Civil Service.

ALLISTON, Charles, 1819, *b.* 1808. Solicitor in London.

ALLISTON, George, 1823, *b.* 1812. Solicitor, deceased.

ALLSOP, Charles Watkinson, 1825, *b.* 1813.

ALMOND, Harry John, 1863, *b.* 1850. Civil Engineer, Costa Rica.

ALSOP, Henry Griffin, 1818, *b.* 1804.

ALSTON, Albert, 1834-37. Scholar of St. John's Coll. Cam. Solicitor; subsequently ordained. Curate of St. Botolph's, Aldgate, Chaplain to the Lord Mayor; deceased.

ALSTON, Herbert, 1854-58, *b.* 1838. St. John's Coll. Cam. Rector of Little Bradley.

AMES, John Carlowitz, 1873-78. Son of G. Ames. Went to the University of Edinburgh.

AMES, Oswald Henry, 1875. Son of Lionel Neville F. Ames, of the Hyde, Luton, Beds, *b.* 1862.

AMOS,* Andrew, 1877. Son of Rev. Jas. Amos, formerly Vicar of St. Stephen's, Southwark, *b.* 1863.

List of Carthusians.

AMOS,* Sheldon, 1848-53. Son of Andrew Amos, Legal Member of the Supreme Council of India, b. 1835. Clare Coll. Cam. Senior Op. 2nd Class Classical Tripos. Barrister, Professor of Jurisprudence, Univ. Coll. London, &c., &c. Author of several legal works.

ANCRUM, George Wayland, 1878. Son of William Rutherford Ancrum, b. 1864.

ANCRUM, Sydney Rutherford, 1874. Brother of the above, b. 1860.

ANDERSON,* Fortescue Lennox McDonald, 1844-51. Son of Rev. James Anderson, Preacher of Lincoln's Inn, b. 1832. Worc. Coll. Oxf. Incumbent of St.Baldred's, North Berwick.

ANDERSON, Herbert Goulburn, 1856-60. Son of Rev. Robt. Anderson, of Brighton, b. 1842. Civil Engineer, d.

ANDERSON, John, 1827. Son of General Anderson, b. 1815. Merton Coll. Oxf. Formerly Rector of Norton le Moors.

ANDERSON, Musgrave Wroughton, 1848-52. Brother of F. L. M. Anderson (above), b. 1836. Governor of the Goldfields, Australia, d. 1870.

ANDERSON,* Noel Robert, 1848-57. Son of Rev. Robert Anderson, of Brighton, b. 1838. Ch. Ch. Oxf. Admiralty Office, d. 1868.

ANDERSON, William, 1820, b. 1807.

ANDREW, Alfred, 1844-45, b. 1827. Merchant at Liverpool.

ANDREWS,* Charles, 1805-11. Son of the Rev. Mr. Andrews, Rector of Great Henny, Essex, b. 1795. Indian Staff Corps, Major-General. Served in Punjab Campaign, &c. Medal and clasps, d.

ANDREWS, Charles, 1834-39. Surgeon at Salisbury. Afterwards to India.

ANDREWS, John Leslie, 1864. Son of Mr. Andrews, of Hatch Street, Dublin, b. 1850.

ANDREWS, John Oneby, 1822. Son of Mr. Andrews, of Watford (Surgeon), b. 1809. House Surgeon to the Lock Hospital.

ANSON,* Arthur Henry, 1827-36. Son of Dr. Frederick Anson, Dean of Chester, b. 1817. Orator. Ball. Coll. Oxf. Fellow of All Souls', Oxf. Holy Orders, d. 1859.

ANSON,* George Henry Greville, 1833-39. Cousin of the above and son of Sir William Anson, Bt., b. 1820. Ex. Coll. Oxf. Curate of the Parish Church, Leeds, 1843-46, Rector of Birch in Rusholme, Archdeacon of Manchester.

ANSON,* Theodosius Vernon, 1819. Son of Sir George Anson, K.C.B., b. 1808. Died young.

ANTROBUS, Edward Gream, 1872-78. Son of Rev. George Antrobus, Vicar of Beighton, Derbysh. b. 1860. Crown Agents Office for the Colonies.

APPLEBEE, Henry, 1809-12, b. 1794. Trin. Coll. Cam.

APPLEWHAITE, Edward Archer, 1812-17. Son of Edward A. Applewhaite, of Barbados, b. 1800. Of Pickenham Hall, Norfolk.

APPLEWHAITE, Philip Lythcott, 1808-14. Brother of the above, of Barbados, b. 1795. Queens Coll. Oxf. Died Barbados, 1835.

APPLEYARD, Robert Boultbee, 1811, b. 1798.

APTHORP, Kendal Pretyman, 1875. Son of Capt. Apthorp.

ARCHDALE, George Fitzroy, 1878. Son of F. Archdale, Baldock, Herts.

ARCHDALE, William Frederick, 1874. Brother of the above.

ARCHER, Charles Goodwyn, 1839-42. Son of Thomas Archer, of Ely, b. 1824. Scholar of Jesus Coll. Cam. Rector of Alderton.

ARCHER, Goodwyn, 1827. Brother of the above, b. 1813. Solicitor at Ely.

ARCHER, Goodwyn Alfred, 1856-60. Son of the above, b. 1841. Emm. Coll. Cam. Rector of Campsey Ash.

ARCHER, Harold, 1858-62. Brother of the above, b. 1845. Solicitor, Ely.

ARMITSTEAD,* Sidney Henry, 1849-56. Son of Rev. J. Armitstead, Vicar of Sandbach, b. 1837. Ch. Ch. Oxf. Vicar of St. John's, Sandbach Heath.

ARMSTRONG, James, 1855-59. Son of Rev. Nicolas Armstrong, b. 1840. Talbot Scholar. Oriel Coll. Oxf.

List of Carthusians. 7

ARMSTRONG, John, 1807-9. Son of Dr. Armstrong, of Bishops Wearmouth, b. 1797.

ARMSTRONG, John, 1827. Son of Dr. Armstrong, an eminent physician, b. 1813. Linc. Coll. Oxf. 3rd Class. Vicar of Tiddenham, Bishop of Grahamstown, d. 1856.

ARMSTRONG, Thomas, 1807-9, b. 1795.

ARNOULD (Sir) Joseph (Knt.), 1826. Son of Joseph Arnould, of Whitecross, Berks, b. 1813. Fellow of Wadh. Coll. Oxf. 1st Class Lit. Hum. Newdegate prize, Judge of the Supreme Court of Bombay. Knighted, 1859.

ARTHUR,* R., 1815.

ARUNDEL, John Brazier, 1821, b. 1807.

ARUNDELL, Hon. Henry, 1823. Son of the 9th Baron Arundel, b. 1811, d. 1857.

ASHHURST, James Henry, 1834-36. Son of W. H. Ashhurst, of Waterstock, Oxon. Ex. Coll. Oxf. Vicar of Waterstock.

ASHHURST, John Henry, 1826. Son of W. H. Ashhurst, of Waterstock, Oxon, b. 1813. Now Squire of Waterstock.

ASHHURST, William Henry, 1823. Brother of the above, b. 1807. Capt. 21st Foot, d. 1843.

ASKEW, John, 1818, b. 1804. Em. Coll. Cam. Holy Orders.

ATHERTON, Edward Sextus, 1816-17, b. 1804.

ATHERTON, Thomas James, 1869-76. Son of Sir William Atherton, b. 1856.

ATHERTON, Walter Hyde, 1868-72. Brother of the above, b. 1855. Caius Coll. Cam. Lieut. 5th Dragoon Guards.

ATHILL, John, 1814-15, b. 1800.

ATKINSON, George, 1818, b. 1809.

ATKINSON, George Clayton, 1823. Son of Matthew Atkinson, Carr's Hill, Durham, b. 1808. J.P. of Northumberland, d. 1877.

ATKINSON, George Dixon, 1854 (see G. D. A. Clark).

ATKINSON, Henry George, 1827, *b.* 1812.

ATKINSON, Isaac, 1823. Brother of Geo. Clayton Atkinson, *b.* 1809, died young.

ATKINSON, Richard, 1826. Brother of the above, *b.* 1812, deceased.

ATKINSON, Thomas, 1854-58. Son of Rev. Wm. Atkinson, Gateshead, *b.* 1840. Univ. Coll. Oxf. Perpetual Curate of Yiewsley, West Drayton.

ATKINSON, William Adair, 1854-59 (see W. A. A. Clark).

AUBERTIN, Daniel, 1827. Son of Rev. Peter Aubertin, Rector of Chipstead, *b.* 1814, *d.* 1831.

AUBERTIN, Paul, 1829. Brother of the above, *b.* 1817. Merchant, London.

AUBERTIN, Peter, 1827. Brother of the above, *b.* 1811. Wadh. Coll. Oxf. Rector of Chipstead.

AUBREY, Samuel Charles, 1827, *b.* 1812.

AUSTIN, Henry, 1801-2.

AUSTIN, William, 1810-11.

AWDRY,* John Dea, 1815-18. Son of Rev. Jeremiah Awdry, Vicar of Felsted, *b.* 1801. Was a Major-Gen. in the Madras Service.

AYLES, John, 1815-16, *b.* 1803.

AYTON, William Alexander, 1830, *b.* 1816. Trin. Coll. Cam. Rector of Scampton, Lincolnshire.

B.

BABINGTON, Arthur, 1812. Son of Wm. Babington, M.D., *b.* 1797. Trin. Coll. Cam. *d.* 1821.

BABINGTON, Benjamin Guy, 1803-7. Brother of the above, *b.* 1794. Pemb. Coll. Cam. M.D. Physician to Charterhouse, *d.* 1866.

BABINGTON, Charles Cardale, 1821. Son of Rev. Joseph Babington, *b.* 1808. St. John's Coll. Cam. Professor of Botany at Cambridge, F.R.S. F.S.A.

BABINGTON, Charles Roos, 1819. Son of Sir Thos. Babington, of Rothley Temple, Leicestershire, M.P. *b.* 1806. E. I. Civil Service, died young.

BABINGTON, Charles Walter, 1852-55, *b.* 1841.

BABINGTON, David, 1812-16. Brother of Arthur Babington, *b.* 1800, died while a medical student at Paris.

BABINGTON, John Hastings, 1852-55, *b.* 1843.

BABINGTON, Stephen, 1804-5. Brother of David Babington. E. I. Civil Service, Bombay. Secy. to Sir M. Nepean, the Governor, died in India.

BABINGTON, Stephen, 1834-36. Son of the above. E. I. Civil Service, Bombay, *d.* 1846.

BABINGTON, Stephen Peile, 1833-39. Son of Dr. B. G. Babington. A merchant in London.

BABINGTON, Thomas Francis, 1852-55, *b.* 1841.

BACK, Henry, 1826, *b.* 1811.

BACON, Reginald Cazalet, 1875. Son of Rev. F. Bacon, of Much Hadham, Herts, *b.* 1861.

BADCOCK, Audry, 1851-53, *b.* 1837.

BADDELEY, Henry Daniell, 1864, *b.* 1851. 1st Lieut. Bombay Marine.

BADDELEY, Paul Frederick Henry, 1820, *b.* 1807.

BADELEY, John Carr, 1808-11, *b.* 1794. Caius Coll. Cam. M.D., of Chelmsford and Brighton, *d.* 1851.

BADEN-POWELL, Baden Fletcher Smyth, 1873-77. Son of Rev. Baden Powell, Savilian Professor at Oxford, *b.* 1860.

BADEN-POWELL,* Robert Stephenson Smyth, 1870-76. Brother of the above, *b.* 1857. Lieut. 13th Hussars.

BADHAM, James, 1823, *b.* 1815.

BAGGE, Edward, 1826. Son of Thos. P. Bagge, of Stradsett Hall, Norfolk, *b.* 1812. Merchant, Mayor of Lynn.

BAGGE, Richard, 1820. Brother of the above, *b.* 1810. Merchant. King's Lynn.

BAGGE (Sir) William (Bart.), 1820. Brother of the above, *b.* 1810. Ball. Coll. Oxf. M.P. for West Norfolk. Created a Baronet 1867.

BAGNEL, Robert, 1808-10. Trin. Coll. Cam.

BAGOT, Alexander, 1837. Son of late Hon. Sir Charles Bagot, G.C.B. *b.* 1822. Lieut.-Col. 15th Bengal Native Infantry, A.D.C. to the Governor-General.

BAGOT, Charles, 1819. Brother of the above, *b.* 1808. Colonel Gren. Guards, retired.

BAGOT, Edward Richard, 1818. Son of the Bishop of Bath and Wells, *d.* 1877.

BAGOT, Hon. William (Lord Bagot), 1820. Eldest son of the 2nd Baron Bagot, *b.* 1811. M.P. for Denbighshire, 1835-52. Succeeded as 3rd Lord Bagot 1856.

BAILEY, John James, 1851-53, *b.* 1837.

BAILEY, Rishton Robinson, 1825, *b.* 1809.

BAILLIE,   , 1805-8.

BAILLIE, Grant, 1821, *b.* 1808, deceased.

BAILLIE, John, 1821, *b.* 1810. Trin. Coll. Cam.

BAINES, Henry Ramsay, 1827, *b.* 1813.

BAKER, 1800-8. Son of M.P. for Canterbury.

BAKER, Brackstone, 1822, *b.* 1810. In business in London.

BAKER, Cecil Cautley, 1868, *b.* 1856. Son of Eric Thomas Baker (below).

BAKER, Cecil Edward, 1872.

BAKER, Eric Thomas, 1823, *b.* 1809.

BAKER, Ernest Edward, 1868. Twin brother of C. C. Baker, *b.* 1856. Went to Felstead School. Mathematical scholar, Clare Coll. Cam.

BAKER, Frank Ernest, 1872.

BAKER, Henry, 1823, *b.* 1811.

BAKER, Herbert, 1858-59. Brother of E. E. Baker, *b.* 1843.

BAKER,* John Julius, 1850-56. Son of Colonel George Baker, *b.* 1838. Ex. Coll. Oxf. Curate of Yoxall.

BAKER, Stephen Cattley, 1822. Brother of Brackstone Baker, *b.* 1811. St. John's Coll. Cam. Vicar of Usk, Monmouthshire.

BAKER, William, 1815-16, *b.* 1801.

BALDWIN, Edmund, 1823, *b.* 1810.

BALFOUR, Henry, 1877. Son of Lewis Balfour, *b.* 1863.

BALLANCE, Josiah Descarrieres, 1845-48. Son of John Ballance, of Clapton, *b.* 1829. Trin. Coll. Cam. 25th Wrangler. Vicar of Horsford, Norfolk.

BANBURY, Edward, 1873. Son of William Banbury, Banker in London.

BANKHEAD, William Robert, 1807, *b.* 1792.

BANNATYNE, Charles, 1817. Son of John Bannatyne, *b.* 1805. Ball. Coll. Oxf. Rector of Aldham, Essex.

BANNISTER, Charles George, 1808-11. Son of J. Bannister, *b.* 1796. Solicitor to the War Office, *d.* 1858.

BANNISTER, Charles William, 1838. Son of the above, *b.* 1826. 2nd Bombay Light Cavalry. Medal. Governor of Maidstone Gaol, *d.* 1874.

BARHAM, Charles Henry, 1821. Son of late Joseph Foster Barham, M.P., *b.* 1809. Ch. Ch. Oxf. M.P. for Appleby 1831-2. Afterwards took Holy Orders, and became Rector of Barming, Kent, *d.* 1878.

BARING, James Drummond, 1822. Son of Henry Baring, and nephew of the first Lord Ashburton, *b.* 1809.

BARKER, 1803.

BARKER, Benjamin, 1826, *b.* 1814. Caius Coll. Cam. Holy Orders. Shipdham, Norfolk.

BARKER, Frederick Hubert, 1878. Son of F. Barker, of Leeds.

BARKER, Henry John, 1851-55, *b.* 1837.

BARKER,* John, 1813-18, *b.* 1800.

BARKER, Joseph Henry, 1822. Son of Joseph Gibbs Barker, *b.* 1809. St. John's Coll. Cam. Wrangler. Chaplain of the County Gaol, Hereford.

BARKER, Richard, 1805-8, *b.* 1791. Solicitor.

BARKER, Richard, 1821. Son of Francis E. Barker, Solicitor, Chester, *b.* 1808. Solicitor at Chester, *d.* 1877.

BARKER, Thomas Francis, 1821. Brother of the above, *b.* 1810. B.N.C. Oxf. Rector of Thornton, Chester, *d.* 1878.

BARKER, William Gibbs, 1822. Brother of Joseph H. Barker *b.* 1809. St. John's Coll. Cam. Senior Op. Incumbent of Trinity Church, New Barnet.

BARKWORTH, Walter Theodore, 1874. Son of Rev. Dr. Barkworth, formerly Vicar of Grey Friars, Reading, *b.* 1859. St. John's Coll. Oxf.

BARLEE,* Reginald, 1855-61, *b.* 1845. Emigrated to Australia.

BARLOW, Charles John, 1876. Son of Rev. J. M. Barlow, Rector of Ewhurst.

BARLOW, Francis, 1813-17. Son of Rev. Francis George Barlow, Rector of Burgh, Suffolk, *b.* 1799. Trin. Hall Cam. Barrister. Senior Master in Lunacy.

BARLOW, Harold, 1874-79. Brother of C. J. Barlow (above). Cooper's Hill Coll.

BARMBY, Cuthbert, 1877. Son of Rev. James Barmby, Rector of Pitlington, Durham.

BARMBY, Francis James, 1877. Brother of the above.

BARNARD, George Martin, 1814-15. Son of Rev. Thos. Barnard, Vicar of Gt. Amwell, Herts, *b.* 1799. Clerk in the Treasury, *d.* 1859.

BARNARD,* Mordaunt, 1806-13. Brother of the above, *b.* 1795. Ch. Coll. Cam. Porteus medallist; late Rector of Preston Bagot. Rural Dean. J.P. for Essex.

BARNARD, Mordaunt Roger, 1843-44. Eldest son of the above, *b.* 1828. To Rugby School. Ch. Coll. Cam. Vicar of Margaretting. Chaplain at Christiania.

BARNARD, Philip Adolphus, 1822. Son of Rev. Robt. Cary Barnard, Rector of Withersfield, Suffolk, *b.* 1811. Served in the 24th Regt. Queen's Messenger.

BARNARD,* Thomas Mordaunt Rosenhagen, 1805-8. Brother of Mordaunt Barnard (above). Royal Navy. Died of his wounds, 1813.

BARNARD, Thomas Mordaunt Rosenhagen, 1843. Son of W. S. Barnard, of Calcutta, *b.* 1829. Ex. Coll. Oxf. Holy Orders. Chipping Ongar, Essex, *d.* 1878.

BARNARD, William Osborne, 1853-5, *b.* 1838. Major 96th Regt.

BARNES, Barrington Syer, 1848-51, *b.* 1834. St. John's Coll. Cam. Rector of Chignal, Essex.

BARNES, James, 1861, *b.* 1851.

BARNES, James Alexander, 1807-14, *b.* 1798. Fellow of Trin. Coll. Cam. Rector of Gilling, Yorks.

BARNES, John, 1807-9. Son of John Barnes, of Finchley, *b.* 1797, *d.* 1841.

BARNES, John Edward, 1843-48. Brother of B. S. Barnes, *b.* 1832. Surgeon at Clare, Suffolk.

BARNES, John Henry, 1844-49, *b.* 1833.

BARNES, Keith, 1815-17. Brother of John Barnes (above), *b.* 1801. Solicitor in London, *d.* 1865.

BARNES, Medley Edward, 1844-48, *b.* 1832.

BARNES, Peter Leather, 1861-62, *b.* 1852.

BARNES, Richard Barnes, 1815. Brother of Keith Barnes (above), *b.* 1804. Stock Broker, *d.* 1845.

BARNES, William Maule, 1822. Brother of the above, *b.* 1811. Trin. Coll. Cam. Holy Orders, *d.* 1848 (circ.).

BARNETT, John Edward, 1875. Son of J. Barnett, Coleraine House, Stamford Hill.

BARNETT, Robert Sydney, 1874. Brother of the above.

BARNETT, Walter, 1878. Brother of the above.

BAROUGH, Alfred Robert, 1861. Son of Mr. Barough, of Hatton Gardens, *b.* 1851.

BARRETT, Edward Moulton, 1820. Son of Edward Moulton Barrett, of Hope End, Herefordshire, *b.* 1807. Drowned at Torquay, 1839.

BARRETT, Joseph Radcliffe, 1820, *b.* 1810.

BARRETT, Samuel Moulton, 1821. Brother of E. M. Barrett (above), *b.* 1812. Died in Jamaica, 1842.

BARRINGTON, Hon. Augustus, 1812-14. Son of 5th Visct. Barrington, *b.* 1798. D.C.L. and Fellow of All Souls', Oxf. Barrister, *d.* 1860.

BARRINGTON,* Charles George, 1837-44. Son of the late Hon. Geo. Barrington, *b.* 1827. Trin. Coll. Cam. The Treasury.

BARRINGTON, Hon. Henry Frederic Francis Adair, 1819. Brother of Hon. Augustus Barrington, b. 1808. Ch. Ch. Oxf. Barrister.

BARRINGTON, John Beatty, 1873. Son of Sir Croker Barrington, Bt., of Glenstal, Limerick, b. 1860.

BARRINGTON, Hon. Lowther John, 1818. Brother of Hon. Augustus Barrington b. 1805. Oriel Coll. Oxf. Rector of Watton, Herts and Hon. Canon of St. Albans.

BARRON, Hunter Jackson, 1867. Son of E. J. Barron, F.S.A., b. 1857. Medical practitioner in London.

BARROW (Sir) George (Bart.), 1819. Eldest son of Sir John Barrow, Bart. b. 1806. Succeeded his father in 1848. Colonial Office. Author of "Ceylon Past and Present," d. 1876.

BARROW,* George Staunton, 1845-53. Son of late Sir George Barrow, Bt. b. 1834. Univ. and Pemb. Coll. Oxf. Vicar of Stowmarket.

BARROW, John, 1819. Brother of Sir George Barrow (above), b. 1808. F.R.S. F.R.G.S. Keeper of the Records at the Admiralty, took an active part in promoting the search for Sir John Franklin. Senr. Major 36th Middlesex Rifles.

BARROW, William, 1820. Brother of the above, b. 1810. Commander R.N. Present at Navarino, d. 1838.

BARROW, William Clarke, 1852-54, b. 1836, d. 1855.

BARROWS, Arthur Murdock, 1878. Son of T. W. Barrows, of Banbury, Oxon.

BARROWS, Harold Murdock, 1874. Brother of the above, b. 1861. Articled to a Solicitor at Birmingham.

BARRY, Douglas, 1864-71. Son of Horace Barry, of Enfield, b. 1853. Ex. Coll. Oxf. Curate of Hitchin.

BARRY, Horace, 1864-68. Brother of the above, b. 1852. King's Coll. London. Merchant.

BARTLETT, John, 1810-12, b. 1797. Went to Westminster School.

BARTON, Aubrey David, 1878. Son of the late Thomas Henry Barton, and grandson of Lord Plunket.

BARTON, Frank, 1854-61, *b.* 1843. Chole Abbey, Isle of Wight.

BARTON, William Henry, 1854-55, *b.* 1840, *d.* 1856.

BARTRUM, Edmund Charles, 1823, *b.* 1810. Solicitor in London.

BARTTELOT, David Smyth, 1837-39. Son of Col. Barttelot, of Stopham, Sussex, *b.* 1821. Jesus Coll. Cam. Scholar of Corpus Coll. Oxon ; died at Sydney, N.S.W. 1852.

BARWELL, John Edric Hayward, 1876. Son of J. Barwell, of Hoveton Hall, Norfolk.

BATCHELOR, Jonathan Trelawny, 1874. Son of Rev. F. T. Batchelor, Rector of Jacobstow, *b.* 1859. Scholar Sid. Suss. Coll. Cam.

BATE, William, 1807-11, *b.* 1794. Trin. Coll. Cam.

BATEMAN, Hugh Athelstan, 1826, *b.* 1810.

BATES,* Charles Cecil, 1801-2, *b.* 1791. Ch. Coll. Cam. Vicar of Castleton, Derbysh.

BATES (Sir) Henry (K.C.B.), 1824. Son of Major Henry Bates, R.A., *b.* 1813. Col. 9th Foot, 1863; General 1877. Medals—Sobraon, Chillianwallah and Goojerat.

BATES, Thomas Holden, 1824, *b.* 1813.

BATHURST,* Allen, 1838-41, *b.* 1827. Royal Navy.

BATTEN, Charles Hamilton, 1842-46, *b.* 1827. St. John's Coll. Cam. Holy Orders, *d.* 1852.

BATTEN,* George Henry Maxwell, 1842-49, *b.* 1832. Bengal Civil Service.

BATTEN,* John Hallett, 1825. Son of Rev. Dr. Batten, F.R.S., Principal of Haileybury College, *b.* 1811. Bengal Civil Service. Officiating Judge of Suddur Court, N.W. Provinces, (retired).

BATTISCOMBE,* William, 1811. Son of Robt. Battiscombe, of Clewer, *b.* 1800. Pemb. Coll. Oxf. Assistant Master. Rector of Horseheath, *d.*

BATTISCOMBE, William Benjamin, 1843-48. Son of the above, *b.* 1830. Major 91st Foot (retired).

BAUGH, Folliott, 1820. Son of the Rev. J. W. Baugh, *b.* 1809. Ex. Coll. and Fellow of All Souls', Oxf. 1st Class Classics, Preacher of Charterhouse, Vicar of Chelsfield, *d.*

BAXENDALE, Francis Richard Salisbury, 1875. Son of Rev. R. Baxendale, St. John's, Maidstone.

BAXTER, George, 1826, *b*. 1813.

BAYLEY,* George Thornton, 1801-6, *b*. 1790. Indian Civil Service.

BAYLEY, Thomas Butterworth Charles, 1825, *b*. 1811.

BAYLEY, Wilton Rees, 1827, *b*. 1812.

BAYLIFF, Richard Lane, 1845-50. Son of Rev. T. T. L. Bayliff, of Albury, *b*. 1833. Army. Served in 33rd Regt. in Crimea. Capt. 100th Regt. Retired 1870.

BAYLIFF, Thomas Lane, 1850-53. Brother of the above, *b*. 1840. Indian Army. Killed in the Mutiny, 1857.

BAYLIFF, Thomas Timothy Lane, 1819. Son of T. G. Bayliff, of Southgate, *b*. 1806. St. John's Coll. Oxf. Vicar of Albury, Herts.

BAYLIFF, William Entwistle Lane, 1846-51. Son of the above, *b*. 1835. H.M. Civil Service.

BAYNES,* Charles Robert, 1820. Son of Col. Baynes, Royal Artillery, *b*. 1809. Madras Civil Service; retired.

BEADON, Richard A'Court, 1820. Son of late Richard Beadon, *b*. 1809. St. John's Coll. Cam. Vicar of Cheddar.

BEALE, William St. John, 1878. Son of Rev. T. Beale, Rector of Hopton Castle.

BEALES, Charles, 1802-5, *b*. 1789. Peter Ho. Coll. Cam. Merchant.

BEALES, Patrick, 1808-11, *b*. 1797. Cambridge. Merchant.

BEASLEY, John Theodore Hume, 1869. Son of John Beasley, of Chapel Brampton, Northants, *b*. 1860. The School, Bedford.

BEASLEY, Joseph Noble, 1845-49. Son of Capt. Wm. Beasley, *b*. 1832, 87th Regt. Bt. Lieut.-Col. 1877. Served in the Indian Mutiny (medal).

BEAUCHAMP,* Maurice, 1811-18. Son of William Henry Beauchamp, of Forthampton, Co. Gloucester, *b*. 1801. Capt. Indian Army.

BEAUCLERK, Aubrey Frederic, 1826. Son of the Rev. Lord Frederick Beauclerk, *b*. 1817. Guards and 7th Foot, *d*. 1852.

BEAUCLERK, Charles William, 1826. Brother of the above, *b.* 1816. Ch. Ch. Oxf. *d.* 1863.

BEAUCLERK, Frederic Amelius, 1864. Son of the late Lord F. Beauclerk, *b.* 1851.

BEAUCLERK (Lord) George Augustus, 1831. Son of the 8th Duke of St. Albans, *b.* 1818. Served with 10th Hussars in the Crimea (medal). Retired as Major 6th Dragoon Guards.

BEAUFORD, Henry William, 1823, of Eaton Socon, Beds. *b.* 1814. Magd. Coll. Cam.

BEAUMONT, Francis William, 1820, *b.* 1809. Trin. Coll. Cam. A.B. 1831.

BEAVAN, Hugh Maurice, 1872, Son of Edward Beavan, of Wimbledon, Barrister, *b.* 1857. Caius Coll. Cam. Lieut. 21st Hussars.

BECHER, George Richard, 1820, *b.* 1808.

BECKFORD, George (Lord Rivers), 1821. Eldest son of Horace W. Beckford, 3rd Lord Rivers, *b.* 1810; succeeded as 4th Lord Rivers 1831, *d.* 1866.

BEDDOES, Charles Henry, 1817. Brother of C. H. Beddoes (below), *b.* 1805. Royal Navy.

BEDDOES, Thomas Lovell, 1817. Son of Dr. Beddoes, and nephew of Maria Edgeworth, *b.* 1803. Pemb. Coll. Oxf. M.D. of Wurzburg. Poet and Dramatist, Author of "The Bride's Tragedy," "Poems," &c. *d.* 1849.

BEDDOME, Richard Henry, 1843-46, *b.* 1830. Col. Madras Staff Corps. Conservator of Forests (Madras).

BEDFORD, John, 1815-17, *b.* 1806.

BEDFORD, Richard Bisse Riland, 1844-48. Son of Rev. W. R. Bedford, Sutton Coldfield, Warwick, *b.* 1830. B.N.C. Oxf. 79th Highlanders; retired. Adjutant 5th Adm. Battn. Staffordshire Rifle Volunteers, 1861.

BEET, John G., 1809-16, *b.* 1800.

BELL, Alexander, 1807-10, *b.* 1794. India Civil Service.

BELL, Cornwallis, 1803.

BELL, George Panton, 1830, *b.* 1820.

BELL, James, 1827, *b.* 1817. Queens Coll. Cam. A.B. 1837.

C

BELL, John William, 1822.

BELL, Melville, 1878. Son of J. R. Bell, a Merchant in Ceylon.

BELL, Richard, 1822, *b.* 1816.

BELL, Robert, 1807-10, *b.* 1793. Lieut.-Col. E. I. Artillery. (Madras)

BELL, William, 1800-6. Went to India.

BELLI, Charles Scott, 1839-42. Son of Rev. C. A. Belli, Preby. of St. Paul's, *b.* 1826. Bengal Civil Service. Retired 1872.

BELLI,* Walter Forbes, 1844-49. Brother of the above, *b.* 1833. Bengal Native Infantry, *d.* 1861.

BELOE, Henry Parr, 1800. Son of Rev. Wm. Beloe, F.S.A., &c., *b.* 1790. C.C.C. Cam. Rector of Guildford, *d.* 1838.

BELSON, James Harwood, 1843-46, *b.* 1829, *d.* 1846.

BELSON, William Eveleigh, 1842-45. Brother of the above, *b.* 1826. Oriel Coll. Oxf. Missionary at the Cape. Vicar of Colemere, Salop.

BENCE, Edward Robert Starkie, 1835-41. Son of Col. H. B. S. Bence, of Thorington Hall, Suffolk. (See below), *b.* 1823. 1st Dragoon Gds. Kentwell Hall, Long Melford.

BENCE, Henry Alexander Starkie, 1826-34. Elder brother of the above, *b.* 1806. Ball. Coll. Oxf. Now of Thorington Hall. J.P. and D.L. of Suffolk.

BENCE, Henry Bence Sparrow, 1802-4. Eldest son of Rev. Bence Sparrow, *b.* 1788. Colonel. Served in 16th Lancers, 60th Rifles, and 7th Dragoon Guards. Wounded at Talavera. Peninsula Medal, *d.* 1861.

BENCE, Thomas Starkie, 1835-42. Son of the above, *b.* 1824. St. John's Coll. Cam. Rector of Thorington.

BENETT, John, 1822. Son of John Benet, M.P., of Pythouse and Norton Bavant, Wilts, *b.* 1809; deceased.

BENNETT, Frederic Debell, 1821, *b.* 1808.

BENNETT, James Robert Abrahall, 1875. Son of Rev. J. H. Bennett. Grammar School, Solihull. Went to London University.

BENNETT, Rowland Nevitt, 1822, *b.* 1809. Solicitor in London.

BENSLEY, Charles Norman, 1877. Son of Dr. Bensley, of Kishnaghur.

BENSLEY, Edwin Edward, 1878. Brother of the above.

BENTLEY, , 1804. (Lived in Red Lion Square).

BENTLEY, Herbert Lowndes, 1871-72. Son of Rev. Samuel Bentley, Vicar of Bosbury, Herefordshire, *b.* 1859. In the Merchant Service.

BENYON, Richard, 1823. (See Fellowes). Son of Wm. Henry Fellowes, of Ramsey Abbey, Hunts, *b.* 1811. Took the name of Benyon. St. John's Coll. Cam. Barrister. Was M.P. for Berks 1860-76.

BERDMORE, Hugh Thomas Matthew, 1825, *b.* 1812.

BERDMORE, St. John Vesey, 1825, *b.* 1813. Army, 63rd Foot.

BERDMORE,* Samuel Charles James, 1819-24. Son of Thomas Berdmore, of Chelsea, *b.* 1807. Orator. Student Ch. Ch. Oxf.

BERDMORE, William de Lisle, 1825, *b.* 1816.

BERE, Montague Classell, 1867. Son of Montague Bere, Q C., of Morebath, Devon, *b.* 1856. In business in London.

BERESFORD, Edward, 1877. Son of G. D. Beresford, M.P. for Armagh, *b.* 1863.

BERESFORD, Henry William de la Poer, 1874. Son of Rev. J. G. Beresford, Bedale, Yorks, *b.* 1862.

BERKELEY,* Charles Paul, 1840-44. Nephew of G. C. Berkeley, *b.* 1828. Land Surveyor, *d.* 1853.

BERKELEY,* George Campion, 1822-32. Son of Chas. Berkeley, of Biggin Hall, Northants, *b.* 1812. Pemb. Coll. Oxf. Vicar of Southminster.

BERNAL (Osborne), Ralph, 1819. Son of Ralph Bernal, M.P. *b.* 1808. Trin. Coll. Cam. 7th Fusiliers, M.P. for Liskeard, &c. Sec. to the Admiralty, 1852-58.

BERNARD, John Frederic, 1826, *b.* 1814. Solicitor in London.

BERNEY, George Duckett, 1826. Son of the late Thomas Trench Berney, of Morton Hall, Norfolk, *b.* 1813. St. John's Coll. Cam. of Morton Hall, Norwich,

BERNEY, Thomas, 1829. Brother of the above, *b.* 1816. St. John's Coll. Cam. formerly Rector of Hockering, Norfolk. Lord of the Manor and Rector of Bracon Ash.

BERRIDGE, James Samuel, 1818, *b.* 1806.

BERRY, George James, 1812-18. Son of John Alexander Berry, *b.* 1800. Emm. Coll. Cam. Barrister of Lincoln's Inn, *d.* 1872.

BERRY, Oswald Philip, 1851-54, *b.* 1843.

BERRY, Richard James, 1821, *b.* 1808.

BERRYMAN, Charles Powell, 1866-67. Son of Rev. J. W. Berryman, Rector of Tydd St. Giles, Cambs. *b.* 1854. St. John's Coll. Oxf. Curate of Ashford.

BESNARD, Julius Cæsar, 1823, *b.* 1809. Trin. Coll. Dublin.

BEST, Francis Whittingham, 1856-57. Son of the following, *b.* 1842.

BEST, George, 1811-17. Son of George Nathaniel Best, of Bayfield Hall, Norfolk, *b.* 1799. Ch. Coll. Cam. Of Eastbury Manor, Guildford.

BEST, Nathaniel, 1812-18. Brother of the above, *b.* 1801. Ball. Coll. Oxf. Holy Orders, *d.* 1841.

BEST, Nathl. Loftus, 1857-62. Son of George Best (above), *b.* 1843.

BEVAN, Charles Dacres, 1818. Son of Charles Bevan, of Bath, *b.* 1805. Ball. Coll. Oxf. Barrister. Judge of County Court, Cornwall, *d.*

BEVAN, Thomas, 1819, *b.* 1806. Holy Orders.

BEVIR, John, 1819, *b.* 1806. Solicitor at Cirencester, *d.* 1860.

BEWES, Anstis John, 1829-32. Son of Thos. Bewes, of Beaumont, Plymouth, *b.* 1814. 8th Foot, *d.* 1835.

BEWES, Cecil Edward, 1831-33. Brother of the above, *b.* 1816. Capt. 85th Foot; retired 1849.

BEWES, Charles Theodore, 1832-35. Brother of the above, *b.* 1817. Solicitor at Stonehouse, Devon.

BICKNELL, Henry, 1811-12, *b.* 1796. Solicitor.

BICKNER, Henry James, 1805-9, *b.* 1796.

BICKNER, Otto, 1805-9, *b.* 1794. Barrister.

BIDDULPH, Theophilus, 1817-18. Son of Rev. Thos. Biddulph, of Bristol, *b.* 1802. Scholar of Corpus Coll. Oxf. 2nd Class Lit. Hum.

BIGNELL, William Philips, 1814, *b.* 1803. Went to Westminster.

BILL, John, 1812-13. Son of John Bill, of Farley Hall. Staffordshire, *b.* 1799. J.P., *d.* 1853.

BINGHAM, Peregrine, 1831. Son of late P. Bingham, Police Magistrate, *b.* 1820. Jesus Coll. Cam. Holy Orders (resigned his Orders).

BINGLEY, Henry Campbell Alchorne, 1876. Son of Rev. R. M. Bingley (below).

BINGLEY, John George, 1847-49. Son of Henry Bingley, of Woodford, *b.* 1834. B.N.C. Oxf. Rector of Snodland.

BINGLEY, Robert Mildred, 1847-48. Brother of the above, *b.* 1829. Trin. Coll. Cam. Rector of Braiseworth.

BIRCH, Charles, 1844-50. Son of Rev. E. Birch, late Rector of Windlesham, Surrey, *b.* 1832. Scholar of St. John's Coll. Cam. Rector of Foots Cray.

BIRCH, Edward, 1844-47. Brother of the above, *b.* 1830. Civil Engineer.

BIRCH, Francis Mildred, 1875. Son of J. W. Birch, Deputy Govr. of the Bank of England.

BIRCH, Frederic Lane, 1825, *b.* 1812. St. John's Coll. Cam. Rector of Wretham.

BIRCH, George Thackeray, 1876. Brother of Francis Mildred Birch (above).

BIRCH, Morley William, 1873. Son of Wm. Birch, of Wimbledon, *b.* 1859, *d.* 1875.

BIRCH,* Walter de Grey, 1851-60. Son of Samuel Birch, LL.D., of the British Museum, *b.* 1842. Talbot Scholar. Trin. Coll. Cam. British Museum.

BIRD, John, 1807, *b.* 1791. Peterhouse Coll. Cam. A.B. 1814.

BIRKBECK, William Lloyd, 1824. Son of George Birkbeck, F.R.S., a physician in London, *b.* 1807. Fellow of Trin. Coll. Cam. 9th Wrangler. Barrister of Lincoln's Inn.

BIRLEY, Hornby, 1824. Son of John Birley, of Manchester, *b.* 1811. 13th and 9th E. I. Company's Regts. Retired 1845, *d.* 1875.

BIRLEY, William, 1826. Brother of the above, *b.* 1813. Oriel Coll. Oxf. Rector of Chorlton. H.M. Inspector of Schools, *d.* 1865.

BIRTWHISTLE,* Alfred, 1859-64. Son of Canon J. B. Birtwhistle, of Beverley, *b.* 1845. Pemb. Coll. Oxf. Holy Orders. Beverley, Yorks.

BISHOP, Archibald Herbert, 1874. Son of the late Rev. Freeman H. Bishop, *b.* 1861.

BISHOP, Charles L. Nepean, 1869. Brother of the above, *b.* 1858. Royal Marine Artillery.

BISHOP, Fred. William Fremantle, 1871. Brother of the above, *b.* 1859. Trin. Hall, Cam.

BISHOP, William Alfred, 1874-77. Brother of the above.

BITTLESTON, Adam Henry, 1858. Son of Sir Adam Bittleston, late Judge at Madras, *b.* 1848. St. John's Coll. Oxf. Barrister.

BITTLESTON, George Hastings, 1867. Brother of the above, *b.* 1856. Lieut. Royal Artillery.

BITTLESTON, John Pattison, 1862. Brother of the above, *b.* 1852.

BITTLESTON, Thomas George, 1856-65. Brother of the above, *b.* 1846. Pemb. Coll. Oxf. Deceased.

BLACKBURNE,* Isaac, 1813, *b.* 1803.

BLACKER, Robert Shapland Carew, 1839-44. Son of the late Wm. Blacker, of Woodbrook, Co. Wrexford, and nephew of the 1st Lord Carew, *b.* 1826. Trin. Coll. Dublin. Rector of Marholm. Hon. Canon of Peterborough.

BLACKETT, Spencer Collinson, 1873-76. R.M. Coll. Sandhurst.

BLACKWOOD,* Percy, 1852-57. Son of Sir Henry Martin Blackwood, Bart., R.N., *b.* 1840. Colonial Sec. for Tobago, *d.* 1866.

BLAIR,* Thomas, 1814-18, *b.* 1802.

List of Carthusians.

BLAKE, Frederick Rodolph (C.B.), 1820. Son of William Blake, of Danesbury Welwyn, Herts, *b.* 1809. Col. 33rd Regt., *d.* 1855.

BLAKE, Henry, 1820, *b.* 1806. Peterhouse Coll. Cam.

BLAKESLEY, Arthur Holmes, 1877. Son of the Very Rev. J. W. Blakesley, Dean of Lincoln.

BLAKESLEY, Philip Holmes, 1862-63. Brother of the above, *b.* 1851. Went to Winchester.

BLAKESLEY, Thomas Holmes, 1860-65. Brother of the above, *b.* 1847. Exhibitioner of King's Coll. Cam. Wrangler. Barrister.

BLAKISTON (Sir) Matthew (Bart.), 1822. Son of Sir M. Blakiston, 3rd Baronet, *b.* 1811. Trin. Coll. Dublin. Succeeded his father 1862.

BLANCHARD, John, 1805-9, *b.* 1790. Jesus Coll. Cam. Rector of Middleton, Yorks.

BLAND,* George Templeman, 1838. St. John's Coll. Cam.

BLAND, Miles, 1841-47. Son of Rev. Miles Bland, DD. of Ramsgate, *b.* 1828. St. John's Coll. Cam. Curate of Saltwood, Kent, *d.*

BLAND,* Robert James, 1825. Son of Rev. Robert Bland, author of several poetical works, *b.* 1814. Jesus Coll. Cam. Vicar of Tutbury. Chaplain in India.

BLAND, Thomas, 1823, *b.* 1810. Solicitor in London.

BLANE,* George Rodney, 1800-5. Son of Sir Gilbert Blane, Bart., Physician to the Prince Regent, *b.* 1791, *d.* 1833.

BLANE, Gilbert Gardner, 1800-4. Brother of the above, *b.* 1787, *d.* 1833.

BLANE (Sir) Hugh Seymour (Bart.), 1803-7. Brother of the above, *b.* 1795. East India Co.'s Service. Succeeded his father 1834, *d.* 1869.

BLANE, Robert, 1820, *b.* 1809. Trin. Coll. Cam.

BLAXLAND, George Cuthbert, 1867-71. Son of George Blaxland, of Lesness Heath, Kent, *b.* 1852. Scholar of Pemb. Coll. Oxf. 1st Class Mods. 2nd Class Lit. Hum. Student of Ch. Ch. Curate of Saffron Walden,

BLENCOWE, Edward, 1815. Son of Saml. Blencowe, of Marston St. Lawrence, Northants, *b.* 1805. Wadham Coll. Oxf. 1st Class Lit. Hum. Fellow of Oriel. Holy Orders, *d.* 1840.

BLENCOWE, Edward Willis, 1820. Son of Robt. Willis Blencowe, *b.* 1810. Army. Drowned at the Cape, 1833.

BLENCOWE, George, 1815-17, *b.* 1803.

BLENCOWE, Robert, 1815-17, *b.* 1801. Barrister.

BLENKIRON, Thomas Walter, 1877. Son of T. Blenkiron, of Horne Park, Lee, Kent, *b.* 1864.

BLOIS, Thomas Francis, 1820. Son of Sir Charles Blois, Bart. of Grundisburgh Hall, Suffolk, *b.* 1807. 11th Bengal Native Infantry. Medal. Retired Lieut.-Col. 1856, *d.*

BLOMFIELD, Charles James, 1874. Son of Arthur W. Blomfield, Architect.

BLOMFIELD,* Edward George, 1865. Son of Rev. Geo. John Blomfield (below), *b.* 1853. Trin. Coll. Oxf. Curate of St. Mary's, Portsea.

BLOMFIELD, Edward Henry, 1840. Son of Rev. Jas. Blomfield, Rector of Orsett, Essex, *b.* 1824. Madras Staff Corps, Major-Genl. retired 1875.

BLOMFIELD,* George James, 1843-50. Son of Rev. G. B. Blomfield, Canon of Chester, *b.* 1831. Ch. Coll. Cam. Rector of Norton, Somerset.

BLOMFIELD,* George John, 1834-41. Brother of E. H. Blomfield (above), *b.* 1822. Ex. Coll. Oxf. Rector of Aldrington, E. Kent, and Rural Dean.

BLORE,* George John, 1848-55. Son of Edwd. Blore, F.R.S. &c. (Architect), *b.* 1835. Gold Medal. Student and Tutor of Ch. Ch. Oxf. 1st Class in Mods. and Lit. Hum. 2nd Class Law, &c. Assistant Master, 1859. Head Master of the King's School, Canterbury.

BLOXAM,* Andrew Roby, 1850-57. Son of Rev. Andrew Bloxam, Twycross, Leicester, *b.* 1839. Worc. Coll. Oxf. Notary Public, Christ Church, New Zealand.

BLOXAM, Frank Richard, 1862-3. Son of Richard Bloxam, of Eltham, *b.* 1850.

BLUNT, Edward Walter, 1875. Son of Major-Genl. Charles H. Blunt, *b.* 1860. R.M. Academy, Woolwich.

BLUNT, George, 1817, *b.* 1805.

BLUNT, Henry, 1817, *b.* 1806.

BLUNT, Herbert Arthur Scawen, 1874. Son of Rev. H. G. S. Blunt, Rector of St. Andrew's, Holborn.

BLUNT, Walter, 1821, *b.* 1809. Caius Coll. Cam. Rector of Bicknor, Maidstone.

BLUNT, Walter Brand Frederick, 1877. Son of the Ven. Archdeacon Blunt, of Scarborough, *b.* 1863.

BODDAM, William Tudor, 1818. Son of Rawson Hart Boddam, Govr. of Bombay, *b.* 1804, *d.* 1876.

BODDINGTON, Reginald Brook, 1821. Son of Benjamin Boddington, of Burcher Titley, Herefordshire, *b.* 1809. Royal Navy, 1824-28. Afterwards 23rd Madras Native Infantry. J.P. and D.L. for Herefordshire, *d.* 1863.

BODE, Edward, 1836-39. Indian Navy, *d.* 1854.

BODE, Henry, 1838-40. Son of William Bode, of Hare Hatch, Berks, *b.* 1825. Clerk in the Foreign Office.

BODE,* John Ernest, 1829-31. Son of Wm. Bode, *b.* 1816. Orator. Student of Ch. Ch. Oxf. 1st Class Lit. Hum. Hertford Scholar. Rector of Castle-Camps, *d.* 1874.

BODE, William, 1826, *b.* 1818. Post Office (Foreign Service).

BOGER, Henry Western Otway, 1878. Son of W. S. Boger (below).

BOGER, Hext, 1847-53. Son of Deeble Boger, *b.* 1837. Solicitor, Stonehouse, Devonport.

BOGER, William Shadforth, 1847-51. Son of George T. Boger, of Hastings, formerly Royal Artillery, *b.* 1833. Emm. Coll. Cam. War Office. Retired 1871.

BOISRAGON, Alfred, 1878. Son of Col. Boisragon, Bengal Staff Corps.

BOLGER, George, 1816-18, *b.* 1800.

BOLTON, William Henry, 1854-56. Son of Thos. Bolton, of Kinver, *b.* 1839. Went to King's College. Scholar of Trin. Coll. Cam. Wrangler. Head Master of Kinver Grammar School.

BOMPAS, Charles Steele Murchison, 1876. Son of G. C. Bompas, *b.* 1862. London University.

BOMPAS, Harold Buckland, 1876. Brother of the above, *b.* 1863.

BONHAM, Edward Walter (C.B.), 1820. Son of Henry Bonham, M.P. *b.* 1809. Foreign Office. Late Consul General at Naples.

BONHAM, Henry Frederic, 1820. Brother of the above, *b.* 1808. Col. 10th Hussars, *d.* 1856.

BONNER, Charles Edward, 1874. Son of C. F. Bonner, of Ayscoughfee Hall Spalding, *b.* 1860. Trin. Hall, Cam.

BONNER, James Tillard, 1845-47. Son of the late Chas. Bonner, of Spalding, *b.* 1830. Linc. and New Colls. Oxf. Vicar of Hale Magna.

BONNEY, Thomas, 1816, *b.* 1802. Orator. Clare Hall, Cam. Holy Orders. Master of Rugely School, *d.* 1853.

BONNEY, Thomas George, 1847-48. Son of the above, *b.* 1833. Fellow and Tutor of St. John's Coll. Cam. 12th Wrangler. Professor of Geology in Univ. Coll. London.

BOODLE, Edward, 1813-18, *b.* 1800. Barrister, *d.* 1873.

BOODLE, Henry Mitford, 1813. Brother of the above, *b.* 1802. Solicitor at London and Tunbridge Wells, *d.* 1878.

BOODLE, John, 1815. Son of John Boodle, Heath Farm, Watford, *b.* 1806. Solicitor in London.

BOODLE, William Chilver, 1817. Brother of the above, *b.* 1808. Conveyancer.

BOONE, James Shergold, 1812-16. Son of Thos. Boone, of Sunbury, *b.* 1798. Gold Medal. Student of Ch. Ch. Oxf. Craven Scholar, &c. Incumbent of St. John's, Paddington, *d.* 1859.

BOOTH,   , 1803.

BOOTHBY * (Sir) Brooke William Robert (10th Baronet), 1819. Son of Sir Willm. Boothby, Bart. *b.* 1809. Ch. Ch. Oxf. Fellow of All Soul's. Succeeded his father 1846. Rector of Welwyn, *d.* 1865.

BOOTHBY, Cecil Brooke, 1824. Brother of the above, *b.* 1813 Ch. Ch. Oxf.

List of Carthusians. 27

BOOTHBY, Charles Edward, 1836-37. Son of Rev. Brooke Boothby, b. 1821. Formerly in the Privy Council Office and Secy. to the late Marquis of Lansdowne and Earl Granville. Ranger of Needwood forest.

BOOTHBY,* Evelyn, 1838-40. Son of Rev. Charles Boothby, Prebendary of Southwell, and Vicar of Sutterton, Lincolnshire, b. 1825. Univ. Coll. Oxf. Rector of Whitwell, d. 1874.

BOOTHBY, Henry Brooke, 1831-36. Brother of C. E. Boothby (above), b. 1816. Orator. Durham University. Vicar of Lissington.

BOOTHBY, John George, 1838-39. Brother of the above, b. 1824. Royal Artillery. Served in the Crimea, &c. Major-Genl. d. 1876.

BOOTHBY, William Henry, 1838-40. Brother of Evelyn Boothby, b. 1823. Corpus Coll. Cam. Vicar of Hawksbury.

BOREHAM, Reginald Thorpe Joseph, 1865-70. Son of W. W. Boreham, of Haverhill, Suffolk, b. 1855. Univ. Coll. Lond., d. 1874.

BOREHAM, Walter Long, 1859. Brother of the above, b. 1848. Ch. Coll. Cam. Barrister.

BOREHAM, William Chalklen, 1859-63. Brother of the above, b. 1846. Melbourne, Australia.

BORRADAILE, Alfred, 1878. Son of A. Borradaile. E.I. Civil Service, b. 1864.

BORRADAILE, Henry Benjamin, 1874. Brother of the above. R.M. Coll. Sandhurst.

BORRER,* Charles Alexander, 1855-62. Son of Rev. C. H. Borrer, of Hurstpierpoint, Sussex, b. 1843. Ch. Ch. Oxf. Rector of Hope Mansell, Herefordshire.

BORRETT, Thomas Percy, 1852-57. Son of Thomas Borrett, of Bryanstone Square, b. 1840. Solicitor in London.

BORRETT,* William Penrice, 1818-22. Son of Giles Borrett, of Great Yarmouth, b. 1803. Gold Medal. Fellow of Caius Coll. Cam. Vicar of Siston, d. 1847.

BORTHWICK, George Augustus, 1874. Son of George Borthwick, b. 1859.

BORTHWICK, William Henry, 1847-48. Son of John Borthwick, of Crookston and Borthwick, Midlothian; b. 1832.

BORTON, Silvanus Key, 1863. Son of the Rev. Canon Borton, b 1853. Talbot Scholar, 1871. King's Coll. Cam. 3rd Class Classical and Theol. Tripos. Curate of S. Saviour's, Eastbourne.

BOSCAWEN, George Henry, 1873. Son of Hon. and Rev. John Townshend Boscawen, b. 1859, of Lamorran, Cornwall.

BOSTOCK, John Ashton (C.B.), 1828. Son of Dr. J. Bostock, b. 1815. Trin. Coll. Cam. Hon. Dep. Surgeon-General, Hon. Surgeon to Her Majesty. Served with the Buffs at the battle of Punniar, 1843 (Bronze Star); with the Scots Guards in the Crimea, Medal and four clasps. Companion of the Bath, &c.

BOSWORTH, Frederick William, 1840-44. Son of T. H. Bosworth, of Westerham, b. 1825. Silver Medal. Post-Master of Merton Coll. Oxf. Barrister, d. 1867.

BOSWORTH, Percy Mackie, 1847-51. Brother of the above, b. 1834. Lieut. 42nd Highlanders. Served in India during the Mutiny. Lucknow Medal. Died in India 1858.

BOULTON, George, 1808-11, b. 1798.

BOULTON, Godfrey, 1871. Son of James Boulton, Solicitor, b. 1858. Trin. Hall, Cam.

BOULTON, Henry Edward, 1824, b. 1812.

BOULTON, Thomas, 1808-11 b. 1798.

BOURCHIER,   , 1801-2.

BOURCHIER, Edward, 1824, b. 1810. Emm. Coll. Cam. Rector of Bramfield, Herts. Father of Sir Geo. Bourchier.

BOURCHIER, Robert Francis, 1817, b. 1804.

BOURDIEU, John Henry, 1822, b. 1811. Indian Artillery.

BOURDILLON, James, 1823. Son of Jas. Bourdillon, Bedford Square, London, b. 1812. Barrister.

BOURDILLON, Stafford, 1823. Brother of the above, b. 1814. Abbotstone, Whiteparish, near Salisbury.

BOURKE,* Walter Longley, 1870. Son of Hon. and Rev. G. W. Bourke, b. 1859.

BOURNE, Cornelius, 1820, *b.* 1807.

BOURNE, Herbert John, 1875. Son of J. S. Bourne, of Camp Hill, Nuneaton.

BOURNE, Joseph Handforth, 1873. Son of Rev. J. G. Bourne, Rector of Broome, Stourbridge, *b.* 1860.

BOUWENS, Charles Augustus Theodore, 1856-61. Son of the late Rev. Theodore Bouwens, *b.* 1842. Ch. Ch. Oxf. Emigrated to Australia, *d.* 1874.

BOVELL, Alfred Farre, 1851-56. Son of John Roach Bovell (below), *b.* 1838. British Museum, *d.* 1860.

BOVELL, John, 1815-17. Son of Mr. Bovell, of Barbados. Medical Practitioner, *b.* 1801, *d.* 1837.

BOVELL, John Roach, 1815. Brother of the above, *b.* 1803. Silver Medal. Trin. Coll. Cam. *d.* 1852.

BOVELL, Michael Nihell, 1815-18. Brother of the above, *b.* 1805. Trin. Coll. Cam. Curate of Windlesham, *d.* 1877.

BOWEN, Charles Andrew, 1846-49. Son of Revd. Edward Bowen, of Taughboyne, Donegal, *b.* 1835. Merchant.

BOWEN,* Edward, 1839-46. Brother of the above, *b.* 1823. Orator. Univ. Coll. Oxf. Archdeacon of Raphoe.

BOWEN* (Sir) George Ferguson (Knt.), 1833-40. Brother of the above, *b.* 1821. Silver Medals. Orator. Scholar of Trin. Coll. Oxf. 1st Class Lit. Hum. Fellow of B.N.C. Chief Sec. to the Government of the Ionian Islands 1854-59. Successively Governor of Queensland, New Zealand, Victoria, and Mauritius (1878). Knighted 1860. G.C.M.G.

BOWER, Charles Uppleby, 1853-56. Son of Thomas Bower, Hankelow Hall, Nantwich, Chesire, *b.* 1837. St. John's Coll. Cam. Junior Opt. Formerly Head Master of Stafford Grammar School. Rector of Wolferlow.

BOWER, Francis Chivers, 1875. Son of Edward Chivers Bower, of Wadworth Hall, Doncaster. —— R.M. Academy, Woolwich.

BOWES, Bernard, 1820, *b.* 1805.

BOWLBY, Henry Thomas, 1877. Son of Rev. H. B. Bowlby, Rector of St. Philip's, Birmingham.

BOWMAN, David, 1810.

BOWYEAR, William Francis, 1823, b. 1815.

Box,* Arthur Gould, 1871-75. Son of Rev. H. A. Box (below), b. 1858.

Box, Henry Adderly, 1835-39. Son of George M. Box, of Doctor's Common, b. 1819. Gold and Silver Medals. Scholar of Wadham Coll. Oxf. Curate of Heavitree, Exeter, d. 1869.

Box, John, 1821. Brother of the above, b. 1807.

Box, Kitson, 1835-40. Brother of the above, b. 1825. Merchant in So. America, d. 1858.

Box, William Frederick, 1835-38. Brother of the above, b. 1821. Indian Navy, d. 1858.

BOYCE, Herbert Ridley, 1869-71. Son of Matthias Boyce, Solicitor, b. 1856.

BOYD * (Sir) Frederick (Bart.), 1831-39. Son of the late Sir John Boyd, Bart., b. 1820. Orator. Univ. Coll. Oxf. Rector of Wouldham, Kent.

BOYD, Frederick Blackhall, 1844-48, b. 1830. Trin. Coll. Cam. Indian Army. Killed in action 1857.

BOYLE,* Cavendish Charles, 1861. Son of Capt. C. S. Boyle (below), b. 1849. Thackeray Prize. Probate Court.

BOYLE,* Cavendish Spencer, 1824. Son of Adml. the Honl. Sir Courtenay Boyle, and nephew of the 8th Earl of Cork, b. 1814. Ch. Ch. Oxf. 48th and 72nd Regts. Retired Capt. 1846. Governor D. M. P., Weedon, 1853, d. 1868.

BOYLE, Charles Fremoult, 1869. Son of Capt. Robert Boyle, R.A. b. 1857. Now in Canada.

BOYLE,* Charles John, 1814. Brother of Cavendish Spencer Boyle (above), b. 1806. Orator. Fellow of All Souls Coll. Oxf. Diplomatic Service.

BOYLE,* Courtenay Edmund, 1857-63. Son of Cavendish Sp. Boyle (above), b. 1845. Orator. Silver Medal, &c. Student Ch. Ch. Oxf. 3rd Class Lit. Hum. Private Sec. to the Lord Lieutenant of Ireland, 1868-73. Inspector Local Govt. Board 1873.

BOYLE, Ernest Patrick, 1874. Son of Chas. John Boyle (above), *b.* 1860. Vancouver's Island.

BOYLE, George David, 1843-47. Son of Rt. Hon. David Boyle, of Shewalton, *b.* 1828. Ex. Coll. Oxf. Vicar of Kidderminster. Hon. Canon of Worcester.

BOYLE, Hon. Robert John Lascelles, 1878. Son of the Earl of Cork and Orrery, K.P. *b.* 1864.

BOYMAN, Richard Pitsdey, 1819-20, *b.* 1806.

BOYS,* Charles, 1820. Son of Capt. Boys, R.N. *b.* 1809. Mert. Coll. Oxf. Vicar of Wing, Rutlandshire.

BOYS,* Edward, 1827, *b.* 1814. St. John's Coll. Cam.

BRACKENBURY, Robert Carr N. 1818. Eldest son of Sir John Brackenbury, formerly H.M. Consul at Cadiz, *b.* 1803. Linc. Coll. Oxf. Rector of Brocklesby Lincolnshire, deceased.

BRACKENBURY,* Walter Charles, 1832-40. Son of Rev. Joseph Brackenbury, *b.* 1822. Indian Army. 30th Madras N.I. Auckland, New Zealand.

BRADBURNE, Charles, 1803-5.

BRADDYLL, Edward Stanley, 1820. Son of Thomas Richmond Gale Braddyll, of Conishead Priory, Lanc. *b.* 1807.

BRADFORD, Charles William, 1846-49. Son of James Bradford, of Swindon, *b.* 1830. B.N.C. Oxf. Vicar of Clyffe-Pypard, Wilts.

BRADFORD, Francis Richard, 1849-51. Brother of the above, *b.* 1835. Lieut. 5th Fusiliers; retired 1857. Registrar of the Supreme Court of Penang.

BRAMLEY, Henry, 1846-48. Son of Richard Bramley, of Leeds, *b.* 1830. Silver Medal. Trin. Coll. Cam. Vicar of Uffculme, Devon.

BRAMLEY, Richard, 1846-48. Brother of the above, *b.* 1829. Scholar B.N.C: Oxf. Incumbent of Kirkdale, York.

BRANDRETH, Frederick, 1823. Second son of late J. P. Brandreth, M.D. *b.* 1812. Scots Guards. Retired Lieut.-Col. 1848. Took the name of Gandy through his marriage with the heiress of James Gandy, Heaves, Westmoreland.

BRANDRETH, William Harper, 1823. Twin brother of the above, *b.* 1812. Ch. Ch. Oxf. Rector of Standish, Wigan. Hon. Canon of Manchester.

BRASSEY,* Gordon, 1837-42, *b.* 1826. Clerk in the Bank of England. 3rd Light Dragoons.

BRASSEY, Nathl. Richard, 1821, *b.* 1806.

BRATHWAITE, Francis Gretton Coleridge, 1849-53. Son of the Ven. F. R. Brathwaite, late Archdeacon of St. Christophers, W. Indies, *b.* 1834. Ball. Coll. Oxf. Curate of St. Mary Magdalene, Munster Square.

BRAUND, George Percival, 1878. Son of George Braund, of Barrow-upon-Soar.

BRETON, George Augustus, 1824, *b.* 1808.

BRIDGE, Thomas Finch Hobday, 1817. Son of Thomas Bridge, of Harwich, *b.* 1807. Ch. Ch. Oxf. Double 2nd Class. Archdeacon of Newfoundland, *d.*

BRIDGER, John, 1823, *b.* 1811. St. Cath. Coll. Cam. Rector of Charlton by Dover.

BRIETZCKE, George John, 1822, *b.* 1809. 49th Bengal N.I. *d.* 1840.

BRIGGS, Adolphus, 1835-38.

BRIGGS, Thomas, 1818, *b.* 1805. Caius Coll. Cam. *d.*

BRIGGS, Thomas Carter, 1822, *b.* 1813. Worc. Coll. Oxf. Barrister.

BRIGGS, William Sturgis, 1828, *b.* 1818.

BRIGHT, John Edward, 1823-29. Son of Dr. John Bright, of Birmingham, *b.* 1810. Gold Medal. Student of Ch. Ch. Oxf. Barrister.

BRINE, James Edward Bouverie, 1865. Son of Rev. J. G. Brine, and grandson of Rev. Dr. Pusey, *b.* 1855. Ch. Ch. Oxf. Holy Orders.

BRINE, Philip Arthur Sherard, 1871. Brother of the above, *b.* 1861.

BRINTON, Selwyn John Curwen, 1872. Son of John Brinton, of Moor Hall, Worcestersh., *b.* 1859. Trin. Coll. Cam.

BRISCOE, William Kyffin Bostock, 1843-46. Son of Richard Briscoe, of Wrexham. *b.* 1828. Scholar and Fellow of Jesus Coll. Oxf. 2nd Class Lit. Hum. Rector of Shipton-on-Stour.

BROADWOOD, Robert George, 1876. Son of the late Thomas Broadwood, of Holmbush, Sussex.

BROCKHURST, Joseph Sumner, 1819, *b.* 1805. St. John's Coll. Cam. Chancellor's Medal for English Verse, 1824. Master of Camberwell Proprietary School.

BROCKMAN, William Lock, 1816. Son of Rev. Julius Drake Brockman, Rector of Cheriton, Kent. *b.* 1803. Emigrated to Australia. Member of the Legislative Council. Died in Australia 1872.

BRODERICK, John Lawrence, 1839-40, *b.* 1825. 18th Foot. Drowned on his passage out to China, 1843.

BRODIE, George, 1854-62. Son of Peter Bellinger Brodie. *b.* 1844. Conveyancer.

BRODIE,* Robert, 1849-58. Brother of the above. *b.* 1840. Gold Medal. Orator, &c. Ball. Coll. Scholar of Trinity, and Student and Tutor of Ch. Ch. Oxf. Head Master of Whitgift School, Croydon.

BROME, Charles John Bythesea, 1826. Son of the late Charles Brome, of West Malling, Kent. *b.* 1811, *d.* 1878.

BROME, John, 1823, *b.* 1809. Gold Medal. Trin. Coll. Cam.

BROOKE, George Nathl., 1821, *b.* 1812.

BROOKS, Benjamin, 1817, *b.* 1802. Solicitor in London.

BROOKS, George, 1822, *b.* 1809.

BROOKS,* James Henry, 1876. Son of James Henry Brooks, of Seychelles. *b.* 1863.

BROOKS, Thomas, 1825, *b.* 1812.

BROOKSBANK,* Charles, 1823. Son of Thomas Constantine Brooksbank. *b.* 1812. Ch. Ch. Oxf. Denyer Prizeman. Formerly Vicar of Blakeney.

BROUGHTON, Henry, 1825, *b.* 1809.

BROUGHTON, Robert, 1838.

BROWN, Charles Edward, 1819, *b.* 1806. Tostock Place, Bury St. Edmund's.

BROWN, Edward Cyril, 1872. Second son of Geo. J. E. Brown, of Tostock, Suffolk. *b.* 1857.

BROWN,* Ernest Faulkner, 1865. Son of William Brown, of Chester. *b.* 1854. Scholar of Univ. Coll. Oxf. 1st Class Mods. Curate of St. Margaret, Anfield, Liverpool.

BROWN,* Francis Faulkner, 1862. Brother of the above. *b.* 1851. Caius Coll. Cam. Curzon Park, Chester.

BROWN, Francis John, 1819, *b.* 1809.

BROWN,* Frederick Hewlett, 1875. Son of Thos. Edwin Burton Brown, M.D. Indian Medical Service.

BROWN, Harry Faulkner, 1869-70. Brother of Francis Faulkner Brown (above). *b.* 1857.

BROWN, James, 1820, *b.* 1808. E. India Company's Service, *d.* 1840.

BROWN, Louis Faulkner, 1859-64. Brother of Harry Faulkner Brown (above). *b.* 1840. Lieut. R.E. Serving in Afghan War.

BROWN, Maurice Theodore Kenworthy, 1876. Son of Rev. T. K. Brown, Rector of Brockhall, Northants. *b.* 1862.

BROWN, Rawdon Lubbock, 1820, *b.* 1806.

BROWN, Robert James, 1823, *b.* 1812.

BROWN, Thomas, 1802-5.

BROWN, Thomas, 1820, *b.* 1807. Magd. Hall, Oxf. Barrister. Newcastle-on-Tyne.

BROWN, William Baker, 1878. Son of Isaac Baker Brown, F.R.C.S. *b.* 1864.

BROWNE, Samuel Sneade, 1821, *b.* 1809.

BROWNE, Thomas Bingley, 1818, *b.* 1808.

BROWNE, Thomas Brame, 1827, *b.* 1813.

BROWNING, Benjamin Russell Hamond, 1850-51, *b.* 1835. Surgeon R.N.

BRUÈRE, Henry Sadlier, 1819. Son of William Sadlier Bruère, of Northumberland. *b.* 1809. Capt. 43rd Regt. *d.*

BRUÈRE, James Graham Sadlier, 1819. Brother of the above. *b*. 1807. East India Civil Service.

BRUÈRE, William Sadlier, 1819. Brother of the above. *b*. 1805. Jes. Coll. Cam. Died 1844.

BRUTTON,* Edward, 1848-54, *b*. 1837. 57th Regt. Crimea. China. Taku Forts New Zealand War. Frequently mentioned in despatches. 2 Medals and Clasps. Retired Captain 1870. Now Head of the Devon County Police.

BRYDEN, James, 1861-63, *b*. 1851.

BRYDEN, William Frith, 1859-64, *b*. 1848.

BUCHANAN, Alfred Morris, 1867-68, *b*. 1856.

BUCHANAN, George Rudolph, 1867-68, *b*. 1855.

BUCKINGHAM, Joseph Charles, 1876. Son of Joseph Hicks Buckingham, 29, Lancaster Gate, London. *b*. 1864.

BUCKLEY, Edmund, 1873. Son of Capt. Buckley.

BUCKLEY, Francis, 1873. Brother of the above.

BUCKLEY,* Henry William, 1814-16. Son of Edward Pery Buckley, of Woolcombe Hall, Dorset. *b*. 1800. B.N.C. and Mert. Colls. Oxf. Rector of Hartshorne, Derbyshire.

BUCKNOR, Richard James, 1823, *b*. 1808.

BUCKWELL, Eustace Arthur, 1863, *b*. 1847.

BUDD, Thomas William, 1814, *b*. 1805. Solicitor in London.

BULKELEY, Llewelyn Thomas, 1851-56. Son of G. T. Bulkeley, of Horton, Bucks. Worc. Coll. Oxf. Holy Orders. Office of the National Society, Westminster.

BULLOCK, Edward, 1831. Son of Rev. John Bullock, Rector of Radwinter. *b*. 1818; died in Canada.

BULLOCK, John Frederick, 1823. Brother of the above. *b*. 1809. Clare Hall, Cam. (B.A. 1831). Rector of Radwinter, d.

BULLOCK, John Frederick Watkinson, 1854-60. Son of the above. *b*. 1840. St. Peter's Coll. Cam. Rector of Radwinter.

BULLOCK, St. George, 1823. Brother of Edward Bullock (above). *b*. 1812. Clare Coll. Cam. Died in Canada.

BULWER, Erasmus Wigget, 1821. Son of Rev. Dr. Augustine Bulwer, Rector of Heydon, Norfolk. *b.* 1809. Pem. Coll. Cam. *d.* 1828.

BULWER (Sir) Henry Lytton (K.C.M.G.), 1850-55. Youngest son of William E. Lytton Bulwer, of Heydon Hall, Norfolk. *b.* 1836. Silver Medal for English Verse. Trin. Coll. Cam. Governor of Natal.

BUNBURY, Hugh Mill, 1814-15, *b.* 1802.

BUNYON, Charles Spencer, 1818. Son of Charles Bunyon, of Bombay. *b.* 1805. New Coll. Oxf. 2nd Class Lit. Hum. Army. Retired 1836.

BURCHELL,   , 1803.

BURD, Edward Lycett, 1875. Son of Dr. Burd, of Shrewsbury.

BURDETT, Francis, 1829. Eldest son of William Jones Burdett, of Copt Hall, Twickenham, Middlesex. *b.* 1813. Trin. Coll. Cam. 17th Dragoons. Lieut.-Col. 1848. Retired.

BURDETT, William Jones, 1829. Son of William Jones Burdett, and grandson of Sir Robert Burdett, D.C.L. *b.* 1814. Trin. Coll. Cam. *d.* 1858.

BURDON, Cotsford Mathews, 1873. Son of C. Burdon, Parkhurst House, Haslemere.

BURGESS, Henry Gilbert, 1837-41. Son of Henry W. Burgess, Artist, of Sloane Street. *b.* 1823. St. John's Coll. Cam. Clerk in Ordnance Office; deceased.

BURGESS, James Robert, 1820. Son of W. R. Burgess, and nephew of Bishop Burgess, of St. David's. *b.* 1809. Oriel Coll. Oxf. Vicar of Streatley, Berks; deceased.

BURNETT, Charles Henry, 1852-55. From Alton, Hants. *b.* 1837. Caius Coll. Cam.

BURNETT, Montague, 1852-59. Brother of the above. *b.* 1851. Scholar of Queens Coll. Cam. Curate of All Saints, Clifton.

BURNSIDE, Francis Rashleigh, 1867-70. Son of Rev. A. W. Burnside, late Vicar of Farningham, Kent. *b.* 1852.

BURNTHORN, William, 1810.

List of Carthusians. 37

BURR, John Macdonald, 1821, *b.* 1808.

BURRELL, Peter Robert (Lord Gwydyr), 1823. Son of Lindsay Merrik Peter Burrell. *b.* 1810.

BURROUGHES, Burkin, 1818, *b.* 1803.

BURROUGHES, Thomas Deye, 1815-18, *b.* 1800. Army. Guards.

BURROWS,* Alfred, 1872. Son of Montagu Burrows, Capt. R.N. and Professor of Modern History at Oxford. *b.* 1860. C. C. C. Oxf.

BURROWS, Basil, 1872. Son of Rev. L. F. Burrows (below). Scholar of Hertford Coll. Oxf.

BURROWS, Leonard Francis, 1834-39. Son of the late Maj.-Gen. Burrows. *b.* 1822. Scholar and Fellow of Wadh. Coll. Oxf. 1st Class Lit. Hum. Assistant Master at Charterhouse and Rugby. Vicar of Witley.

BURROWS, Leonard Hedley, 1872. Son of the above. New Coll. Oxf.

BURTON, Arthur George Teer, 1875. Son of J. S. Burton, Woodland Lodge, Blackheath.

BURTON, Charles Eneas, 1820. Son of Major Charles William Burton. *b.* 1812. E. I. Co. Service.

BURTON, Clarke Watkins, 1841-45, *b.* 1828. Clare Coll. Cam. Rector of Cliburn, Penrith.

BURTON, Francis, 1824, *b.* 1809.

BURY, Charles, 1815. Son of James Bury, of St. Leonards, Nazing, Essex. *b.* 1804. Bengal Civil Service, *d.* 1876.

BURY, Edmund, 1809-14. Brother of the above. *b.* 1797. East India Company's Service; died in India 1824.

BURY, Horatio, 1815. Brother of the above. *b.* 1806. 3rd Bombay Cavalry. Killed in action in India 1842.

BURY, James Frederick, 1809-13. Brother of the above. *b.* 1796. No profession; *d.* 1860.

BURY, William Shepherd, 1810-15. Brother of the above. *b.* 1798. Major Indian Army, *d.* 1852.

BUSFEILD, Charles Johnson, 1817. Son of the Rev. J. A. Busfeild, D.D. *b.* 1804.

BUSFEILD, William, 1816-17. Brother of the above. *b.* 1802. Univ. Coll. Oxf. Rector of Keighley, Yorks, *d.* 1878.

BUSHBY, William John, 1802-7. Son of William Bushby, of Kirkmichael, Dumfriesshire. *b.* 1793. E. I. Co's. Service. Drowned in India.

BUSHE-FOX, Loftus Henry Kendal, 1878. Son of Major Bushe-Fox.

BUSHNELL,* George Alexander, 1864, *b.* 1851.

BUSSELL,* Frederick William, 1876. Son of the late Rev. Frederick Bussell, Vicar of Marlow, Bucks. *b.* 1862.

BUTLER, Ferdinand Dick, 1845-47, *b.* 1837.

BUTLER, Francis, 1846-49, *b.* 1833.

BUTLER, Henry Richard, 1872. Son of Philip Butler, 40, Queen's Gate Terrace, Kensington. *b.* 1859. Lieut. R.A.

BUTLER, William John Chesshyre, 1877. Brother of the above.

BUTT, Augustine Henry, 1873. Son of Rev. G. Butt, Vicar of Chesterfield, Derbyshire.—C. C. Coll. Cam.

BUTTER, Albert, 1858-61. Son of Archibald Butter, of Faskally, Perthshire. *b.* 1844. Banker in Edinburgh.

BUTTER,* James, 1853-61. Brother of the above. *b.* 1843. Talbot Medal. Orator. Ball. Coll. Oxf. Assist. Master. Formerly Rector of Horseheath, Cam. Vicar of St. Michael and All Angels, Coventry.

BUTTS, Edward B., 1831, *b.* 1819. Vicar of Melplash, Bridport, *d.*

BYNG, Edmund Henry, 1874. Son of Hon. and Rev. F. C. Byng, Chaplain to the House of Commons.

BYNG,* Francis Russell, 1865. Son of late Major the Hon. Robt. B. P. Byng, and nephew of Viscount Torrington. *b.* 1853.

BYNG,* John Morice, 1858. Son of Rev. John Byng, Rector of Boxford. *b.* 1846. Jesus Coll. Cam. Rector of Wymondham.

BYRON, Cecil, 1824. Son of Thomas Byron, M.P., of Bayford House, Herts. *b.* 1812. Emigrated to Australia; died on his way home, 1849.

BYRON,* Hon. William, 1841-50. Son of the 7th Lord Byron. *b.* 1831. Ball. Coll. and Fellow of All Souls', Oxf. Rector of Stow-Langtoft.

C.

CADDELL, Walter, 1818. Son of Dr. Philip Caddell. *b.* 1806, deceased.

CAINES, James Thomas, 1827, *b.* 1814. Merchant at St. Kitts.

CAM, Charles Coxall, 1825, *b.* 1810. Holy Orders.

CAMERON, Charles Hay, 1865. Son of the late Mrs. Cameron, Freshwater, Isle of Wight. *b.* 1849. Coffee planter in Ceylon.

CAMERON, Edward Alexander, 1857-59, *b.* 1843.

CAMERON,* Hardinge Hay, 1859-65, *b.* 1846. Univ. Coll. Oxf. Assistant Govt. Agent Kaltura, Ceylon.

CAMERON, Henry Herschel Hay, 1865. Brother of Charles Hay Cameron (above). *b.* 1852. Coffee planter in Ceylon.

CAMPBELL,* Augustus Almeric, 1858-62, *b.* 1846.

CAMPBELL, Charles Ramsay, 1872. Son of Rev. J. Campbell, Rector of Aston, near Rotherham. Died at Charterhouse, 1873.

CAMPBELL, Donald, 1873. Son of Hon. and Rev. Archd. G. Campbell, Rector of Knipton, 2nd son of 1st Earl of Cawdor. *b.* 1860. B.N.C. Oxf.

CAMPBELL, Duncan, 1818. Trin. Coll. Cam. Holy Orders.

CAMPBELL, Hugh Walter George, 1876. Brother of Donald Campbell. *b.* 1863.

CAMPBELL, John, 1817, *b.* 1804.

CAMPBELL,* John Gordon Drummond, 1877. Son of the late Col. Archibald N. Campbell. *b.* 1864.

CAMPBELL,* Walter Douglas Somerset, 1851-56. Son of Walter Fredk. Campbell, of Islay. *b.* 1840. 79th Highlanders. Now on the Staff of the Lord Lieut. of Ireland.

CAMPBELL, William, 1821, *b.* 1809.

CAMPBELL, William Alexander, 1817, *b.* 1806.

CAMPBELL, William James Charles, 1820, *b.* 1808.

CAMPION,* Charles Thomas, 1875. Son of Henry Campion, M.R.C.S. Manchester. *b.* 1861.

CANE, Arthur Beresford, 1878. Son of the late Capt. Arthur B. Cane, 10th Regt. *b.* 1864.

CANNAN, John Hay, 1820, *b.* 1809.

CANNAN, Thomas, 1820, *b.* 1807.

CAPE, Gervas, 1809, *b.* 1797, *d.* 1814.

CAPEL, Hon. Arthur Algernon, 1878. Son of the 6th Earl of Essex. *b.* 1864.

CAPEL-CURE,* Edward Capel, 1874. Son of Rev. L. G. Capel-Cure. Abbess Roothing, Ongar. *b.* 1860.

CARDALE, Alfred, 1860-62. Son of the late J. B. Cardale, of Albury. *b.* 1845. Farmer at Canterbury, New Zealand.

CARDALE, George, 1854-58. Brother of the above. *b.* 1839. Mathematical Medal. Oriel Coll. Oxf. Called to the Bar 1864. Admitted a Solicitor 1877. 2, Bedford Row.

CARDEN, John Rutter, 1826, *b.* 1810.

CAREW, William Henry Pole, 1824-27. Son of the Rt. Hon. Reginald Pole Carew and grandson of the 1st Lord Lyttleton. *b.* 1811. Oriel Coll. Oxf. M.P. for E. Cornwall 1845-52. High Sheriff of Cornwall 1854.

CAREY, Hewett, 1822. Eldest son of Peter Carey. *b.* 1811. Oriel Coll. Oxf. Holy Orders; deceased.

CAREY, John, 1816, *b.* 1804.

CAREY, John, 1821, *b.* 1810. Trin. Coll. Cam.

CARMICHAEL (Sir) James Robert (Bart.), 1829. Son of Major-Genl. Sir James Carmichael Smyth, Bart. *b.* 1817. Was formerly an officer in the Army, D.L. of Kent, Chairman of the Submarine Telegraph Company, &c. Re-assumed (1841) the name of Carmichael only, in lieu of that of Carmichael-Smyth.

CARNE, Joseph, 1824. Of Penzance, Cornwall. *b.* 1809. Trin. Coll. Cam. Holy Orders; *d.* 1836.

CARPENTER, George Edward, 1852-58. Son of R. C. Carpenter (below). *b.* 1842. Solicitor. 4, Trafalgar Square.

CARPENTER, Harry Stanley, 1873-75. Son of Col. Carpenter. *b.* 1857. Keble Coll. Oxf.

List of Carthusians. 41

CARPENTER, Richard Cromwell, 1825, *b.* 1812. Architect. Late of 4, Carlton Chambers; *d.* 1855.

CARPENTER, Richard Herbert, 1851-57. Son of the above. *b.* 1841. Architect. 4, Carlton Chambers.

CARPENTER, Thomas, 1826, *b.* 1812.

CARR,* Arthur Fortescue, 1858-63. Son of Andrew Morton Carr. *b.* 1846. Bank of Bengal, Lucknow.

CARR,* Henry Morton, 1863-66. Brother of the above. *b.* 1851.

CARR, Reginald Childers Culling, 1878. Son of Francis Culling Carr-Gomm, Madras Civil Service. *b.* 1864.

CARR,* Walter Raleigh, 1857-62. Brother of Henry Morton Carr (above). *b.* 1843. Pemb. Coll. Oxf. Vicar of Foleshill, Coventry.

CARRINGTON,* Henry 1826, *b.* 1814. Caius Coll. Cam. Dean and Rector of Bocking, Essex.

CARRINGTON, William, 1819, *b.* 1808.

CARSON, William, 1828, *b.* 1814.

CARTER,* Arthur Shaen, 1851-58, *b.* 1840. Capt. 51st Regt.

CARTER, Berkeley Luce, 1853-58. Son of W. Carter, Coroner for Surrey. *b.* 1842, *d.* 1862.

CARTER, Crescens, 1810-15, *b.* 1802.

CARTER,* Ernest Courtenay, 1869. Son of Rev. G. Carter, Rector of Compton Beauchamp. *b.* 1858.

CARTER,* George Charles, 1865. Son of Rev. J. Carter, Vicar of Linton, Kent. *b.* 1853. Assistant Master, Charterhouse, Godalming. Holy Orders.

CARTER, Horace, 1852. Brother of B. L. Carter (above). *b.* 1841, *d.* 1854.

CARTER, Hugh Adolphus, 1874. Son of Rev. W. A. Carter, Rector of Worplesdon, Surrey. *b.* 1860. Articled to a Solicitor.

CARTER, John George, 1867. Son of Rev. George Carter, Rector of Falkingham, Linc. *b.* 1854. Trin. Coll. Cam. Holy Orders. Assistant Master at the King's School Ely.

CARTER, Laurance, 1873. Brother of the above.

CARTER, Samuel Robert, 1829-38. Son of Capt. Carter and nephew of Rev. W. H. Chapman. *b.* 1819. Gold Medal. Fellow of Emm. Coll. Cam. B.D. Rector of Brantham, Suffolk, *d.*

CARTER, Thomas Stead, 1810-12, *b.* 1796. Trin. Hall, Cam. LL.B. 1817, *d.* 1856.

CARTER, William, 1854-60. Brother of B. L. and Horace Carter (above). *b.* 1845, *d.* 1862.

CARTER, William Henry, 1838-41, *b.* 1825. Solicitor.

CARTWRIGHT, Richard Aubrey, 1822. Son of William R. Cartwright, M.P. of Aynhoe. *b.* 1811. Rector of Aynhoe.

CARTWRIGHT, Robert, 1818. Brother of the above. *b.* 1804. Ch. Ch. Oxf. Barrister.

CARTWRIGHT, Stephen Ralph, 1818. Brother of Robert Cartwright. *b.* 1806. Ch. Ch. Oxf. Rector of Aynhoe, *d.* 1862.

CARY, Joseph, 1818, *b.* 1810. Solicitor in London.

CARY, Samson, 1818.

CASE, Charles Hesketh, 1826. Son of Henry Case, of Shenstone, Staffordsh. *b.* 1812. B.N.C. Oxf. Went to India.

CASE,* EDWARD, 1802-7, *b.* 1790. Indian Army.

CASE, John Dean, 1801-3. Merchant in Liverpool.

CASS, Claude William Culley, 1875. Son of Rev. F. C. Cass, Rector of Monken Hadley, Middlesex. *b.* 1862.

CASTLE, Richard Feild, 1872-78. Son of R. H. B. Castle, of Sevenoaks. *b.* 1860. Pemb. Coll. Cam.

CATES, John, 1813-14, *b.* 1799. (Of St. Omers).

CATHCART, Hon. Charles, 1874. Son of the 3rd Earl Cathcart. *b.* 1859. 2nd Lieut. 82nd Foot.

CATHCART, Hon. George, 1875. Brother of the above. *b.* 1862.

CATOR, Peter, 1807-10, *b.* 1796. Trin. Coll. Cam.

CATTLEY, Henry Thomas, 1844-46. Son of John Henry Cattley, of York. *b.* 1827. St. John's Coll. Oxf. Holy Orders. Fulford, York.

CAUTLEY, Edmund, 1878. Son of Henry Cautley, of Bramley, Yorks. *b.* 1864.

CAUTLEY,* Henry Strother, 1876. Brother of the above. *b.* 1862.

CAUTLEY (Sir) Proby Thomas (K C.B.), 1813-18. Son of Rev. T. Cautley, Rector of Roydon, Suffolk. *b.* 1802. Col. in the E. I. Co.'s Service, Bengal. Knighted 1854. Member of Council of India 1858, *d.* 1871.

CAVENDISH, Hon. William Edwin, 1875. Son of the 2nd Baron Chesham. *b.* 1862.

CAYLEY, Digby William, 1876. Son of Geo. A. Cayley, and grandson of Sir Digby Cayley, Bt. *b.* 1862.

CAYLEY, Francis Melville, 1821. Son of John Cayley, of Petersburg. *b.* 1809. Of East Grinstead, Sussex.

CAYLEY, William, 1821. Brother of the above. *b.* 1807. Ch. Ch. Oxf. Emigrated to Canada.

CAZALET, William W., 1820, *b.* 1808. Trin. Coll. Cam. Holy Orders.

CAZENOVE, Henry, 1843-45. Eldest son of Philip Cazenove (below). *b.* 1829. Stock Exchange.

CAZENOVE, Philip, 1813-15, *b.* 1798. Merchant in London.

CEELY Arthur James, 1850-54. Son of James Henry Ceely, F.R.C.S. of Aylesbury. *b.* 1834. Caius Coll. Cam. Lieut. 42nd Highlanders. Served through the Indian Mutiny Campaign (Medal and Clasp) and died on his way home to England, 1866.

CHADWICK, William, 1817-18, *b.* 1803. Solicitor in London.

CHALMERS, Charles Marshall Sidney, 1873. Clough House, Rotherham, Yorks.

CHAMBERS, George Wilton, 1826. Son of Robt. Joseph Chambers, of Rotherham, formerly a Police Magistrate in London. *b.* 1812. Univ. Coll. Oxf. Barrister of Middle Temple.

CHAMBERS, James Polhill, 1818. Brother of the above. *b.* 1809, *d.* in India 1830.

CHAMPNEYS,* Basil, 1854-60. Son of the Very Rev. W. W. Champneys, Dean of Lichfield. *b.* 1842. Gold Medal. Scholar of Trin. Coll. Cam. 2nd Class Classical Tripos. Architect.

CHAMPNEYS, Montague Storr, 1854-59. Brother of the above. *b.* 1840. Gold Medal. Ex. Coll. Oxf. Bengal Civil Service; *d.* 1868.

CHAMPNEYS, Weldon, 1852-58. Brother of the above. *b.* 1839. Talbot Scholar. B.N.C. Oxf. Vicar of Haslingden, Lanc.

CHAPMAN, Arthur Robert, 1848-53. Son of Henry Chapman, of Canterbury, late of the Indian Medical Service. *b.* 1836. Major Bengal Staff Corps.

CHAPMAN, Benjamin Bovill, 1810-13, *b.* 1798. Ch. Coll. Cam. Vicar of Leatherhead.

CHAPMAN, Charles William Robert, 1833-38. Son of Capt. Chas. Matthew Chapman, R.N. *b.* 1823, *d.*

CHAPMAN, D'Arcy Richard, 1872. Lieut. 29th Regt.

CHAPMAN, Edward, 1819, *b.* 1804. Solicitor in London.

CHAPMAN, Edward Henry, 1817, *b.* 1803. Merchant at Mauritius.

CHAPMAN, Henry, 1812-13. Son of Rev. William Chapman, Vicar of St. John's, Margate. *b.* 1800. Surgeon.

CHAPMAN, Henry William, 1844-50. Brother of Arthur Robert Chapman (above). *b.* 1834. Capt. 28th Bengal N. I. Retired.

CHAPMAN, John, 1809-11, *b.* 1797. Merchant. Now living at Folkestone.

CHAPMAN, John, 1819, *b.* 1805.

CHAPMAN, Thomas, 1824, *b.* 1812. Ex. Coll. Oxf.

CHAPMAN, Vaughan Godfrey St. John, 1871. Son of the late George Chapman, Solicitor. *b.* 1858.

CHAPMAN, William Henry, 1829. Son of Rev. Samuel Chapman. *b.* 1819.

CHAPMAN, William Herbert, 1812. Son of Rev. Willliam Herbert Chapman, Vicar of Balsham, for 27 years a Master in the School. *b.* 1807. Emm. Coll. Cam. Vicar of Bassingbourne, Cam. *d.* 1861.

CHAPMAN, William Herbert, 1850-51. Son of the above. *b.* 1834. Emm. Coll. Cam. Rector of Eydon, Northants.

List of Carthusians.   45

CHAPMAN, William Robert, 1819, b. 1806.

CHATAWAY, Henry Howard, 1873. Son of Rev. J. C. Chataway, Rector of Rotherwick.

CHATAWAY, Thomas Drinkwater, 1878. Brother of the above. b. 1864.

CHATER, John Andrew, 1870-71, b. 1855.

CHATFIELD, Allen William, 1820. Son of the Rev. Robert Chatfield, LL.D. b. 1808. Trin. Coll. Cam. Bell's Univ. Scholar. Member's Prizeman, &c. Vicar of Much Marcle, co. Hereford.

CHATFIELD, Frederick, 1874. Of Kingston, Surrey.

CHATFIELD, Robert Money, 1821. Brother of A. W. Chatfield (above). b. 1804. Scholar of Trin. Coll. Cam. Junior Opt. and 5th in 1st Class Classical Tripos. Vicar of Woodford, Salisbury.

CHATFIELD, Thomas Kyrle Ernle, 1821. Brother of the above. b. 1806. Trin. Coll. Cam. Barrister, d. 1836.

CHATTERTON, Abraham, 1875. Son of A. T. Chatterton, of Dublin.

CHEPMELL, Charles William James, 1874. Son of Dr. Chepmell.

CHERMSIDE,* Walter Frederic, 1861-65. Son of Rev. R. S. C. Chermside, Vicar of Wilton, Wilts. b. 1848. Ex. Coll. Oxf.

CHERRY, Walter Alexander, 1872.

CHESTER,* Charles, 1814. Son of the late Sir Robert Chester. b. 1803. E. I. Co. Army, Bengal.

CHESTER, Charles Montagu, 1827. Of Chicheley Hall, Bucks. b. 1815. Capt. 90th Regt. Major Royal Sussex Artillery.

CHESTER, Harry, 1815. Brother of Charles Chester (above). b. 1806. Clerk in the Privy Council Office, d. 1868.

CHESTER,* William, 1829. Son of George Chester, E.I.C.S. b. 1815. Univ. Coll. Oxf.; died in India 1837.

CHESTER, William Henry Clinton, 1818, b. 1809. Em. Coll. Cam. Rector of Elstead, Sussex, d. 1841.

CHETWODE,* Charles, 1804-8. Son of Sir John Chetwode, Bart. b. 1794. Deceased.

CHETWODE,* George, 1802-10. Brother of the above. *b.* 1791. B.N.C. Oxf. Rector of Ashton-under-Lyne, *d.* 1870.

CHEVALLIER, Barrington, 1832-37. Eldest surviving son of late Rev. John Chevallier, of Aspall, Suffolk. *b.* 1818. Scholar of B.N.C. Oxf. M.D. Several years Mayor of Ipswich.

CHEVALLIER, John, 1832-34, *b.* 1817. Caius Coll. Cam. Holy Orders, *d.* 1854.

CHEVALLIER, Charles Henry, 1839-42. Third son of late Rev. John Chevallier. *b.* 1823. Trin. Coll. Oxf. Holy Orders. Vicar of Aspall, Suffolk.

CHILCOTE, Henry, 1818, *b.* 1806.

CHILCOTE, Paul, 1818, *b.* 1808.

CHILD, Arthur, 1837-39, *b.* 1824. Merchant.

CHILD, Charles Henry, 1837-39, *b.* 1823. Solicitor.

CHILD, George Augustus, 1837-40, *b.* 1826.

CHILD, Sydney C., 1837-40, *b.* 1828.

CHILDERS, Charles, 1818. Son of Col. John W Childers, M.P. of Cautley, Doncaster. *b.* 1806. Ch. Ch. Oxf. 2nd Class Lit. Hum. Vicar of Cautley. Chaplain at Nice. Canon of Gibraltar 1866.

CHILDERS, Leonard, 1818. Brother of the above. *b.* 1804. Diplomatic Service; died at Panama 1826.

CHILTON, George, 1809. Son of George Chilton, a Master of the Exchequer. *b.* 1796. Queens Coll. Oxf. 2nd Class Lit. Hum. Barrister. Q.C. Recorder of Gloucester, &c., *d.* 1852.

CHOLMELEY,* Norman Goodford, 1876. Son of the late Col. Montague Cholmeley. *b.* 1863.

CHOLMELEY, Randolph Lucas, 1875. Son of Stephen Cholmeley, of Kingston Hill, Surrey. *b.* 1861.

CHURCH, Adolphus Edgar, 1844-48. Son of J. H. Church, Solicitor, Colchester. *b.* 1830. Solicitor. Coroner for Colchester.

CHURCH, Henry John, 1844-45. Brother of the above. *b.* 1829. St. Bees Coll. Barrister 1874. Deputy Coroner for Colchester, &c.

CHURTON,* Edward, 1810-18. Son of the Ven. Ralph Churton, Archdeacon of St. David's. *b* 1800. Gold Medal. Ch. Ch. Oxf. 2nd Class Lit. Hum. Rector of Crayke. Archdeacon of Cleveland. Author of History of the Early English Church, &c., &c., *d.* 1874.

CHURTON, Henry Burgess Whitaker, 1822-28. Brother of the above. *b.* 1810. Scholar of Ball. Coll. Oxf. 1st Class Lit. Hum. Fellow of B.N.C. Bampton Lecturer, &c. Preacher of Charterhouse. Rector of Icklesham, Sussex. Prebendary of Chichester.

CHURTON, John, 1814. Brother of the above. *b.* 1803; died at Charterhouse 1814.

CHURTON.* Joshua Watson, 1851-57. Son of Edward Churton (above). *b.* 1839. Scholar of Univ. Coll. Oxf. *d.* 1860.

CLAPCOTT, William George Coleridge, 1875. Son of Major Clapcott.

CLARE,* George Thomas, 1820. Son of Rev. Thos. George Clare. *b.* 1808. Fellow of St. John's Coll. Oxf. Rector of Bainton.

CLARK, George Dixon Atkinson—(see Atkinson). 1854. Son of William Atkinson Clark, of Belford Hall, Northumberland. *b.* 1836. Univ. Coll. Oxford. J.P. for Northumberland.

CLARK, George Elliott, 1824, *b.* 1811. Trin. Coll. Cam. Barrister.

CLARK,* George Thomas, 1819-25. Son of Rev. Geo. Clark, A.M., of Trin. Coll. Cam. *b.* 1809. Col. in Chief of the 2nd Batt. Glamorgan R.V. Magistrate and D.L. of Glamorganshire. Sheriff of the County 1868.

CLARK, Henry, 1815-17, *b.* 1803.

CLARK, Henry McGregor, 1827, *b.* 1813. Solicitor in London, *d.* 1850.

CLARK,* I. Hew Warrender, 1866. Son of Genl. Clark. *b.* 1853.

CLARK, William Adair Atkinson—(see Atkinson), 1854-59. Brother of G. D. Atkinson Clark (above). *b.* 1842.

CLARK, William Falconer Clark, 1874. Son of W. F. Clark, Medical Practitioner, of Rose Hill, Dorking. *b.* 1860.

CLARKE, Arthur Francis, 1846-48. Son of Rev. Thos. Clarke, of Mitcheldever, Hants. *b.* 1836. Ship-broker.

CLARKE,* Arthur Frederic, 1861-67. Son of Seymour Clarke, of Northcotts, Essex. *b.* 1848. Trin. Coll. Oxf. Holy Orders. Diocesan Inspector of Schools, Diocese of Worcester.

CLARKE, Charles, 1819, *b.* 1805. Trin. Coll. Cam. Vicar of Takeley, Essex, *d.*

CLARKE (Sir) Charles (Bart.), 1821. Son of Sir Charles Mansfield Clarke, Bart., M.D., &c. *b.* 1812. Trin. Coll. Cam. Formerly Rector of Hanwell. Worlingham Hall, Suffolk.

CLARKE, Charles Granville, 1843-52. Brother of Arthur F. Clarke (above). *b.* 1833. Scholar of Worc. Coll. Oxf. Vicar of Langley Fitzurse, Wilts.

CLARKE, Charles Robert Meyricke, 1815, *b.* 1804.

CLARKE, Denison Leslie, 1867. Brother of Arthur Frederic Clarke (above). *b.* 1854. Magd. Coll. Oxf.

CLARKE, Edmund Ludlow, 1816, *b.* 1805. Holy Orders. Resided at Cheltenham.

CLARKE, Edward John Bellingham, 1824, *b.* 1814. Royal Navy.

CLARKE, Edward Nalder, 1871, *b.* 1856.

CLARKE, Frederic Christian, 1818, *b.* 1807.

CLARKE, Henry Stephenson, 1849-55, *b.* 1839.

CLARKE, James Smith, 1817, *b.* 1802.

CLARKE, John, 1869, *b.* 1855.

CLARKE,* Melville, 1848-52, *b.* 1834. Indian Army.

CLARKE, William Edmund Grey, 1876. Son of Rev. T. G. Clarke, Vicar of Odiham, Hants. *b.* 1864.

CLARKE, William Henry, 1817, *b.* 1803. Cath. Hall, Cam.

CLARKSON, Townley Lebeg, 1820, *b.* 1809. Ch. Coll. Cam. Rector of South Elham, *d.* 1877.

CLAY, Aiskew, 1852-56, *b.* 1840. Indian Army.

CLAY (Sir) George (Bart.), 1844-48. Son of Sir William Clay, 1st Bart., M.P. *b.* 1832. Served in the Crimea with the 19th Regt. Retired Lieut.-Col. 1875. Succeeded to the Baronetcy 1876, *d.* 1878.

CLAY, John Gough, 1821. Son of Thomas Clay. *b.* 1809. Jesus Coll. Oxf. Chaplain at Siena.

CLAYTON, Henry Reginald, 1866. Son of John Clayton. *b.* 1855.

CLAYTON, John Essex, 1866-70. Brother of the above. *b.* 1852.

CLAYTON, John Whitehead, 1860-64, *b.* 1848.

CLEAVER, William Wilfrid Mackworth, 1877. Son of Rev. W. H. Cleaver, Willesden. *b.* 1865.

CLEEVE, Egerton Stewart, 1875. Son of Colonel Cleeve.

CLEEVE, Frederic John Stewart, 1874. Brother of the above. R.M. Academy, Woolwich.

CLEMENS, James, 1803-8.

CLEMENTS, Charles Topham, 1876. Nephew of H. T. Clements (below).

CLEMENTS, Henry Topham, 1845-47. Son of Rev. J. C. Clements. *b.* 1830. 14th King's Light Dragoons. Served in Persia, and Indian Mutiny. Medals and Clasps. Retired Captain 1861.

CLEMENTS, Hon. Francis Nathaniel, 1826. Son of the 2nd Earl of Leitrim. *b.* 1815. Oriel Coll. Oxf. Vicar of Norton, and Hon. Canon of Durham, *d.* 1870.

CLERKE,* Charles Carr, 1809-15. Son of the Rev. Sir William Henry Clerke, Bart. *b.* 1798. Student of Ch. Ch. Oxf. Rector of Milton, Berks. Archdeacon of Oxford. Canon of Ch. Ch. Author of several theological works, *d.* 1875.

CLERKE,* Francis, 1808. Brother of the above. *b.* 1797. B.N.C. and Fellow of All Souls, Oxf. Rector of Eydon.

CLERKE,* William Henry (Bart.), 1803-5. Brother of the above. *b.* 1793. Lieut.-Col. 52nd Regt. Waterloo, *d.* 1861.

CLEVELAND, Henry Francis, 1875.

CLIFFORD,* Charles Cavendish, 1831-38. Son of Admiral Sir Aug. Clifford, Bart. *b.* 1821. Ch. Ch. and Fellow of All Souls, Oxf. Private Sec. to Lord Palmerston. M.P. for the Isle of Wight 1858 and 60; for Newport 1870 and 75.

CLIFFORD, Henry Frederick, 1835. Son of Mr. Clifford, of Great Portland Street.

CLIFTON, Anthony Crole, 1826, *b.* 1812. Surgeon.

CLIFTON, Charles, 1878. Son of G. F. Clifton, of Constantinople.

CLIFTON, Charles Frederick, 1874. Son of E. N. Clifton (below).

CLIFTON, Edward Norton, 1828, *b.* 1817. Architect.

CLIFTON, Percival Robert, 1849-53. Son of Rev. Robert Cox Clifton, Canon of Manchester. *b.* 1834. Scholar of Linc. Coll. Oxf. Assistant Master in Sherborne School, *d.* 1873.

CLIFTON, Raymond George, 1854. Brother of the above. *b.* 1843, *d.* 1859

CLINCH, Edward, 1850-53, *b.* 1837.

CLIVE, Theophilus, 1821. Son of Theophilus Clive, of Whitfeld, Hereford. *b.* 1808. Ch. Ch. Oxf.

CLOGSTOWN, Samuel, 1801-5.

CLOWES, Edmund, 1842-45, *b.* 1828; died at Rio de Janeiro 1852.

CLUTTERBUCK, John Lyon, 1837-41. Son of John Clutterbuck, of Warkworth, Northumberland. *b.* 1824. 37th Regt., died in India.

COATES, John, 1813-15, *b.* 1804.

COATES, Samuel, 1822. Son of John Coates, of Ripon. *b.* 1807. Jes. Coll. Cam. Perpetual Curate of Thirsk, Yorks. Hon. Canon of York, *d.* 1878.

COATES, Thomas, 1813-15. *b.* 1802.

COBB, Edward Winstanley, 1874-77. Son of Mr. Cobb a Merchant in Portugal.

COBBE, Charles, 1827. Eldest son of Chas. Cobbe, of Newbridge House, Co. Dublin. *b.* 1810. Ex. Coll. Oxf. Barrister. D.L. and High Sheriff for Co. Dublin, 1841.

COBBE, Henry, 1829. Brother of the above. *b.* 1817. Oriel Coll. Oxf. Rector of Milton Bryant.

COBBE, Thomas, 1828. Brother of the above. *b.* 1813. B.N.C. Oxf. Barrister. Easton Lys, Petersfield.

COBBOLD, Edward Augustus, 1838-44. Second son of Rev. R. Cobbold, Rector of Wortham, Author of Margaret Catchpole, &c. *b.* 1825. Trin. Coll. Cam. Formerly Vicar of Yaxley, Suffolk.

COBBOLD, Henry Chevallier, 1847-50. Son of T. C. Cobbold, M.P., of Holy Well, Ipswich. *b.* 1832. Solicitor at Ipswich, deceased.

COBBOLD, Thomas Clement (C.B.), 1848-51. Brother of Henry C. Cobbold (above). *b.* 1833. Diplomatic Service. M.P. for Ipswich.

COBBOLD, Thomas Spencer (F.R.S.), 1843-44. Brother of E. A. Cobbold (above). *b.* 1828. M.D. Edinburgh, &c., &c. Author of numerous works on Entozoa, &c.

COBBOLD,* William Nevill, 1877. Son of Rev. E. A. Cobbold, of Dry Hill Park, Tunbridge (above). *b.* 1863.

COCK, 1803.

COCKBURN, Robert, 1873. Son of Sir Edward Cludde Cockburn, Bart., of Pennoxstone Ross, Herefordshire. *b.* 1861.

COCKER, George Henry, 1818, *b.* 1810.

COCKEY, Edward, 1825. Son of Edward Cockey, of Frome, Somerset. *b.* 1809. Fellow of Wadham Coll. Oxf. 2nd Class Lit. Hum.; 1st Class Math. Rector of Fryerning, Ingatestone.

COCKLE (Sir) James (Knt.), 1829. Son of the late James Cockle, of Gt. Oakley, Essex. *b.* 1819. Trin. Coll. Cam. Barrister. Chief Justice of Queensland. Knighted 1869.

COCKS, Charles Richard Somers, 1826 (see Somers-Cocks).

COCKSHOTT, Harold, 1875. Born in Australia.

COCKSHOTT, John, 1825. Son of John Cockshott, of Warrington. *b.* 1809. Of Mark's Gate, Dagenham, Essex.

COCKSHOTT, William Evans, 1875-77. Son of Rev. J. W. Cockshott, Vicar of Burwell, Cambs. *b.* 1862.

CODD, Henry, 1827, *b.* 1813.

CODDINGTON, Henry Hallet, 1852-55. Son of Rev. Henry Coddington, Vicar of Ware. *b.* 1839. Trin. Coll. Cam. Goldsmith's Co Exhibitioner. Vicar of High Cross, Herts.

CODDINGTON, John George Thornton, 1855. Brother of the above. *b.* 1841. Civil Engineer. Public Works Dept., India.

CODRINGTON, Robert Henry, 1845-48. Son of Rev. Thos. Stretton Codrington, of Wroughton, Wilts. *b.* 1830. Scholar and Fellow of Wadham Coll. Oxf. Holy Orders. Head of the Melanesian Mission, 1871-77.

COFFIN, Edmund, 1841. Son of Robert Coffin, of Broadwater, Sussex. *b.* 1824. Ch. Ch. and Demy of Magd. Coll. Oxf. Holy Orders (resigned).

COKAYNE, Brien Ibrican, 1878. Son of George Edward Cokayne, Lancaster Herald. *b.* 1864.

COLDWELL,* William Edward, 1835-39. Son of Rev. W. E. Coldwell, Rector of Stafford and Preby. of Lichfield. *b.* 1825. Ch. Ch. Oxf. 3rd Class Lit. Hum. Vicar of Sandon, Staffs. Chaplain to the Duke of Marlborough.

COLDWELL,* William St. George, 1869. Son of the above. *b.* 1857. Messrs. Lloyd's Bank, Stafford.

COLE, Allen Summerly, 1857. Son of Sir Henry Cole, C.B. *b.* 1846.

COLE, Arthur Willoughby George Lowry, 1875. Son of Col. A. Lowry Cole, of Wimbledon.

COLE, George, 1872, *b.* 1857. Left 1874.

COLE, George Beauchamp, 1821. Son of Stephen Thomas Cole, of Twickenham. *b.* 1807. D.L. for Middlesex.

COLE, James George, 1820, *b.* 1807.

COLE, John Griffith, 1817. Son of Rev. Dr. Cole, Chaplain of Greenwich Hospital. *b.* 1805. Gold Medal. Fellow of Ex. Coll. Oxf. 3rd Class Lit. Hum. Holy Orders; deceased.

COLE, Owen Blaney, 1821. Son of the late Major H. Cole, of Twickenham. *b.* 1808. Ch. Ch. Oxf. Was High Sheriff of Co. Monaghan 1843.

List of Carthusians. 53

COLE-HAMILTON,* Arthur Henry, 1857-65. Son of Major A. W. Cole-Hamilton, of Beltrim. *b.* 1846. Pemb. Coll. Oxf. Rector of Scaldwell, Northampton.

COLEBROOKE, Edward Lotherington, 1873. Son of Dr. H. Colebrooke, of Southboro', Tunbridge Wells.

COLEBROOK, John Henry, 1819, *b.* 1810.

COLERIDGE, Derwent Moultrie, 1843-46, *b.* 1828. Emigrated to Australia.

COLES, , 1801-2.

COLES,* Charles Edward Norman, 1872. Son of Rev. E. Norman Coles, Rector of Pottesgrove. *b.* 1861. In a Merchant's House.

COLES,* Edward Charles, 1830, *b.* 1818.

COLES,* George Godwin, 1842-50. Son of Rev. G. Coles, Vicar of St. James', Croydon. *b.* 1831. Emigrated to Australia, *d.* 1854.

COLES,* Rogers Lyons Cowper, 1871. Son of the late Capt. Cowper Coles, R.N., who was drowned in H.M.S. Captain. *b.* 1860. R.M. Coll. Sandhurst.

COLES, Thomas, 1818. Of Norwood. *b.* 1806. Capt. in the Army; died on his way home from India.

COLES, William, 1806-7, *b.* 1793.

COLLIE, John Norman, 1873.

COLLIER,* Clarence Augustus, 1842-46. Son of Adml. Henry T. B. Collier. *b.* 1830. Lieut.-Col. Bombay Staff Corps; retired.

COLLINS, Thomas, 1841-44. Second son of Rev. T. Collins, of Knaresborough. *b.* 1826. Wadh. Coll. Oxf. Barrister. Late M.P. for Knaresborough.

COLLINS, William, 1801-2. Youngest son of James Collins, of Kirkman Bank, Yorks. *b.* 1787. Formerly Captain of Wakefield Militia.

COLLINS, William, 1845-48. Son of William Collins, of Knaresboro'. *b.* 1830. Ex. Coll. Oxf. Vicar of Freiston, Linc.; deceased.

COLLINSON, Alfred Cockburn, 1862, *b.* 1849.

COLLYER, John, 1814-18. Son of the late Ven. John Bedingfeld Collyer, of Hackford Hall, Norfolk, Archdeacon of Norwich. *b.* 1801. Fellow of Clare Coll. Cam. Senior Opt. Barrister. County Court Judge, *d.*

COLLYER, John Monsey, 1853. Son of the above. *b.* 1840. Went to Rugy School. Univ. Coll. Oxf. 2nd Class Lit. Hum. Barrister. Hackford Hall, Norfolk.

COLLYER, Robert, 1821. Brother of John Collyer (above). *b.* 1804. Trin. Coll. Cam. Junior Opt. Rector of Warham, Norfolk, and Hon. Canon of Norwich, *d.*

COLLYER, Thomas, 1809-11, *b.* 1799. St. John's Coll. Cam. Rector of Gislingham, Suffolk.

COLQUHOUN, James, 1815-16, *b.* 1803.

COLT, Frederick Everard, 1875. Son of F. H. Colt, of Hampstead.

COLTMAN, William Joseph. 1805-11. Son of Wm. Joseph Coltman—B.N.C. Oxf.

COLVIN,* Elliot Graham, 1875-78. Son of B. W. Colvin, E.I.C.S., Member of the Legislative Council. *b.* 1861.

COMBE, Charles William, 1821, *b.* 1808.

COMBE, Lionel, 1873. Son of Major-Gen. James John Combe, of Cippenham House, Slough. *b.* 1862.

COMMELIN, John Dethic, 1807-11, *b.* 1795.

COMPTON, Charles Francis, 1822. Son of Sir Herbert Compton, Chief Justice of Bombay. *b.* 1810. Indian Army. Capt. retired, 1847.

CONDELL, Charles, 1819, *b.* 1806. Solicitor.

CONDELL, William, 1819, *b.* 1808.

CONEY, Henry Tudway, 1873-78. Son of Rev. Thomas Coney, Senior Chaplain to the Forces, S.W. District. *b.* 1860. Entered at Keble Coll. Oxf.

CONEY, William John, 1816-18. Son of Rev. W. J. Coney, of Cookham, Berks. *b.* 1807. Clare Hall, Cam. Rector of Wrington, Somersetshire, *d.*

CONGREVE, William, 1875. Left 1877.

CONNELL,* Alexr. Richard Campbell, 1864. Son of Rev. J. Connell, of Monks Eleigh. *b.* 1851. Trin. Coll. Oxf. B.A. 1876.

CONNOP, Richard, 1876. Son of Newell Connop, of Kingsnympton Park, Devon. *b.* 1863.

CONOLLY, William Philip, 1844-46, *b.* 1829. 46th Bengal N I. deceased.

CONROY,* (Sir) Edward (Bart.), 1820. Son of Sir John Conroy, Bart. *b.* 1809. Ch. Ch. Oxf. Assistant Registrar-General, *d.* 1869.

CONSTABLE, Charles Quayle, 1823, *b.* 1807. Trin. Coll. Cam. A.B. 1830; deceased.

CONSTABLE, John Jolly, 1814-17, *b.* 1801.

COODE, Edward, 1806-9. Eldest son of Edward Coode, of St. Anstell, Cornwall. *b.* 1792. Solicitor. Clerk of the Peace and County Treasurer of Cornwall, *d.* 1865.

COODE, Henry, 1806-11. Brother of the above. *b.* 1795. Solicitor in London, *d.* 1844.

COOK, Alfred, 1847-49, *b.* 1836. Went to Westminster School.

COOK, Herbert George Graham, 1876. Son of T. W. Cook, of Braemar House, Cromwell Road, London.

COOKE, Charles Brand, 1807-16. Son of Rev. Charles Cooke, Rector of Semer, Suffolk. *b.* 1799. St. John's Coll. Cam. *d.* 1820.

COOKE, Edward, 1823. Son of Thos. Cooke, of Peterboro'. *b.* 1808. Queens Coll. Oxf. Barrister.

COOKE, George, 1816. Brother of Charles B. Cooke (above). *b.* 1807. Clare Hall, Cam.

COOKE, George Frederick, 1838. Solicitor and Parliamentary Agent.

COOKE, James Young, 1812. Brother of Charles B. Cooke (above). *b.* 1804. Clare Hall, Cam. Rector of Semer, Suffolk, *d.* 1875.

COOKE, John Parry, 1820, *b.* 1806.

COOKE, Robert Matthew, 1824, *b.* 1810.

COOKE, William Davis Octavius, 1827, *b.* 1812. Royal Navy.

COOKSON, Arthur James, 1826. Son of Isaac Cookson, of Meldon Park, Northumberland. *b.* 1813. Royal Navy, and afterwards in the Merchant Service, *d.* 1847.

COOKSON, George John, 1855. Son of W. I. Cookson (below). J.P. In business in Newcastle-upon-Tyne.

COOKSON, Isaac Thomas, 1821. Son of Thomas Cookson, of Hermitage, Co. Durham. *b.* 1809. Canterbury, New Zealand, *d.* 1872.

COOKSON, William Brian, 1854-58. Son of W. I. Cookson (below). *b.* 1840. Univ. Coll. Oxf. Drowned at Oxford 1859.

COOKSON, William Isaac, 1825. Brother of Arthur J. Cookson (above). *b.* 1812. J.P. for Northumb. and Notts. Worksop Manor, Retford.

COOMBS, Thomas, 1866-69, *b.* 1852. Solicitor at Dorchester.

COOPE, John Frederick, 1873-75. Went to King's Coll. London.

COOPER (Sir) Astley Paston (Bart.), 1810-13. Son of Rev. Saml. L. Cooper and nephew of the eminent surgeon. *b.* 1798. Trin. Coll. Cam. Succeeded to the Baronetcy 1841; *d.* 1866.

COOPER, Astley Paston, 1842-42. Son of Bransby Cooper. *b.* 1827. Caius Coll. Cam. Admiralty Office. Paymaster of H.M. Dockyard, Devonport.

COOPER, Godfrey Charles, 1876. Son of Charles John Cooper, of Bridgenorth. *b.* 1863.

COOPER, Henry Charles, 1810-12, *b.* 1795. Medical Practitioner, *d.* 1819.

COOPER, Lovick Henry, 1843-49. Son of Bransby Cooper. *b.* 1832. Lieut. 1st European Regt., Bengal, died at Meerut 1851.

COOPER, Robert, 1876. Son of Rev. R. J. Cooper, Rector of Fylingdales, Yorks.

COOPER, Samuel Lovick Astley, 1842-46. 3rd son of Sir Astley Cooper, Bart. *b.* 1827. B.N.C. Oxf. Rector of Croxton and Vicar of Eltisley.

COOPER, Sydney, 1874. Son of H. Cooper, of Forest Lodge, Shooter's Hill. *b.* 1862.

COOPER, William Rickford Astley, 1841-44. Son of Sir Astley Cooper, Bart. *b.* 1826. Univ. Coll. Oxf. Vicar of Froyle, Hants, *d.* 1876.

COOPER, William Way, 1860, *b.* 1847. St. John's Coll. Cam. Junior Op. Solicitor in London.

CORBETT, Frank, 1845-47, *b.* 1833. Army. Formerly 33rd Regt.

CORBETT,* James Wortley, 1826-34. Son of Archdeacon Stuart Corbett, of Wortley, Sheffield. *b.* 1814. Orator. Mert. Coll. Oxf. Rector of Wigginton, Yorks.

CORNEWALL,* Herbert Somerset Hamilton, 1839-43, *b.* 1826. Formerly Rifle Brigade.

CORNISH, Charles John, 1872. Son of Rev. C. Cornish, Vicar of Debenham.

CORRANCE, Henry Clemence, 1873. Son of Rev. C. T. Corrance, Vicar of Parham, Suffolk. Ch. Ch. Oxf.

CORRIE, Alfred Wynne, 1872. Son of J. Corrie. Articled to a Solicitor.

CORRIE, John William, 1874. Son of William Corrie, 26, Cleveland Square.

CORRIE, William Byron, 1824, *b.* 1811.

CORY, Charles William, 1872. Son of Alexander Turner Cory, Assistant Sec. Education Department. *b.* 1857. Emigrated to Durban, Natal.

COSTER, George, 1810-12, *b.* 1793. St. John's Coll. Cam. Archdeacon of New Brunswick.

COTTON, Henry James, 1825. Son of the Very Rev. J. H. Cotton, Dean of Bangor. *b.* 1811. Worc. Coll. Oxf. Rector of Dalbury.

COTTON, Joseph John, 1827, *b.* 1813. Indian Civil Service.

COTTON,* Richard Lynch, 1805-12. Son of Henry C. Cotton, Whitchurch, Oxon. *b.* 1794. 2nd Class Lit. Hum. Scholar, Fellow and Provost (1839) of Worc. Coll. Oxf.

COTTON, Thomas Dicey, 1808-12, *b.* 1797.

COTTON, William Charles, 1825. Son of the late William Cotton, and brother of Sir Henry Cotton. *b.* 1813. Went to Eton, Newcastle Scholar. Student of Ch. Ch. Oxf. Vicar of Frodsham.

COULSON, Thomas, 1819, b. 1808. In business at Liverpool.

COURTENAY,* Edward Reginald, 1864. Son of Capt. G. H. Courtenay. b. 1853. Lieut. 20th Hussars.

COVENTRY, Hon. Henry Amelius, 1825. Son of the 8th Earl of Coventry. b. 1815, d. 1873.

COWIE,* Alexander Hugh W. 1874-78. Son of H. C. Cowie, Figtree Court Temple. b. 1860. R.M. Academy, Woolwich.

COWIE, Arthur Thomas Carnsew, 1862. Son of the Very Rev. Benjn. Morgan Cowie, Dean of Manchester. b. 1849. Oriel Coll. Oxf. Assistant Master in St. Edward's School, and Curate of SS. Philip and James, Oxford.

COWIE,* Donald William Garden, 1877. Brother of Alexander H. W. Cowie (above). b. 1863.

COWPER, Harry Villiers, 1875. Son of H. A. Cowper, 46, Cambridge Terrace.

COWPER-SMITH, Arthur Monro, 1877. Son of Rev. T. F. Smith, DD. late Rector of Horsington, Linc. b. 1863.

COWPER-SMITH, Frederick Evan, 1874. Brother of the above. b. 1861. Lieut. Royal Artillery.

Cox, Herbert Vaughan, 1872-77. Son of Rev. F. Cox, Rector of Upper Chelsea.

COXE, William Henry, 1852-58. Son of Rev. H. O. Coxe, Libr. of the Bodleian Library. b. 1840. Ball. Coll. Oxf. Boden Scholar. British Museum. Professor of Sanskrit King's Coll. London, d. 1869.

COXHEAD, Algernon Barnaby, 1864. Son of John Coxhead, 47, Russell Square. b. 1853. In business in London.

COYLE, Lewis Henry, 1842-44. Son of Rev. Miles Coyle. b. 1826. Wadh. Coll. Oxf. Holy Orders, d. 1862.

CRANFIELD, Edward, 1818.

CRASTER, Thomas William, 1875. Eldest son of John Craster, of Craster, Northumberland. b. 1860.

CRANFORD, Thomas Robertson, 1811-12, b. 1803. Went to Eton.

CRESSWELL (Sir) Cresswell Easterby (Knt.), 1806-8. 4th son of Francis Easterby, of Blackheath, who assumed the name of Cresswell on his marriage. *b.* 1793. Em. Coll. Cam. Barrister. M.P. for Liverpool 1837-41. Justice of the Court of Common Pleas 1842. (Knighted). Judge of the Probate and Divorce Court. Governor of Charterhouse, *d.* 1863

CRESSWELL, Edward John, 1845-48. Son of Wm. Cresswell, and nephew of Sir C. Cresswell (above). *b.* 1829. 49th Regt. Crimea, W. Indies, &c. Deputy Judge Advocate to the Forces. Retired Capt. 1868.

CRESSWELL,* Frederick, 1859-61. Son of Rev. O. J. Cresswell. *b.* 1848. Sarum Theol. Coll. Curate of St. John's, Clerkenwell.

CRESSWELL, George, 1845-48. Brother of E. J. Cresswell (above). *b.* 1832. 89th Regt. Was paralysed from exposure in the trenches (Crimean War). Medal and pension. Capt. of Invalid's Royal Hosp., Kilmainham.

CREWE,   , 1800. Left the same year.

CROFT, Richard, 1822. Son of Sir Richard Croft, Bart. *b.* 1808. Ball. Coll. and Fellow of Ex. Coll. Oxf. 2nd Class Lit. Hum. Vicar of Hillingdon, Middlesex.

CROFTON, Edward (First Baron Crofton), 1820. Son of Sir Edward Crofton, Bart. *b.* 1806. Succeeded to the peerage, 1817. Elected a representative Peer of Ireland, 1840, *d.* 1869.

CROHAN, George Birmingham, 1824, *b.* 1811. Trin. Coll. Cam.

CROMMELIN, Charles Barker, 1805-9, *b.* 1790. E. I. Co.'s Service.

CROOME, James, 1844-45. Son of Robert Croome. *b.* 1828. B.N.C. Oxf. Barrister.

CROPPER, James, 1877. Son of Edward William Cropper, of Fearnhead, Great Crosby, Liverpool. *b.* 1862.

CROPPER, John, 1878. Brother of the above. *b.* 1864.

CROSS, John William, 1820, *b.* 1807.

CROSS, Richard Powell, 1819, *b.* 1809.

CROSSE, Edward Algernon, 1867. Son of E. W. Crosse, of Doctor's Commons. *b.* 1855.

CROSSE, Lionel, 1874. Brother of the above.

CROSSE, Richard Reader, 1821, *b.* 1808. Solicitor.

CROUGHTON, William Peel, 1827, *b.* 1817. Of Heronden House, Tenterden.

CROWDEY, James William, 1827, *b.* 1813. 47th Regt. Capt. 1840.

CROWDY, William Slater, 1825. Son of William Crowdy, Highworth, Wilts. *b.* 1814. Linc. Coll. Oxf. Curate of Thursford, Norfolk.

CROWE, John Henry Verinder, 1876. Son of Edward Frederick Crowe, of Gresham Lodge, Hammersmith. *b.* 1862.

CROZIER, James, 1817, *b.* 1802.

CUNDILL, John Ponsonby, 1857-61. Son of Rev. Canon Cundill, Rector of St. Margaret's, Durham. *b.* 1843. Capt. Royal Artillery. Assistant Instructor Royal Laboratory, Woolwich.

CUNNINGHAM, Henry Hutt, 1865-69. Son of H. D. P. Cunningham, R.N., Bury House, Alverstoke, Hants. *b.* 1850. Clare Coll. Cam. Junr. Opt. 1874. Barrister.

CUNINGHAM, William, 1851-54, *b.* 1836.

CUNYNGHAME,* James Joseph Myrton, 1843-51. Son of Sir David Cunynghame, Bart. *b.* 1832. St. John's Coll. Oxf. Rector of Horseheath, Cambs.

CUPPAGE,* Burke, 1846-52. Son of General Cuppage. *b.* 1836. Indian Army. Killed in the Mutiny 1857.

CUPPAGE, Robert Burke, 1842-47. Brother of the above. *b.* 1830. E. I. Co's. Civil Service. Killed in the Mutiny 1857.

CURE, Edward Capel, 1874. (See Capel-Cure).

CURREY,* Eliott Scarlett, 1848-50. Son of Sir Edmund Currey, Equerry to the late Duke of Gloster. *b.* 1836. Civil Engineer.

CURREY, Frederick William, 1873. Son of Arthur Currey.

CURREY, George, 1824. Son of the Rev. James Currey, Preacher of Charterhouse. *b.* 1816. Gold Medal. St. John's Coll. Cam. Bell Scholar, 14th Wrangler, and 1st Class Tripos. Fellow and Tutor of the College. D.D. Preacher at Whitehall 1845. Hulsean Lecturer 1850. Preacher of Charterhouse 1846. Master of Charterhouse 1871. Prebendary of St. Paul's.

CURREY, George Evelyn, 1875. Son of Edmund C. Currey, of Malling Deanery, Sussex. *b.* 1864.

CURREY, James Edmund, 1826, *b.* 1818. Army Surgeon 23rd Regt. *d.* 1861.

CURREY, John Swaine, 1821. Elder brother of the Rev. Dr. Currey, the Master. *b.* 1813, *d.* 1821.

CURREY, William Samuel, 1823. Brother of the above. *b.* 1814. Solicitor. Parliamentary Agent, *d.* 1858.

CURREY, William Vincent, 1821. Son of Col. Currey, of Lismore Castle. Agent to the Duke of Devonshire. *b.* 1808, *d.* 1822.

CURRIE, Charles, 1844-46, *b.* 1829. Civil Commissioner at Allahabad, *d.* 1878.

CURRIE (Sir) Frederick (Bart.), 1808-17. Son of Mark Currie. *b.* 1799. E. I. Co's. Civil Service. Secretary to the Govr.-Genl. of India. Created a Baronet 1846. Chairman of East India Company. Vice-President of the Council of India, *d.* 1875.

CURRIE, Mark John, 1804-6. Brother of the above. *b.* 1795. Admiral, *d.* 1874.

CURRIE, William, 1801-8. Eldest brother of Sir Fredk. Currie, Bart. (above). *b.* 1791, *d.* 1869.

CURTIS, Augustus John, 1827, *b.* 1815. Indian Army, *d.*

CURTIS, Charles George, 1836-40. Son of John Curtis. *b.* 1821. Gold Medal. Post-Master of Mert. Coll. Oxf. Assist. Master in the School. Chaplain at Constantinople. Canon of Gibraltar.

CURTIS, Henry Charles, 1823, *b.* 1812.

CURTIS, John Edmund Lawrence, 1859-62, *b.* 1845.

CURTIS, John Edward, 1851-56, *b.* 1840.

CURTIS, William, 1836-40. Cousin of C. G. Curtis (above). *b.* 1821. Silver Medal. Scholar of St. John's Coll. Cam. Wrangler. Chaplain to the Priory, Roehampton. Formerly Assistant Math. Master in the School.

CURWEN, Edward Darcy, 1878. Son of H. F. Curwen, of Workington Hall, Cumberland.

CURZON, Hon. Edward Cecil, 1823. Son of the Hon. Robt. Curzon and the Baroness De la Zouche. *b.* 1812. Ch. Ch. Oxf. Barrister. D.L. and J.P. for Middlesex. Chairman of Kensington Sessions, &c.

CURZON, Hon. Robert (Lord De la Zouche), 1821. Elder brother of the above. *b.* 1810. Ch. Ch. Oxf. Private Secy. to Lord Stratford de Redcliffe when Ambassador at Constantinople. Joint Commissioner with Sir Fenwick Williams at the Conference at Erzeroum for settling the boundaries between Russia, Persia and Turkey. Succeeded to the title 1870, *d.* 1873. Author of 'Monasteries of the Levant,' &c.

CURZON,* Robert Lothian William, 1868. Son of Col. the Hon. Ernest Curzon, and nephew of Earl Howe. *b.* 1857.

CUTHBERT, William, 1825, *b.* 1813.

D.

DAINTRY, George Smith, 1823. Son of John Smith Daintry, of North Rode, Cheshire. *b.* 1810. J.P. for Cheshire. North Rode Grange.

D'ALBIAC, George Charles, 1819. Son of the late Major D'Albiac, of Buckham Hill, Sussex. *b.* 1807. Capt. 4th Light Dragoons, *d.*

D'ALBIAC, Henry Eardley Aylmer, 1819. Brother of the above. *b.* 1808. J.P. for Sussex. Durrington Manor, Worthing.

DALDY,* Frederick Francis, 1869. Son of Fred. R. Daldy, of Belvedere, Kent. *b.* 1857. Scholar of Pemb. Coll. Cam. Senior Opt.

DALTON,* Edward Charles, 1856-64. Son of Rev. C. B. Dalton, Vicar of Highgate, &c. *b.* 1846; deceased.

DALZEL, , 1806-8.

DALZELL, George, 1802-4.

DAMER,* (see Dawson Damer).

DAMES, Edward Travers Longworth, 1874. Son of Francis Travers Longworth Dames, Q.C., of Dublin. *b.* 1862.

DAMES,* Francis Longworth, 1874. Brother of the above. *b.* 1862.

DANCE,* Charles, 1808-11, *b.* 1795, *d.* 1862.

DANIELL, Charles Astell, 1845-49, *b.* 1833. 8th Bengal Light Cavalry, died 1855.

DANIELL, Percy, 1874. Son of Major Daniell.

DANIELS, William Pottinger, 1853. Left the same year, *b.* 1839.

DANN, Henry, 1822. Son of Richard Dann. *b.* 1810. St. John's Coll. Oxf.

DANN, Richard, 1820, *b.* 1807.

DARBY, Charles William, 1808, *b.* 1794.

DARBY,* John Charles Homfray, 1878. Son of Rev. J. C. S. Darby, Machen Rectory, Newport. *b.* 1864.

DARBY, William John, 1807, *b.* 1793.

DARLEY, Henry Brewster, 1825. Son of Henry Darley, Adby Park, Yorks. *b.* 1809.

DARLING, John, 1835-39. Son of late Dr. Darling, of Russell Square. *b.* 1821. Ch. Ch. Oxf. Barrister, *d.* 1858.

DARLING, Thomas, 1828. Brother of the above. *b.* 1816. St. John's Coll. Cam. Rector of S. Michael Royal, London.

DARNELL, James, 1821, *b.* 1804. Trin. Coll. Cam. A.B. 1826. Holy Orders. Tunbridge Wells.

DASHWOOD,* James Edward Bateman, 1843-48. Son of Adml. Dashwood, of Ringwood, Hants. *b.* 1833. Foreign Office.

DAUGHTREY, John Roberts, 1826, *b.* 1818.

DAVENPORT, Cyril James, 1860-61. Son of Capt. Charles E. Davenport, of Monk's Hill, Pontefract. *b.* 1848. Assistant Librarian British Museum. Formerly in the War Office.

DAVEY, William Harrison, 1836-44. Son of William Davey. Scholar of Linc. Coll. Oxf. Denyer Prize. Vice-Principal Theol. Coll. Lampeter.

DAVIDSON, George, 1814-17. Brother of W. F. Davidson (below). *b.* 1804. Army.

DAVIDSON, Hugh Morgan, 1874. Son of S. Davidson, of Alburgh, Suffolk, and nephew of the above.

DAVIDSON, William Francis, 1815-16. Brother of G. Davidson (above). *b.* 1800. Solicitor in London.

DAVIES, Arthur Templer, 1871. Son of Herbert Davies, M.D., of London. *b.* 1858. Trin. Coll. Cam.

DAVIES, Ernest Reuter, 1875. Brother of the above. *b.* 1862.

DAVIES,* Gerald Stanley, 1856-64. Son of Admiral Davies. *b.* 1845. Gold Medal. Orator. Scholar of Ch. Coll. Cam. 2nd Class Class Tripos. Assistant Master in the School.

DAVIES,* Herbert Wyatt, 1866. Brother of E. R. Davies (above). *b.* 1854. Prize Scholar 1869. Pemb. Coll. Cam. 2nd Class Class Tripos.

DAVIES, Richard Banks, 1873-77. Son of Rev. J. Davies, of Moor Court, Kington, Herefordshire.

DAVIES, Robert, 1804-5, *b.* 1793. Clare Coll. Cam. A.B. 1811.

DAVIES (Sir) Robert Henry (K.C.S.I.), 1835-40. Son of Sir David Davies, K.C.H. *b.* 1824. E. I. Civil Service. Lieut.-Govr. of the Punjab till 1877. Knighted 1874.

DAVIES, William, 1863. Left the same year, *b.* 1846.

DAVIES,* William Henry, 1835-44. Brother of Sir Robt. H. Davies (above). *b.* 1825. Orator. Ch. Ch. Oxf. Chaplain to St. George's Hospital, *d.* 1868.

DAVIS, Arthur Holdsworth, 1875. Son of B. Goodwin Davis, of St. John's Wood Park. *b.* 1863.

DAVIS, William Lloyd, 1875. Son of W. Davis.—deceased.

List of Carthusians. 65

DAVISON, George, 1814-17, b. 1804.

DAVISON, James, 1803-4.

DAWES, William Rutter, 1812-13, b. 1799.

DAWKINS,* Charles Digby, 1812-18. Son of Henry Dawkins, M.P. for Aldborough. b. 1800. Ch. Ch. Oxf. Indian Army, d. 1846.

DAWSON, Baker, 1817. Son of John Dawson. b. 1800. B.N.C. Oxf.

DAWSON,* Herbert James, 1877. Son of James Dawson, of Gipsy Hill. b. 1864.

DAWSON, Hugh Pudsey, 1821, b. 1808.

DAWSON, Samuel Francis, 1812, b. 1798, d. 1816.

DAWSON-DAMER, John William George, 1846-49. Son of the Hon. Willm. Dawson-Damer, and grandson of the 3rd Earl of Portarlington. b. 1834. Capt. R.N. Served at Sweaborg and Cronstadt, and in the Black Sea 1854. d. 1869.

DAWSON-DAMER,* Lionel Digby William, 1845-51. Brother of the above. b. 1832. Orator. Gold Medal. Scholar of Trin. Coll. Oxf. Vicar of Gt. Canford, Dorset.

DAY,* Charles Henry, 1862. Son of Rev. George Day, Rector of Baldwyn Brightwell, Oxon. b. 1849. Pemb. Coll. Oxf. Indian Medical Service.

DAY, Charles James, 1869, b. 1858. Pemb. Coll. Oxf. d. 1870.

DAY, Edward Augustus, 1823, b. 1809.

DAY, Francis Hermitage, 1875. Son of Rev. H. C. Day, of Frindsbury, Kent. b. 1861. Entered at Keble Coll. Oxf.

DAY, Frederick, 1824, b. 1814. Pemb. Coll. Cam.

DAY, John Nash, 1823, b. 1818.

DAY, Thomas, 1821, b. 1809.

DAY, William, 1824. Son of Rev. George Day. b. 1812. Mert. Coll. Oxf. Holy Orders.

DEAKIN, Egerton, 1872. Son of J. B. Deakin, of Darwen. b. 1856.

F

DEAN,* Charles Augustus Brietzke, 1819. Son of the Chairman of Commissioners of Customs. *b.* 1808. Barrister; deceased.

DEAN, Richard Ryder, 1822. Son of Richard Bettenson Dean. *b.* 1810. Ch. Ch. Oxf.

DEANE, Henry, 1820. Son of William Deane. *b.* 1807. Ex. Coll. Oxf. Chaplain at Canton. Rector of Hintlesham.

DEANE, Henry Allen Murray, 1840-42, *b.* 1825. Lieut. 4th Regt. Retired on half pay.

DEANE, Hugh Pollexfen, 1848-54. Son of Rev. J. B. Deane, Mathematical Master at Merchant Taylor's School. *b.* 1836. Went into the Army.

DEARE, Frederick Arthur, 1874. Son of F. D. Deare, of Wentworth, Ditton Hill, Surrey.

DEAS, Francis William, 1875. Son of the late Sir David Deas, K.C.B., M.D. *b.* 1862.

DE BRISAY, Henry Le Stock Delacour, 1874. Son of Rev. H. D. de Brisay, of Oxford.

DE CRESPIGNY,* Heaton Champion, 1806-11. Son of Sir Wm. C. De Crespigny, Bart. M.P. *b.* 1796. Was formerly in the Royal Navy. Afterwards ordained.

DE GREY, Hon. Frederick, 1821. Son of the 4th Baron Walsingham. *b.* 1811. St. John's Coll. Cam. Rector of Copdock, Ipswich.

DE GREY, Hon. George, 1821. Brother of the above. *b.* 1812.

DELHOSTE,* Donald Charles Augustus, 1840-45. *b.* 1829. Formerly in 63rd Regt.

DE MOLEYNS, Edward Henry, 1873-76. Son of Edward Henry de Moleyns, Solicitor to the Bank of Ireland. *b.* 1859. Trin. Coll. Dublin.

DEMPSEY, Henry Blundell, 1878. Son of Arthur Dempsey, St. George's Mount, New Brighton, Cheshire. *b.* 1864.

DEMPSEY, Hugh Paul, 1875. Brother of the above. *b.* 1862.

DENDY, Samuel, 1827. Son of Arthur Dendy. *b.* 1813. Trin. Coll. Oxf. Holy Orders. Lattisford House, Wincanton.

DENNIS, George, 1828, *b.* 1814.

DENNIS, John Gwennap, 1827, *b.* 1812; *d.* 1830.

DENNISON, Mark Byam, 1821, *b.* 1812.

DENT, Stanley Marseille, 1873-77. Son of Stanley Dent, of Mayfield, Upper Tooting. *b.* 1861. Merchant.

DENT, William, 1873-77. Brother of the above. *b.* 1860. Wine Merchant.

DE SOYRES,* Francis, 1817. Son of Rev. Francis de Soyres. *b.* 1804. Mert. Coll. Oxf. Holy Orders. 13, Victoria Terrace, Mt. Radford, Exeter.

DES VOEUX, Alfred Anthony, 1842-46. Son of Rev. Henry Des Voeux and brother of Sir Henry Des Voeux, Bart. *b.* 1830. Lieut.-Col. 5th Bombay N.I.

DES VOEUX, Edward Alfred, 1876. Son of the above.

DES VOEUX,* George William, 1846-53. Brother of Alf. A. Des Voeux (above). *b.* 1834. Orator. Ball. Coll. Oxf. Lieut.-Governor Fiji Islands.

DEVENISH, Henry Weston, 1873. Son of Henry Devenish, of Whitchurch, Hants. Ex. Coll. Oxf.

DEVEREUX, Hon. Humphrey de Bohun, 1824. Son of the 15th Visct. Hereford. *b.* 1812. E. I. Co's. Service. The High Wood, Leominster.

DEVEY, William Giffard, 1875. Son of C. H. Devey.

DEWAR,* William Wemyss Methven, 1840-48. Son of the late Sir John Dewar. *b.* 1829. Orator. Ball. Coll. Oxf. Formerly Capt. Oxfordshire Militia. D.L. for Oxon. Middleton Stoney, Bicester.

DEWRANCE, John, 1872-74. Son of John Dewrance, of The Green Hills, Tilford, Surrey. *b.* 1858. Mechanical Engineer.

D'EYNCOURT,* Ashton Lovett Tennyson, 1874. (See Tennyson D'Eyncourt). B.N.C. Oxf.

DE ZOETE, Charles Septimus, 1873. Son of Samuel Herman de Zoete, of Hayes, Kent.   Mert. Coll. Oxf.

DICKEN,* Charles Rowland, 1814. Son of Rev. Perry Dicken, of Witheridge, Devon. *b.* 1801. Corpus Coll. Cam. Assist. Master. Reader and Librarian to Charterhouse. Rector of Balsham, Cambs. *d.* 1873.

DICKEN, Charles Shortt, 1855-58. Son of William Stevens Dicken, M.D. *b.* 1841. Holds a Government appointment at Brisbane, Queensland.

DICKEN, Edmund Ashton, 1824. Brother of Charles Rowland Dicken (above). *b.* 1808. Sid. Suss. Coll. Cam. Holy Orders; deceased.

DICKEN, Frederick Rowland, 1858-59. Son of Rev. A. Dicken, D.D. *b.* 1845. Commander R.N. H.M.S. Arab.

DICKEN, George Perry, 1860-61. Brother of Charles Shortt Dicken (above). *b.* 1848. Emigrated to Queensland.

DICKEN, Purefoy Huddleston, 1860-61. Brother of Frederick Rowland Dicken (above). *b.* 1850; deceased.

DICKEN,* William Charles Henry, 1842-47. Son of Rev. Charles Rowland Dicken (above). *b.* 1829. War Office. Retired on a pension. Resides at Bengeo, Herts.

DICKEN, William Popham, 1849-51. Brother of Charles Shortt Dicken (above). *b.* 1834. Major Madras Staff Corps.

DICKINSON, Arthur Lowes, 1873. Son of Lowes Dickinson, of Hanwell. Scholar of King's Coll. Cam.

DICKINSON,* Goldsworthy Lowes, 1876. Brother of the above. *b.* 1862.

DICKINSON, Thomas Malcolm, 1878. Son of Major-Genl. William Rice Dickinson. *b.* 1864.

DICKSON, Thomas Briggs, 1819, *b.* 1804. Fellow of Em. Coll. Cam. Vicar of Eastchurch, Kent.

DICKSON, Walter Collin, 1864, *b.* 1841.

DILLON, Hon. Arthur Edmund Denis, 1825. Son of the 13th Visct. Dillon. *b.* 1812. Trin. Coll. Oxf. Home Office.

DINGWALL, Walter Molyneux, 1878. Son of Charles Dingwall, of Caterham, Surrey. *b.* 1863.

DISBROWE,* Henry Sharpe, 1832-41. Son of the Rev. H. Disbrowe. *b.* 1822. Orator. Univ. Coll. Oxf. Rector of Bennington, Lincolnsh.

DIXON, Charles Steward, 1821, *b.* 1808.

DIXON, George, 1878. Son of John Dixon, C.E., of Surbiton. *b.* 1864.

DIXON, George Blackett, 1828, *b.* 1812.

DIXON, John Spofforth, 1826, *b.* 1813. Banker in London. Chancery Lane.

DOBBIE, Charles Francis, 1876. Son of Maj.-Genl. Dobbie, of Budleigh Salterton, N. Devon.

DOBBIE, Herbert Hugh, 1872. Brother of the above. *b.* 1859. R.M. Coll. Sandhurst.

DOBINSON, Joseph, 1804-9. West India Merchant.

DOBINSON, Joseph, 1842-45, *b.* 1827. Deceased.

DOBSON, Francis, 1818, *b.* 1804.

DOBSON, William, 1822, *b.* 1809. Fellow of Trin. Coll. Cam. 1st Class. Vicar of Tuxford, Notts. Principal of Cheltenham Coll. *d.* 1868.

DOBSON, William Burdett, 1803-5.

DOCKER, Thomas Robert, 1816-18, *b.* 1803. Pemb. Coll. Cam. Formerly Rector of Froxfield, *d.*

DODD, Charles William, 1811-12. Went to Westminster School.

DODD, Rose, 1819-20, *b.* 1806.

DODSON, James, 1825. Son of George Dodson. *b.* 1813. Ch. Ch. Oxf.

DOLLMAN, Francis, 1835-40. Son of Rev. Francis Dollman (below). *b.* 1824. Solicitor in London. Bexley Heath, Kent.

DOLLMAN, Francis, 1806-10, *b.* 1791. Trin. Coll. Cam. Formerly Vicar of St. Mark's, Myddleton Square, London, and Vicar of Loders, Dorset, *d.* 1869.

DOLPHIN,* Henry, 1816. Son of Rev. J. Dolphin, Rector of Wakescoln and Pebmarsh, Essex. *b.* 1806. Entered the E. I. Co's. Service, but was drowned the day after his arrival at Bombay.

DONNITHORNE, Edward George Moore, 1853-54. Son of E. H. Donnithorne, of Ewhurst, Surrey. *b.* 1842. Capt. 2nd Royal Dragoons. Served in New Zealand War as Lieut. R.A.

DORLING, Francis, 1863-68. Son of H. Dorling, of Croydon. *b.* 1850. Capt. 96th Regt.

DORLING, Horace Norman, 1874. Brother of the above.

DORLING, Lionel, 1873. Brother of the above. R.M. Coll. Sandhurst.

DORLING, Walter, 1867. Brother of the above. *b.* 1855.

DOUGLAS, Archibald Charles, 1875. Son of the late Rt. Rev. H. A. Douglas, Bishop of Bombay. *b.* 1861.

DOUGLAS, Edward Algernon Stuart, 1861, *b.* 1848.

DOUGLAS, Henry, 1841-47. Son of the Rev. Canon Douglas, of Durham. *b.* 1828. Merchant in London.

DOUGLAS, Henry Dighton, 1877. Son of the above. *b.* 1864.

DOUGLAS, James William, 1865, *b.* 1852.

DOUGLAS,* John, 1819, *b.* 1805.

DOUGLAS, John, 1822, *b.* 1811. Went to India.

DOUGLAS, Percy, 1842, *b.* 1833. Left the same year.

DOUGLAS,* Robert Stopford, 1856-58, *b.* 1844. Grenadier Guards.

DOUGLAS, William Frederick, 1823, *b.* 1813. Ch. Coll. Cam. Vicar of Shefford, *d.*

DOWBIGGIN,* Montague Hamilton, 1846-48. Son of Col. W. H. Dowbiggin and nephew of Lord Dalhousie. *b.* 1832. Served with the 71st, 4th and 99th Regts. (Crimea). Lieut.-Col. *d.* 1866.

DOWELL, Thomas, 1824. Son of Thomas Dowell. *b.* 1811. Oriel Coll. Oxf. Vicar of Evancoyd, Radnorshire.

DOWN, Edward Arthur, 1875. Son of James Dundas Sommers Down, of Oakridge, Dorking. *b.* 1862.

DOWN, Everleigh Langdon, 1874-77. Son of J. Langdon-Down, M.D. *b.* 1861. London University (1879).

DOWN, Richard, 1830-34. Son of H. Down, Banker, of London. *b.* 1816. Inspector-General of Customs, Victoria. Retired, 1876.

DOWNES, William, 1850-53. Son of Rev. John Downes. *b.* 1837. Ex. Coll. Oxf. F.G.S. Curate of Kentisbeare, Collumpton.

List of Carthusians.

DOWNING, Benjamin Joshua Evans, 1847-49, b. 1832.

DRAKE, John D'Urban Tyrwhitt, 1877.
DRAKE, Fredk. E. Tyrwhitt, 1840. } See Tyrwhitt-Drake.
DRAKE, Alg. Fredk. Tyrwhitt, 1872.

DRAKE,* William Montague, 1841-47, b. 1830. Solicitor.

DREW, Ernest Young, 1870. Son of Rev. William H. Henry Drew (King's Coll. London). b. 1857. Stock Exchange.

DREW,* William Wilson, 1869. Brother of the above. b. 1855. King's Coll. Cam. E. India Civil Service.

DRUCE, Charles Carey, 1874. Son of Edwd. Read W. Druce, of Dover.

DRUCE, George Claridge, 1873. Son of Alexander Devas Druce, Solicitor.

DRUCE, Hubert Arthur, 1874. Brother of the above.

DRUMMOND,* Charles Spenser, 1846-53. Eldest son of the late Rev. Arthur Drummond. b. 1834. Worc. Coll. Oxf. Emigrated to Canada.

DRUMMOND, Heneage, 1819. Son of John Drummond. b. 1810. Ball. Coll. Oxf. 4th Class Lit. Hum. Rector of Leckhamsted.

DRUMMOND, Hugh, 1819. Brother of the above. b. 1807. Clerk in the Colonial Office, d. 1829.

DRUMMOND, Spencer, 1819. Brother of the above. b. 1808. Clerk in the Treasury, d. 1869.

DRUMMOND, Hon. William Henry (7th Visct. Strathallan), 1822. Son of the 6th Viscount. b. 1810. Succeeded his father 1851; is a representative Peer for Scotland.

DRUMMOND, Hon. William Henry, 1856-58. Son of the above. b. 1845.

DRUMMOND-HAY, Edward, 1827.
DRUMMOND-HAY, John, 1828. } See Hay.

DU CANE (Sir) Charles (K.C.M.G.), 1836-42. Son of Captain Charles Ducane, R.N. of Braxted Park, Essex. b. 1825. Ex. Coll. Oxf. 4th Class. M P. for Maldon, North Essex. Was a Lord of the Admiralty, 1866-69. Governor of Tasmania.

List of Carthusians.

Du Cane, Louis Charles, 1876. Son of Richard Du Cane, of Roehampton. *b.* 1863.

Du Cane, Richard Dacre Guest, 1876. Brother of the above. *b.* 1862.

Dudding, Horatio Nelson, 1821. Son of Edward Barr Dudding. *b.* 1808. Fellow of Ex. Coll. Oxf. 1st Class Lit. Hum. Vicar of St. Peter's, St. Albans.

Dumaresque,* Algernon Edward, 1845-48, *b.* 1833.

Dumergue, Charles, 1824 Son of Charles Dumergue, of 42, Albemarle Street, London. *b.* 1811. Indian Civil Service, Madras, *d.* 1837.

Dumergue, Herbert Walter, 1874. Son of Rev. Walter Scott Dumergue, Vicar of Farnham. *b.* 1860. C.C.C. Cam. (1879).

Dumergue, John Shore, 1826. Brother of Charles Dumergue (above). *b.* 1812. Indian Civil Service, Bengal. Judge; retired, 1862.

Duncan, Douglas Charteris, 1875. Son of Henry Cairncross Duncan, of Bromborough, Cheshire. *b.* 1862.

Duncan, Percival Jenour, 1874. Brother of the above.

Dundas, Robert James, 1845-52. Son of William Pitt Dundas, of Edinburgh. *b.* 1833. Ex. Coll. Oxf. Rector of Albury. Formerly Chaplain to the Bishop of Columbia.

Dunlop, Andrew Robert, 1823. Son of James Dunlop. *b.* 1810. Ch. Ch. Oxf. *d.* 1830.

Dunn,* Ronald, 1863. Son of Isaac Dunn, of Patrington, Yorks. *b.* 1850. Caius Coll. Cam. Curate of Swinton.

Dunnage, Charles, 1825, *b.* 1809. Solicitor.

Dunsford,* William Henry, 1823, *b.* 1813. Clare Hall, Cam. Of Tiverton, Devon.

Dunsmure, James, 1819, *b.* 1805. Clerk in the India House.

Durham, Patrick Francis, 1823, *b.* 1809. Capt. 37th Regt. Retired.

Duthoit, Henry Causer, 1876. Son of William Duthoit, D.C.L. Indian Civil Service. *b.* 1862.

DYKEN, Joseph Lawes, 1806. Left in ill-health, 1808.

DYNE, William Tylden, 1874. Son of Rev. Dr. Dyne, Preby. of St. Paul's—Oriel Coll. Oxf.

DYNELEY,* Douglas, 1842-48. Son of Major-Genl. Dyneley, R.H.A. *b.* 1831. 23rd Regt. Crimea. Killed in the attack on the Redan, 8th Sept., 1855.

DYNELEY, Henry Ellenborough, 1842-44. Brother of the above. *b.* 1829. Lieut.-Col. Commanding 4th Madras Light Cavalry.

DYSON, George William, 1877. Son of George Dyson, Corn Bank, Netherton, Yorks. *b.* 1864.

DYSON,* Henry Wilcocks, 1804-9, *b.* 1793.

DYSON, Thomas James, 1875. Brother of G. W. Dyson (above). *b.* 1862.

E.

EADY, Richard Moorhouse, 1875. Son of T. W. Eady, of Richmond, Surrey. *b.* 1861.

EAGLE, Francis King, 1800-2. Of Bury St. Edmunds, *b.* 1784. Trin. Coll. Cam. LL.B. Barrister.

EAGLE, Robert, 1800-1. Died young.

EAGLE, William, 1800-5. Trin. Coll. Cam. Barrister of the Temple.

EAMER,* Henry Scott, 1817. Son of Sir John Eamer, Knt. *b.* 1803. Deceased.

EARDLEY, William, 1878. Son of Rev. William Eardley, Vicar of Cantley, Yorks. *b.* 1863.

EARDLEY-WILMOT,* Edward Parry, 1855.
EARDLEY-WILMOT,* Ernest Augustus, 1862. } See Wilmot.
EARDLEY-WILMOT, Hugh Eden, 1862.
EARDLEY-WILMOT, William Assheton, 1853.

EARLE, Edward Robert, 1808-9, b. 1795. Ch. Coll. Cam. Vicar of Wardley, Rutlandshire.

EARLE (Sir) Hardman (Bart.), 1804-9. Son of Thomas Earle, of Spekelands, Lancashire. b. 1792. Merchant in Liverpool. Created a Baronet, 1869; d. 1877.

EARLE, Henry, 1802-5.

EARLE, James, 1802-4.

EARLE, Richard, 1807-14. Brother of Sir Hardman Earle (above). b. 1796. St. John's Coll. Cam. Senior Op. Barrister. Poor Law Commissioner in Ireland, d. 1848.

EASTLAKE (Sir) Charles Locke (Knt.). Son of the late George Eastlake, Judge Advocate at Plymouth. b. 1793. President of the Royal Academy. F.R.S. Director of the National Gallery, &c., d. 1865.

EASTLAKE,* William, 1868-71. Son of William Eastlake, of Plymouth, Deputy Judge Advocate to the Fleet. b. 1855. Solicitor at Plymouth.

EASTON, Francis Henry Tytherley, 1873. Son of Charles Easton, Holton Hall, Holdsworth. b. 1859. Trin. Coll. Cam.

EASTWICK, Edward Backhouse (C.B.), 1827. Son of late Robt. Wm. Eastwick. b. 1814. Post-Master of Merton Coll. Oxf. Indian Army and Civil Service. F.R.S. 1851. Late M.P. for Penryn and Falmouth. Made a C.B. for his Services in Persia, 1859. Author of several translations and works on Oriental literature, &c.

EATON, Thomas, 1818. Son of Thomas Eaton, R.N. b. 1805. Trin. Coll. Cam. Rector of W. Kirby. Canon of Chester. Formerly Rector of St. Mary's, Chester.

EBDEN, John Watts, 1823. Eldest son of John Bardwell Ebden, of Capetown. b. 1810. Fellow of Trin. Hall, Cam. Formerly Attorney Genl. and a Judge of the Supreme Court, Cape of Good Hope.

EBDEN,* Leonard Powney, 1878. Eldest son of Richard Powney Ebden, of the Colonial Office. b. 1864.

EDDIS, John Elwin, 1873. Son of Arthur Shelly Eddis, 19, Old Sq., Lincoln's Inn.   Trin. Hall, Cam.

EDDIS, Kenneth Hubert, 1878. Brother of the above. b. 1865.

List of Carthusians.

EDEN, Hon. Francis Fleetwood, 1877. Son of the 4th Baron Auckland. *b.* 1865.

EDEN, Reuben, 1834-36. Left in ill-health.

EDGAR,* Edward Alexander Kerr, 1822. Son of the late Capt. Edgar, R.A. *b.* 1811. Civil Service. Retired 1871.

EDGELL, Harry, 1823, *b.* 1810. St. John's Coll. Cam. Rector of Nacton.

EDGELL, William Charles, 1826. Son of Henry Edgell. *b.* 1813. St. John's Coll. Oxf. Rector of Uggeshall, Norfolk.

EDGEWORTH, Francis Beaufort, 1819-25. Son of R. L. Edgeworth, of Edgeworth's Town, Co. Longford, and nephew of Miss Edgeworth, the authoress. *b.* 1809. Trin. Coll. Cam. *d.* 1846.

EDGEWORTH, Michael Pakenham, 1823-25. Brother of the above. *b.* 1812. Bengal Civil Service. Retired 1859. Author of many works and papers on Oriental languages, Botany, &c.

EDIS, Robert Wilkie, 1876. Son of Robert W. Edis, F.S.A.

EDMONDS, Walter John Rastall, 1866-68, *b.* 1853.

EDWARDS, Andrew, 1809-11, *b.* 1794. Caius Coll. Cam. Afterwards Fellow of Magd. Coll. Oxf. 2nd Class. Holy Orders. B.D. 1828.

EDWARDS, Arthur George, 1874.

EDWARDS, Edward James Justinian George, 1819. Son of James Edwards. *b.* 1811. Went to Shrewsbury School. Ball. Coll. Oxf. Hebrew Scholar. Vicar of Trentham.

EDWARDS, Fitzjames Maine, 1874. Son of James Edwards, M.D., of Benarth, Carnarvonshire. *b.* 1861.

EDWARDS, Henry Rodie, 1826, *b.* 1816.

EDWARDS, James, 1819, *b.* 1809.

EDWARDS, John Alabaster, 1821, *b.* 1813.

EDWARDS, Lawrence Tucker, 1820, *b.* 1807. Trin. Hall, Cam. Rector of Waltham, Essex.

EDWARDS, Lushington, 1804-7.

EDWARDS,* Spencer Henry Hutchins, 1833-40, *b.* 1822. 98th Regt. Served in the Punjab Campaign, &c. 2 Medals and Clasps. Lieut.-Col., retired.

EDWARDS, William Horatio, 1826. Son of Thomas Spencer Edwards, of Antigua. *b.* 1810. B.N.C. Oxf. Holy Orders. Died in Antigua.

EGERTON, Cecil Martin, 1874-77. Son of Lieut.-Col. the Hon. Arthur Egerton. *b.* 1859.

EGERTON, Granville George Algernon, 1872-74. Brother of the above. R.M. Coll. Sandhurst.

ELDER, Edward, 1826-30. Son of John W. Edward Elder, of Barbados. *b.* 1812. Scholar of Ball. Coll. Oxf. 1st Class Lit. Hum. Head Master of Durham School. Head Master of Charterhouse, 1853, *d.* 1858.

ELLABY, William Francis, 1826, *b.* 1817.

ELLIOT, Hugh, 1877. Son of Frederick Eden Elliot, E. I. Civil Service. *b.* 1863.

ELLIOT, Norman Bruce, 1863. Left the same year, *b.* 1848.

ELLIOTT, Joseph, 1825, *b.* 1817.

ELLIS, Bernard, 1874. Son of C. Ellis, of Beddingham, Sussex. Articled to a Solicitor.

ELLIS, Clement George Lumley, 1878.

ELLIS, Francis Jervoise, 1822. Son of Rev. Francis Ellis. *b.* 1809. Mert. Coll. Oxf. M.A. 1835.

ELLIS,* Frederick John, 1838-43, *b.* 1828. 58th Bengal Native Infantry. Retired Major-General 1876.

ELLIS, George Henry, 1831-37, *b.* 1820. Indian Civil Service, Madras.

ELLIS, Godin, 1818, *b.* 1805.

ELLIS,* Henry Augustus Lewis, 1835-42. Son of the Hon. Henry Ellis. *b.* 1823. Ex. Coll. Oxf. 1st Bengal Light Cavalry. A.D.C. to Lord Hardinge, *d.* 1852.

ELLIS, John Chute, 1860-61, *b.* 1848.

ELLIS, Robert, 1803-5, *b.* 1790. Trin. Coll. Cam. J.P. of N. and E. Ridings and Vicar of Acaster-Malbis, Yorks.

ELLIS, Robert Keate Alves, 1853-54, *b.* 1835. Gold Medal. Scholar of Trin. Coll. Oxf. County Court Office, Sunderland.

ELLIS, Robert Staunton (C.B.), 1838-40, *b.* 1826. Madras Civil Service. C.B. 1860; *d.* 1877.

ELLIS, Thomas Chute, 1860-61, *b.* 1849.

ELLIS, Walter James Elley, 1823, *b.* 1808. Caius Coll. Cam.

ELLMAN, Henry John, 1815-17. Son of John Ellman, of Glynde, Sussex. *b.* 1799. Wadh. Coll. Oxf. B.C.L. 1828. Rector of Carlton, Beds, *d.* 1862.

ELRINGTON, Robert Fenwick, 1869-70. Son of Rev. R. B. F. Elrington. *b.* 1855. Lieut. Cornwall Miners Artillery Militia.

ELWES, Henry Robert Harrington Carey, 1820, *b.* 1808. Of Billing Hall, Northampton. Was in the Army; deceased.

ELWYN, Richard, 1836-45. Son of Rev. W. Elwyn, Vicar of Loose, near Maidstone. *b.* 1827. Scholar and Fellow of Tin. Coll. Cam. Bell and Craven Scholarships. Members Prizeman. Junr. Opt. and Senior Classic, &c. Head Master of Charterhouse, 1858. Head Master of S. Peter's School, York, 1864. Prebendary of York. Vicar of Ramsgate. Hon. Canon of Canterbury.

ELWYN,* William, 1834-41. Brother of the above. *b.* 1822. Ch. Coll. Cam. 58th Bengal Native Infantry. Retired Major-Gen. 1874; *d.* 1876.

EMERIS, William Charles, 1877. Son of Rev. John Emeris, Rector of Upton St. Leonard, Gloucester. *b.* 1863.

EMERSON, Alexander Lyon, 1827. Son of Alexander Lyon Emerson, of Retford. *b.* 1812. Pemb. Coll. Oxf.

EMPSON, , 1804-5.

EMPSON,* Walter, 1867. Son of Rev. Arthur John Empson, Rector of Eydon, and grandson of Dean Hook. *b.* 1856. Trin. Coll. Oxf.

ENGLAND, George Fuller Ashbridge, 1875.

ENGLAND, William Henry Russell, 1877. Son of Capt. Russell England.

ENGLEHEART, Evelyn Linzee, 1875. Son of Gardiner D. Engleheart, Vice-Chancellor of the Duchy of Lancaster. *b.* 1862.

ERSKINE,* Henry Adeane, 1867. Son of Rev. Thomas Erskine, Rector of Alderley, Cheshire. *b.* 1857.

ERSKINE, James Francis, 1875. Son of Henry David Erskine, of Cardross, Perthshire. *b.* 1862.

ERSKINE,* James Hay, 1858-60. Son of Capt. George Keith Erskine, Bombay Cavalry. *b.* 1845. Emigrated to New Zealand; deceased.

ERSKINE, Keith David, 1876. Son of Major George Elphinstone Erskine, Bombay Cavalry. *b.* 1863.

ESCOMBE, Rowland Lingard, 1877. Son of Rowland Escombe, of Blackheath. *b.* 1863.

ESDAILE, Edward Margrave, 1851-53. Brother of James K. Esdaile (below). *b.* 1842. Merchant.

ESDAILE, James Kennedy, 1818. Son of James Esdaile, of Bunhill Row, London. *b.* 1803; deceased.

ESDAILE, James Kennedy, 1850-53. Son of Edward Esdaile, of Ockley, Surrey. *b.* 1840. St. Peter's Coll. Cam. Of Saint Hill Place, Sussex.

ESDAILE, John, 1818. Left the same year. Son of James Esdaile, of Bunhill Row, London. *b.* 1805; deceased.

ESPINASSE, Isaac, 1842-49. Son of James Espinasse, of Maidstone. *b.* 1829. Solicitor, Richmond and Hemel, Hemstead.

ESPINASSE, Richard, 1846-50. Brother of the above. *b.* 1832. Ch. Ch. Oxf. Vicar of Westhampnett, Sussex.

ESPINASSE, Richard Talbot, 1874. Son of the above. *b.* 1864.

ESTEN, James Christie Palmer, 1820, *b.* 1805.

ESTEN, John Hamilton, 1820, *b.* 1808. Rifle Brigade. Major, retired. Settled in Canada.

ESTLIN, George Stuckey, 1822, *b.* 1809. Of Bristol.

ESTRIDGE, John Julius, 1815-17, *b.* 1799. St. John's Coll. Cam. Rector of Puncknowle, Bridport.

ESTRIDGE, William, 1816, *b.* 1804.

List of Carthusians.

EVAN-THOMAS, Llewelyn, 1874. Son of Chas. Evan-Thomas, Barrister of the Inner Temple. *b.* 1859. Ball. Coll. Oxf.

EVAN-THOMAS, Owen Grant, 1874. Brother of the above. *b.* 1861.

EVANS, Arthur, 1851-56. Son of Herbert Norman Evans, M.D. *b.* 1840, *d.* 1854.

EVANS, Arthur Benoni, 1827, *b.* 1813. Surgeon. E. I. Co's. Service. Drowned in India.

EVANS, Arthur Robertson, 1849-55. Son of Richard David Jones Evans, of Hertford. *b.* 1840. Oriel Coll. Oxf. Domestic Chaplain to the Bishop of Ely.

EVANS, George Randell, 1877. Son of G. Evans, of Richmond. *b.* 1864.

EVANS, John, 1818, *b.* 1803. Pemb. Coll. Cam. Formerly Secy. to S.P.C.K. Prebendary of St. Paul's; (*d.* 1879).

EVANS, Lewis James, 1851-52. Brother of Arthur Evans (above). *b.* 1838. Naval Cadet, *d.* 1852.

EVANS, Neville, 1852-56. Son of Rev. T. S. Evans, Vicar of Shoreditch. *b.* 1839. Marine Engineer.

EVANS, Turberville, 1852-58. Brother of the above. *b.* 1838. Ex. Coll. Oxf. Vicar of Buckland, Dover.

EVELEGH, Henry John, 1817, *b.* 1802.

EVELYN, William Arthur, 1874. Son of the late Francis Evelyn, of Corton, Radnorshire. *b.* 1860. Caius Coll. Cam. (1879).

EVERARD, Edward John, 1826. Son of Rev. Dr. Everard, of The Wick, Brighton. *b.* 1814. Went to Eton. St. John's Coll. Cam. Rector of Tormarton.

EVERETT, Charles, 1823, *b.* 1811.

EVERETT, William, 1820, *b.* 1810.

EVERSLEY, Edmund Jordan, 1813-16. Son of S. W. Eversley, of Barbados. Solicitor. *b.* 1800, *d.* at Bath, 1859.

EVERSLEY, Edward Welch, 1813-16, Brother of the above. *b.* 1803. Capt. 60th Rifles.

EWART, Charles Henry, 1854. Left the same year, *b.* 1839.

EWBANK, William, 1827, b. 1815.

EWBANK, William Withers, 1825. Son of Rev. William Ewbank, Rector of North Witham, Lincolnshire. b. 1807. Ch. Coll. Cam. Bell Scholar, &c. Perpet. Curate of Everton, d. 1854.

EWEN, Thomas L'Estrange, 1802-5. Son of Thomas Ewen, of Norwich. b. 1791. St. John's Coll. Cam.; deceased.

EWING, Guy Beaumont, 1877. Son of Rev. J. A. Ewing, of West Mill Rectory, Buntingford. b. 1863.

EWING, Wentworth Hugh Alexander, 1877. Brother of the above. b. 1864.

F.

FAGAN, Christopher George, 1820. Son of Col. G. H. Fagan, Adj.-General of the Bengal Army. b. 1812. 8th Bengal Cavalry. Lieut.-Col. retired; deceased.

FAGAN, Christopher Weston, 1820. Son of Major-General Christopher Fagan, Bengal Army. b. 1811. Bengal Civil Service, d. 1856.

FAGGE (Sir) John (Bart.), 1812-16. Son of Sir John Fagge, of Mystole, Kent. 6th Bart. b. 1798. Ch. Ch. Oxf. Succeeded his father 1822. d. 1873.

FAGGE, John William, 1812. Brother of the above. b. 1801, d. 1840.

FAIR, James Alexr. Stretton, 1877. Son of Thomas Fair, of Lytham, Lanc. b. 1863.

FAIRBAIRN, Thomas James Alexander Browne, 1820, b. 1808.

FAIRLES, Gustavus William, 1859-63, b. 1847.

FAIRLIE, Frank Archibald, 1878. Son of Robert Francis Fairlie, Woodlands, Clapham. b. 1864.

FAIRLIE,* Herbert James, 1841-42, b. 1830. 10th Hussars. 4th Dragoons. Turkish Contingent.

FAIRLIE, James Ogilvie, 1820. Son of William Fairlie, of Coodham. *b.* 1809. Formerly in the 2nd Life Guards. Of Coodham, Ayrshire, *d.*

FAIRLIE, Robert George, 1877. Brother of F. A. Fairlie (above).

FALCON, Robert Worgan, 1875. Son of Antony B. Falcon, of Cheltenham. *b.* 1864.

FALKNER,* Henry, 1825, *b.* 1815. Solicitor at Southwell, Notts.

FANE, Arthur, 1823. Son of Genl. Sir Henry Fane, G.C.B. of Fulbeck, Lincolnshire. *b.* 1809. Ex. Coll. Oxf. Rector of Fulbeck, Lincoln. Domestic Chaplain to the Earl of Westmoreland. Prebendary of Salisbury, *d.* 1872.

FANE,* Charles Thorold, 1832-38. Son of Rev. E. Fane, Rector of Fulbeck. *b.* 1822. Partner in Messrs. Child's Bank, Temple Bar.

FANE, Frederick Adrian Scrope, 1823. Son of John Fane, of Wormsley, Oxfordshire. *b.* 1810. Trin. Coll. Oxf. Perpet. Curate of Norton Mandeville, Essex.

FANE, Henry Edward Hamlyn, 1832. Eldest son of Rev. E. Fane, of Fulbeck, Linc. *b.* 1817. 17th Regt. Major 4th Light Dragoons. Took the additional name of Hamlyn on his marriage. M.P. for South Hants 1865-68, *d.* 1868.

FANE, Henry Prinsep, 1835-39. Son of William Fane (below), Bengal Civil Service, 1842-68. *b.* 1822. Fulbeck Hall, Grantham.

FANE, Robert George Cecil, 1808-13. Son of the Hon. Henry Fane, and grandson of 8th Earl of Westmoreland. *b.* 1796. Demy and Fellow of Magd. Coll. Oxf. 1st Class Lit. Hum. Commissioner of the Court of Bankruptcy, *d.* 1864.

FANE,* Walter (C.B.), 1839-44. Son of Rev. E. Fane, Rector of Fulbeck. *b.* 1826. Commandant of "Fane's Horse." Lieut.-Col. 19th Bengal Light Cavalry. C.B. 1871. Retired Major-General.

FANE,* William, 1801-6. Son of the Hon. Henry Fane, of Fulbeck. *b.* 1789. Bengal Civil Service; *d.* 1839.

FANE, William Dashwood, 1830. Son of the above. *b.* 1816. St. John's Coll. Cam. Wrangler. Barrister. Legal Assistant at the Board of Trade, 1856-67. Melbourne Hall, Derby.

FANE, William John Jervis, 1824, *b.* 1808.

FANSHAWE, Charles, 1828. Son of Lieutenant-General E. Fanshawe, C.B. *b.* 1817. Major-Gen. R.E.

FANSHAWE, Hew Dalrymple, 1828. Twin brother of the above. *b.* 1817. Lieut.-Col. unatt. Retired 1859.

FARNALL,* Harry Burrard (C.B.), 1813. Son of Capt. Harry Farnall, R.N. *b.* 1802. Downing Coll. Cam. Poor Law Inspector.

FARQUHAR, James, 1817, *b.* 1805. Solicitor in London.

FARQUHAR, Thomas Newman, 1818, *b.* 1808. Solicitor in London.

FARR, Samuel Athill, 1827, *b.* 1811.

FARRAR, Henry, 1813-14. Son of Thomas Farrar. *b.* 1798. Ex. Coll. Oxf. Barrister.

FARRE, Alfred, 1818. Son of the late John R. Farre, M.D. *b.* 1808, *d.* 1820.

FARRE, Arthur (F.R.S.), 1821-27. Brother of the above. *b.* 1811. Caius Coll. Cam. M.D. 1841. F.R.C.P.L. Holds many distinguished appointments. Physician Extraordinary to the Queen. Physician Accoucheur to H.R.H. the Princess of Wales, &c.

FARRE, Benjamin, 1827. Brother of the above. *b.* 1817. Settled in Australia, *d.* 1872.

FARRE, Frederic John, 1814-23. Brother of the above. *b.* 1804. Captain of the School. Gold Medal. St. John's Coll. Cam. Wrangler. M.D. 1837. F.R.C.P.L. Physician to St. Bartholomew's, 1835. Physician to Charterhouse. Treasurer of the College of Physicians, &c.

FARRE, Henry William Richard, 1809-16. Brother of the above. *b.* 1799. Resides in Madeira.

FARRE, John Richard, 1822. Brother of the above. *b.* 1813. St. John's Coll. Cam. M.D. 1837. Holy Orders, *d.* 1868.

FARROW, William Morley, 1853-56, *b.* 1838. Barrister.

List of Carthusians. 83

FAULKNER, Staffard Bett, 1878. Son of the late Colonel Henry D. Faulkner. *b.* 1864.

FAUSSETT, Godfrey Trevelyan Godfrey- 1853-55. ⎫ See Godfrey-
FAUSSETT, John Toke Godfrey- 1848-53. ⎭ Faussett.

FAWSSETT, Richard, 1822. Son of John Fawssett, of Horncastle. *b.* 1807. Linc. Coll. Oxf. Vicar of Smeeton Westerly, Lincolnshire.

FAWSSETT, Thomas, 1824. Cousin of the above (also of Horncastle). *b.* 1810. Holy Orders.

FAWSSETT, Walter Barham, 1822, *b.* 1810. Died at Cambridge.

FELLOWES, Edward, 1821. Son of the late W. H. Fellowes, M.P., of Ramsey Abbey, Hunts. *b.* 1809. St. John's Coll. Cam. Formerly Lieut. 15th Hussars. M.P. for Huntingdonshire since 1837.

FELLOWES, Richard, 1823. (See Benyon). Brother of the above.

FELLOWES, William Henry, 1819. Brother of the above. *b.* 1806, *d.* 1836.

FERGUSON, Edwin Augustus, 1877. Son of Lieut.-Col. George Arthur Ferguson, of Pitfour, Aberdeenshire. *b.* 1864.

FFITCH, Samuel, 1812-13, *b.* 1804.

FIELDING, Henry Johnes, 1847-52. Son of Rev. G. Fielding, Rector of North Ockenden, Essex. *b.* 1834. Ex. Coll. Oxf.

FINCH, Louis Robert, 1877. Son of Rev. R. Finch, Rector of Pangbourne. *b.* 1862.

FINCH-HATTON, Nigel Montagu, 1873. Son of Rev. W. R. Finch Hatton, Rector of Weldon, Wansford.

FINNIMORE, Benjamin Kington, 1873. Son of the late Major B. K. Finnimore, of the Bombay Artillery. *b.* 1859. Cooper's Hill College.

FIRTH,* Frederick Henry, 1865-74. Son of Frederick Thomas Firth. *b.* 1855.

FIRTH, Henry, 1815, *b.* 1801.

FISHER, Charles, 1820, *b.* 1806. St. John's Coll. Cam.

FISHER,* Edmund Conroy, 1838-42. Son of Rev. William Fisher, 1809 (below). *b.* 1828, *d.* 1842.

FISHER, Edward, 1872. Son of E. K. Fisher, Market Harboro'.

FISHER, Edward, 1876. Son of Rev. Osmond Fisher, Rector of Harleton, Cambs. *b.* 1863.

FISHER,* Francis, 1833-40. Son of the Ven. John Fisher, Archdeacon of Berks. *b.* 1822. Em. Coll. Cam. Vicar of Hillmarton, Wilts, *d.* 1858.

FISHER, George Ruggles, 1841-43. Son of Rev. Charles J. Fisher, Rector of Ovington, Essex. *b.* 1827. Jes. Coll. Cam. Indian Army. Chaplain to the Forces.

FISHER, George William, 1846-48. Son of Geo. Fisher, of Cambridge. *b.* 1835. Ch. Coll. Cam. Wrangler. Dioc. Inspector of Schools. Diocese of Rochester and St. Albans.

FISHER,* Herbert William, 1837-44. Son of the Rev. Wm. Fisher, Canon of Sarum (below). *b.* 1826. Orator. Gold Medal. Student of Ch. Ch. Oxf. 1st Class Lit. Hum. Tutor and Sec. to H.R.H. the Prince of Wales. Vice-Warden of the Stannaries of Cornwall and Devon.

FISHER,* John, 1802-6. Son of Rev. Dr. Fisher, Master of Charterhouse. *b.* 1788. Ch. Coll. Cam. Archdeacon and Canon of Sarum.

FISHER, John Turner, 1839-41. Son of Rev. C. J. Fisher, of Ovington. *b.* 1822. Univ. Coll. Oxf. Holy Orders. Hessenford, St. Germains, Cornwall.

FISHER,* Philip Manly, 1814. Son of Samuel Fisher, M.D. of Bath, and nephew of the Master. *b.* 1803, *d.* 1817.

FISHER,* Philip Scott, 1805-11. Son of Dr. Philip Fisher. *b.* 1794. Univ. Coll. Oxf. Law Scholar.

FISHER, Roger Horman, 1830. Son of late Roger S. Horman Fisher, of Freshford, Somerset. *b.* 1819. Ch. Ch. Oxf. Barrister.

FISHER, Thomas Cathrew, 1848. Son of Geo. Fisher, of Cambridge. *b.* 1833. Cath. Hall, Cam. Died in Sydney, N.S. Wales, 1860.

FISHER,* Wilfred, 1844-51. Son of Rev. William Fisher (below. 1809), *b.* 1832. Ch. Ch. Oxf. Assistant Master. Rector of Westwell, Burford.

FISHER,* William, 1809-15. Son of Rev. Dr. Fisher, the Master. *b.* 1798. Student of Ch. Ch. Oxf. 2nd Class Lit. Hum. Rector of Poulshot, Wilts. Canon of Sarum.

FISHER, William, 1831-37. Son of the Venl. John Fisher (above). *b.* 1820. 10th Bengal Light Cavalry. Killed at Moodkee, 1845.

FISKE-HARRISON, 1806. (See Harrison).

FITZGERALD, Charles Cellarius, 1814, *b.* 1804.

FITZ-HERBERT, Alleyne, 1824. Third son of late Sir Henry Fitzherbert, Bart. *b.* 1815. S. John's Coll. Cam. Wrangler. Holy Orders, *d.* 1860.

FITZ-HERBERT, Anthony, 1828. Son of the late Sir Henry Fitz-Herbert, Bart. *b.* 1818. Went to Harrow School.

FITZ-HERBERT, Richard Henry, 1819. Brother of the above. *b.* 1809. Rifle Brigade. Major, retired, 1847.

FITZHERBERT (Sir) William (Bart.), 1819. Eldest brother of the above. *b.* 1808. Succeeded his father, 1858. Tissington Hall, Ashbourne.

FITZ-JAMES, James John, 1823. *b.* 1808. St. John's Coll. Cam. Barrister. Drowned off Corunna in the Solway Steamer, 1843.

FITZ PATRICK, Bernard Gowran, 1865. Son of J. Fitz-Patrick, Surgeon-Major Madras Army. *b.* 1850. Trin. Coll. Dublin. Curate of Coneysthorpe, Yorks. Formerly Clerk in the War Office.

FITZROY, Augustus, 1822. Son of Lord Henry Fitzroy. *b.* 1809. Trin. Coll. Cam. Rector of Fakenham, *d.* 1869.

FLEET, Ernest James, 1859-62, *b.* 1850.

FLEET, Frederick Rooke, 1859-64, *b.* 1849.

FLETCHER,* Miles Douglas, 1863, *b.* 1853. Keble Coll. Oxf. Curate of St. Thomas, Salisbury.

FLOYD,* Charles Greenwood, 1841-49. Son of Major-Gen. Sir Henry Floyd, Bart. *b.* 1830. Orator. Gold Medal. Student of Ch. Ch. Oxf. Rector of Runcton-Holme.

FLOYD,* Henry Ridout, 1846-52. Brother of the above. *b.* 1835. 25th Regt. Major, retired, 1873.

FLOYER, Ernest Ayscoghe, 1865. Son of the Rev. A. Floyer, Vicar of Marshchapel, Lincs. *b.* 1852. Inspector-Genl. of Egyptian Telegraphs.

FOLLETT, Frederick Charles, 1828. Son of Andrew Tucker Follett, of the Manor House, Paddington. *b.* 1815. Barrister.

FONBLANQUE, Albany William, 1801. Son of J. de Grenier Fontblanque, Q.C. *b.* 1793. Chief of the Statistical Department of the Board of Trade. Editor of the Examiner, &c. *d.* 1872.

FONBLANQUE, Alfred, 1850-52. Son of the above. *b.* 1839. Capt. R. Marines. China, Taku Forts. Medal and Clasps.

FONBLANQUE,* Bentham Albany, 1843-50. Brother of the above. *b.* 1832. Civil Service, *d.* 1870.

FOOTE, John Andrews, 1840-42. Son of William Foote, Surgeon, of Edgeware. *b.* 1827. M.A. Cantuar. Curate in charge of S. Michael and All Angels, Beckenham.

FOOTE,* John Alderson, 1860. Son of Capt. Foote, R.N. *b.* 1848. Prize Scholar. St. John's Coll. Cam. 1st Class Classical Tripos. Chancellor's Legal Medallist, &c., &c.

FORBES, Alexander, 1820. Son of James Forbes, of Kingareloch, Co. Argyle. *b.* 1810. East India Civil Service, Bengal. Judge.

FORBES, Charles Henry, 1819. Brother of the above. *b.* 1808. Of Kingareloch. J.P. and D.L. Argyleshire, *d.* 1876.

FORBES, Francis, 1820. Son of Bartholomew Forbes, Merchant of London. *b.* 1808. Indian Army. Brevet Major.

FORBES, George Forrest Greenlaw, 1874.

FORBES, Hugh, 1819, *b.* 1807.

FORBES, William Greenlaw, 1874.

FORBES-ROBERTSON Johnston, 1865-68. Son of John Forbes Robertson. *b.* 1853. Painter and Player.

FORDER, Percy Drake, 1874.

FORDER, Charles, 1872.

FORESTER, Hon. Charles Robert Weld, 1822. Son of the 1st Baron Forester. *b.* 1811. Royal Horse Guards. Assistant Military Sec. in Ireland, *d.* 1852.

FORMAN, Edward, 1805-11, *b.* 1796.

FORMAN, Richard, 1820, *b.* 1808.

FORMAN, Thomas Seaton, 1800-7, *b.* 1791. Was M.P. for Bridgwater 1841-7.

FORMAN, William Henry, 1800-8, *b.* 1793. Partner in the Tredegar Iron Works.

FORMBY, Henry, 1833-34. Son of H. Formby. Scholar of B.N.C. Oxf. Holy Orders (resigned).

FORMBY, Richard Edward, 1837-38. Son of Rev. James Formby, Vicar of Frindsbury, Kent. B.N.C. Oxf. Rector of Latchingdon.

FORSHALL, William Hayes, 1837-40. Son of late Rev. J. Forshall, of the British Museum. *b.* 1827. Indian Army.

FORSTER, Charles Manners, 1818, *b.* 1806. Left in ill health after a few days.

FORSTER, Charles Thornton, 1850-55. Son of Rev. Charles Forster, Rector of Stistead, Essex. *b.* 1836. Talbot Scholar and Medallist. Fellow of Jesus Coll. Cam. 1st Class Classical and Divinity Tripos. Vicar of Hinxton. Chaplain to the Earl of Leven and Melville.

FORSTER, Edward Morgan Llewellyn, 1861-65. Brother of the above. *b.* 1847. Trin. Coll. Cam. 2nd Class Classical Tripos. Architect.

FORSTER, Henry Thornton, 1850-58. Brother of C. T. Forster (above). *b.* 1838. Talbot Scholar and Medallist. Scholar of Trin. Coll. Cam. 1st Class Classical Tripos. Assistant Master, 1861, *d.* 1865.

FORSTER, James William Doane, 1853-55. Brother of the above. *b.* 1841, *d.* 1857.

FORSTER,* John Arthur Fox, 1848-53. Son of Matthew Forster. *b.* 1837. Commander-in-Chief's Office, Horse Guards (retired).

FORSTER, William Howley, 1863-64. Son of Rev. C. Forster, Rector of Stisted. *b.* 1851. Trin Coll. Cam.

FORT, John, 1841-43. Son of the late John Fort, M.P. for Clitheroe. *b.* 1828. 5th Dragoon Guards. Retired 1850.

FORTESCUE,* George, 1860-62. Son of Rev. E. B. Fortescue. *b.* 1847.

FORTESCUE, Henry, 1805-6. Son of Capt. Fortescue, R.N. *b.* 1796.

FORTUNE, Fitzfrederick, 1810-11. Went to Westminster School.

FOSTER, Arthur, 1876. Son of William Francis Foster, 7, Lower Berkeley-street. *b.* 1864.

FOSTER, Claude, 1876. Son of Rev. R. Foster, Vicar of Burpham, Sussex.

FOSTER, Francis, 1876. Brother of Arthur Foster (above). *b.* 1862.

FOSTER, Henry, 1870. Brother of the above. *b.* 1856. In business in London.

FOSTER, James, 1862, *b.* 1850. Chichester Theol. Coll. Rector of Authorpe, Linc.

FOSTER, Richard, 1820. Son of William Foster, Lanwithan, Cornwall. *b.* 1808. Ex. Coll. Oxf. *d.* 1869.

FOUNTAINE, Andrew, 1821. Eldest son of the late Andrew Fountaine. *b.* 1808. Ch. Ch. Oxf. Narford Hall, Norfolk, *d.* 1874.

FOUNTAINE, Thomas William, 1822. Brother of the above. *b.* 1811.

FOWLE, Thomas Welbank, 1853-54. Son of Thomas Fowle, Mount Pleasant, Northallerton. *b.* 1835. Scholar of Oriel Coll. Oxf. 2nd Class Lit. Hum. Rector of Islip, Oxon.

FOWLER, Alfred, 1821, *b.* 1810.

FOWLER, James, 1819, *b.* 1809. Solicitor.

FOX, John Elliot, 1858. Son of Rev. W. Fox, of Demarara. *b.* 1845. Scholar of Ch. Coll. Cam. Vicar of Bourne, Cambs.

FOX,* Maxwell Sinclair, 1841-46. Son of Richard Fox, of Auch Au Bawn, Co. Cavan. *b.* 1831. Ensign 27th Regt. Madras N.I. *d.* 1853.

Fox, William, 1824, *b.* 1808.

Fox, Wilson Henry, 1876. Son of Wilson Fox, M.D. of London. *b.* 1863.

Fox-Strangways, Maurice Walter, 1875. Son of Lieut.-Col. Fox Strangways, R.E.

Frame, Henry George, 1821, *b.* 1807.

Francis, George, 1815-18. Son of George Francis, Henley, Oxon. *b.* 1799. Queens Coll. Oxf.

Francis, George Henry, 1826, *b.* 1815.

Francis, Henry Clement, 1870. Son of Clement Francis, of Quy Hall, Cambs. *b.* 1857. Emigrated to South Australia.

Francis, James, 1867-71, *b.* 1856.

Francklin, John, 1821. Son of Richard Francklin, of Great Barford. *b.* 1808. Of Gonalston, Notts, *d.* 1858.

Franklyn, Alexander Allen, 1819, *b.* 1809.

Franks, Armand, 1803. Died young.

Fraser, Herbert Charles, 1876.

Fraser, Hugh, 1873. Son of Thomas Fraser, of Blackheath.

Freckleton, George, 1807-8, *b.* 1792. Trin. Coll. Cam. M.D. 1819. Resided at Liverpool.

Frederick,* Arthur, 1811. Son of Lieut.-Col. Thomas Frederick. *b.* 1800. Of the Exchequer, *d.* 1866.

Freeling* (Sir) George Henry (Bart.), 1800-5. Son of Sir Francis Freeling, Bart. *b.* 1789. New Coll. Oxf. A Commissioner of the Customs, *d.* 1841.

Freeling (Sir) Henry Hill (Bart.), 1828. Eldest son of the above. *b.* 1818. 8th Madras Light Cavalry. Succeeded his brother 1845, *d.* 1871.

Freer, Nigel James, 1876. Son of Major W. R. Freer, of Eckington Manor, Wilts. *b.* 1862.

Freese, Arthur, 1813-18, *b.* 1802.

Freese, John Wellington, 1827-31. Son of John Henry Freese, of Brazil. *b.* 1812. Gold Medal. Ball. Coll. Oxf. Trin. Coll. Cam.

FRENCH, George Edward, 1820, b. 1808.

FRENCH, George William, 1816. Son of Capt. William French. b. 1805. Capt. 82nd Regt. Died in Canada.

FRENCH, John Gilmore, 1820, b. 1806.

FRENCH, William Henry, 1821, b. 1810.

FREND, Alfred Henry, 1872.

FRERE,* Bartle Henry Temple, 1875. Son of Rev. H. T. Frere, Rector of Burston, Norfolk. b. 1862.

FRERE, George, 1820. Son of Geo. Frere, of Lincoln's Inn. b. 1810. Foreign Office. Slave Trade Commissioner at the Cape of Good Hope, d. 1878.

FRERE, George Edward (F.R.S.), 1821. Son of the late Edward Frere, of Llanelly, Co. Brecon. b. 1807. Edinburgh University. Barrister. Succeeded to the estates of his uncle, the late Rt. Hon. John Hookham Frere, Roydon Hall, Norfolk.

FRERE, Walter Howard, 1877. Son of the late Philip Howard Frere, Fellow of Downing Coll. Cam. b. 1863.

FRESHFIELD, Charles Kaye, 1822. Son of James William Freshfield, F.R.S., of Mynthurst, Surrey. b. 1808. For many years Solicitor to the Bank of England. M.P. for Dover.

FRESHFIELD, Henry Ray, 1824. Brother of the above. b. 1814. Solicitor to the Bank of England, Kidbrooke Park, Sussex.

FRESHFIELD, John Sims, 1824. Brother of the above. b. 1811. Lieut.-Col. Madras Cavalry, d. 1860.

FRITH, Reginald Cokayne, 1877. Son of Major Cokayne Frith. b. 1863.

FRITH, Robert William, 1824, b. 1811.

FRITH, Warren Hastings Leslie, 1826, b. 1814. Lieut.-Col. Bengal Artillery.

FRITH,* William Edward Cokayne, 1872-78. Brother of R. C. Frith (above). b. 1859. Ch. Ch. Oxf. Holford Exhibitioner.

FROST, George Joseph, 1813-14, b. 1799.

FRY, , 1803.

FRY, , 1803.

FULLER,* Henry, 1809-18. Son of Dr. John Fuller, Uckfield, Sussex. b. 1799. Univ. Coll. Oxf.

FULLER,* Oswald William, 1854-60. Son of Edmond Fuller, of Hastings. b. 1844. Probate Court. Died in Ceylon, 1878.

FULLER, Robert Fitzherbert, 1805-13. Son of Thos. Trayton Fuller, of Ashdown House, Sussex. b. 1795. B.N.C. Oxf. Rector of Chalvington, Sussex.

FULTON, Edington, 1821, b. 1807.

FULTON, Henry, 1822, b. 1814.

FULTON, James, 1821, b. 1811.

FULTON, John Atkinson, 1819. Son of Edington Fulton. b. 1805. Gold Medal. Queens Coll. Oxf.

FULTON, Mark, 1821, b. 1809. Lived in Charterhouse Square.

FULTON, Thomas, 1821. Brother of the above. b. 1811.

FURBER, Henry Aubrey, 1874. Son of Charles Furber, of Upper Hamilton Terrace. b. 1860. Surveyor.

FURBER, Edward Price, 1877. Brother of the above. b. 1864.

FURLONGE, Thomas Berry, 1819, b. 1804.

FURLONGE, William, 1815-17, b. 1799.

FURZE, Henry, 1836-37. Brewer in Whitechapel.

G.

GAGE, Francis Edward, 1873. Son of Genl. the Hon. E. T. Gage, R.A., and grandson of the 4th Visct. Gage. b. 1850. Went to Wellington College.

GAHAGAN, Albert, 1840-41. Son of Mr. Gahagan, of Regent Street. b. 1828. Went to Highgate School. Lieut.-Col. Madras Staff Corps, retired.

GALE, Alexander Robinson, 1828. Son of Alex. Robinson Gale. *b.* 1811. Wadham Coll. Oxf.

GALPIN, Sidney Clement, 1873-78. Son of T. D. Galpin. *b.* 1860. New Coll. Oxf.

GALSWORTHY, Edwin Henry, 1874. Son of Edwin Henry Galsworthy, J.P. for Middlesex. *b.* 1861. Entered at Caius Coll. Cam.

GALSWORTHY, Frederick Trevor, 1877. Son of Frederick Thomas Galsworthy, of 8, Queen's Gate, S.W. *b.* 1865.

GANDELL, Sidney Graham Kerr, 1875. Son of Rev. R. Gandell, Professor of Arabic, Oxford. *b.* 1861.

GANDELL,* Thomas Pearse, 1864. Brother of the above. *b.* 1853. St. John's Coll. Oxf. 4th Class Lit. Hum.

GANDY, Frederick, 1823. (See Brandreth, Fredk.).

GARCIA, Nicholas, 1826, *b.* 1810.

GARDNER, Alan Edward, 1874-76. Son of Rear-Adml. Alan Henry Gardner. *b.* 1861.

GARDNER, Henry Willoughby, 1876-78. Son of Henry Gardner. *b.* 1861. Leech Prizeman.

GARDNER,* Herbert Calthorpe, 1832-40. Son of Genl. the Hon. William Henry Gardner. *b.* 1822. 38th Bengal N. Infantry. Served in the Indian Mutiny. Died near Delhi, 1857.

GARDNER, Richard, 1826. Son of Robert Gardner, Merchant, of London. *b.* 1813. Wadh. Coll. Oxf. Barrister. Elected M.P. for Leicester, 1847, but unseated on petition; deceased.

GARDNER, William, 1826, *b.* 1815. In business in Manchester.

GARDNER, William, 1843-46, *b.* 1828. Brewer.

GARDNER, William Bethell, 1825. Brother of H. C. Gardner (above). *b.* 1815. Royal Artillery. General (retired).

GARNETT, Charles, 1878. Son of Jeremiah Garnett, The Grange, Bolton. *b.* 1865.

GARRETT, Joseph Payne, 1868, *b.* 1856.

GARROW, Edward William, 1827. Son of Rev. D. W. Garrow, D.D. and grandson of the Rt. Hon. Sir William Garrow. *b.* 1815. B.N.C. Oxf. Rector of Bilsthorpe, Notts.

GARROW,* George William, 1830-37. Brother of the above. *b.* 1818. Worc. Coll. Oxf. D.D. Chaplain R.N. Died of yellow fever, 1847.

GARSTIN, Charles, 1819. Son of Genl. Garstin, E.I.C.S. *b.* 1803. Bengal Civil Service (retired).

GASKELL, John, 1826. Son of Henry Gaskell, of Southworth House, Wigan. *b.* 1811, *d.* 1837.

GASKELL, Richard, 1832, *b.* 1817.

GATTY, Alfred, 1825. Son of Robert Gatty. *b.* 1813. Ex. Coll. Oxf. D.D. Vicar of Ecclesfield. Sub-dean of York.

GATTY, Charles, 1803. Son of William Gatty. *b.* 1789. Clerk in the Exchequer Court. Assistant Registrar of Charterhouse, *d.* 1871.

GATTY,* Charles Tindal, 1863. Son of the Rev. Dr. Alfred Gatty (above). *b.* 1851. Curator of Meyer's Museum, Liverpool.

GATTY, Edward, 1805. Brother of Charles Gatty (above). *b.* 1792. Solicitor; *d.* 1872.

GATTY, Henry, 1803. Brother of the above. *b.* 1790. Army Surgeon. Royal Artillery; *d.* 1858.

GATTY,* Robert Henry, 1838-47. Brother of the above. *b.* 1828. Orator. Trin. Coll. Oxf. Vicar of Buckden, Hants.

GATTY, William Henry Caryer, 1873. Son of the above. *b.* 1861.

GAUTIER, Gay Grant Aristides, 1810-11.

GAY, Henry, 1821, *b.* 1810. Solicitor in London.

GAY, John, 1873-78. Son of John Gay, F.R.C.S. *b.* 1861.

GEDDES, Archibald Perrin, 1820, *b.* 1803.

GELL, John Franklin, 1864. Son of Rev. J. P. Gell, Rector of Buxted, Sussex. *b.* 1851. Caius Coll. Cam. 3rd Senr. Opt. M.B. Court of Wards, Madras.

GEORGE, Francis, 1825, *b*. 1814.

GEPP, Thomas Morgan, 1820, *b*. 1806. Solicitor at Chelmsford.

GIBBARD, John, 1826. Son of John Gibbard, of Sharnbrook, Beds. *b*. 1814. Of Sharnbrook House, Bedford. J.P. D.L.

GIBBON, William Jacomb, 1870.

GIBBONS, , 1804-6.

GIBBONS, Clifford, 1875. Son of Sills Gibbons, of Lindfield, Sussex.

GIBBS, Antony, 1838-39. Son of George Henry Gibbs, of Aldenham House, Herts. Senr. partner in the House of Antony Gibbs and Sons, Merchants, of London. *b*. 1822. Worc. Coll. Oxf.; *d*. 1856.

GIBBS, Charles, 1839-43. Brother of the above. *b*. 1829. 2nd Regt. Lieut.-Col. 1877; retired.

GIBBS, Francis, 1844-52. Brother of the above. *b*. 1834. Ex. Coll. Oxf. *d*. 1857.

GIBBS, George, 1838-46. Brother of the above. *b*. 1827. Ex. Coll. Oxf. Drowned at Oxford, 1846.

GIBBS, John Lomax, 1846-47. Brother of the above. *b*. 1832. Ex. Coll. Oxf. Vicar of Exwick, Devon.

GIBBS, William Lloyd, 1845-47. Brother of the above. *b*. 1830. Ex. Coll. Oxf. *d*. 1860.

GIBSON, Alan Bethel, 1870, *b*. 1857.

GIBSON, Arthur, 1867-72, *b*. 1856.

GIBSON,* Arthur Charles, 1876. Son of Rev. Richard Hudson Gibson, Rector of Lound, Norfolk. *b*. 1862.

GIBSON, Arthur Edward, 1877. Son of James Edward Gibson, of West Cowes, Isle of Wight. M.R.C.S. *b*. 1863.

GIBSON, Douglas, 1870, *b*. 1859.

GIBSON,* Edgar Charles Sumner, 1859-67. Son of the Rev. Wm. Gibson. *b*. 1848. Trin. Coll. Oxf. Vice-Principal of Wells Theol. Coll. 1875. Lecturer of the Clergy School, Leeds, 1876.

List of Carthusians. 95

GIBSON, Henry Frederick, 1865, *b.* 1854.

GIBSON, Thomas Milner B. (the Rt. Hon.), 1819. Son of the late Major Thomas Milner Gibson, of the 37th Foot. *b.* 1807. Trin. Coll. Cam. M.P. for Ipswich 1837; for Manchester 1841; for Ashton-under-Lyne 1857-68; President of Board of Trade 1859-66.

GIFFARD,* Arthur, 1836-42. Son of the late Sir Ambrose Hardinge Giffard. *b.* 1827. Capt. 21st Bombay N. Infantry. Killed in India during the Mutiny, 1858.

GIFFARD, Edward, 1825. Brother of the above. *b.* 1812. Pemb. Coll. Oxf. Sec. of the Transport Board. Author of "Travels in Greece," &c. Kilcorrall, Co. Wexford.

GIFFARD,* Edward Walter, 1872. Son of the above. *b.* 1861.

GIFFARD,* William, 1828-36. Brother of Arthur Giffard (above). *b.* 1818. Univ. Coll. Oxf. Rector of Weybridge; *d.* 1855.

GILBEE, , 1805-8.

GILBERT, Herbert Henry, 1853-59. Son of W. A. Gilbert, of Cantley Manor, Norfolk. *b.* 1840. Magd. Coll. Oxf. Lieut. 18th (Royal Irish) Regt.

GILBERT, Samuel Richardson, 1822, *b.* 1809.

GILBERT, William Alexander, 1843-46. Brother of H. H. Gilbert (above). *b.* 1831. Late Lieut. West Essex Militia.

GILES, Alfred, 1826. Son of Francis Giles, C.E. *b.* 1816. Civil Engineer. M.P. for Southampton 1878. Created a Knight of the Order of Dannebrog by the late King of Denmark.

GILES, Francis George, 1826. Son of Francis Giles, C.E. *b.* 1815. Of Upper Clatford, Andover.

GILES, Herbert Allen, 1859-63. Son of John Allen Giles (below). *b.* 1845. Acting Consul at Amoy.

GILES, John Allen, 1824. Eldest son of Wm. Giles, of Southwick House, Mark, Somersetshire. *b.* 1808. Fellow of Corpus Coll. Oxf. Double 1st Class. D.D. Head Master of the City of London School. Rector of Sutton, Surrey. Author and Editor of many classical works.

GILES, John Douglas, 1827. Son of John Giles, of Southwick House. *b.* 1812. Corpus Coll. Oxf. Vicar of Willoughby, Linc. Archdeacon of Stow; deceased.

GILES, William, 1825. Brother of John Allen Giles (above). *b.* 1810. Trin. Coll. Dub. Registrar of Courts at Taunton, *d.* 1875.

GILLETT, , 1803.

GILLETT, Leonard Francis, 1874. Son of Francis Calvert Gillett, C.E. of Borrowash, Derby. *b.* 1861. Entered at Pemb. Coll. Oxf.

GILLETT, Richard Clay, 1877. Brother of the above.

GILLHAM, Herbert William Chowne, 1873.

GILLIAT, John Henry, 1815-16, *b.* 1801. Holy Orders in the American Episcopal Church, *d.*

GILLIAT, William Henry, 1815-16. Cousin of the above. *b.* 1801. Merchant in Liverpool; *d.* 1853.

GILLIES, Robert, 1817, *b.* 1806.

GILLING-LAX, Edward Percival, 1877. Son of Rev. G. R. Gilling-Lax, Rector of Fitzhead, Taunton. *b.* 1863.

GILLING-LAX, George Robert, 1876. Brother of the above. *b.* 1861. Keble Coll. Oxf.

GILMORE, Allan, 1820, *b.* 1809. Merchant at Calcutta; *d.* 1867.

GILMORE, Mungo Smith, 1820. Brother of the above. *b.* 1810. East India Civil Service, Bengal. Retired.

GILSON, Thomas, 1825, *b.* 1810.

GINSBURG, Benedict William, 1874. St. Cath.'s Coll. Cam.

GIPPS,* Algernon Henry, 1867. Son of the following. *b.* 1855.

GIPPS, Frederick, 1843-46. Son of Rev. Henry Gipps, Canon of Carlisle. *b.* 1827. Univ. Coll. Oxf. Vicar of Corbridge, Northumb. *d.* 1874.

GIPPS, George, 1823. Son of George Gipps, M.P. for Ripon. *b.* 1812. Univ. Coll. Oxf. Of Howlett's, near Canterbury.

List of Carthusians.   97

GIPPS, Henry B. 1832-33.   Brother of the above. *b.* 1817; *d.* 1836.

GIPPS, Thomas, 1825.   Brother of the above. *b.* 1814.   St. John's Coll. Cam.

GIRDLESTONE,* Charles Edward Ridgway, 1852-57.   Son of Rev. E. Girdlestone, Canon of Bristol. *b.* 1839.   Elective Scholar.   Sch. of Pemb. Coll. Oxf.   India Civil Service.

GIRDLESTONE, Charles Richey, 1878.   Son of Rev. Robert Baker Girdlestone (below). *b.* 1864.

GIRDLESTONE, Frederic Kennedy Wilson, 1856-63, *b.* 1844. Prize Scholar.   Demy Magd. Coll. Oxf.   1st Class Mods.   Assistant Master in the School.

GIRDLESTONE,* Robert Baker, 1850-55.   Son of Rev. Charles Girdlestone, of Kingswinford. *b.* 1836.   Ch. Ch. Oxf. 3rd Class Lit. Hum.   Principal of Wycliffe Hall, Oxf.

GLADSTONE, John McAdam, 1819-20, *b.* 1808.   Civil Engineer. Pupil of George Stephenson.   Drowned at sea.

GLASGOW, Nevile George, 1875.

GLASSE,* William Bulkeley, 1815.   Son of the Rev. John Glasse. *b.* 1806.   Barrister, Q.C.

GLEICHEN (Count) Albert Edward Wilfred, 1877.   Son of Count Gleichen, St. James Palace. *b.* 1863.

GLEIG,* Charles Edward Stuart, 1835-41.   Son of Rev. G. R. Gleig, Chaplain-General to the Forces. *b.* 1825.   14th Regt.   Lieut.-Col. h.p.

GLEN, Alexander, 1858-68.   Son of W. C. Glen, Barrister at Law. *b.* 1850.   Scholar of Ch. Coll. Cam.   Wrangler. Barrister.   Midland Circuit.

GLEN, Augustus Cunningham, 1870.   Brother of the above. *b.* 1860.   Went to Westminster School.

GLEN, Reginald Cunningham, 1865.   Brother of the above. *b.* 1855.   Ch. Coll. Cam.   Law Tripos.   Student of the Middle Temple.

GLYNN, John, 1827, *b.* 1812.

GODDARD, Charles Samuel, 1822, *b.* 1812.

H

GODFREY, , 1804.

GODFREY, Arthur Hill, 1877. Son of John Richard R. Godfrey, of Franklands, Weybridge. *b.* 1863.

GODFREY-FAUSSETT, Godfrey Trevelyan, 1853-55. Only son of Rev. Bryan Faussett, of Heppington, Kent. *b.* 1840. 76th Regt.; retired 1865. H.M. Inspector of Factories 1867. Major of Gloucestersh. Artillery Volunteers.

GODFREY-FAUSSETT, John Toke, 1848-53. Son of Rev. Godfrey Faussett, D.D. of Heppington, Kent, Canon of Ch. Ch. &c. *b.* 1835. Student of Ch. Ch. Oxf. Inner Temple. District Registrar of the Probate Court at Lichfield.

GODING, William, 1808-13. Son of Thomas Goding. *b.* 1798. The Priory, Burnham, Bucks.

GODWIN, William, 1811-14, *b.* 1803. Rector of St. Martin's, Chester.

GOLDNEY,* Charles, 1856-63. Son of Rev. Adam Goldney. *b.* 1844. Gold Medal. Scho. of Linc. Coll. Oxf. 3rd Class Law. Chaplain of Stafford Gaol.

GOLDSMID, Nathaniel, 1818. Son of Edward Goldsmid. *b.* 1807. Ex. Coll. Oxf. 2nd Class Lit. Hum. Barrister; *d.* 1860.

GONNE, Arthur Edward, 1878. Son of Charles Gonne. E. I. Civil Service. *b.* 1864.

GONNE, Charles Melville, 1875. Brother of the above.

GOOCH, Arthur, 1828, *b.* 1816.

GOOD, , 1803.

GOODE, Alexander, 1811. Left the same year. *b.* 1796.

GOODE, Benjamin Geldart, 1833-38, *b.* 1822.

GOODE, Frederick, 1811-12, *b.* 1796.

GOODE, Philip Benjamin, 1831-33, *b.* 1817. Solicitor in London.

GOODEVE, Henry Hills, 1854-55. Son of Henry Hurry Goodeve, M.D., of Cooks Folly, near Bristol. *b.* 1840. Major Royal Artillery.

List of Carthusians. 99

GOODWIN, Francis Cornelius, 1826, *b.* 1813.

GORDON,* Alexander Henry, 1824, *b.* 1813.

GORDON,* Arthur Henry Wyndham, 1864. Son of Lord Cecil Gordon-Moore, and grandson of the 9th Marquis of Huntly. *b.* 1853.

GORDON,* Charles Alex. Boswell, 1833-41. Son of Alex. Gordon, of Hampton Court. *b.* 1823. Ex. Coll. Oxf. Lieut.-Col. h.p. 60th Regt. Assist. Adj. and Qr. Mr.-General, Portsmouth. Served in India and the Crimea. (Medals and Clasps).

GORDON, Cosmo, 1823. Younger son of late Sir William Duff-Gordon, Bart. *b.* 1812; *d.* 1876.

GORDON, Francis Alexander, 1855-61. Son of Charles Gordon, 13, Grenville Place, S.W. *b.* 1844. Lieut. 60th Rifles. Died at Calcutta, 1868.

GORDON (Lord) Francis Arthur, 1821. Youngest son of the 9th Marquis of Huntly. *b.* 1808. 1st Life Guards. Lieut.-Col. 1855; *d.* 1857.

GORDON,* Francis Frederick, 1849-55. Son of the above. *b.* 1839. Admiralty.

GORDON, Hamilton, 1830. Son of Thomas Gordon, of Harperfield, Lanarkshire. *b.* 1815.

GORDON,* Hubert George, 1868. Brother of Arthur H. W. Gordon (above). *b.* 1858.

GORDON,* James Henry, 1849-56. Son of Adam Gordon, of Abergeldie. *b.* 1839. Major Madras Staff Corps.

GORDON, John, 1824, *b.* 1809.

GORDON,* Laurence George Frank, 1877. Son of Lieut.-Col. Geo. Grant Gordon, Scots Guards. *b.* 1864.

GORDON,* Leslie, 1868-71, *b,* 1855. Emigrated to Canada.

GORDON, Newton Roberts, 1862. Brother of Francis Alex. Gordon (above). *b.* 1850. No profession.

GORDON, William Henry, 1859-63. Brother of the above. *b.* 1846. 28th Regt. Ashantee War. Medal and Clasp. Assist. Commissioner Famagusta, Cyprus.

GOSS, Stephen Weston, 1814, *b.* 1805.

GOSSIP-WILMER, Thomas George, 1822, *b.* 1808. Trin. Coll. Cam. Took the name of Wilmer. Holy Orders.

GOSSIP-WILMER, Wilmer, 1813, *b.* 1804. Solicitor.

GOUGH,* John Charles, 1832, *b.* 1821.

GOULD, Lionel Francis, 1870, *b,* 1859.

GOULD, Owen, 1867-72, *b.* 1856.

GOVETT, Lionel Arthur, 1875. Son of Charles Albert Govett, of Richmond, Surrey. *b.* 1863.

GOVETT,* William Romaine, 1820. Son of Mr. Govett, Surgeon at Tiverton. *b.* 1807. Government Surveyor, Sydney, Australia.

GOWAN, George Mauleverer, 1829, *b.* 1818.

GRABHAM, Arthur Illingworth, 1878. Son of G. W. Grabham, M.D., Earlswood, Surrey. *b.* 1865.

GRANT, Alexander, 1825. Son of Edward Grant (below). *b.* 1817. Trin. Coll. Cam. Rector of Manningford, Wilts.

GRANT, Alexander Charles, 1810-12, *b.* 1798. Navy.

GRANT, Alexander Ronald, 1874. Son of Rev. A. R. Grant, Rector of Hitcham, Suffolk. *b.* 1861.

GRANT, Charles, 1818. Left the same year. E. India Civil Service.

GRANT, Edward, 1810-12. Son of Alexander Grant, a West Indian Proprietor, and D.L. for Banffshire. *b.* 1795. E. Indian Judge; deceased.

GRANT, Frederick John Robert, 1820, *b.* 1807. Solicitor.

GRANT, George, 1818, *b.* 1805.

GRANT, Henry, 1818, *b.* 1806.

GRANT, Horace, 1810-12, *b.* 1800.

GRANT, James, 1800-4. Son of George Grant, of Drumferrich, Banffshire.

GRANT, Montague Harvey, 1810-13, *b.* 1797.

GRANT, Oliver, 1818, *b.* 1809.

List of Carthusians.

GRANT, Robert, 1800-4. Brother of James Grant (above).

GRANT, William Francis, 1818, b. 1806.

GRAVES, William, 1823, b. 1808.

GRAY, George, 1843-46. Son of Geo. Gray, of Bowerswell, near Perth. b. 1829. Studied law in Edinburgh. Sheep farmer in N.S. Wales.

GRAY, Henry, 1822, b. 1809.

GRAY,* Russell John, 1852-60, b. 1842. Clerk in the London and Co. Bank.

GRAYDON, John, 1836-38. 44th Bengal N. Infantry.

GRAYDON, William, 1836-39. Brother of the above. b. 1821. 16th Bengal N. Infantry.

GREATOREX,* Edward, 1836-42. Son of Thomas Greatorex. b. 1823. Pemb. Coll. Oxf. Rector of Croxdale, Durham.

GREEN, Arthur Gordon, 1876. Son of Thomas Henry Green, of Dalecote, Coventry. b. 1863.

GREEN, Charles Alfred Howell, 1878. Son of Rev. Alfred John Morgan Green, Rector of Warren, Pembroke. b. 1864.

GREEN, Edward Ernest, 1875. Son of J. P. Green, of Hucking Hill, Sittingbourne. b. 1861.

GREEN, John, 1829. Son of Rev. J. C. Green, Vicar of Rustington, Sussex. b. 1817. Eman. Coll. Cam. Rector of Little Leighs, Essex.

GREEN,* Malcolm Schrimshire (C.B.), 1837-41. Son of Rear-Adml. Sir Andrew P. Green, K.C.H. b. 1824. Colonel Indian Army. Served in the Crimea, Central India and Persia. (Medals). Consul at Muscat 1862.

GREEN,* William Sebright Saunders, 1842-48. Of Huntingdon, b. 1829. Solicitor. Went to India.

GREENALGH, James, 1811-12, b. 1794. Peterho. Coll. Cam.

GREENE, Francis Ernest, 1873. Son of Thomas Greene, Avonmore, Co. Dublin. b. 1859. Trin. Coll. Dublin.

GREENING, Henry, 1821, b. 1809.

GREENWAY, Charles, 1875-77. Eldest son of Rev. Charles Greenway, of Over Darwen, Lancashire. b. 1860. 2nd Lt. 5th Royal Lancas. Militia. R.M. Coll. Sandhurst.

GREENWAY, Davenham, 1875. Brother of the above. *b.* 1862.

GREGG,* John, 1801-8. Son of Thomas Gregg. *b.* 1790. Student of Ch. Ch. Oxf. Drowned at Oxford 1813.

GREGORY, Richard, 1819, *b.* 1809.

GREGSON, William, 1803-6. Son of John Gregson. B.N.C. Oxf. Barrister. Law Writer of the London Gazette.

GREGSON,   , 1803. Drowned in the Tagus.

GREIG, James Arthur, 1873.

GREIG, Woronzow, 1820. Son of Mr. Commissioner Greig and Mrs. Greig (afterwards Mrs. Somerville). *b.* 1805. Trin. Coll. Cam. Barrister. Clerk of the Peace for Co. of Surrey.

GREY,* Arthur John, 1840-44. Son of Rt. Rev. Edward Grey, Bishop of Hereford. *b.* 1829. Lieut. Royal Navy; died 1854.

GREY, Egerton Spencer, 1875. Son of Lieut.-Col. Grey, Ludgrove, Barnet.

GREY,* Francis Lennox George, 1849-56. Son of John Grey. *b.* 1839. Oriel Coll. Oxf. 96th Regt.; deceased.

GREY, William Thomas, 1820. Son of Lieut.-Col. William Grey, and nephew of Earl Grey. *b.* 1808. Wine Merchant; *d.* 1864.

GRIFFINHOOFE, Benjamin, 1843-44. Son of Rev. T. S. Griffinhoofe, Vicar of Arkesden, Essex. *b.* 1828; *d.* 1844.

GRIFFINHOOFE, Thomas John, 1838-39. Brother of the above. *b.* 1820. Pemb. Coll. Oxf. Vicar of Arkesden, Essex; *d.* 1869.

GRIFFITH, Charles, 1803-6, *b.* 1792. A.M. Cantab.

GRIFFITH,* Charles, 1817. Son of Rev. Charles Griffith, Brecknock. *b.* 1792. Ch. Ch. Oxf. Rector of Talachddu, Brecons. Prebendary of St. David's. J.P. for Brecon.

GRIFFITH, Charles Higman, 1839-47. Son of John William Griffith, of Bruce Castle, Tottenham. *b.* 1829. St. John's Coll. Cam. Formerly in the Rifle Brigade. Now Rector of Stratfield Turgiss, Hants.

GRIFFITH, George Frederick, 1820, *b.* 1808.

GRIFFITH, Henry Darby- (C.B.), 1820. Son of Maj.-Gen. Matthew Chitty Darby-Griffith, *b.* 1809. 5th Royal Irish Lancers. General.

GRIFFITH, John Cobham, 1807-8, *b.* 1795.

GRIFFITH, John Walter, 1873. Treforgan, Cardigan, So. Wales.

GRIFFITH,* Percy Wynn, 1867-71, *b.* 1855.

GRIFFITH, William, 1803. M.A. Cantab.

GRIFFITH, William Stokes, 1878.

GRIFFITHS, Frederick Robertson, 1866-72. Son of C. Robertson Griffiths, Barrister. *b.* 1853. Law Student.

GRIGG, Frederick Hawker, 1850-51. Son of Mark Grigg, of Plymouth. *b.* 1838. Went to Winchester School.

GRIGNON, James, 1827, *b.* 1813. 37th Regt.

GRIMES, William, 1831, *b.* 1817.

GROOM, Frederick Edward, 1876. Ashwicken Hall, King's Lynn.

GROOME, John Hindes Henry, 1860-63. Son of the Ven. Archdeacon Groome, of Earl Soham. *b.* 1847. Scholar of Pemb. Coll. Cam. Formerly Curate of Reydon and Wangford.

GROOME, William Hubert, 1862-63. Brother of the above. *b.* 1849. St. Pet. Coll. Cam. Curate of Stockbury, Kent.

GROTE, Andrew, 1808. Re-entered 1814-16. Son of George Grote, of Badgemoor, Oxon. *b.* 1799. E. I. Civil Service, Bengal.

GROTE, Charles, 1819. Brother of the above. *b.* 1805. Banker in the Firm of Prescott and Co., London; *d.* 1854.

GROTE, Frederick, 1820, *b.* 1807.

GROTE, George, 1804-10. Brother of Andrew Grote (above). *b.* 1794. Banker in the City. M.P. for London 1832 to 41. Author of The History of Greece, &c.; *d.* 1871.

GROTE, Henry, 1806-10.

GROVER, Malcolm Henry Stanley, 1874. Son of C. E. Grover, of Hemel, Hempstead.

GROWSE, Edward Frederick, 1872. From Brentwood. Indian Civil Service.

GUILDING, Edward Lainson, 1871. Son of Edward Wingfield Guilding, of 19, Great Russell Street. *b.* 1858. Bracketed Scholar of Pemb. Coll. Oxf. Passed into Sandhurst first on the list. 44th Regt.

GUILLEMARD,* Laurence Nunns, 1875. Son of Rev. W. H. Guillemard, D.D., Vicar of St. Mary the Less, Cambridge. *b.* 1862.

GUINNESS, Gerald Seymour, 1874. Son of Richard Seymour Guinness, of Dublin. *b.* 1862. Trin. Coll. Dublin.

GUINNESS, Henry Thomas, 1875.

GUISE,* Henry John Wright, 1871. Son of Major Henry John Guise, H.E.I.C.S. *b.* 1857. R.M. Coll. Sandhurst.

GULICH, John Percival, 1878. Son of Hermann Gulich, of Wimbledon. *b.* 1864.

GUNN, Bassett Charles Edward Fitzgerald, 1872. Son of William Gunn, M.D. (Royal Navy). *b.* 1858. Medical Student at University Coll. Hospital, London.

GUNNING,* George Orlando, 1807-11. Second son of Sir Geo. Gunning, 2nd Bart. *b.* 1796. Capt. 10th Hussars. Killed at Waterloo.

GUNNING,* Henry John (Bart.), 1808-16. Son of Sir Geo. W. Gunning, Bart. *b.* 1797. Ball. Coll. Oxf. Rector of Wigan 1833-64. Succeeded his brother as 4th Bt. 1862. Horton, Northampton.

GUNNING, Octavius, 1815. Brother of the above. *b.* 1804. Captn. 52nd Regt.

GURDON, Philip Richard Thornhagh, 1877. Son of Lieut.-Col. E. P. Gurdon, Bengal Staff Corps. *b.* 1863.

GUTHRIE, Charles Seton James Lister, 1874. Of Caterham.

GWILLIM, Francis Garbett, 1828, *b.* 1816.

GWILLYM, Richard, 1814-17. Son of Richard Gwillym. *b.* 1802. B.N.C. Oxf. Rector of Ulverstone; *d.* 1867.

H.

HACON, William Llewelyn, 1874.

HADFIELD,* George Horatio, 1818. Son of Joseph Hadfield. *b.* 1805. Fellow of Pemb. Coll. Oxf. Double 2nd Class. Formerly Curate of Whitchurch; *d.* 1854.

HADFIELD, Octavius, 1829, *b.* 1814. Bishop of Wellington, New Zealand.

HAGGARD, Christopher, 1841-47. Son of John Haggard, L.L.D. of Doctor's Commons. *b.* 1829. Ch. Ch. Oxf. Rector of Filleigh.

HAGGARD, Edward, 1848-51. Brother of the above. *b.* 1836. Barrister. Lincoln's Inn.

HAGGARD, George, 1844-49. Brother of the above. *b.* 1832. Major Madras Artillery. Retired 1871.

HAHN, John Frederick, 1821, *b.* 1810. Died in Mexico 1865.

HAHN, Henry George, 1826. Brother of the above. *b.* 1812. Died in Mexico.

HAIG, George Andrew, 1817. Son of John Haig, of Bonnington, Midlothian. *b.* 1803. Of Maulsden, Forfarshire. Edinburgh University. Resident at Torquay.

HAIG, John, 1813-14. Son of Robert Haig, of Roebuck, Dublin. *b.* 1801. Trin. Coll. Dublin. Gold Medallist 1820. Barrister; *d.* 1837.

HAIG, Thomas, 1817-18. Brother of George Andrew Haig (above). *b.* 1804. Distiller at Brentford; *d.* 1858.

HAINES, Frederick William Henry, 1866, *b.* 1852. Worc. Coll. Oxf. Holy Orders. Assist. Master at St. John's School, Leatherhead.

HAINES, Henry Jackson, 1874. Son of H. Haines, The Pool House, Stourport. *b.* 1859. Trin. Coll. Cam.

HAINES, Robert Lewis, 1869, *b.* 1855. Lieut. Royal Artillery. 4th Battn.

HAINES, Thomas, 1826, *b.* 1813. Indian Army, Madras.

HAINES, William Clarke, 1823, b. 1810.   Caius Coll. Cam. A.B. 1833.

HAINES, Willoughby Charles, 1868, b. 1858.

HALCOMBE, John Joseph, 1845-50, b. 1832. Scholar of Magd. Coll. Cam. Formerly Reader and Librarian at Charterhouse. Rector of Balsham, Cambs.

HALE, George Herbert, 1841-50. Son of Archdeacon Hale. b. 1832. Indian Army. 4th Bengal Cavalry, d.

HALE, James Charles, 1856-58. Brother of the above. b. 1840. Trin. Coll. Cam. Rector of Castle Camps, d.

HALE, John Godwin, 1841-48. Brother of the above. b. 1830. Oriel Coll. Oxf. Vicar of Tottenham 1861-70. Rector of Therfield, Herts.

HALE, Lonsdale Augustus, 1845-48. Brother of the above. b. 1834. Lieut.-Col. R.E. Professor of Fortification. R.M. Coll. Sandhurst.

HALE, William Hale, 1807-11, b. 1795. Oriel Coll. Oxf. Double 2nd Class. Archdeacon of London, Canon of St. Paul's, Master of Charterhouse, d.

HALE,* William Palmer, 1835-42. Son of the above. b. 1824. Orator. Ch. Ch. Oxf. Scholar of Trin. Hall, Cam. Barrister, d.

HALFORD, Charles Douglas, 1805-8. Son of late James Halford, of Laleham, Middlx. b. 1793. Jesus Coll. Cam. Barrister of Lincoln's Inn; d. 1865.

HALIBURTON, Alexander Fowden, 1825. Son of Alex. Haliburton, of Whitley, near Wigan. b. 1809. St. John's Coll. Cam. Of Grafton, Torquay, and J.P. for Lancashire; d. 1873.

HALIFAX, John Savile, 1817, b. 1804. Trin. Coll. Oxf. Rector of Groton, Suffolk.

HALL, Arthur, 1875. Of Ely.

HALL, Charles Percy, 1876.

HALL, Edmund, 1843-47. Son of G. Hall, of Ely. b. 1828. Scholar of Emm. Coll. Cam. Rector of Myland, Essex.

HALL, Gerald, 1858-62. Of Ely, b. 1844.

HALL, George Hall, 1854-57. Son of Alexander Hall Hall, of Watergate, Sussex. *b.* 1841. Trin. Coll. Cam. Late Ensign 4th (King's Own) Regt. Solicitor in London.

HALL, John, 1874. Son of John Hall, 30, Porchester Sq., W.

HALL,* John Cecil, 1816. Son of the Rev. Dr. Hall, Dean of Ch. Ch. *b.* 1803. Ch. Ch. Oxf. Rector of Kirk Andrews, Isle of Man. Archdeacon of Man; *d.* 1844.

HALL, Seymour Gilbert, 1847-49, *b.* 1832. Civil Engineer.

HALL, Tansley, 1827, *b.* 1811. St. John's Coll. Cam. Rector of Boylestone, Derbyshire.

HALL,* Thomas Francis, 1805-13, *b.* 1795. Trin. Coll. Cam. Vicar of Hatfield, Broad Oak, Essex.

HALL,* William, 1809-12, *b.* 1796. Solicitor at Walden, Essex; deceased.

HALL, William George, 1866-70, *b.* 1854.

HALLETT, Shackleton, 1854-56. Son of Thomas P. Luxmore Hallett, late Fellow of Trin. Hall, Cam. *b.* 1842. Barrister of Lincoln's Inn.

HALLETT, Holt Samuel, 1854-56. Brother of the above. *b.* 1841. Civil Engineer in H.M. Indian Service at Rangoon.

HALLETT, Lyttleton, 1859-64. Brother of the above. *b.* 1846. M.R.C.S. Died at Shanghai 1876.

HALLOWELL,* Benjamin, 1812. Son of Adml. Sir B. Hallowell. *b.* 1802. Died in India.

HALLOWELL, William Henry, 1820, *b.* 1809.

HALLWARD,* Frederick Leslie Charles, 1874. Son of Rev. John William Hallward. *b.* 1862.

HALLWARD,* Nathaniel William, 1808-14. Son of Rev. John Hallward, Vicar of Assington, Suffolk. *b.* 1797. Worc. Coll. Oxf. Rector of Milden, Suffolk.

HALSEY, Edward Joseph, 1853. St. John's Coll. Oxf.

HAMILTON, Alexander Edmund, 1817, *b.* 1806.

HAMILTON, Alfred George, 1876. Son of the late Rev. George Hamilton, Incumbent of Christ Church, Bloomsbury. *b.* 1861. Engineer Student.

HAMILTON, Arthur Henry Cole, 1857. (See Cole-Hamilton).

HAMILTON, Augustus Terrick, 1830. Youngest son of Wm. Richd. Hamilton, Under Secy. of State. Minister at Naples. *b.* 1818. Capt. 71st Regt.

HAMILTON, Charles Antony, 1824, *b.* 1809. Council Office.

HAMILTON (Sir) Charles John James (Bart.), 1823. Son of Sir Charles Hamilton, 2nd Bart. *b.* 1810. Formerly Col. Scots Fusilier Guards. Alma, &c. (C.B.). Succeeded his father 1849.

HAMILTON, John James Edward, 1821. Son of Admiral Sir Edward Hamilton, Bart. K.C.B. *b.* 1808; *d.* 1847.

HAMILTON, Henry, 1817, *b.* 1808.

HAMILTON, Henry, 1828, *b.* 1816.

HAMILTON, John, 1819-20. Son of John Hamilton, of Sundrum, Ayrshire. *b.* 1806. Edinburgh University. E. Indian Company's Navy. Late Lieut.-Col. Commanding Ayrshire Yeomanry Cavalry. Sundrum, Ayr. N. B.

HAMILTON, John, 1823, *b.* 1809.

HAMILTON, Walter Archibald, 1877. Grosvenor Hill, Wimbledon, *b.* 1862.

HAMILTON, William John, 1817, *b.* 1805.

HAMLIN, James, 1801-7, *b.* 1790. Solicitor. A Pensioner of the Charterhouse.

HAMLYN-FANE, Henry Edward, 1832. (See Fane).

HAMMICK,* Ernest Austin, 1861. Son of Sir Vincent L. Hammick, Bart. *b.* 1850. Ex. Coll. Oxf. Rector of Forrabury, Cornwall.

HAMMICK,* Murray, 1866-69. Brother of the above. *b.* 1854. King's Coll. London, 1870. Indian Civil Service.

HAMMOND, Egerton, 1876.

HAMMOND, James John, 1826, *b.* 1811.

HAMMOND, John, 1813-14, *b.* 1798.

HAMMOND, William Farrar, 1841-42, *b.* 1824. St. John's Coll. Cam. *d.* 1850.

List of Carthusians. 109

HAMPSON, Charles Seymour, 1874. Son of the late Rev. William Seymour Hampson, of Stubton, Lincolnshire. *b.* 1861.

HAMPSON,* George Francis, 1871. Brother of the above. *b.* 1860.

HANBURY, Bernard Kingscote, 1878. Son of Edgar Hanbury, of Eastrop, Wilts. *b.* 1865.

HANCOCK, Philip, 1822, *b.* 1809. Of Ford House, Wivelscombe, Somerset, *d.* 1870.

HANDLEY, Benjamin, 1802-8. Son of B. Handley, of Sleaford. 9th Light Dragoons. Served in the Peninsula. Drowned at Lisbon.

HANDLEY, Henry, 1805-7. Brother of the above. Banker at Sleaford. *b.* 1797. Went to Eton. Ch. Ch. Oxf. M.P. for S. Lincolnshire; *d.* 1846.

HANDLEY, William, 1803-6 Cousin of the above, *b.* 1792. Formerly M.P. for Newark-on-Trent.

HANDLEY, William, 1820. Nephew of the above. *b.* 1806. St. John's Coll. Cam. Rector of Winthorpe, Notts.

HANKEY, Algernon Alers, 1876. Son of Jameson Alers Hankey, of Upton, Kent. *b.* 1862.

HANMER, Thomas, 1826. Third son of late Thos. Hanmer, and brother of present Lord Hanmer. *b.* 1813. B.N. Coll. Oxf. Barrister of the Middle Temple; *d.* 1869.

HANMER, Wyndham Edward, 1823. Brother of the above. *b.* 1810. Capt. Royal Horse Guards. Stockgrove, Bucks and Rushmere Lodge, Beds.

HANNAM, Edward Lawton, 1844-48. Son of Rev. Edward Pett Hannam, Vicar of Borden, Kent. *b.* 1830. Proctor in Doctors' Commons. Of Oakfield Lodge, Sussex.

HANNAM, Frederic, 1827, *b.* 1812.

HANNAM, George Emilius, 1823. Eldest son of George Hannam, of Bromstone, Kent. *b.* 1810. J.P. for Kent. Bromstone House, St. Peter's, Ramsgate.

HANNAM, Henry, 1812-14, *b.* 1798. Farmer near Wallingford.

HANNAM, Henry Backhouse, 1842-47. Son of Henry Jessard Hannam. *b.* 1828. Ex. Coll. Oxf. Emigrated to Australia.

HANSARD, Alfred Ogle, 1827, b. 1817. Lieut. R.N. d. 1851.

HANSARD, Frederick, 1828, b. 1818. Solicitor, Gray's Inn; d. 1844.

HANSARD, George, 1825, b. 1812. Barrister of Lincoln's Inn.

HANSELL, Arthur David, 1874. Son of Rev. Edward Hansell, Rector of East Ilsley, Berks. b. 1863. Articled to a Solicitor.

HANSELL,* Edward William, 1868. Brother of the above. b. 1856. Holford Exhibitioner. Ch. Ch. Oxf. 2nd Class Mods.

HANSELL, Reginald Goddard, 1873. Brother of the above. b. 1861. Articled to a Surveyor.

HANSELL, Walter Edward, 1873-78. Son of P. E. Hansell, Solicitor, Thorpe, Norwich. b. 1860. Articled to a Solicitor.

HANSLIP, Robert, 1859-61. Son of Charles Hanslip, Solicitor, of London. b. 1846. Interpreter to the British Consulate, Friendly Islands.

HANSON, Alfred Atkinson, 1844-48. Son of late George Hanson, of Chigwell. b. 1833. Royal Navy.

HANSON, James Oliver, 1843-48. Brother of the above. b. 1831. Merchant. Constantinople. Deceased.

HANSON,* John Clarke, 1867-73, b. 1854. Prize Scholar 1869. St. John's Coll. Cam. Cuddesdon Theol. Coll.

HARDING, Henry, 1825, b. 1810.

HARDING,* John, 1863-65. Son of Wyndham Harding and nephew of the late Sir J. D. Harding. b. 1851. Of Rockfield, Monmouth.

HARDING (Sir) John Dorney (Knt.), 1821. Son of Rev. J. Harding. b. 1809. Oriel Coll. Oxf. 2nd Class Lit. Hum. D.C.L. 1837. Barrister. Advocate-General. Knighted 1852; d. 1868.

HARDING, John Ward, 1814-16, b. 1804.

HARDING,* William, 1818. Son of Rev. William Harding. b. 1805. Univ. Coll. Oxf. Vicar of Sulgrave, Northampton.

HARDINGE, Heler Thomas, 1851, b. 1836.

HARDMAN, Charles Edward Shirley, 1873. Son of Charles Alexander Hardman, of Wimbledon Park.

HARDMAN, Edward Trevor, 1874. Brother of the above. *b.* 1861.

HARDY, John Richard, 1820, *b*, 1807.

HARE, Gustavus Edward Cockburn, 1821. Son of Francis Hare-Naylor, of Hurstmonceux, Sussex. *b.* 1811. A Judge in Australia. Formerly in the Prussian Army.

HARE, Humphrey John, 1820. Son of late Rev. Humphrey J. Hare, of Docking Hall, Norfolk. *b.* 1811. Wadham Coll. Oxf. Barrister of the Inner Temple.

HARE, Julius Charles, 1806-12. Son of Francis Hare-Naylor, of Hurstmonceux, Sussex. *b.* 1795. Fellow of Trin. Coll. Cam. Rector of Hurstmonceux, Sussex. Archdeacon of Lewes. The well-known Author; *d.* 1855.

HARENC,* Herbert Benjamin, 1860-65. Son of Rev. A. F. Harenc, formerly of Longcot, Berks. *b.* 1849. Lieut. Kent Artillery Militia; *d.* 1878.

HARINGTON, Charles, 1875. Son of Sir Richard Harington, Bart. *b.* 1862.

HARKINGS, Charles, 1824, *b.* 1812.

HARLAND, George Brighton, 1876. Son of John Harland, of Hull. *b.* 1861. Articled to a Solicitor.

HARMAN, Ezekiel Dickinson, 1815-16, *b.* 1800.

HARNY, Edward Francis, 1824, *b.* 1814.

HARPER, Henry, 1812-13, *b.* 1798.

HARPER, Henry Lacon, 1874. Engineer.

HARPER, Samuel Thomas, 1820, *b.* 1808.

HARRIS, Thomas, 1811-14, *b.* 1798.

HARRIS, William, 1817, *b.* 1805.

HARRISON, Arnold Sanders, 1876. Son of Charles Whitmore Harrison, of Whitmores, Beckenham. *b.* 1863.

HARRISON, Charles King, 1876. Son of Charles Harrison, M.P., of Aveley Court, Stourport. *b.* 1863.

HARRISON, Cyril, 1877.

HARRISON, Fiske Goodeve Fiske- 1806-10. Son of late John Haynes Harrison, of Copford Hall, Essex, who assumed the additional name of Fiske in 1839. *b.* 1793. St. John's Coll. Cam.; *d.* 1872.

HARRISON, George, 1826, *b.* 1814.

HARRISON, Henry Bashcomb, 1859-62, *b.* 1848.

HARRISON, John Haynes, 1805-10. Son of Rev. John Harrison. *b.* 1792. Of Copford Hall, Essex; *d.* 1839.

HARRISON, John Moseley Gilbert, 1876.

HARRISON, Thomas, 1808-10, *b.* 1797.

HARRISON, Walter Harry, 1861-63, *b.* 1846.

HARTLEY, Perceval, 1826. Son of James Hartley, Solicitor of London. *b.* 1814. Scholar of Trin. Hall, Cam. LL.B. Rector of Creeton, Lincolnshire.

HARTSHORNE,* Bertram Fulke, 1857-63. Son of Rev. Chas. Henry Hartshorne. *b.* 1844. Pemb. Coll. Oxf. Indian Civil Service. Retired. Barrister.

HARTWELL,* Brodrick, 1800-4. Son of Sir Francis John Hartwell, Bart. *b.* 1788, *d.* 1810.

HARVEY, Beauchamp, 1802-4, *b.* 1792.

HARVEY,* Charles Musgrave, 1850-55. Son of Rev. Canon Harvey, Rector of Hornsey. *b.* 1837. Orator. Ch. Ch. Oxf. Rector of Acton, Middlesex.

HARVEY, George Ludford, 1810-13, *b.* 1798. Sid. Suss. Coll. Cam. Rector of Yate, Gloucester.

HARVEY, James Vigors, 1802-3, *b.* 1788. Of Killiane, Co. Wexford.

HARVEY, Onley, 1806-13. (See Savill-Onley).

HARWOOD, Basil, 1874.

HASTINGS (Lord) Francis Theophilus Henry, 1823. Son of the 12th Earl of Huntingdon. *b.* 1808. Succeeded his father as 13th Earl 1828; *d.* 1875.

HASTINGS,* Hon. Richard Godolphin Henry, 1832-38. Son of the 11th Earl of Huntingdon. *b.* 1820. Univ. Coll. Oxf. Rector of Hertingfordbury, Herts; *d.* 1864.

List of Carthusians. 113

HATCHARD, Francis Sumner Utterton, 1874. 81, Queen's Gate, S.W.

HATHAWAY, Philip, 1843-46, *b.* 1832. Went to Bath School. Solicitor in London.

HATHORN, Hugh Vans, 1817, *b.* 1804. East India Civil Service. A Judge in Bengal; *d.* 1842.

HAVELOCK (Sir) Henry (K.C.B.), 1804. Son of William Havelock, of Ingress Park, Kent. *b.* 1795. Major-General Sir Henry Havelock, K.C.B. of Lucknow; *d.* 1857.

HAVELOCK, Thomas, 1809-11. Brother of the above. *b.* 1800. Served in Spain under Sir De Lacy Evans; *d.* 1836.

HAVELOCK, William (K.H.) 1804-9. Brother of the above. *b.* 1793. Lieut.-Col. 14th Light Dragoons. Wounded at Waterloo. Killed in action at Ramnugger 1848.

HAVELOCK, William Waller Carrington, 1873. Son of the late William H. Havelock, Member of Bombay Council. *b.* 1859. Army Student.

HAVERFIELD,* John, 1822. Son of Lieut.-Col. Haverfield, of Kew. *b.* 1810; died young.

HAVERS, John Cory, 1853-58. Son of Dr. Havers, of Guildford Street. *b.* 1843. Medical Practitioner.

HAWKE (Hon.) Stanhope Harvey- (Lord Hawke), 1813-14. Son of the 3rd Baron Hawke. *b.* 1804. Capt. in the Army 1826. Succeeded his brother as 5th Lord Hawke 1869 and *d.* 1870.

HAWKER,* Charles Frederick, 1833-38. Son of Col. Hawker. *b.* 1821. Ordnance Office.

HAWKER, Edward Williams, 1845-50. Son of W. H. Hawker, of Plymouth. *b.* 1833. Bank of England.

HAWKES, Frederick, 1818. Of Norwich. *b.* 1808.

HAWKINS, Anthony Nicholl, 1823. Son of Anthony Montonnier Hawkins, M.D. of London. *b.* 1809. Barrister of the Middle Temple.

HAWKINS, Charles, 1824-28. Brother of the above. *b.* 1812. Fellow of the Royal College of Surgeons of England. Inspector of Schools of Anatomy, &c.

HAWKINS, Charles John Sidney, 1859-62. Son of C. S. Hawkins (below). *b.* 1845. Magd. Hall, Oxf. Lieut. W.I. Regt. *d.* 1868.

I

HAWKINS, Charles Sidney, 1834-36. Son of John S. Hawkins, F.S.A. *b.* 1818. Magd. Hall, Oxf. Major Worcestershire Militia. Wroughton House, Swindon.

HAWKINS, Edward, 1826, *b.* 1814. Trin. Coll. Cam. Law.

HAWKINS, Edward, 1846-50. Son of Rev. Dr. Hawkins, Provost of Oriel Coll. Oxf. *b.* 1833. Ball. Coll. Oxf. Holy Orders, *d.*

HAWKINS, Henry Archer, 1859-63. Brother of C. J. S. Hawkins (above). *b.* 1847. Late Lieut. Worcester Militia.

HAWKINS, Henry Theodore, 1876. Royal Military Academy, Woolwich.

HAWKINS, Major Rohde, 1831-37. Son of Edward Hawkins, of the British Museum. *b.* 1821. Architect. Council Office, Whitehall.

HAWKINS, Sidney Barrington Robson, 1859-63. Son of C. S. Hawkins (above). *b.* 1848. Capt. Worcester Militia.

HAWKS, Frederick Augustus, 1878. Son of Augustus Hawks, Springfield, Hertford. *b.* 1865.

HAWORTH,* Henry, 1857-61. Son of Capt. Haworth, of Barham Wood, Herts. Queen's Messenger. *b.* 1845.

HAWORTH,* Martin Leslie, 1849-55. Brother of the above. *b.* 1839. Foreign Office.

HAWORTH, Walter Stuart Stevens, 1874. R.M. Coll. Sandhurst.

HAY, David, 1872. Son of Col. Hay, Waltham Abbey.

HAY (Sir) Edward Hay Drummond (Knt.), 1827. Son of E. W. A. Drummond-Hay. *b.* 1815. Colonial Office. Governor of the Virgin Islands 1839, St. Kitts 1850, St. Helena 1855. Retired 1863.

HAY (Sir) John Hay Drummond (K.C.B.), 1828. Brother of the above. *b.* 1816. Min. Plenip. at the Court of Morocco.

HAYDON, Thomas Horatio, 1878. Son of Dodsworth Haydon, Castlegate, Guildford. *b.* 1865.

HAYES, Horace Milman, 1875. Of Avoca, Co. Wicklow.

HAYES,   , 1803.

HAYNES,* John Hardcastle, 1801-6, *b.* 1791. Student of Ch. Ch. Oxf. Drowned at Oxford 1813.

HAYTER, Francis Goodenough, 1874. Son of Henry Goodenough Hayter.

HAYTER, Henry Hayter, 1837. Son of Henry Hayter, of Edendale, Wilts. Government Statist, Victoria. Author of Works on New Zealand and Victoria.

HAYTER, Henry William Goodenough, 1876. Brother of Francis Goodenough Hayter (above).

HAYTER, William Thomas Baring, 1873. Son of Harrison Hayter, C.E. B.N. Coll. Oxf.

HEAD, Charles Howard, 1875. Son of Henry Head, Stamford Hill, *d.* 1877.

HEAD (Sir) Frank Somerville (Bart.), 1827. Eldest son of the late Sir Francis Head, Bart. *b.* 1817. Bengal Civil Service.

HEAD, Henry, 1875. Brother of Charles Howard Head (above). *b.* 1861.

HEAD, Hugh Stanley, 1878. Brother of the above. *b.* 1864.

HEALEY,* James, 1804, *b.* 1794.

HEATH,* William Emanuel, 1847-51, *b.* 1835.

HEATHER, Henry, 1810-13, *b.* 1797; deceased.

HEATON, Beresford Rimington, 1876. Son of J. D. Heaton, M.D., of Claremont, Leeds. *b.* 1863.

HEBDEN, Robert James, 1826, *b.* 1813. St. John's Coll. Cam. A.B. 1839.

HEBERDEN, Frederick, 1820. Son of William Heberden, M.D., Physician to King George III. *b.* 1810. St. John's Coll. Cam. A.B. 1832. Vicar of Wilmington, Dartford; *d.* 1876.

HEBERT, Charles, 1822. Son of Robert Hebert, Merchant, of London. *b.* 1807. Gold Medal. Trin. Coll. Cam. Wrangler and 1st Class Classical Tripos. D.D. Vicar of Ambleside.

HEDGES, Septimus, 1874. Of Sunbury on Thames.

HELME, Robert, 1846. Son of R. Helme, of Walthamstow. *b*. 1830. Trin. Coll. Cam. 6th Senr. Opt. Formerly Vicar of Leverstock-Green, &c.

HELME, Robert Masterman, 1876. Son of the above. *b*. 1862.

HELPS, Henry, 1822. Son of Thomas Helps. *b*. 1807. Magd. Coll. Cam.; *d*. 1853.

HENLEY, Arthur Keith, 1875. Son of Hon. and Rev. Robert Henley, Vicar of Putney. *b*. 1863.

HENNIKER, Aldborough, 1833-39. Eldest son of Aldborough J. B. Henniker, of Catcott, Somerset. *b*. 1821. Q.C. Treasurer of Gray's Inn 1877.

HENNIKER, Frederick, 1835-40. Brother of the above. *b*. 1823. Merchant; died in Australia.

HENNIKER, John, 1837-41. Brother of the above. *b*. 1825. R. Navy; *d*. 1854.

HENNIKER, Robert, 1844-52. Brother of the above. *b*. 1833. Gold Medal. Scholar of Trin. Coll. Oxf. 1st Class Lit. Hum. &c. Vicar of Frocester. Head Master of Rossall School 1869-75.

HENNIKER, Rowland, 1849-54. Brother of the above. *b*. 1835. Trin. Hall. Cam. Holy Orders; *d*.

HENRIQUES, David, 1807-8, *b*. 1792.

HENRY, Arnold Jabez, 1825, *b*. 1813.

HENRY, Thomas Ethrington, 1825, *b*. 1814.

HERBERT, Magnus William Morton, 1872. Son of the late Capt. Herbert, 48th Regt. *b*. 1859. Army Student.

HERIOT, Charles Hambro, 1878. Son of Robert Heriot, of Mulgrave House, Sutton, Surrey. *b*. 1864.

HERIOT, Walter James, 1876. Brother of the above.

HERON, Francis Arthur, 1878. Son of Arthur P. Heron, of Lonsdale House, Dorking. *b*. 1864.

HERRING, Nathaniel Rogers, 1823, *b*. 1809. Trin. Coll. Cam. Holy Orders; *d*.

HERTSLET, Cecil, 1864.

HERVEY,* Granville Walter, 1864. Son of Rev. Lord Charles A. Hervey, Rector of Chesterford, Cambridgeshire. *b.* 1852. Clare Coll. Cam.

HESKETH, Wickham, 1818, *b.* 1806.

HESSING, George William, 1833-35, *b.* 1819. Army; died in India 1841.

HEWETT, Cornwallis, 1800-4. Trin. Coll. Cam. M.D. Fellow and Medical Professor of Downing Coll. Physician to St. George's Hospital, &c.; *d.* 1841.

HEWETT, Douglas, 1876. Son of Robert Hewett, Roden Lodge, Barking, Essex. *b.* 1862.

HEWETT, Graham, 1875. Brother of the above. *b.* 1862.

HEWETT, Robert Muirhead, 1871. Brother of the above. *b.* 1860.

HEWLETT,* Joseph Thomas James, 1812-18. Son of Joseph Hewlett. *b.* 1800. Worc. Coll. Oxf. Vicar of Little Stambridge, Essex. Author of "Peter Priggins," &c.; *d.* 1846.

HICKMAN, Devereux Edward, 1873.

HICKS, Edward, 1825. (See Simpson, Edward).

HIGGINS, James Robert, 1824, *b.* 1810. Medical Practitioner.

HIGGINSON, Jonathan, 1821, *b.* 1807.

HILL, Edward Johnson, 1827, *b.* 1811. Drowned 1829.

HILL, George Henry Hawtrey, 1864. Army. Highland regt.

HILL, John Frederick, 1824, *b.* 1809.

HILLIARD, Frederick Joseph, 1811-13, *b.* 1797. Peterhouse Coll. Cam. Rector of Little Wittenham, Berks.

HILLIARD, John Ashby Stafford, 1844-47. Son of the above. *b.* 1830. St. John's Coll. Oxf. Rector of Little Wittenham.

HILLS, Henry Thomas Snow, 1847-48. Son of Walter Hills, Barrister. *b.* 1837. Emm. Coll. Cam. Died at Rome 1858.

HILLS, Walter Alfred, 1844-52. Brother of the above. *b.* 1835. Trin. Coll. Oxf.

HILLS, William Jefferys, 1843-47. Brother of the above. *b.* 1829. Trin. Coll. and Scholar of Jesus Coll. Oxf. Vicar of Cookham Dean.

HILTON, Arthur Denne, 1838-43. Son of Rev. John Hilton, Vicar of St. Nicholas, at Wade, Kent. *b.* 1824. Wadh. Coll. Oxf. Incumbent of St. John's, Uxbridge Moor.

HINCHLIFFE,* William, 1814-20, *b.* 1803.

HIND, Charles, 1820, *b.* 1806. Lieut.-Genl. Formerly of 45th Regt.

HIND, William, 1820. Son of Martin Hind. *b.* 1804. Univ. Coll. Oxf. 1st Class Math. Holy Orders.

HINDS, Philip, 1802-5, *b.* 1791.

HINDS, Samuel, 1801-7, *b.* 1789. Pemb. Coll. Cam.

HINDS, Samuel, 1803-12. Son of Abel Hinds, of Barbados. *b.* 1795. Queens Coll. Oxf. 2nd Class Lit. Hum. Dean of Carlisle 1848. Bishop of Norwich 1849. Resigned 1857; *d.* 1872.

HINDS, Thomas Maxwell, 1807-13, *b.* 1799.

HIRTZEL, Francis, 1811-16, *b.* 1801.

HOBART, George Bertie Benjamin, 1850-55. Son of the Hon. and Very Rev. H. L. Hobart, D.D., Dean of Windsor. *b.* 1838. Major Royal Horse Artillery. China 1860. Medal and Clasps. Military Secy. to the Governor of Madras.

HOBART, Robert Henry, 1849. Brother of the above. *b.* 1836. Trin. Hall, Cam. War Office. Private Secretary to the Marquis of Hartington.

HOBART,* Hon. William Arthur, 1840-45. Son of the 6th Earl of Buckinghamshire. *b.* 1828. 26th Bombay Native Infantry. Holy Orders. Rector of Conisholme, Linc.; *d.* 1874.

HOBBS, Charles James, 1878. Son of Joseph Hobbs, 9, Kensington Gardens Square. *b.* 1866.

HOBBS, Joseph Scovell, 1874. Brother of the above.

HOBHOUSE, Thomas Benjamin, 1821. Son of Sir Benj. Hobhouse, Bart., and brother of Lord Broughton. *b.* 1807. Ball. Coll. Oxf. 2nd Class Lit. Hum. Barrister. M.P. for Chatham 1837-41; for Lincoln 1848-52; *d.* 1877.

List of Carthusians.   119

HODGE, Thomas Durell Powell, 1851-53, b. 1835. Joined Garibaldi's Army.

HODGES,* Charles William Henry, 1822, b. 1808.

HODGES, John, 1804-5.

HODGES, Nethersole, 1821, b. 1808.

HODGKINSON, Edward, b. 1812.

HODGKINSON, Samuel Brandram, 1828, b. 1817.

HODGKINSON, Thomas Mather, 1874.

HODGSON, Anthony John, 1825, b. 1814.

HODGSON,   , 1805-7. Royal Engineers.

HODGSON, Ellis, 1805-7.

HODGSON,* James Thomas, 1857-64. Son of Rev. Francis Hodgson. b. 1846. Univ. Coll. Oxf. Assistant Master at Charterhouse.

HODGSON, John Fisher, 1820. Son of C. Hodgson, Secretary and Treasurer Queen Anne's Bounty. b. 1812. Went to Westminster School. Ch. Ch. Oxf. 3rd Class Lit. Hum. Vicar of Horsham.

HODGSON, Kirkman Daniel, 1826. Son of John Hodgson, of The Elms, Hampstead. b. 1814. Merchant in London. Director of the Bank of England, &c. M.P. for Bristol, &c.; d. 1879.

HODGSON, William, 1850-57. Son of the Rev. Dr. Hodgson, Master of St. Peter's Coll. Cam. b. 1839. St. Peter's Coll. Cam. Vicar of Plaistow, Kent.

HODSON, Charles Frederick, 1863, b. 1847.

HODSON, Grenville Heber Frodsham Elton, 1831-40. Son of Rev. Dr. Hodson, Principal of B.N.C. Oxf. b. 1821. B.N.C. Oxf. Rector of Michaelchurch.

HOGARTH, John Rayer, 1821, b. 1811.

HOLBERTON, Richard R. 1822. Ex. Coll. Oxf. Holy Orders; deceased.

HOLDSHIP,* James Michael, 1816, b. 1803. Registrar's Office, Chancery Lane.

HOLDSWORTH, Arthur Bastard E. 1823. Son of A. H. Holdsworth, M.P. for Dartmouth. *b.* 1808. Capt. 6th Dragoons; *d.* 1875.

HOLLAND, Henry Lancelot, 1821. Eldest son of Colonel Holland. *b.* 1808. Went to Harrow School. A Governor of the Bank of England.

HOLLAND, Percy, 1875. Son of Rev. C. Holland, Rector of Petworth. R. M. Coll. Sandhurst.

HOLLAND, Thomas Edwardes Mytton, 1808-11 Son of Saml. Holland. *b.* 1793. Ball. Coll. Oxf. Vicar of Stoke Bliss, Herefordshire.

HOLLAND,* William, 1808-15. Son of Rev. William Holland. *b.* 1797. Ch. Ch. Oxf. Rector of Cold Norton, Essex; *d.* 1868.

HOLLOWAY,* Edward Vere Peregrine, 1816, *b.* 1806. Lieut.-Col. Indian Army; *d.* 1877.

HOLLOWAY, Meryon, 1823, *b.* 1812. Drowned at Charterhouse 1829.

HOLLWAY, Geoffrey Fynes, 1874. Son of Major Jas. Hollway, Stanhoe Grange, Norfolk. *b.* 1861. Articled to a Solicitor.

HOLLWAY, John Majendie, 1876. Brother of the above. *b.* 1863.

HOLLYON, James Blatch Philip, 1825, *b.* 1811. Wadh. Coll. Oxf. Banker.

HOLMAN, Henry Martin, 1874. Son of G. Holman, of Reigate.

HOLME, James Wetheral, 1858, *b.* 1844. Merchant's Office.

HOLMES, Marcus Edward, 1877.

HOLROYD, Edward, 1806-11. Son of Sir George S. Holroyd, Judge of the Court of King's Bench. *b.* 1794. Trin. Coll. Cam. Barrister. Late Senior Commissioner of Bankruptcy.

HOLT,* Charles Reginald Cooper, 1874. Son of Rev. Robert Holt, of Hillesden, Bucks. Scholar of Hertford Coll. Oxf.

HOLWORTHY, Wentworth Samuel, 1825. Son of Rev. Samuel Holworthy, Rector of Croxall, Derbyshire. *b.* 1812. Trin. Coll. Cam.

HOOD, Thomas Pelham, 1802-4.

HOOLE, James, 1826, *b.* 1814.

HOOMAN, Thomas Charles, 1863-68, *b.* 1850.   27, Clement's Lane, E.C.

HOOPER, Thomas James, 1849, *b.* 1833.

HOPE, David Boyle, 1847-50.   Second son of James Hope, and nephew of the late Rt. Hon. John Hope-Vere, Lord Justice Clerk of Scotland. *b.* 1833.   Scotch Advocate.

HOPE-VERE, Charles Edward, 1843-48.   Son of J. J. Hope Vere, and grandson of 4th Marquis of Tweedale. *b.* 1828. Mercantile House.

HOPEGOOD, Andrew Edward, 1823, *b.* 1814.   Trin. Coll. Cam. A.B. 1836.

HOPKINS, Everard, 1873.   Son of Manley Hopkins, Oak Hill, Hampstead. *b.* 1860.   Artist.

HOPKIRK, Charles Thomas, 1863-7.   Son of Thos. Hopkirk. *b.* 1849.   St. Edmund's Hall, Oxf.

HOPPER, Arthur Quin, 1823, *b.* 1811.   34th Bengal N.I.

HOPPER, Harman Baillee, *b.* 1819.   31st Bengal N.I.   Severely wounded at Kelat, 13th Nov. 1839.

HOPWOOD, Arthur Robert, 1855-60, *b.* 1845.   Captain Rifle Brigade.   Ashanti Medal and Clasp.

HOPWOOD, Henry Aubrey, 1876.

HORDER, Thomas William, 1822, *b*, 1812.

HORE, Charles Clavell, 1864.   Son of Charles Hore, of Dulwich, Solicitor. *b.* 1851.   Barrister of Lincoln's Inn.

HORNE, Arthur, 1821, *b.* 1807.   25, Avenue Rd., N.W.

HORNE, Frederick William, 1878.   Son of Rev. Frederick Edward Horne, Rector of Drinkstone, Suffolk. *b.* 1866.

HORNER, John Stuart Hippisley, 1822.   Second son of Thos. Strangways Horner, of Mells Park, Somerset. *b.* 1810. M.A.   Ex. Coll. Oxf.   Holy Orders.   Rector of Mells, and Preb. of Wells ; *d.* 1874.

HORROCKS, Edgeworth, 1840-44.   Son of Peter Horrocks, of Penwortham Lodge, Preston, Lanc. *b.* 1829.   Of Mascalls, Kent, and Hill House, Oxon.

HORSLEY, Francis, 1810-13, *b.* 1799. Ch. Coll. Cam. Vicar of Matching, Essex.

HORSLEY, John, 1809-12, *b.* 1796. E. I. Civil Service.

HORTON, Robert, 1821, *b.* 1810. Army.

HOSE, Henry Christian, 1865, *b.* 1853.

HOSKINS,* Haviland George, 1838-40. Son of Rev. Henry Hoskins, of North Perrott, Somerset. *b.* 1826; *d.* 1840.

HOTHAM, Henry, 1825. Son of the Hon. and Rev. Fred. Hotham, and grandson of 2nd Lord Hotham. *b.* 1814. Royal Artillery. Jesus Coll. Cam. Rector of Woodensborough, Kent.

HOTHAM, John Hallett, 1825. Brother of the above. *b.* 1811. Demy. of Magd. Coll. Oxf. Vicar of Sutton, Kent.

HOULTON, Ellis Hart Torrianna, 1856-59. Son of George Fredk. Houlton, of the Bengal Civil Service. *b.* 1841.

HOUSTON, William, 1824, *b.* 1811.

How, Charles Christian, 1877. Son of Rt. Rev. Walsham How, Bishop Suffragan of London. *b.* 1864.

HOWARD, Charles William, 1873-77. Son of Charles Howard, of Hampstead. *b.* 1860.

HOWARD, George Percy, 1873-78. Brother of the above. *b.* 1861. Nethershall Terrace, Hampstead.

HOWARD, Hon. Henry Thomas, 1820. Son of the 16th Earl of Suffolk. *b.* 1808. Capt. in the Army 1830. M.P. for Cricklade 1841; *d.* 1851.

HOWARD,* Hon. James Kenneth, 1827. Brother of the above. *b.* 1814. Foreign Office. M.P. for Malmesbury 1841-52. Commissioner of Woods and Forests 1855.

HOWARD, Hon. John, 1822, *b.* 1811.

HOWARD, John Ernest, 1877. Brother of C. W. Howard (above). *b.* 1864.

HOWARD,* Thomas Bowes, 1857-60. Son of Capt. the Hon. H. T. Howard, M.P. *b.* 1847. Royal Navy; *d.* 1864.

HOWE, Thomas, 1807-9, *b.* 1792. Solicitor.

HOWELL, Alexander, 1829, *b.* 1811.

HOWELL, Oswald John, 1823, *b.* 1810. Chaplain to the Sussex County Hospital.

HOWELL (Sir) Thomas (Knt.), 1815-16. Son of Thomas Howell, of Clapham. *b.* 1802. Was Director of Contracts in the War Office 1855-74. Knighted 1876.

HOWES, George, 1825. Son of Rev. George Howes, Rector of Spixworth, Norfolk. *b.* 1811 ; *d.* 1827.

HOWLETT, John Henry, 1821. Son of Rev. J. H. Howlett, Chaplain of the Chapel Royal, Whitehall. *b.* 1810. Fellow of St. John's Coll. Cam. Bell Scholar. Wrangler and 2nd Class Classical Tripos. Rector of Meppershall, Beds.

HOWLETT, Robert, 1809-16. Son of Samuel Howlett. *b.* 1797. Pemb. Coll. Oxf. Formerly Vicar of Hopton, St. Margaret.

HOWORTH, Humphrey, 1826, *b.* 1813. Indian Army.

HUBAND, Hugo Richard, 1876. Son of the late Capt. Geo. Joseph Huband, 8th Hussars. *b.* 1862.

HUDDLESTONE, Andrew Fleming, 1808. Son of Andrew Huddlestone, of Hutton John, Cumberland. *b.* 1796. Madras Civil Service. J.P. for Cumberland ; *d.* 1861.

HUDSON, George Isaac, 1821, *b.* 1811.

HUDSON, Thomas Keith, 1845-46, *b.* 1836.

HUDSON, William Bankes, 1824, *b.* 1812. Apothecary.

HUGHES, Albert, 1851-54. Son of Walter Hughes. *b.* 1835. St. John's Coll. Oxf. Rector of Woodford, Essex.

HUGHES, George, 1820, *b.* 1805.

HUGHES, John Carlyon, 1824. Son of the late Capt. John Hughes, Capt. 52nd Regt. *b.* 1811. Wine Merchant, 58, Fenchurch Street.

HUGHES, John Stanley, 1876.

HUGHES, Rathbone Duncan, 1821, *b.* 1808.

HUGHES, William, 1823, *b.* 1813.

HUGHES, William John Marjoribanks, 1821. Son of Capt. Philip Hughes, R.N. *b.* 1808. Formerly Captain 5th Dragoon Guards. Assumed the name of Loftus Otway 1873.

HUGHES-ONSLOW, Denzil, 1877. Second son of late Henry J. Hughes-Onslow, of Balkissock, Co. Ayr. *b.* 1863.

HULKES, Cecil James Gladdish, 1876. Son of Jas. Hulkes, Little Hermitage, Rochester. *b.* 1863.

HULL, Francis James, 1838-45, *b.* 1826. Univ. Coll. Durham. Curate of Netherbury, Dorset.

HULL, Henry Mitchell, 1874. Son of John Winstanley Hull (below).

HULL, Henry Mitchell, 1838-46. Son of W. W. Hull, Barrister. *b.* 1827. Ball. Coll. and Scholar of Univ. Coll. Oxf. Double 1st Class; *d.* 1853.

HULL, John Winstanley, 1836-44. Brother of the above. *b.* 1824. B.N. Coll. Oxf. Vicar of N. Muskham, Newark-on-Trent.

HULL, Thomas Hillman, 1825, *b.* 1809.

HULL, William Wilson, 1836-39. Brother of J. W. and H. M. Hull (above). *b.* 1822. * Student of Ch. Ch. Oxf. 2nd Class Lit. Hum. *d.* 1846.

HULME, Samuel Joseph, 1833-42. Son of Robert Hulme. *b.* 1824. Scholar and Fellow of Wadh. Coll. Oxf. 2nd Class Lit. Hum. Rector of Bourton-on-the-Water, Gloucestershire.

HULTON, Henry, 1867-71. Son of Rev. Campbell Bassett Arthur Grey Hulton, Rector of Emberton, Bucks. *b.* 1854. Fiji Islands.

HULTON, Reginald Edward, 1871. Brother of the above. *b.* 1857. Birmingham.

HULTON, Richard, 1824, *b.* 1810.

HULTON, Samuel Fletcher, 1875. Brother of Reginald Edward Hulton (above). *b.* 1862.

HULTON, William Preston, 1820, *b.* 1806. Went to Eton. Incumbent of St. Paul's, Southampton; *d.* 1870.

HULTON,* William Stokes, 1863-69. Brother of Samuel Fletcher Hulton (above). *b.* 1852. Residing at Hanover.

HUMFREY, Charles, 1819. Son of Mr. Humfrey, Banker at Cambridge. *b.* 1807. Downing Coll. Cam. Solicitor.

HUMPHREYS, Gardiner, 1878. Son of Thomas Humphreys, of Dover. *b.* 1865.

HUMPHREYS, John James Hamilton, 1827. Son of Major John Humphreys, of Mitown House, Co. Tyrone. *b.* 1816. Ex. Coll. Oxf. Barrister.

HUMPHREYS, Thomas William Drummond, 1835-41, *b.* 1824. Trin. Coll. Oxf. J.P. for Tyrone.

HUMPHRIES,* Henry, 1810, *b.* 1796. Solicitor; *d.* 1833.

HUMPHRIES,* John, 1809-14. Brother of the above. *b.* 1795. Trin. Coll. Cam.

HUMPHRYS,* George, 1810-16, *b.* 1800.

HUMPHRYS,* Josiah, 1814, *b.* 1802.

HUNT, Arthur, 1854-56, *b.* 1840. Went to New Zealand. Late Capt. 10th Hussars. Capt. Middlesex Militia.

HUNT,* Charles Anthony, 1807-16, *b.* 1797. Mert. Coll. Oxf. Holy Orders.

HUNT, George Jenkyns, 1849-53, *b.* 1836.

HUNT,* John, 1802-5, *b.* 1789. Navy; *d.* 1806.

HUNT,* Robert Shapland, 1828-36. Son of Henry Holdsworth Hunt, of Waterford. *b.* 1817. Ex. Coll. Oxf. Rector of Mark Beech, Kent.

HUNT, Walter Robert, 1876. Son of the late Rt. Hon. Geo. Ward Hunt. *b.* 1864.

HUNTER, Henry Charles Vickers, 1876. Nephew of W. Hunter, Kilburne Hall, Derby.

HUNTER,* Mark William, 1847-55, *b.* 1836. Prize Scholar. Trin. Coll. Cam. Barrister. Telhurst, Ryde.

HUNTER, Perceval William, 1827. Son of David Hunter. *b.* 1812. Mert. Coll. Oxf.

HUNTER, Richard Henry, 1878. Son of Richard H. Hunter, of Isleworth (below). *b.* 1864.

HUNTER, Richard Henry, 1848-54, *b.* 1838. Surgeon, M.R.C.S. Isleworth.

HURLE, Henry Allen, 1816, *b.* 1807.

HURRELL, William Philip, 1873.

HURST, Nicholas Edward, 1828, *b.* 1814.

HUSSEY, Edward, 1821. Son of Edward Hussey, of Scotney Castle, Sussex. *b.* 1807. Ch. Ch. Oxf. Scotney Castle, Lamberhurst. J.P. and D.L. for Kent.

HUTCHINS, Edward John, 1821. Son of E. Hutchins, of Briton Ferry, Co. Glamorgan. *b.* 1809. St. John's Coll. Cam. M.P. for Penryn 1840. For Lymington 1850; *d.* 1877.

HUTCHINSON,* Ernest R., 1858-59. Son of Rev. B. Hutchinson, of St. Albans. *b.* 1847.

HUTCHINSON, Horace Gordon, 1872. Son of General Hutchinson, of Wellesbourne, Bideford.

HUTSON, Henry, 1824. Son of H. Hutson, of Demarara, Medical Practitioner. *b.* 1812.

HUTSON, John Richard Farre, 1810-13. Brother of the above. *b.* 1797. M.D. Edinb.; deceased.

HUTTON,* Charles Henry, 1807-8. Son of Rev. H. Hutton, D.D., Rector of Beaumont, Essex. *b.* 1794. Fellow of Magd. Coll. Oxf. D.D. 1843.

HUTTON,* Henry, 1807-16. Brother of the above. *b.* 1797. Ball. Coll. Oxf. Rector of Filleigh, Devon; *d.* 1875.

HUXLEY, Thomas, 1815-17, *b.* 1801. St. John's Coll. Cam.

HUXLEY,* Thomas Christopher, 1865, *b.* 1853. Coffee Planter in Ceylon.

HYSLOP, Maxwell, 1820. Son of John Hyslop, of Lochend, Kirkcudbright. *b.* 1809. Lieut.-Col. Bengal Infantry.

I.

IEVERS,* James Wentworth, 1849-53, *b.* 1835.

ILBERG, James William Henry, 1824, *b.* 1811.

ILBERT,* Donald, 1863-66. Son of Rev. Peregrine A. Ilbert, Rector of Thurlestone, Devon. *b.* 1850. Emigrated to California.

ILDERTON, Robert Mitford, 1871. Son of Thomas Ilderton (below). *b.* 1858.

ILDERTON, Thomas, 1824. Son of Sanderson Ilderton, of Ilderton. *b.* 1811. St. Peter's Coll. Cam. Rector of Ilderton, Northumberland.

ILES, Henry Wilson, 1878. Son of Francis H. W. Iles, M.D., of Watford. *b.* 1865.

IMBERT-TERRY (see Terry).

INGE,* Francis George, 1853-59, Son of Rev. Wm. Inge, of Benn Hill, near Atherstone. *b.* 1840. Ch. Ch. Oxf. Assistant Master in the School. Curate of Alrewas, Lichfield.

INGE, John Walter, 1853-56. Brother of the above. *b.* 1839. Capt. Royal Artillery.

INGLIS,* Charles George, 1867-71. Son of Major-Genl. Sir John E. W. Inglis, K.C.B., and grandson of the 1st Lord Chelmsford. *b.* 1855. Coffee planter in Ceylon.

INGLIS,* John Frederick, 1864. Brother of the above. *b.* 1853. Lieut. 62nd Regt.

INGPEN, Edward Lockyer, 1849-53, *b.* 1835. St. Mark's Coll. Chelsea.

INGRAM,* Edward John Winnington, 1863, *b.* 1849.

INGRAM, Horace Walter Walpole, 1876, *b.* 1863.

INMAN,* James Lipson, 1855-58, *b.* 1844.

INNES, Lewis Charles, 1839-41, *b.* 1825. Judge of High Court of Judicature, Madras.

IRVINE, Archibald Henry, 1860-63. Son of Lt.-Col. Archibald Irvine, C.B. *b.* 1847. Civil Engineer.

IRVINE, Charles Thomas, 1842-46. Son of Rev. Andrew Irvine, of St. Margaret's, Leicester, formerly an Assist. Master in the School. *b.* 1827. Admiralty; *d.* 1850.

IRVINE,* John William, 1846-55. Brother of the above. *b.* 1836. Orator. Ch. Ch Oxf. Assistant Master. Rector of St. Mary's, Colchester.

IRVINE, Octavius Butler, 1846-53. Twin brother of the above. *b.* 1836. Judge of the High Court, Madras.

IRVINE,* Robert Hamilton, 1819, *b.* 1806.

IRVING,* Frederick Sumner, 1840-48. Son of Rev. Matthew Irving, D.D. Canon of Rochester. *b.* 1830. Trin. Coll. Cam. Solicitor. One of the Poor-law Auditors.

IRVING, John, 1820, *b.* 1805.

IRVING, Robert, 1823, *b.* 1810.

IRWIN, John Lewis, 1822, *b.* 1808.

ISAACSON,* Anthony Allett, 1803-12. Son of Anthony Isaacson. *b.* 1793. Worc. Coll. Oxf. Vicar of St. Woolos, Newport. Mon. *d.* 1843.

ISAACSON, Henry Whitehead, 1856-59. Son of Rev. John Fredk. Isaacson, Rector of Freshwater, Isle of Wight. *b.* 1843, Merchant.

ISAACSON, John Frederick, 1855-58. Brother of the above. *b.* 1842. Fellow of St. John's Coll. Cam. 3rd Senr. Opt. Senr. Classic. Rector of Freshwater, Isle of Wight.

ISAACSON, Thomas Charles, 1817, *b.* 1804.

IVATT, Alfred Edgar, 1875. Son of the late Rev. Alfred William Ivatt, Rector of Coveney, Cambs. *b.* 1861.

IVESON, , 1806-7.

IVESON, , 1806-7.

J.

JACKSON, Alfred, 1819, *b.* 1805.

JACKSON, Arthur Aubert, 1878. Son of Thos. Jackson, of Amwell, Ware. *b.* 1864.

JACKSON, Charles Edward, 1863-64, *b.* 1852.

JACKSON, Cyril, 1876. Son of Lawrence Morris Jackson, of Beckenham. *b.* 1863.

JACKSON, Edward, 1857-63. Son of Rev. James Jackson, Vicar of St. Sepulchre, London. *b.* 1845. Civil Engineer. Government Dockyard, Singapore.

JACKSON, Ellis Charles, 1851-56. Brother of the above. *b.* 1841. Army; *d.*

JACKSON, Francis Arthur, 1857. Brother of the above. *b.* 1847. Emigrated to Australia.

JACKSON, Freeman Henry, 1852-60. Brother of the above. *b.* 1842. Capt. Bombay Army. Assist. Resident, Baroda.

JACKSON, Henry Radcliffe Todd, 1874. Son of H. W. Jackson of Haverhill, Suffolk.

JACKSON, John Edward, 1820. Son of James Jackson, Banker, of Doncaster. *b.* 1805. Capt. of the School. B.N. Coll. Oxf. 2nd Class Lit. Hum. Rector of Leigh Delamere, Chippenham. Hon. Canon of Bristol.

JACKSON, John Houlton, 1852-54. Son of Rev. James Jackson, Vicar of St. Sepulchre, London. *b.* 1837. Clerk in the War Office.

JACKSON, Landon Dealtry, 1875. Brother of Arthur Aubert Jackson (above). *b.* 1862. R.M. Academy, Woolwich.

JACKSON, Randle, 1812, *b.* 1799. East India Company's Service.

JACKSON, Samuel, 1812, *b.* 1797. East India Company's Service.

JACKSON, William, 1812-13, *b.* 1800.

K

JACKSON, William Minchin, 1875-77. Brother of Landon Dealtry Jackson (above). Merchant.

JACOBS, Henry, 1834-41. Son of W. H. Jacobs. *b.* 1824. Fellow of Queens Coll. Oxf. 1st Class Lit. Hum. Dean of Christchurch, New Zealand.

JACOBS, Hugh, 1838-9. Brother of the above. *b.* 1827. Went to St. Paul's School. Queens Coll. Oxf.; *d.* 1850.

JACOBS, Leonard, 1836-39. Brother of the above. *b.* 1826. In business in New York.

JACQUES, James Kinton, 1878. Son of Rev. Kinton Jacques, Vicar of Westhoughton. *b.* 1865.

JACQUES, John, 1874.

JAGO,* William, 1816. Son of Rev. John Jago. *b.* 1802. Gold and Silver Medals. Ch. Ch. Oxf. Died 1823.

JAMES, Charles Pope, 1842-46, *b.* 1829. Surgeon.

JAMES, Ernest Edward, 1875.

JAMES,* Henry Gardner, 1847-53. Son of John James, 85th Regt. *b.* 1835. Civil Service. (Retired).

JAMES, Isaac, 1826, *b.* 1812.

JAMES,* John Burleigh, 1821. Son of John James, Canon of Peterborough. *b.* 1811. St. John's Coll. Cam. Formerly Perpet. Curate of St. Paul, Knowbury.

JAMES, Robert David, 1826, *b.* 1813.

JAMES, Thomas Andrew, 1823, *b.* 1812.

JAMES, William Rhodes, 1831-36, *b.* 1820. Surgeon. Went to India; *d.* 1844.

JEAFFRESON, Henry Gordon, 1869-75. Son of the late Henry Jeaffreson, M.D., Senior Physician of St. Bartholomew's Hospital. *b.* 1857. Pemb. Coll. Cam. Law Student, Inner Temple.

JEBB,* Richard Claverhouse, 1855-58. Son of Robert Jebb, Barrister, late Counsel to the Revenue for Ireland. *b.* 1841. Prize Scholarship. Gold Medal. Trin. Coll. Cam. Fellow. Craven Scholar. Porson Prize. Senior Classic, &c. Public Orator of the University 1869-76. Professor of Greek at the University of Glasgow.

JELF, George Edward, 1847-52. Son of Rev. Dr. Jelf, Canon of Ch. Ch. and Principal of King's Coll. London. *b.* 1834. Student of Ch. Ch. Oxf. 1st Class Mods. Vicar of Saffron-Walden. Hon. Canon of St. Albans.

JELLETT, Matthew Barrington, 1874. Son of H. P. Jellett, of Dublin. Trin. Coll. Dublin.

JENKIN, George, 1823, *b.* 1809.

JENNER, Arthur Charles William, 1878. Son of Sir Wm. Jenner, Bart., K.C.B. *b.* 1860.

JENNER, Edward Francis, 1826. Son of the Rt. Honl. Sir Herbert Jenner-Fust. *b.* 1814. Registrar of the Court of Probate.

JENNER, Walter Kentish William, 1874. Brother of A. C. W. Jenner (above). *b.* 1864. R.M. Coll. Sandhurst.

JENNEY, Archibald Offley, 1878. Son of A. H. Jenney, of Ditchingham Lodge, Bungay, Norfolk. *b.* 1864.

JENOUR, Maynard Edward, 1842. Left the same year. *b.* 1833. Ch. Coll. Cam. Rector of Evedon, Sleaford.

JEPHSON, Richard, 1815-18. Son of the late Rev. John Jephson. *b.* 1799.

JERVIS, Charles, 1858-59, *b.* 1843. Medical Practitioner.

JESSOPP, Francis Johnson, 1827. Son of Francis Jessopp, of the Wardwick House, Derby. *b.* 1814. Solicitor at Derby; *d.* 1867.

JESSOPP, William, 1836-40. Brother of the above. *b.* 1822. Ch. Coll. Cam. Capt. Derbyshire Militia; *d.* 1867.

JINKIN, James, 1821, *b.* 1810.

JODRELL, John William, 1821. Son of Francis Jodrell, and grandson of the 1st Earl Bathurst. *b.* 1808. Of Yeardsley, Cheshire; deceased.

JOHNS, Sydney Eustace, 1872. Son of J. W. Johns, Arbor Hill, Slough.

JOHNSON,   , 1802-3.

JOHNSON, Frederick Thomas, 1822, *b.* 1808.

JOHNSON, Hugh Walters Beaumont, 1878. Son of Capt. W. Victor Johnson, of King's Mead, Windsor. *b.* 1865.

JOHNSON, Victor George Ralph, 1874. Brother of the above. *b.* 1861. Army Student.

JOHNSON, William Henry, 1821. Son of Rev. Robt. Henry Johnson. *b.* 1810. Worc. Coll. Oxf. Vicar of Witham on the hill.

JOHNSTON, Bertram Masterson, 1875. Son of Francis John Johnston, of Lamas, Chiselhurst.

JOHNSTON,* Christian Fredk. Charles Alexr. James, 1804-10, *b.* 1792.

JOHNSTON, Edward, 1851-52. Son of Rev. W. D. Johnston (below). *b.* 1838. 96th Regt. Afterwards Wine Merchant in York.

JOHNSTON, Francis Alexander, 1878. Brother of Bertram Masterson Johnston (above). *b.* 1864.

JOHNSTON, Frederick, 1820, *b.* 1806. Jesus Coll. Cam. M.B. 1829.

JOHNSTON, John George Jubilee, 1825, *b.* 1809.

JOHNSTON, John Lewis, 1824, *b.* 1817.

JOHNSTON, Patrick, 1842-46. Son of the late Patrick Johnston, Banker, of 189, Fleet Street. *b.* 1829. Solicitor. Holmwood House, Kingston, Surrey.

JOHNSTON, Patrick Francis, 1820, *b.* 1810.

JOHNSTON, William Boys, 1849-53. Son of Rev. W. D. Johnston (below). *b.* 1835. Ch. Ch. Oxf. Vicar of Hoo, Kent.

JOHNSTON, William Downes, 1819, *b.* 1805. St. John's Coll. Cam. 2nd Class Lit. Hum. Rector of Milton, next Gravesend.

JOLLIFFE, Charles, 1820, *b.* 1810.

JOLLIFFE, George, 1823. Brother of the above. *b.* 1812.

JONES, Algernon Burdett, 1826, *b.* 1810.

JONES, Bertram, 1824, *b.* 1812.

JONES, Champion, 1807-8, *b.* 1795. Ball. Coll. Oxf.

JONES, Charles, 1809-11, *b.* 1794. Caius Coll. Cam.

JONES, Charles, 1817, *b.* 1804.

JONES, Charles Hyndman, 1871, b. 1855.

JONES, David, 1824 (of Pantglas). Eldest son of the late John Jones, of Blaenos. b. 1810. Ch. Ch. Oxf. M.P. for Carmarthen 1852; d. 1869.

JONES, Denis Edward, 1818. Son of Denis Ward Jones. b. 1807. Linc. Coll. Oxf. Rector of St. John's, Stamford.

JONES, Frederick de Castro, 1826, b. 1812.

JONES, Hastings Fowler, 1843-45, b. 1828. 1st Regt. (Royals); deceased.

JONES, Henry Berkley, 1825, b. 1813. St. John's Coll. Cam. Holy Orders; deceased.

JONES, James Trevor Evan, 1876.

JONES, John Thomas William, 1824, b. 1813. 43rd Regt.

JONES, Joseph, 1823. Son of Dr. J. F. D. Jones, of Barbados. b. 1809. Caius Coll. Cam. M.B.; d. 1865.

JONES, Mostyn, 1812, b. 1799. Army.

JONES, Owen, 1818.

JONES, Richard Minshull, 1820, b. 1808. Solicitor in London.

JONES, Thomas Oliver, 1874.

JONES,* Walter, 1813-16, b. 1802.

JONES, William, 1825. Brother of David Jones, of Pantglas (above). b. 1811. J.P. and D.L. Of Glandenys, Cardigan.

JONES, William Fowler, 1843-47, b. 1830. 57th Regt.; d. 1854.

JONES, William Oliver, 1872. Son of the following. b. 1858. In the Service of the Eastern Telegraph Extension Company.

JONES, William Samuel, 1846-49. Son of William Samuel Jones, one of the Masters in the Court of Queen's Bench. b. 1831. Caius Coll. Cam. Barrister. J.P.

JONES, Wordsworth Everard, 1867-71, b. 1856. Went to St. Paul's School.

JORDAN, Joseph William, 1801-7, b. 1789. Trin. Coll. Cam. A.B. 1812.

JOSEPH, Hugh Gore, 1864. Son of S. F. Joseph. *b.* 1854. New Coll. Oxf.

JOSSELYN, John, 1812-16. Son of John Josselyn, of Sproughton, Suffolk. *b.* 1802. Land Agent and Surveyor, Ipswich; *d.* 1869.

JOSSELYN, John Henry, 1849-52. Son of George Josselyn, of Sproughton, Suffolk. *b.* 1834. Solicitor at Ipswich.

JOWERS, Fredk. Henry Matthew, 1873. Son of F. W. Jowers, of Brighton.

JOYCE,* George Hayward, 1878. Son of Rev. Francis Hayward Joyce, Vicar of Harrow. *b.* 1864.

JOYCE,* William Henry, 1828. Son of Rev. James Joyce. *b.* 1817. Univ. Coll. Oxf. Rector of Dorking; *d.* 1871.

JOYNES, John, 1839-43. Son of Rev. Dr. Joynes, Rector of Frindsbury, Kent. *b.* 1826. Emm. Coll. Cam. Vicar of S. James, Gravesend.

JOYNES, Richard, 1830-36. Brother of the above. *b.* 1818. Corpus Coll. Oxf. Rector of Great Holland, Colchester.

JOYNES, Robert, 1836-39. Brother of the above. St. John's Coll. Cam. Rector of Gravesend.

JULIUS, Alfred Alexander, 1824. Son of Dr. Julius, of Richmond, Surrey. *b.* 1813; deceased.

JULIUS, Frederick Gilder, 1823. Brother of the above. *b.* 1811. M.D. The Hermitage, Clewer.

JULIUS, Henry Richard, 1824. Brother of the above. *b.* 1816. St. John's Coll. Cam. Vicar of Wrecclesham, Surrey.

JULL, John, 1805-7. Son of John Jull, of Ash, near Sandwich, Kent. *b.* 1789. St. John's Coll. Cam. Assumed the name of Godfrey by Royal Licence 1810. J.P. and D.L. for Kent. Brooke House, Ash; *d.* 1861.

JUPP, Ernest Holroyd, 1877. Son of David Jupp, of Palmyra, Surbiton. *b.* 1863.

K.

KANE, James Percy, 1850-52, *b.* 1832. Trin. Coll. Oxf. Curate at Brighton.

KARSLAKE, William Heberden, 1820. Son of Rev. William Karslake, Rector of Dolton. *b.* 1803. Oriel Coll. Oxf. Rector of Meshaw, So. Devon. Prebendary of Exeter. Chairman of Quarter Sessions; *d.* 1878.

KAY, Richard Smith, 1813, *b.* 1802. C.C.C. Oxf.

KAYESS, Walter, 1877. Son of James Kayess, Bourton House, Streatham, S.W. *b.* 1863.

KEANE, Augustus Daniel, 1848-50. Son of Daniel Keane, Solicitor of Lincoln's Inn Fields. *b.* 1840. 74th Highlanders; died at Delhi 1858.

KEANE, Howard, 1868. Brother of the above. *b.* 1851. Medical Practitioner.

KEANE, Robert Keane Charles, 1867, *b.* 1856.

KEANE,* William, 1828, *b.* 1818. Emm. Coll. Cam. Rector of Whitby, Yorks. Formerly Canon of St. Paul's, Calcutta, *d.*

KEATE, Charles Robert, 1876.

KEAYS, Robert, 1823, *b.* 1809.

KEELING, Albert Stanley, 1877. Son of Alfred Keeling, of East Moulsey. *b.* 1862.

KEEN, Grinham Frederick, 1871. Son of Grinham Keen, of 27, Harewood Square, London. *b.* 1858. Caius Coll. Cam.

KEENE, Henry Augustus, 1878. Son of Samuel Wolfe Keene, of Barnes, Surrey. *b.* 1864.

KEIGHTLEY, Archibald, 1807-10. Son of Archibald Keightley, of Liverpool, Solicitor. *b.* 1795. Solicitor. Registrar of Charterhouse; *d.* 1877.

KEIGHTLEY, Archibald, 1873. Son of Alfred Dudley Keightley, of Old Hall, Milnthorpe, Westmoreland. *b.* 1859. Pemb. Coll. Cam.

KEIGHTLEY, Bertram, 1872. Son of William Tristram Keightley, of Birkenhead. *b.* 1860. Trin. Coll. Cam.

KEIGHTLEY, George Donaldson, 1872. Son of G. W. Keightley (below). *b.* 1858. Trin. Coll. Oxf.

KEIGHTLEY,* George Wilson, 1840-44. Son of the late Lieut.-Col. Keightley, of Pickhill Hall, Wrexham. *b.* 1825. Pemb. Coll. Oxf. Rector of Great Stambridge, Essex.

KEIGHTLEY, William Henry, 1840-42. Son of W. T. Keightley, of Birkenhead. *b.* 1826. Wadh. Coll. Oxf.; deceased.

KEITH, Herbert, 1867-68. Son of Thomas William Keith, Accountant-General at the India Office. *b.* 1852. Solicitor in London.

KEITH-FALCONER, Cecil Edward, 1875. Son of Major the Hon. Charles James Keith-Falconer. *b.* 1860.

KEITH-FALCONER, Charles Adrian, 1875. Brother of the above. *b.* 1861.

KELLY, Edmund Pentheny, 1813, *b.* 1800.

KELLY, George, 1813, *b.* 1801.

KELLY, Henry Plimley, 1846-51. Son of the late Rev. Anthony Plimley Kelly, Incumbent of St. John's, Hoxton. *b.* 1832. Scholar of Caius Coll. Cam. Vicar of Christ Church, Hoxton.

KEMBALL, Charles Arnold, 1874. Son of Charles G. Kemball, Judge in High Court, Bombay. *b.* 1860.

KEMPE, Richard Russell, 1805-7, *b.* 1794.

KEMPE, William, 1805-7, *b.* 1792.

KENNEDY, Frederick Rivers, 1872. Of Brighton.

KENT,* Charles James, 1853-56. Grandson of Bishop Blomfield. *b.* 1843. Royal Navy.

KENT, Ernest Nield, 1875. Son of G. Barton Kent, 31, Lancaster Gate.

KENT, Ridley William, 1861-62, *b.* 1848.

KENYON, George, 1823. Son of the Hon. Thomas Kenyon, of Pradoe, Salop. *b.* 1811. Commander R.N.; *d.* 1866.

KENYON, John Robert, 1819. Brother of the above. *b.* 1807. Fellow of All Souls', Oxf. D.C.L. Barrister. Vinerian Professor of Civil Law. Q.C.

KEPPEL, Hon. Derek William George, 1876. Son of Viscount Bury, C.M.G. *b.* 1863.

KERR, Arthur Herbert, 1874. Son of Admiral Lord Frederic Herbert Kerr, of Crookham, Farnham. *b.* 1862.

KERR, Charles Wyndham Rodolph, 1864-69. Son of Lord Charles Lennox Kerr. *b.* 1849. 33, Mount Street.

KERR,* Walter Montagu, 1864. Brother of the above. *b.* 1851. Civil Engineer.

KERR, William Frederick, 1814-18. Son of General John Marcus Kerr. *b.* 1806. St. John's Coll. Cam. Rector of Marston-Sicca, Gloucestershire; *d.* 1878.

KEY, Aston Turner Powell, 1841-43, *b.* 1826. Civil Engineer.

KEY, William Down, 1825, *b.* 1812. Queens Coll. Cam.; *d.* 1836.

KIDD, Thomas George, 1817-18, *b.* 1803. Caius Coll. Cam. Rector of Catwick, Yorks, *d.*

KIMPTON, William, 1825, *b.* 1811. Trin. Coll. Cam. Barrister; *d.* 1843.

KINDERLEY, George Herbert, 1822, *b.* 1809. Solicitor in London, *d.*

KINDERLEY, John, 1823, *b.* 1811. Capt. 97th Regt.

KINDERSLEY, Lucius Graham, 1827, *b.* 1815. Ball. Coll. Oxf. Trin. Hall, Cam. Barrister of Lincoln's Inn.

KING,* Arthur, 1870. Son of Rev. R. H. King, Rector of Little Glemham, Suffolk. *b.* 1860.

KING, Arthur Hamilton, 1878. Son of Henry Samuel King, of the Manor House, Chigwell, Essex. *b.* 1866.

KING, Charles, 1824, *b.* 1814.

KING, Charles Edward, 1850-52, *b.* 1834. Emigrated to Australia; *d.* 1853.

KING, Edward Newman, 1867, *b.* 1852.

KING, Harold Robertson, 1863. Brother of Arthur Hamilton King (above). *b.* 1853. East Indian Agent.

KING, Henry, 1831, *b.* 1816. Scholar and Fellow of Wadham Coll. Oxf. 2nd Class Lit. Hum. Barrister of the Inner Temple.

KING,* Henry Seymour, 1862-70. Brother of H. R. King (above). *b.* 1852. Orator. Gold Medal. Ball. Coll. Oxf. Banker.

KING, Isaac, 1815, *b.* 1804. Ch. Ch. Oxf. Rector of Bradenham.

KING, John Thornton, 1872, *b.* 1857.

KING, Joseph Berry, 1819, *b.* 1803. Ex. Coll. Oxf.

KING, Joseph Edmund Shepherd, 1860-65, *b.* 1845.

KING,* Magrath, 1836-40, *b.* 1825. Royal Artillery.

KING, Richard Blakeway, 1866-69. Brother of Henry Seymour King (above). *b.* 1855. Went to Chigwell School. Emigrated to Texas.

KING, Thomas, 1847-51, *b.* 1836.

KING, Walter Edward, 1852-53, *b.* 1837.

KING, William Bevan Davis, 1855-57, *b.* 1842.

KING, William Smyth, 1824. Son of Hulton Smyth King, of Borris Castle, Queen's County. *b.* 1810. Page of King George IV. Canon of St. Patricks. Dean of Leighlin.

KING-HARMAN, Lawrence William, 1877. Son of Colonel E. R. King-Harman, M.P., of Rockingham, Co. Roscommon. *b.* 1863.

KINGSCOTE,* John Bloomfield, 1863. Son of Col. Thos. H. Kingscote, of Kingscote, Gloucestershire. *b.* 1851. Land Agent. Bryansford, County Down.

KINLOCH (Sir) George (Bart.), 1814-16. Son of George Kinloch, M.P. *b.* 1801. University of Edinburgh. Barrister. Created a Baronet 1873.

KIRBY, William Lee, 1868-70, *b.* 1851.

KIRKHAM,* William Gillmore, 1866-72. Son of Rev. W. Kirkham, Rector of Llanbrynmair. *b.* 1853. Ch. Ch. Oxf. Curate of St. John Baptist, Cardiff.

KIRKPATRICK, William, 1875. Son of John Kirkpatrick, of Horton Park, Hythe, Kent. *b.* 1861. Oxford.

KITCHIN, Thomas Milward, 1848. Son of Rev. Isaac Kitchin, Rector of St. Stephens, Ipswich. *b.* 1833. Stock Exchange. Great Down, near Farnham.

KITCHINER, William Brown, 1818, *b.* 1804.

KITSON, Ellis Puget, 1827, *b.* 1813. Ball. Coll. Oxf. *d.*; 1840.

KNAPP, John, 1811-18. Son of Rev. Primatt Knapp, Vicar of Shenley. *b.* 1800. M.D. of Edinburgh; *d.* 1857.

KNAPP, Primatt, 1811-17. Brother of the above. *b.* 1799. Merton Coll. Oxf. Rector of Shenley Mansell, Bucks.

KNAPP, William Frederick, 1856-58, *b.* 1842. Army Surgeon, India. Professor of Anatomy.

KNAPP, William Jerome, 1819. Son of Jerome Knapp. *b.* 1809. Barrister of the Middle Temple.

KNIGHT, Frederick Winn, 1828. Son of John Knight, of Wolverley, Worc. *b.* 1812. Secretary to the Poor Law Board 1852. Has been M.P. for West Worcestershire since 1841.

KNIGHTON (Sir) William Wellesley (Bart.) 1822. Son of Sir William Knighton, Bart. *b.* 1811. Ch. Ch. Oxf. Blendworth Lodge, Hants.

KNOLLYS, William Wallingford, 1873. Eldest son of Major William W. Knollys, and grandson of Sir W. Knollys. *b.* 1862.

KNOX,* Henry, 1835-39, *b.* 1823. Late of the 84th Regt.

KNOX, Thomas Vesey Melville, 1878. Son of Charles J. Knox, of the Indian Civil Service. *b.* 1865.

KNYVETT, George Henry Williams, 1823. Son of Charles Knyvett, Instructor of Music to the Royal Family. *b.* 1813. Ch. Ch. Oxf. Registration Office, Somerset House; *d.* 1840.

KNYVETT,* Sumner Felix, 1852-56, *b.* 1839.

KOE, Lancelot Charles, 1876. Son of Stephen L. Koe, 8, St. Michael's Place, Brighton.

KYMER, John, 1823, *b.* 1810. Finished his education at Geneva. No Profession; died 1878.

KYNASTON, Spencer William, 1818, *b.* 1808. Writer in India; *d.* 1829.

L.

LACEY, Charles James, 1864. Son of William Charles Lacey, of Wareham, Dorset. *b.* 1852. Solicitor at Bournemouth.

LACEY, Howard George, 1868. Brother of the above. *b.* 1856. Caius Coll. Cam.

LACY, Seymour De Lacy, 1848-53. Son of the Rev. Charles Lacy, Rector of All Hallows, London Wall. *b.* 1839. Capt. Royal Artillery.

LACY, Spencer De Lacy, 1847-48. Brother of the above. *b.* 1835. Lieut. R.N. Died at sea 1858.

LA FARGUE, George Henry Leith, 1873.

LAFONT, Ogle Russell, 1837-46, *b.* 1827. St. John's Coll. Oxford. Rector of Hinxworth, Herts.

LAFOREST, Edward, 1815-16, *b.* 1800.

LAFOREST, Edward William Carew, 1845, *b.* 1829. Wine Merchant.

LAING, Robert, 1807-10, *b.* 1794; died 1811.

LAKE, Alexander, 1813-14. Son of W. C. Lake, Merchant of Liverpool. *b.* 1800. Died in South America 1826.

LAMB, Alexander, 1811-15, *b.* 1799. Ex. Coll. Oxf.

LAMB, John, 1805-7, *b.* 1789. Fellow and Master of Corpus Coll. Cam. Dean of Bristol; died 1850.

LAMB, Robert Boyd, 1873. Son of Robert Boyd Lamb, late Consul in the West Indies. *b.* 1858. Engaged in the Tea Trade in India.

LAMB, Thomas Davis, 1824, *b.* 1815. S.C.L. Oxon. Formerly Rector of West Hackney, &c.

LAMBE, , 1865.

LAMBE, David, 1811. Son of William Lambe, M.D., of London and Henwood, Herefordshire. *b.* 1803; deceased.

LAMBE, Lacon William, 1810-15. Brother of the above. *b.* 1797. Caius Coll. Cam. Tancred Scholar 1817. M.D. 1825; *d.* 1871.

LAMMIN, Archer Davison, 1863-69. Son of William Henry Lammin, of Shorrolds, Fulham. *b.* 1852.

LAMMIN, Percy Belasyce, 1865. Brother of the above. *b.* 1853.

LANDON, George, 1819. Son of the Very Rev. Whittington Landon, D.D., Dean of Exeter and Provost of Worcester Coll. Oxf. *b.* 1805. Worc. Coll. Oxf. B.C.L. 1834. Rector of Richards Castle, Salop; *d.* 1875.

LANE, Thomas, 1802-4.

LANE,* John Fraser, 1800-6, *b.* 1788. E. I. Civil Service.

LANE, Thomas Reynell, 1878, *b.* 1864.

LANE-FOX,* William Augustus, 1868. Son of Col. Lane-Fox, Uplands Merrow, Guildford. *b.* 1858.

LANGDALE, William John, 1809-12. Son of Marmaduke Langdale, of 17, Doughty Street, London. *b.* 1796. Cath. Hall, Cam. Holy Orders.

LANGDON-DOWN, Everleigh, 1874. (See Down).

LANGHAM, Henry Burdett, 1819. Son of Sir Jas. Langham, Bart. *b.* 1808. St. Alban's Hall, Oxf.; *d.* 1876.

LANGHAM, William Samwell, 1819. Brother of the above. *b.* 1810. Life Guards.

LANGLEY, Algernon Arthur, 1877. Son of Henry Langley, late 2nd Life Guards. *b.* 1863.

LANGSTAFF, Francis, 1826, *b.* 1810.

LANGSTAFF, Frederick, 1826, *b.* 1811.

LANT, John, 1860-63. Of Nailcote Hall, Coventry, *b.* 1845.

LARCOM, Thomas Henry, 1851-53. Son of the Rt. Hon. Sir Thos. A. Larcom, Bart. *b.* 1842. Went to Rugby School. Commander R.N.; *d.* 1877.

LARKINS, Colin Robertson, 1827, *b.* 1817. 20th Regt. Bengal N.I.; *d.* 1835.

LARKINS, John Gladstone, 1830, *b.* 1815, *d.* 1833.

LAST,* Arthur John, 1876. Son of Frederic Last, Regent's Park Terrace, London. *b.* 1862.

LATHAM, George Nix, 1875. Son of George Latham. *b.* 1860.

LATHAM, Frederic Nix, 1878. Brother of the above.

LATTER, Oswald Hawkins, 1878. Son of Rev. Arthur Simon Latter, Vicar of North Mymms, Herts. *b.* 1864.

LATTER, Robert Booth, 1814. Son of Edward Latter, of Pixfield, Bromley, Kent. *b.* 1805. Solicitor.

LAW, Edward Downes, 1853-54. Son of the Hon. Henry Spencer Law. *b.* 1841. Commander R.N. Retired.

LAW,* George John, 1804-9. Son of Rt. Rev. George Henry Law, D.D., Bishop of Chester and Bath and Wells. *b.* 1794. Went to India; *d.* 1811.

LAW, William (C.B.), 1834-38. Son of late Rev. H. Law, Rector of Standon, Herts. Clerk in the Treasury. Private Secretary to Lord Palmerston.

LAWES,* Edward, 1829, *b.* 1817. Special Pleader; *d.* 1852.

LAWRELL, Walter Glyn, 1853-61. Son of Rev. J. Lawrell, of St. Matthew's, City Road. *b.* 1844. Capt. 4th Hussars.

LAWRENCE, Ernest Frederick, 1876. Son of F. W. Lawrence, Oakleigh, Beckenham.

LAWSON, Thomas, 1821, *b.* 1810. Solicitor in Paris.

LAWSON, William Frederick, 1828, *b.* 1813. Clerk of the Peace for Surrey; *d.* 1839.

LEA,* William, 1876. Son of Rev. Josiah Turner Lea, Far Forest Vicarage, Bewdley, Worcestershire. *b.* 1862.

LEACH, Edward, 1818, *b.* 1802.

LEACH, John Frederick, 1819, *b.* 1804. B.N.C. Oxf. Barrister.

LEACH, Kenneth Henry, 1876. Of Winchester, *b.* 1863.

LEACH, Maurice Mackenzie, 1878. Brother of the above. *b.* 1865.

LEADER, John Temple, 1823, *b.* 1810. Gold Medal. Ch. Ch. Oxf. M.P. for Westminster 1837.

LEAKE, Stephen Martin, 1875. Son of Stephen Martin Leake, Barrister, of Marshalls, Ware, Herts. *b.* 1862.

LEARY, Joseph, 1822, *b.* 1812. Librarian to the House of Lords; deceased.

LEATHLEY, William Henry, 1824, *b.* 1811.   Trin. Coll. Cam. B.A. 1834.

LEAVER, Benjamin, 1818, *b.* 1806.

LEAVER, Samuel, 1818, *b.* 1808 ; *d.* 1818.

LE BAS, Henry Vincent, 1842-47. Son of Rev. Charles Webb Le Bas, of Haileybury College. *b.* 1828. Univ. Coll. Oxf. Preacher at Charterhouse.

LE BAS, Reginald Vincent, 1871. Son of the above. *b.* 1856.

LE BLANC, Arthur, 1825, *b.* 1813. Solicitor.

LE BLANC, Frederick, 1821. Brother of the above. *b.* 1809. Leamington.

LECHE, John Hurleston, 1819. Son of Wm. Leche, of Carden, Cheshire. Of Carden Park, Cheshire. *b.* 1805. High Sheriff of Cheshire in 1832 ; *d.* 1848.

LECHE, William Edward, 1843-45. Third son late J. H. Leche, of Carden (above). *b.* 1830. 17th Regiment; *d.* 1848.

LECHMERE,* (Sir) Edmund Anthony Harley (Bart.), 1837-44. Son of Sir E. H. Lechmere, Bart. *b.* 1826. Ch. Ch. Oxf. M.P. for Tewkesbury 1866-68 ; for W. Worcestershire 1876. Rhyd Court, Upton upon Severn.

LECKIE,* John Warrington, 1876. Son of Lieut.-Col. John Davies Leckie. *b.* 1862.

LECKIE, Robert Lindsay, 1817. Son of John Lindsay Leckie, of Bombay. *b.* 1806. Banker in Bombay; *d.* 1865.

LEECH, John, 1825-32, *b.* 1817. The Celebrated Caricaturist; *d.* 1864.

LEECH,* John Charles Warrington, 1866. Son of John Leech (above). *b.* 1856. Went to Australia. Drowned at sea 1875.

LEECH, Thomas, 1831, *b.* 1822.

LEEDS, George William, 1820. Son of Sir George William Leeds, Bart., of Croxton Park, Cambs. *b.* 1807 ; *d.* 1864.

LEESON, Hubert Seymour, 1852-58, *b.* 1841. Barrister of Lincoln's Inn.

LEGARD,* Frederick, 1823. Son of the Rev. William Legard, Vicar of Ganton. *b.* 1811. Emm. Coll. Cam. Vicar of Ganton, Yorks.

LEGGE, Augustus George, 1845-53. Son of Rev. Henry Legge (below). *b.* 1835. Silver Medal. Ch. Ch. Oxf. Vicar of North Elmham, Norfolk.

LEGGE,* Henry, 1815. Son of the Hon. and Rev. A. G. Legge, Rector of Wonston, Hants. *b.* 1803. Ch. Ch. Oxf. Rector of East Lavant, Sussex. (Died 1879).

LEGGE, Henry Edward, 1844-49. Son of the above. *b.* 1831. Ch. Ch. Oxf.; died at Algiers 1861.

LEGGE, Walter Douglas, 1878. Son of Rev. A. G. Legge (above). *b.* 1865.

LEGH, William Dawson, 1843-45. Son of Rev. Edmund Dawson Legh. *b.* 1834. Went to Harrow School. Holy Orders; *d.* 1858.

LEGH, John Pennington, 1840-46. Brother of the above. *b.* 1827. Wadh. Coll. Oxf. Norbury Booths Hall, Knutsford.

LEGREW, Arthur, 1824, *b.* 1812. St. John's Coll. Cam. Formerly Curate of Chaldon.

LEIGH, John Frederic, 1873. Son of the following. *b.* 1858. St. John's Coll. Cam.

LEIGH, Richard, 1820, *b.* 1807. B.N.C. Oxf. Rector of Walton on the hill, Liverpool.

LE MESURIER, Alexander, 1818-12, *b.* 1798. Navy.

LE MESURIER, Augustus, 1809-16, *b.* 1799. Recorder of Bombay.

LE MESURIER, George Paul, 1813-17, *b.* 1802.

LE MESURIER,* John James, 1819, *b.* 1807; deceased.

LEMOS, William, 1826, *b.* 1812.

LENNARD, George Barrett, 1806-11. Son of Sir Thomas Barrett Lennard, Bart., of Belhus. *b.* 1796. Barrister; died 1870.

LENNARD, Henry Barrett, 1807-11. Brother of the above. *b.* 1798. Holy Orders; died at Fontainebleau 1870.

LENNARD, John Barrett, 1803-4. Brother of the above. *b.* 1789. Chief Clerk Privy Council Office; deceased.

LENNOX, Arthur Charles Wriothesley, 1852-54. Son of Lieut.-Col. Lord Arthur Lennox. *b.* 1842. Royal Navy; *d.* 1876.

LESLIE, Charles, 1823, *b.* 1810. Ch. Ch. Oxford.

LESLIE, John William, 1809-12, *b.* 1796. Army.

LESLIE, Shirley Conyers, 1809-12, *b.* 1797. Army.

LESLIE, Hon. Thomas Jenkins, 1821. Son of the third Countess of Rothes. *b.* 1813. Army; *d.* 1849.

LEVINSON, Sigismund, 1831, *b.* 1816.

LEWES, John, 1873. Son of Lt.-Col. John Lewes, of Llanear, Cardiganshire. *b.* 1860. Lieut. Royal Artillery, serving in India.

LEWIN,* Reginald Wynford Elphinstone, 1847-53. Son of Sir Gregory Lewin, Q.C. *b.* 1835. Pemb. Coll. Oxf. Late of the Probate Office. Now in America.

LEWIS, Claud Edmund, 1877. Son of S. Lewis, of the Orchard, Chigwell, Essex. *b.* 1863.

LEWIS, James Dacres, 1814-16, *b.* 1799.

LEWIS, James Henry, 1819, *b.* 1804.

LEWIS, William Edgar, 1875.

LEWIS,* William John, 1844-49, *b.* 1832. War Office; drowned.

LEY, Herbert, 1873.

LIDDELL, Charles Lyon, 1874. Son of Charles Liddell, 4, Cornwall Terrace, N.W.

LIDDELL, Henry George, 1823-29. Son of the Hon. and Rev. Henry G. Liddell. *b.* 1811. Student and Tutor of Ch. Ch. Oxf. Double 1st Class. Head Master of Westminster 1846. Dean of Christ Church 1853.

LIDDELL, Hon. Robert, 1820. Son of the Earl of Ravensworth. *b.* 1808. Ch. Ch. and Fellow of All Souls', Oxf. Vicar of S. Paul's, Knightsbridge.

LIDDELL, William Wren, 1836-42. Brother of H. G. Liddell (above). *b.* 1823. Ch. Ch. Oxf. Rector of Cowley, Gloucestershire.

LIGNE, Philip Edward, 1825, *b.* 1811. Trin. Coll. Cam.

LILLY, John Arnold, 1868-72, *b.* 1854. Clare Coll. Cam.

LINCOLN, William, 1807-9, *b.* 1791.

LINDE, Daniel Bayliffe, 1821, *b.* 1808.

LINDSAY,* Arthur Fergusson, 1853-57, *b.* 1841. Capt. Bengal Cavalry.

LINDSAY, George, 1852-53. Son of the late Martin Lindsay, of the East India Civil Service. *b.* 1838. Ensign 1st Bengal Native Infantry. Murdered at Cawnpore in the Mutiny 1857.

LINDSAY,* Robert Grant, 1851-58, *b.* 1840. Univ. Coll. Oxf.

LINZEE, Charles Arthur, 1875-78. Son of R. G. Linzee, of Broxmore Park, Romsey. *b.* 1861.

LIPSCOMB, Godfrey, 1876. St. Philip's Rectory, Birmingham.

LISTER, George Coryton, 1876. Son of Thomas Villiers Lister, Assistant Under-Secretary of State for Foreign Affairs. *b.* 1863.

LISTER, William Cunliffe, 1825, *b.* 1810. Trin. Coll. Cam. M.P. for Bradford; *d.* 1841.

LISTER, William Short, 1827, *b.* 1813.

LITCHFIELD, Percivall Edmund, 1819, *b.* 1804. Trin. Coll. Cam.

LITTLE (Sir) Archibald (K.C.B.), 1822. Son of Archibald Little, of Shabden Park, Surrey. *b.* 1811. Lieut.-Genl. Col. 9th Lancers. Late Col. 11th Hussars.

LITTLE, William, 1822, *b.* 1809. Merchant.

LITTLEDALE, Edward, 1819, *b.* 1805. Major 1st Dragoons. Retired. (16, St. James Square).

LITTLEPAGE, Allen Williams, 1824, *b.* 1812.

LIVEING, Edward Henry, 1866. Son of Edward Liveing, M.D., of 52, Queen Anne Street, London. *b.* 1855. Mining Engineer. Associate of the Royal School of Mines. First in the 1st Class in Mineralogy.

LLANOS, Charles, 1825, *b*. 1812. Indian Army.

LLOYD,* Arthyr Grey, 1863. Son of Rev. Henry Robert Lloyd, Rector of Clyffe at Hoo, Kent. *b*. 1851. Lieut. 4th Dragoon Guards. (Died at Cape Town 1879).

LLOYD,* Charles Coppe, 1818, *b*. 1808. Orator; died 1838.

LLOYD, Edward Harvey, 1822. Son of Wm. Lloyd, of Aston, Salop. *b*. 1811. Lieut. Rifle Brigade. Retired 1835; *d*. 1870.

LLOYD, Ernest Thomas, 1873. Civil Service.

LLOYD, Eusebius Arthur, 1842-46, *b*. 1829. Indian Army.

LLOYD, Francis, 1809-14, *b*. 1795. Ch. Ch. Oxf. Assistant Master in the School.

LLOYD, Henry, 1809-16, *b*. 1800.

LLOYD,* Rowley Young, 1833-38. Pemb. Coll. Oxf. M.A. 1843. Barrister, *d*.

LLOYD, Vaughan, 1805-7, *b*. 1795.

LLOYD, William, 1814-16, *b*. 1800.

LLOYD, William, 1815-16, *b*. 1804.

LOCH, George, 1823. Son of James Loch, of Uppat, Sutherlandshire. *b* 1811. Barrister of the Middle Temple. Q.C. M.P. for the Wick Burghs 1868-72; *d*. 1877.

LOCH, George, 1824. Cousin of the above. Son of William Loch, of the Bengal Civil Service. *b*. 1815. E. I. C. S. Judge of the High Court of Calcutta; retired 1872.

LOCH, William Adam, 1826. Son of James Loch, of Uppat. *b*. 1814. Barrister.

LOCKER,* Arthur, 1842-47. Son of Edward Hawke Locker, Commissioner of Greenwich Hospital. *b*. 1828. Pemb. Coll. Oxf. Editor of The Graphic.

LOCKER,* William Algernon, 1877. Son of the above. *b*. 1863.

LOCKETT, Hugh Barnett, 1839-43, *b*. 1825. E. I. C. S. Died in India 1860.

LOCKLEY, John, 1819, *b*. 1806.

LOCKWOOD, Henry John Arthur, 1840-43. Son of Robert Manners Lockwood, and grandson of the Earl of Arran. *b.* 1826. The Admiralty.

LORD, , 1806-9.

LOVE, John Henry, 1826, *b.* 1812. Caius Coll. Cam.

LOVEGROVE, Charles Arthur, 1873. Son of C. Lovegrove, of Downe, Kent.

LOVELESS, Charles James, 1872.

LOWDER, William Henry, 1841-48. Son of Charles Lowder, of Frome, Somerset. *b.* 1831. St. Edm. Hall, Oxf. Vicar of St. George's, Hyde, Cheshire.

LOWNDES, Henry, 1809-13, *b.* 1795. Ball. Coll. Oxf.

LOWNDES, Henry Bartholemew, 1875. Son of Lieut.-Col. Lowndes, Braunston, Rugby. *b.* 1862. Army Student.

LOWTHER, Harold Arthur, 1878. Son of Honl. W. Lowther, M.P., of Lowther Lodge, Kensington Gore. *b.* 1864.

LOYD, William Kirkman, 1820. Son of William Loyd, of London. *b.* 1809. Lieut.-Col. Madras Artillery. Twice mentioned in despatches for distinguished service in the field.

LUARD, Thomas William, 1807-9. Son of John Luard. *b.* 1796.

LUARD, William Richards, 1843-45. Son of Henry Luard, a Banker. *b.* 1829. 5, Montagu Place, London.

LUCAS, Charles Arthur, 1872. Of Upper Tooting, Surrey.

LUCAS, Charles Pierpoint, 1838. Son of Rt. Hon. Edward Lucas, of Castle Shaen, Co. Monaghan. *b.* 1825. Captain Bengal Native Infantry.

LUCAS, Fitzherbert Dacre, 1838. Brother of the above. Died 1857 of a wound received at Lucknow, where he was serving as a Volunteer.

LUCAS, George, 1820, *b.* 1806.

LUCK, Edward Thomas, 1813-15. Son of Thomas Luck, of Went House, West Malling, Kent. *b.* 1799. Royal Navy; deceased.

LUCK, Everard Thomas, 1858-60. Son of Edward Thomas Luck, of West Malling. *b.* 1844. St. John's Coll. Cam. Barrister. Capt. West Kent Light Infantry Militia. Went House, West Malling, Kent.

LUCY, Frederick Henry, 1873. Son of William Charles Lucy, of The Wynstones, Gloucestershire.
R.M. Coll. Sandhurst.

LUDBY, Thomas, 1825, *b.* 1810. Rector of Cranham, Essex.

LUKIN,* Cecil Edward George, 1823-28, *b.* 1811. Orator. Government Office, India Board; deceased.

LUMB, William Eedson, 1822. Son of William Lumb. *b.* 1806. Trin. Coll. Cam. Formerly 2nd Master of the Grammar School, Ripon. Vicar of Halford, Shropshire.

LUSHINGTON,* Charles, 1815. Son of Sir Henry Lushington, Bart. *b.* 1805. Student of Ch. Ch. Oxf. 3rd Class Lit. Hum. Vicar of Walton on Thames. Chaplain at Naples.

LUSHINGTON, Edmund Law, 1823-27. Son of Edm. Henry Lushington, of Park House, Maidstone. *b.* 1811. Fellow of Trin. Coll. Cam. Senior Medallist. Professor of Greek at Glasgow 1838.

LUSHINGTON, Edward, 1804-7.

LUSHINGTON, Henry, 1823-28. Brother of Edmund Law Lushington (above). *b.* 1812. Gold Medal. Fellow of Trin. Coll. Cam. 1st Class Classical Tripos. Sec. of State at Malta; *d.* 1855.

LUSHINGTON, Richard Henry, 1824. Son of the Rt. Hon. Stephen R. Lushington, formerly Governor of Madras. *b.* 1809.

LUSHINGTON, Thomas Davies, 1826. Brother of Henry Lushington (above). *b.* 1813. India Civil Service, Madras; *d.* 1858.

LUSHINGTON,* William John, 1817. Son of William John Lushington, of Rodmersham Lodge, Sittingbourne. *b.* 1806. India Civil Service in Ceylon; died 1831.

LUTWYCHE, Alfred James Peter, 1824, *b.* 1810. Queens Coll. Cam. Barrister.

LUXFORD, George Curteis, 1825. Son of John Luxford, of Higham, Sussex. *b.* 1810. Trin. Coll. Cam. Formerly Rector of Middleton, Sussex.

LUXFORD, John Odiarne, 1820. Brother of the above. *b.* 1808. Of Higham, Sussex. J.P. Formerly of the Royal Dragoons ; deceased.

LYNE,* Clavering Mordaunt, 1863-64. Son of Francis Lyne, of Cheltenham. *b.* 1849. Gloucester Theological Coll. Curate of Biddlestone, Wilts.

LYON, Edmund Herbert, 1875. Son of Rev. Samuel Edmund Lyon, of Stratton, Hants. *b.* 1861.

M.

MACAN, Francis William, 1864. Son of John Macan, Q.C., Judge of the Court of Bankruptcy, &c., Ireland. *b.* 1851. Merchant in London.

MACAN, Reginald Walter, 1864-68. Brother of the above. *b.* 1848. Student of Ch. Ch. Oxf. 1st Class Mods. and Lit. Hum.

MACARTNEY, Henry John Ellison, 1873. Son of J. W. E. Macartney, M.P., of Clogher Park, Tyrone. *b.* 1859. Telegraph Engineer.

MACAULAY, Charles Zachary, 1822. Son of the late Zachary Macaulay. *b.* 1813. Treasurer at Mauritius. Secy. to Sanitary Board of London.

MACAULAY, Henry William, 1822. Brother of the above. *b.* 1806. Commissioner at Sierra Leone ; deceased.

MACDONALD, Alexander, 1828, *b.* 1813. Lieut.-Col. 68th Foot. Retired 1854.

MACDONALD, Harry Lindsay Somerled, 1876.

MACDONALD, Norman Hilton, 1817. Son of Sir John Macdonald, Adjut.-Genl. *b.* 1806. Oriel Coll. and Fellow of All Souls', Oxf. Private Secretary for Ireland.

MACDOUGALL, James, 1825. Son of Alexander Macdougall, Solicitor of London. *b.* 1812. B.N.C. Oxf. 3rd Class Lit. Hum. Vicar of Hanney, Oxon.

MACDOUGALL, William Church, 1814-17. Brother of the above. *b.* 1800. Trin. Coll. Cam. Barrister. A Judge in Jamaica.

MACGEORGE, Harry, 1873. Of Glasgow.

MACGREGOR,* Evan, 1853-58. Son of the late Sir John Atholl Bannatyne MacGregor, Bart. *b.* 1842. Clerk in the Admiralty.

MACIVER, Ivan Ian, 1868-71, *b.* 1853. Lieut. 3rd King's Own Hussars.

MACKENZIE,* Francis William, 1862. Left same year. *b.* 1851.

MACKENZIE,* Harry Murray, 1860-67. Son of Colonel Mackenzie. *b.* 1850. Lieut. Bengal Staff Corps. Late 21st Hussars.

MACKENZIE, John Andrew, 1814-17, *b.* 1804.

MACKENZIE, John Kenneth, 1874.

MACKENZIE,* Kenneth Augustus Muir, 1857-64. Son of Sir John W. P. Muir Mackenzie, Bart. *b.* 1845. Prize Scholar. Talbot Medal. Ball. Coll. Oxf.

MACKENZIE, Kenneth John, 1875. Eldest son of Sir Kenneth Smith Mackenzie, Bart., of Gairloch. *b.* 1861.

MACKENZIE, Montague Johnstone Muir, 1860-66. Brother of K. A. Muir Mackenzie (above). *b.* 1847. Barrister of Lincoln's Inn.

MACKENZIE, Samuel John Crawford, 1841-45, *b.* 1826. St. John's Coll. Cam.

MACKENZIE, William, 1807-11, *b.* 1795.

MACKENZIE, William, 1816-18, *b.* 1805.

MACKINNON, Alan Murray, 1874. Son of Major-Genl. David Henry Mackinnon, late 16th Lancers. *b.* 1860. Trin. Coll. Oxf.

MACKINNON, Edmund Daniel, 1820. Son of Daniel Mackinnon, of Binfield, Berks. Left the same year. *b.* 1808. Late of the 2nd Life Guards (*d.* 1879).

MACKINNON, William Henry, 1820. Brother of the above. *b.* 1806. Drowned at Boulogne 1825.

MACKNESS, George Owen Carr, 1875. Son of Rev. G. Mackness, D.D., Rector of S. Mary's, Boughton Ferry, N.B. *b.* 1861. Ch. Ch. Oxford.

MACLAGAN, Walter Douglas Dalrymple, 1876. Son of the Bishop of Lichfield.

MACLARAN, George Gordon, 1864, *b.* 1851. Coffee Planter, Ceylon.

MACNAGHTEN (Sir) Edmund Charles Workman (Bart.), 1800-6. Son of Sir Francis Macnaghten, Bart. *b.* 1790. Trin. Coll. Dublin. Master in Equity to the Supreme Court of Calcutta. M.P. for the County of Antrim 1847-52; *d.* 1875.

MACNAGHTEN,* Elliot Henry, 1850-55. Son of the late Francis Macnaghten. *b.* 1839. Capt. Bengal Cavalry. Killed in Action 1878.

MACNAGHTEN (Sir) William Hay (Bart.), 1803-6. Brother of Sir Edmund Macnaghten (above). *b.* 1793. Bengal Civil Service. Created a Baronet 1839. Assassinated at Cabul 1841.

MACONOCHIE, Alan, 1878. Son of Alexander Maconochie, of 24, Lingfield Road, Wimbledon. *b.* 1864.

MACPHERSON, William Charters, 1876. Son of William Macpherson, 120, Westbourne Terrace.

MACPHERSON, William Hugh, 1877. Son of A. G. Macpherson, 51, Gloucester Place, W.

MACTAGGART, William Charles, 1875. Son of William Mactaggart, of Eskbank, Eltham, Kent. *b.* 1861. Trin. Coll. Cam.

McCLINTOCK, George Frederick, 1821, *b.* 1808.

McCONAGHEY, Allen, 1877. Son of Matthew Allen McConaghey, of the Indian Civil Service. *b.* 1864.

McCONNEL, Henry Morewood, 1876. Son of Frederick McConnel, Clenchead, Annan, N.B. 59, Upper Brook Street, Manchester.

McCONNEL, James Irving, 1876. Brother of the above. *b.* 1863.

McCULLUM,   , 1834-35. 7th Madras N.I.

McGEE, Henry William, 1875.

McGILDOWNY, Robert, 1878. Son of J. M. G. McGildowny, Abbeylands, Whiteabbey, Belfast. *b.* 1864.

McKRAITH, Hugh James, 1803-7.

McNEILL,* Duncan, 1877. Son of Malcolm McNeill, of North Manor Place, Edinburgh. *b.* 1864.

McNEILL, Duncan Alexander, 1875. Son of Capt. McNeill, of Ardeen House, Shillalagh, Co. Wicklow.

McNISH, David, 1825, *b.* 1812.

McPHERSON, William, 1824, *b.* 1812. Trin. Coll. Cam. Barrister.

McTAVISH, William, 1809. Left the same year.

MADAN, George, 1818. Son of Rev. Spencer Madan, D.D., Canon of Lichfield. *b.* 1807. Ch. Ch. Oxf. 1st Class Math. Rector of Dursley, Gloucestershire, and Hon. Canon of Bristol.

MADDEN,* Frederic William, 1851-56. Son of Sir Fredk. Madden, F.R.S. *b.* 1839. British Museum. Author of several works on Coins. Secretary to Brighton College.

MADDEN, George Ernest Phillipps, 1856. Brother of the above. *b.* 1841. 61st Regt. Deputy Assist. Commissary Genl. *d.* 1865.

MADDOCK, Henry, 1821, *b.* 1808.

MADDOCK, John, 1821, *b.* 1810.

MAGNIAC, Claude Hollingworth, 1877. Son of Charles Magniac, of Colworth, Bedford. *b.* 1863.

MAINGAY, Bonamy Cecil, 1878. Son of William Bonamy Maingay, 9, Southwick Crescent, London. *b.* 1864.

MAINGAY, Courtney Cyril, 1873. Brother of the above. *b.* 1859.

MAINWARING,   , 1805-6.

MAINWARING, Edward Frank Charles, 1827. Son of Capt. Charles Mainwaring, R.N. *b.* 1813.

MAINWARING, Stapleton Thomas (Bart.), 1851-53. Son of Sir Harry Mainwaring, Bart. *b.* 1837. Lieut. Coldstream Guards; *d.* 1878.

MAITLAND, Frederick Coulthurst, 1821, *b.* 1808. Army.

MAITLAND, Frederick Thomas, 1817. Son of Genl. Fredk. Maitland. *b.* 1807. Colonel, retired.

MAITLAND, Lauderdale, 1825. Eldest son of late John Busby Maitland, M.P. *b.* 1809. Of Eccles, Co. Dumfries.

MAJENDIE, Severne Andrew Ashhurst, 1856-59. Son of Rev. Henry Lewis Majendie, Vicar of Great Dunmow. *b.* 1843. Ex. Coll. Oxf. Chaplain to the Duke of Buccleuch.

MALCOLMSON, James Grant, 1875. Son of Capt. John Grant Malcolmson, V.C. *b.* 1862.

MALCOLMSON, Kinloch Gordon, 1877. Brother of the above. *b.* 1863. 17, Kensington Gardens Square.

MALDEN,* Henry Melville Scott, 1875. Son of Henry Charles Malden, of Windlesham House, Brighton. *b.* 1862. Exhibitioner to Cambridge.

MALET, George Grenville, 1819. Son of Sir Charles Warre Malet, Bart. *b.* 1805. Lieut.-Col. 3rd Bombay Light Cavalry. Killed in action at Bushire 1856.

MALKIN,* Herbert Charles, 1848-55. Son of Sir Benjamin Heath Malkin, Knt. *b.* 1836. Scholar of Trin. Coll. Cam. Assistant Master in the School 1862 and 63. Clerk of Public Bills, House of Lords.

MALTBY, Henry, 1820, *b.* 1807. Solicitor.

MALTBY, John, 1827, *b.* 1813.

MAMMATT,* Arthur Simmonds, 1862-67. Son of Edward Mammatt, of Ashby de la Zouche. *b.* 1848. Ball. Coll. Oxf. Domestic Chaplain to the Earl of Loudoun.

MAMMATT, Edward Frederic, 1858-60. Brother of the above. *b.* 1843. Solicitor at Ashby de la Zouche.

MAN, Frederick Henry Dumas. 1875. Son of F. Man, of Beckenham.

MAN, Henry, 1825, *b.* 1815.

MANDERSON,   , 1834-35. Born in India.

MANGIN, Henry Mark, 1824, *b.* 1809. Of the Castle, Dublin; deceased.

MANGIN, John Cailland, 1824, *b.* 1811.

MANN, John Howard, 1851-55, *b.* 1841. Killed by a fall while walking in his sleep, 6 Feb. 1868.

MANN, Joseph F., 1861, *b.* 1849.

MANSEL, Francis Montague, 1874.

MANSEL, William Lort, 1802-3. Son of the Bishop of Bristol. Imprisoned with Capt. Wright by Napoleon; died at sea.

MANT, Frederick Woods, 1818. Son of the Bishop of Down and Connor. *b.* 1809. Royal Navy.

MANT, Walter Bishop, 1818. Brother of the above. *b.* 1807. Oriel Coll. Oxf. 3rd Class Lit. Hum. Archdeacon of Down.

MANTELL, Hugh Fraser, 1878. Son of Edward Walter Mantell, Architect, of Golden Manor, Hanwell.

MANTON, John Augustus, 1824, *b.* 1809.

MAPLES, Charles, 1864-67. Son of Frederick Maples. *b.* 1849. Cotton Broker at Liverpool. Drowned off the Welsh Coast 1878.

MAPLES, Chauncy, 1865-69. Brother of the above. *b.* 1852. Univ. Coll. Oxf. Missionary at Zanzibar.

MAPLES, William, 1858-61. Brother of the above. *b.* 1844. Solicitor in London.

MARCH, Charles, 1817, *b.* 1806.

MARCH, John Cumming Lade, 1864, *b.* 1848.

MARCH, William, 1817, *b.* 1804.

MARJORIBANKS, Coutts, 1822. Son of Edward Majoribanks, of Greenlands. *b.* 1810. St. John's Coll. Cam.; *d.* 1829.

MARJORIBANKS, Edward, 1827. Brother of the above. *b.* 1814. Ch. Ch. Oxf. Banker. Partner in Messrs. Coutts & Co. The Hall, Bushey, Watford.

MARKBY, Thomas, 1873. Son of Henry Markby, 155, Westbourne Terrace, W. *b.* 1860. Articled to a Solicitor.

MARRIOTT, Fitzherbert Adams, 1824. Son of George Wharton Marriott, Chairman of the Middlesex Sessions. *b.* 1811. Oriel Coll. Oxf. Vicar of Chaddesley-Corbett, Kidderminster. Formerly Archdeacon of Hobart Town.

MARRIOTT, George Robert, 1821. Brother of the above. *b.* 1809. Oriel Coll. Oxf. 2nd Class Lit. Hum. Barrister; deceased.

MARRYAT, Albert Palliser, 1852-54, *b.* 1837. Army.

MARSHALL, Arthur, 1875. Son of Robert Marshall, 35, Connaught Square. *b.* 1863.

MARSHALL, Edward James, 1874. Son of James Charles Marshall, 29, Pembridge Gardens. *b.* 1860. Tea Broker.

MARSHALL, Francis Eden, 1876. Son of Rev. Jenner Marshall, of Westcott Barton Manor, Oxon. *b.* 1863.

MARSHALL, George, 1826-36. Son of James Marshall, of London. *b.* 1817. Gold Medal. Student, Tutor and Censor of Ch. Ch. Oxf. Craven Scholar, &c. 2nd Class Lit. Hum. Rector of Milton, Berks.

MARSHALL, Henry, 1873. Brother of Arthur Marshall (above). *b.* 1859. Lawyer.

MARSHALL, Henry Johnson, 1830, *b.* 1817. Pemb. Coll. Oxf. A Priest of the Roman Catholic Church; *d.* 1877.

MARSHALL, James, 1829-38, *b.* 1820. Gold Medal. Ch. Ch. Oxf. Rector of Pyrton, Oxon. Formerly Assist. Master in Westminster School.

MARSHALL, Jenner Guest, 1875. Brother of F. E. Marshall (above). Student of Civil Engineering.

MARSHALL, Thomas William, 1827, *b.* 1815.

MARSHALL, Walter Douglas, 1875.

MARSLAND, John, 1849-52. Son of John Marsland, of Henbury Hall, Chester. *b.* 1835. Capt. 1st Warwickshire Militia, Leamington.

MARSLAND, William Edward, 1849-55. Brother of the above. *b.* 1838. Lt.-Col. 5th Dragoon Guards.

MARTEN, Hubert Binden, 1878. Son of Edward B. Marten, of Pedmore, Stourbridge. *b.* 1865.

MARTEN, Thomas Powney, 1820. Son of George Sulivan Marten, of Marshalls Wick, Herts. *b.* 1807. Bengal Civil Service. J.P. for Herts.

MARTIN, Francis Offley, 1818. Son of Henry Martin, M.P., of Colton Basset, Notts. *b.* 1805. Caius Coll. Cam. Barrister. Charity Commissioner. Formerly an Assistant Tithe Commissioner.

MARTIN, James, 1820. Son of John Martin, M.P., of Overbury Court, Worcester. *b.* 1807.

MARTIN, Robert, 1819. Brother of the above. *b.* 1808. Ex. Coll. Oxf. Banker in London. J.P. for Worcester.

MARWOOD, Arthur Octavius, 1864. Son of Thomas Marwood, of Whitby. *b.* 1848. Merchant of Whitby, Yorks.

MASFEN,* Edward Bellasis, 1844-51, *b.* 1834; died 1863.

MASON, Francis John Mills, 1831-36. Son of Adml. Sir Francis Mason, K.C.B. *b.* 1821. Major in the Indian Army. Retired. Willoughby House, Rugby.

MASON, James Oliver, 1825, *b.* 1815.

MASON, James Wood, 1857-64, *b.* 1845.

MASSEY,* Robert John, 1820. Of an Essex family. *b.* 1806. Drowned in Spain.

MASTER, Gilbert Nathaniel, 1875. Son of Charles Hoskins Master, of Barrow Green House, Surrey. *b.* 1860.

MASTER, Robert Streynsham, 1874. Of Croston Rectory, Preston.

MASTERMAN, Charles Edward, 1872. Son of Henry Masterman, of The Mall, Wanstead, Essex.

MASTERS, George, 1831, *b.* 1819. Worc. Coll. Oxf. Holy Orders.

MASTERS, James Herbert, 1878. Son of Rev. James Hoare Masters, Vicar of Lower Beeding, Sussex. *b.* 1863.

MATCHAM, George Henry Eyre, 1876. Son of William Eyre Matcham, of Newhouse, near Salisbury, *b.* 1862.

MATHER, J. C. V. 1876. Left same year.

MATHIAS,* Duncan L'Estrange, 1871. Son of the late Rev. G. H. Duncan Mathias, Vicar of East Molesey. *b.* 1860. Clerk in Coutts' Bank.

MATHIAS, John Daniel, 1824, *b.* 1811. Ball. Coll. Oxf. Curate of Norton Malreward, Somerset; died at Charterhouse 1866.

MATHISON, Archibald Stirling, 1825. Son of Gilbert Mathison, of Jamaica. *b.* 1812. Indian Civil Service. J.P. for Surrey. Lockner Hill, Chilworth.

MATHISON, Walter George, 1819. Brother of the above. *b.* 1804. East India Civil Service, Ceylon; died at Trincomalee 1832.

MATTHEWS, Henry Lumley, 1864, *b.* 1852. St. John's Coll. Cam.

MATTHEWS, Robert Sutton, 1825, *b.* 1811; deceased.

MATTHEWS, William Macdonald, 1865, *b.* 1851.

MATTHEWS,   , 1802. Left the same year.

MATTHEY, Cyril George Rigby, 1877. Son of Edward Matthey, Warwick Crescent, London. *b.* 1864.

MAUD, Charles Theobald, 1809-13. Son of John Primatt Maud, of Hillingdon, Middlesex. *b.* 1797. Ball. Coll. Oxf.; died at Bath 1878.

MAUD, Sidney Ashmore Stuart, 1874. Son of Rev. Henry Landon Maud, Vicar of Assington, Suffolk. *b.* 1861. Finished his education at the Institute of Commerce at Antwerp.

MAUDE, Ernest Henry, 1877. Son of Charles Henry Maude, 19, St. George's Square, S.W. *b.* 1863.

MAUDE, Cyril Francis, 1876. Brother of the above.

MAUDE, Frederick, 1819, *b.* 1806.

MAUDE, Joseph, 1817, *b.* 1805. Fellow of Queens Coll. Oxf. 1st Class Math. Hon. Canon of St. Asaph, &c. Vicar of Chirk, Denbighshire; deceased.

MAULE, Fox (Earl of Dalhousie), 1809. Son of the first Lord Panmure. *b.* 1801. Capt. 79th Regiment. M.P. for Perthshire. Secretary of State for War 1855-8. Governor of Charterhouse, &c.; *d.* 1874.

MAURY, Rutson, 1817, *b.* 1805.

MAWHOOD, Charles, 1813. Left the same year, *b.* 1801.

MAXWELL, George, 1802-4.

MAY, Augustus Wakeford, 1856-58, *b.* 1842.

MAY, Bowen Alexander, 1856-64, *b.* 1846. Worc. Coll. Oxf.

MAY,* William, 1876. Son of George May, Junior F.R.C.S., of Reading. *b.* 1863.

MAYHEW, Edward Jeremiah, 1852-54, *b.* 1838. Solicitor.

MAYNE, Frederick Randal, 1873.

MAYOW,* Augustus Edward Stanley Wynell, 1870. Son of Rev. M. W. Mayow, Rector of Southam, Warwick. *b.* 1859. King's Coll. London. The Oratory, Birmingham.

MAZZINGHI, Thomas John, 1826, *b.* 1811. Trin. Coll. Cam. Barrister.

MEADE, William, 1835-39, *b.* 1821. Ball. Coll. Oxf. Assist. Master in the School. Rector of Binegar, Somerset.

MEDDOWCROFT, Edmund, 1809-13, *b.* 1799. Barrister.

MEDDOWCROFT, William, 1809-10, *b.* 1796.

MEDHURST, Francis William Hastings, 1856-57. Son of Francis Hastings Medhurst. *b.* 1844. Lieut. R.A. Of Kippax Hall, Yorks.

MEDLICOTT, Samuel, 1874. Son of J. G. Medlicott, late Inspector of Schools in India. *b.* 1860.

MEE, Charles John Cowper, 1875. Son of John Cowper Mee, of East Retford. *b.* 1861. Army Student.

MEEKE, William, 1819, *b.* 1806.

MENDHAM, Frederick, 1812-16, *b.* 1804.

MENDHAM, George, 1811-13, *b.* 1801.

MENDHAM, Henry, 1811-12, *b.* 1799.

MERCER, George Elphinstone, 1878. Son of Major-General Thomas Warren Mercer, of Clayton, Sussex.

MEREWETHER, Edward Christopher, 1830, *b.* 1820. Univ. Coll. Oxf.

MEREWETHER, Herbert Walton, 1825, *b.* 1816. Solicitor.

MEREWETHER, John Robert, 1827, *b.* 1817. Royal Navy. Drowned at the Cape in saving persons shipwrecked 1841.

MERRIMAN, Henry Gunthorpe, 1872. Son of John J. Merriman, Surgeon, of London. *b.* 1858; deceased.

MERRIMAN, John William Conyers, 1868-71. Brother of the above. *b.* 1854. Surgeon, 42, Kensington Square.

MERRIMAN,* Septimus, 1849-54. Brother of the above. *b.* 1836. Lloyd's Office. Manager of the Marine Insurance Company.

MERYWEATHER, William Stephens Turner Mellish, 1823, *b.* 1809. Trin. Coll. Cam. Barrister. Took the name of Turner in addition to that of Meryweather; *d.* 1841.

MESSENT, Philip Glynn, 1876. Son of Philip John Messent, Civil Engineer, of Tynemouth. *b.* 1862.

MESSITER, Henry, 1815, *b.* 1803. Capt. in the Army. Died in Bombay 1844.

METHOLD, Henry, 1818. Son of Rev. Thomas Methold, Rector of Stonham-Aspal. *b.* 1803. Solicitor. One of the Masters of The Court of Common Pleas; died 1869.

METHOLD,* John, 1806-12, *b.* 1794. Army.

MEYER, John, 1810-13, *b.* 1798. Merchant.

MIDDLETON, Boswell, 1820. Son of Empson Middleton, of Waltham Abbey, Essex. *b.* 1805. Attorney-General of Jamaica; *d.* 1854.

MIDDLETON, James, 1819. Brother of the above. *b.* 1804. Solicitor; *d.* 1854.

MIDDLETON, Joseph Empson, 1820. Brother of the above. *b.* 1806. Trin. Coll. Cam. Vicar of Belton, Loughborough.

MIDDLETON, Joseph Pedder, 1863. Son of the above. *b.* 1849. Buenos Ayres.

MIDDLETON, Reginald Empson, 1858-61. Brother of the above. *b.* 1844. Civil and Mechanical Engineer.

MILDMAY, Walter Hervey, 1873. Son of Rev. Charles Arundell Mildmay, Rector of Alvechurch, Worcester. *b.* 1860.

MILES, Falconer Robert James, 1823, *b.* 1812.

MILES, Herbert Charles, 1842-48. Son of John Miles, Medical Officer at Charterhouse. *b.* 1833. Surgeon in the Army; deceased.

MILES, John, 1842-44. Son of General William Miles, of Cheshunt, Herts. *b.* 1829. Lieut.-Colonel Bombay Staff Corps. Served in the Indian Mutiny, &c. Medal and Clasp.

MILES, Joseph, 1842-44. Brother of the above. *b.* 1830. Bombay Staff Corps. Major-Genl. Retired. Served in Persia. Medal and Clasp.

MILES, William, 1837-41. Brother of the above. *b.* 1825. 19th Bombay Native Infantry; deceased.

MILES, William Augustus, 1806. Left the same year. *b.* 1796.

MILLARD,* Jeffery Watson, 1841-49, *b.* 1830. Worc. Coll. Oxf. Rector of Shimpling, Norfolk.

MILLER, Charles Davidson, 1875. Son of Gerald F. Miller. Of Cheam, Surrey.

MILLER, Gerard Champion, 1873. Brother of the above. *b.* 1859.

MILLER, Leslie Creery, 1876. Son of Alexander Edward Miller, Q.C., of Stanmore, Middlesex. *b.* 1862.

MILLIGAN, Duncan, 1805-10. Son of R. Milligan, of Rosslyn House, Hampstead, and the W. India Docks. deceased.

MILLIGAN, Henry Duncan, 1804-8. Brother of the above. deceased.

MILLIGAN,* William Henry, 1844-52. Son of Capt. W. Milligan, 2nd Life Guards. *b.* 1833. Univ. Coll. Oxf. Ecclesiastical Commission.

MILLIKEN, Ernest, 1878. Son of Ernest Milliken, of Putney. *b.* 1862.

MILLS, Charles Augustus, 1865-67, *b.* 1850.

MILLS, John, 1816. Left the same year. *b.* 1805.

MILLS, Richard, 1839-44. Son of Richard Mills, of Eltham, Taxing Master in Chancery. *b.* 1826. B.N.C. Oxf. Solicitor.

MILLS, Thomas Wilgress, 1843-50. Brother of the above. *b.* 1831. B.N.C. Oxf. War Office.

MILLWARD, Francis Broadbelt, 1809-12, *b.* 1794. Emm. Coll. Cam.

MILNE, Edgar Astley, 1877. Son of Alfred Milne, of Chiddingfold, Surrey. *b.* 1863.

MILNER, George Ernest John, 1877. Son of Rev. John Milner, Beechhurst, Sussex. *b.* 1863.

MILNER, William Arthur, 1878. Brother of the above. *b.* 1864.

MILNES, Thomas Hercules, 1820, *b.* 1806.

MINOT, William Griffith, 1822, *b.* 1808.

MINTER,* John Surtees, 1868-72. Son of Dr. John Minter, of Plympton, Devon. Inspector-General of Hospitals. *b.* 1856. Royal Artillery.

MITCHELL,* Herbert Edward, 1876. Son of William Charles Mitchell, 2, Sumner Place, So. Kensington. *b.* 1861. Civil Service.

MITCHELL, John, 1823, *b.* 1810.

MITCHELL, Muirhead, 1823, *b.* 1810. Univ. Coll. Oxf. One of H.M. Inspectors of Schools; *d.* 1877.

MOGG, John George, 1826. Son of George Mogg, of Farrington-Gourney. *b.* 1813. Oriel Coll. Oxford.

MOGG, Charles Baker Coxeter Rees, 1868. Son of William Rees Mogg (below). *b.* 1857.

MOGG, Henry James Rees, 1865. Brother of the above. Ex. Coll. Oxf. Curate of Litton, Somersetshire.

MOGG, John Rees, 1821. Son of Rev. John Rees Mogg. *b.* 1806. Solicitor.

MOGG, Leyson Rees, 1868. Son of the following. *b.* 1855.

MOGG, William Rees, 1829. Brother of John Rees Mogg (above). *b.* 1815. Of Cholwell House, Somerset.

MOGG, William Wooldridge Rees, 1863. Son of the above. *b.* 1848.

MOLESWORTH-ST. AUBYN, Hugh, 1878. (See St. Aubyn).

MOLYNEUX, Hon. Francis George, 1816-17. Son of the 2nd Earl of Sefton. *b.* 1805. Went to Eton. Trin. Coll. Cam. Secy. of Legation to the Germanic Confederation. J.P. for Kent and Sussex. Earl's Court, Tunbridge Wells.

List of Carthusians. 163

MONCKTON, Hon. Augustus William, 1820. Son of the 5th Viscount Galway. *b.* 1808. Commander R.N. Lost in H.M.S. Calypso 1833.

MONCKTON, Charles Falkland, 1877.

MONCKTON, Hon. Edmund Gambier, 1820. Brother of the Hon. A. W. Monckton (above). *b.* 1809. Capt. Rifle Brigade, and Col. West York Militia. Hodroyd Hall, Wakefield ; *d.* 1872.

MONCKTON, John Lionel Alexander, 1876.

MONCKTON, Stephen Lancelot, 1875. Son of Stephen Monckton, M.D., of Maidstone.

MONEY, David Inglis, 1821. Son of the late Sir William Taylor Money, M.P. *b.* 1808. Trin. Coll. Cam. Bengal Civil Service. Judge of the Supreme Court, Calcutta. Retired 1860. Stodham Park, Petersfield.

MONINS, Eaton, 1804-8. Son of John Monins, of Canterbury. *b.* 1796. 52nd Regt. Waterloo Medal. Major-Genl. ; *d.* 1861.

MONINS, Henry, 1814-16. Brother of the above. *b.* 1801 ; died 1818.

MONINS, John, 1800-3. Brother of the above. St. John's Coll. Cam. Rector of Ringwould, Kent; died 1853.

MONINS, Richard, 1800-1. Brother of the above. Royal Navy. Afterwards served in 52nd Regt. in the Peninsula; also of the Middle Temple ; died 1848.

MONINS, Richard Eaton, 1823. Son of Rev. John Monins (above). *b.* 1813. St. John's Coll. Cam. Rector of Glemham, Suffolk; *d.* 1852.

MONINS, William, 1801-7. Brother of Richard Monins (above). Entered the 52nd Regt. as a Volunteer. Served at Waterloo with the 17th Lancers ; deceased.

MONTGOMERY,* Alfred, 1824. Son of the late Sir H. Conyngham Montgomery, Bart. *b.* 1814. Dep. Chairman Inland Revenue Office.

MONTGOMERY, Hugh, 1819. Brother of the above. *b.* 1809. Major Madras Army ; *d.* 1852.

MONTGOMERY, Richard Thomas, 1826. Son of Rev. Alexr. J. Montgomery, of Beaulieu. *b.* 1813. Trin. Coll. Dub. 3rd Light Dragoons. Was High Sheriff for Louth 1855.

MOODY, George, 1820, *b.* 1808. St. John's Coll. Cam. Rector of Gilston, Herts.

MOORE, Edmund Fitz, 1813. Son of Richard Moore, of Hampton Court Palace. *b.* 1801. Caius Coll. Cam. Barrister. Q.C. Bencher of the Inner Temple. Author of several legal works ; deceased.

MOORE, Henry, 1817, *b.* 1805.

MOORE,* John Russell, 1834-38. Son of Thos. Moore, the Poet. *b.* 1823. Indian Army ; *d.* 1842.

MOORE, Lewis, 1817. Left the same year. *b.* 1804.

MOORE,* Thomas Lansdown Parr, 1829-36. Brother of J. R. Moore (above). *b.* 1818. In the French Service in Algeria ; *d.* 1846.

MOORE, William Richard, 1845-46, *b.* 1832. Indian Civil Service, Bengal. Killed in India during the Mutiny.

MORGAN, Arthur Middlemore, 1844-50. Son of Francis Morgan, of the E. I. Civil Service, and Catherington House, Hants. *b.* 1831. Ex. Coll. Oxf. 3rd Class Law, &c. Rector of Huish, N. Devon. Author of three Volumes of English Poems.

MORGAN, Charles Jeffrey, 1869-72, *b.* 1856. Went to Univ. Coll. School.

MORGAN, Charles Lewis, 1875. Son of Col. Morgan.

MORGAN, Henry, 1873.

MORGAN,* John Woodroffe, 1804-11, *b.* 1793. Univ. Coll. Oxf. M.A. 1817. Holy Orders.

MORGAN, Seymour Horace, 1845-50. Brother of Arthur M. Morgan (above). *b.* 1833. Hants Militia. Emigrated to Canada.

MORGAN, Thomas John, 1823, *b.* 1807.

MORGAN, William Howard, 1876. Son of William Pitt Morgan, of St. Aubyn's, Cliftonville, Brighton. *b.* 1862.

MORLAND, Henry Servante, 1878.

MORLAND, Thomas Lethbridge Napier, 1878, *b.* 1865.

MORLEY, Joseph, 1823, b. 1817.

MORRELL, Robert Price, 1819. Son of Baker Morrell, of Oxford. b. 1805. Demy of Magd. Coll. Oxf. Rector of Woodham Mortimer, Essex; d. 1872.

MORRIS, Edmund, 1807-11, b. 1795. Trin. Coll. Cam.

MORRIS, Edward Ashurst, 1876.

MORRIS, Frederick John, 1824, b. 1810. E. I. Civil Service.

MORRIS, Robert, 1821. Son of Robert Morris, of Brunswick Square, London. b. 1807. Ch. Ch. Oxf. 1st Class Math. Rector of Friern-Barnet, Middlesex.

MORRIS, William Cholmeley, 1808-11, b. 1793. Queens Coll. Oxford.

MORRISON, Frank Cecil, 1874. Son of G. Carter Morrison, of Reigate.

MORRISON, Walter Granville, 1874. Brother of the above.

MORSE, Charles, 1819, b. 1805.

MORSE, Francis, 1819, b. 1804. Rector of Baxterley.

MORSE, Gilbert, 1878.

MORSE, Thomas Robert, 1824. Son of Capt. Thomas Aubrey Morse, of Glanogwr. b. 1808. Lieut.-Col. Indian Army; retired 1856.

MORTIMER, Charles Smith, 1823. Son of the late Charles Mortimer, Treasurer to the Hon. East India Company, of Streatham. b. 1808. Of Wigmore, Surrey.

MORTIMER, Edward, 1806-8. Son of Charles Smith Mortimer, of Eastbourne. b. 1792; d. 1863.

MORTIMER, Henry, 1823. Brother of C. S. Mortimer (above). b. 1809; died 1879.

MORTIMER, William, 1823. Son of John Mortimer, of Eastbourne. b. 1809. Of the Valley, Bromley, Kent. Has been Master of the Old Surrey Foxhounds since 1842.

MORTLOCK, John Frederick, 1820, b. 1809.

MORTLOCK, Henry, 1802-7, b. 1789.

MOZLEY, Thomas, 1820, b. 1806. Fellow of Oriel Coll. Oxf. Rector of Plymtree, Devon.

MUDGE, Zachary, 1827. Son of Admiral Zachary Mudge. b. 1813. Oriel Coll. Oxf. Barrister. Of Sydney Plympton, Devon; d. 1867.

MUNRO, Henry Acland, 1878. Son of Alexander Munro. b. 1865.

MUNRO,* John Arthur Ruskin, 1876. Brother of the above. b. 1864.

MURDOCH (Sir) Thomas William Clinton (K.C.M.G.), 1819. Son of Thomas Murdoch, F.R.S. b. 1809. Colonial Office. Chief Secy. in Canada, &c. Knighted 1870.

MURRAY, Hon. Allan David, 1877. Son of the Viscount Stormont. b. 1864.

MURRAY, Anthony George, 1846-48. Son of Anthony Murray, of Dollerie, Perthshire. b. 1830. Edinburgh University. Civil Engineer. Served as a Volunteer during the Indian Mutiny.

MURRAY, Hamilton George Dunmore, 1854-58. Son of late Lt.-Col. Samuel Hood Murray. b. 1841.

MURRAY, John, 1819. Son of the late John Murray, of Albemarle Street. b. 1808. Edinburgh University. Publisher.

MURRAY,* Leveson Granville, 1854-59. Brother of Hamilton G. D. Murray (above). b. 1843.

MURRAY,* William Keith, 1850. Left the same year. b. 1837.

MYERS, Jaques, 1825, b. 1812. Merchant in Liverpool; d. 1868.

MYERS, Jerusalem Gedaliah, 1856-60, b. 1848.

MYERS, John, 1821, b. 1807.

MYERS, John Simpson, 1811. Left the same year. b. 1794. St. John's Coll. Cam. Holy Orders.

MYERS, William, 1823, b. 1810.

MYERS, William Thomas, 1811. Left the same year. b. 1794. Jesus Coll. Cam. Holy Orders; d. 1841.

MYTTON, John, 1823. (See Thornycroft).

N.

NALDER, Francis, 1872. Son of Howard Nalder, of Shrublands, Croydon. *b.* 1858.

NAPIER, Alfred Gerard, 1872. Son of Admiral Gerard John Napier. *b.* 1860. R.M. Academy, Woolwich.

NAPIER, Charles George, 1842-46, *b.* 1829. King's Coll. London.

NAPIER, Gerard Codrington, 1875. Brother of Alfred G. Napier (above). *b.* 1863.

NARES, George Walter Adams, 1820. Of Pembrokesh. *b.* 1806; deceased.

NASH, Andrew John, 1822, *b.* 1807. Downing Coll. Cam.

NEAL, Arthur Stanley, 1870, *b.* 1856.

NEATE, Albert, 1845-47, *b.* 1831. Solicitor.

NEATE, Charles, 1838. Left the same year. *b.* 1827. Went to Sutton Valence School.

NEATE, John, 1837-40, *b.* 1824. Solicitor.

NEAVE, Edgar, 1823. Son of John Neave, an Indian Judge, and grandson of Sir Richard Neave, Bart. *b.* 1810.

NEED, Walter John, 1878. Son of Capt. Walter Need, R.N., of Mansfield, Woodhouse, Notts. *b.* 1864.

NEISH, George Watson, 1860-65, *b.* 1849.

NEISH, James, 1866-70, *b.* 1854.

NELSON, Arthur, 1872. Left same year. *b.* 1860.

NELSON, Crighton, 1876. Son of J. C. Nelson, 9, St. Andrew's Place, Regent's Park.

NEPEAN,* Charles Edward Burroughes, 1861-69. Son of Rev. Evan Nepean, Canon of Westminster. *b.* 1851. Univ. Coll. Oxf. Vicar of Lenham, Kent.

NETHERCOTE, Henry Osmund, 1828. Son of John Nethercote, of Moulton, Northants. *b.* 1820. Went to Harrow School. Ball. Coll. Oxf. Moulton Grange, Northamptonshire.

NETHERCOTE, John Rowland, 1827, *b.* 1816; *d.* 1837.

NETTLESHIP,* Henry, 1854. Gold Medal. Scholar of Corpus and Fellow of Linc. Coll. Oxf. 1st Class Mods. Hertford and Craven Scholar, &c. Master at Harrow School.

NEVINSON,* Charles, 1827. Son of Dr. Nevinson, of Hampstead. *b.* 1816. Scholar and Fellow Wadh. Coll. Oxf. 1st Class Lit. Hum. Warden of Browne's Hospital, Stamford.

NEVINSON, Edward, 1826. Brother of the above. *b.* 1813. Barrister of Lincoln's Inn; *d.* 1852.

NEWDICK, Shirley, 1811-14, *b.* 1798. Merchant.

NEWELL,* Thomas Blackman, 1805-11, *b.* 1793. Ch. Ch. Oxf. Holy Orders. Resided at Cheltenham.

NEWILL, Robert Augustus, 1876. Son of Robert Daniel Newill, of Admaston, Wellington, Salop. *b.* 1862.

NEWMAN, Dudley, 1871, *b.* 1859.

NEWMAN, George Herbert, 1871, *b.* 1860.

NEWMARCH, Oliver Richardson, 1849-53, *b.* 1834. Talbot Scholar. Postmaster of Merton Coll. Oxf. Major Indian Army.

NEWSON, Walter Alexander, 1878. Son of Thomas Newson, of East Moulsey. *b.* 1863.

NEWTON, George Bolland, 1848-50, *b.* 1838.

NEWTON, James, 1823, *b.* 1810; *d.* 1829.

NICHOLL, Thomas, 1813-14, *b.* 1796. Emm. Coll. Cam. and Ex. Coll. Oxf.

NICHOLLS, Robert Devereux, 1823, *b.* 1811. Trin Coll. Cam.

NICHOLSON, Charles Millens, 1813-15, *b.* 1799.

NICHOLSON, Charles Norris, 1871. Son of William Norris Nicholson (below). *b.* 1857. Trin. Coll. Cam. 3rd Class Law Tripos. Law Student.

List of Carthusians. 169

NICHOLSON, Frederick, 1877. Brother of the above. *b.* 1864.

NICHOLSON, George Harvey, 1876. Son of William Smith Nicholson (below). *b.* 1862.

NICHOLSON, Hugh Smith, 1874.

NICHOLSON, Robert Isaac, 1873.

NICHOLSON, Stuart James, 1851-54. Son of W. H. Nicholson, of Rochester. *b.* 1837. Major Royal Horse Artillery.

NICHOLSON, William Norris, 1830-34. Son of Isaac Nicholson, Official Assignee in Bankruptcy. *b.* 1815. Trin. Coll. Cam. 7th Senior Opt. Barrister of Lincoln's Inn. A Master in Lunacy.

NICHOLSON, William Smith, 1846-52. Brother of S. J. Nicholson (above). *b.* 1834. Ch. Ch. Oxf. Hoo Lodge, Rochester. J.P. for Kent.

NICOLL, Alexander Charles, 1866. Son of the late C. R. Nicoll, M.D., formerly Surgeon-Major Grenadier Guards. *b.* 1850. Barrister.

NICOLL, Thomas, 1821, *b.* 1809.

NICOLL, Thomas Vere, 1866-67. Brother of Alexander C. Nicoll (above). *b.* 1856. Medical Practitioner

NIND, Philip Henry, 1820. Son of the Rev. Philip Trant Nind. *b.* 1806. Student of Ch. Ch. Oxf. Vicar of South Stoke, Wallingford, Oxon.

NISBETT, Alfred Ernest, 1817, *b.* 1806.

NIVINS, Henry, 1824, *b.* 1815.

NIVINS, James, 1824, *b.* 1813. An Artist.

NOAD,* George Frederick, 1824, *b.* 1812. Worc. Coll. Oxf. 2nd Class Lit. Hum. Rector of Cold Norton, Essex; *d.* 1876.

NORMAN, George, 1824. Son of Richard Norman, of Melton Mowbray, and grandson of 4th Duke of Rutland. *b.* 1811. Goadby Hall, Leicester. J.P.

NORMAN, William Clewin, 1867-68, *b.* 1853.

NORRIS, Charles, 1801-7. Son of William Norris, President of the Royal College of Surgeons. *b.* 1791. E. I. Co. Civil Service. For 25 years Secretary to the Government at Bombay. Retired 1836; died 1842.

NORRIS, Edward John, 1875. Son of Rev. J. P. Norris, Vicar of St. Mary, Redcliffe, and Canon of Bristol. *b.* 1860. Trin. Coll. Cam.

NORRIS, Hugh Littleton, 1876. Brother of the above. *b.* 1863.

NORRIS, Plaisted, 1803-8. Brother of Charles Norris (above). *b.* 1792. Stock Exchange; died 1843.

NORRIS, Walter Harry, 1877. Son of James Norris, of Bletchingley, Surrey. *b.* 1863.

NORRIS (Sir) William, 1804-10. Brother of Plaisted Norris (above). *b.* 1793. Chief Justice of the Supreme Court at Ceylon; died at Ashurst, Sunninghill, 1859.

NORRIS, William Foxley, 1873. Son of Rev. William F. Norris, Vicar of Buckingham.

NORTON, Edward, 1824, *b.* 1809.

NORTON, Henry, 1826, *b.* 1813.

NORTON, Robert, 1817-18, *b.* 1806. Died young.

NOTT, Percy Wemyss Phillips, 1849-50. Son of Maj.-Genl. Francis Percy Nott. *b.* 1838. Trin. Coll. Cam. Vicar of Kew.

NOWELL, Ralph Assheton, 1845-48. Son of Rev. J. Robinson, whose widow assumed the name of Nowell. *b.* 1830. B.N.C. Oxf. Lieut.-Col. Bengal Staff Corps. Retired 1875. Netherside, Skipton.

NUGENT, Albert, 1852-53, *b.* 1839. Royal Navy.

NUGENT,* Cecil Lyndhurst, 1849-55, *b.* 1837.

NUGENT, Charles Edmund, 1824. Son of late Sir George Nugent, Bart. *b.* 1811. Went to Eton.

NUGENT,* Thomas, 1803-7, *b.* 1792.

NUNN, Thomas, 1814. Son of Thomas Nunn, of Lawford Hall, Manningtree. *b.* 1805. Banker. J.P. for Essex; died 1858.

NUTTALL, John Parker, 1815, *b.* 1803. St. John's Coll. Cam.

O.

OAKLEY, Benjamin, 1810-13, *b.* 1798. Stock Exchange; deceased.

OAKLEY, Edward Banner, 1818, *b.* 1806.

OAKELEY, Arthur, 1823. Son of Rev. Herbert Oakeley, of Oakeley, Prebend. of Worcester. *b.* 1815. New Inn Hall, Oxf. Holy Orders; deceased.

OAKELEY, Herbert, 1823. Brother of the above. *b.* 1813. Army; deceased.

O'BEIRNE, Francis Stuart, 1857. Left same year. *b.* 1841.

O'BEIRNE, Lewis Ornsby, 1857. Left same year. *b.* 1843.

O'BRIEN, Joseph, 1805-7, *b.* 1790. Rear Admiral. Late of Yew House, Hoddesden.

O'CONNOR, Roderick, 1800. Left same year.

OGDEN, Aylmer, 1862-64, *b.* 1849.

OGDEN,* Charles Winslow, 1865, *b.* 1854.

OGDEN,* Lyndhurst, 1857-65, *b.* 1847. Trin. Coll. Cam.

OGDEN,* Richard Tynwald, 1856-64, *b.* 1845. Trin. Coll. Cam. Curate of West Derby, Liverpool.

OGILBY, Alexander Beaufort, 1817, *b.* 1804.

OGLE,* Charles, 1811-16. Son of Rev. John Savile Ogle, of Kirkley Hall. *b.* 1799. Ch. Ch. Oxf.; deceased.

OGLE, Robert, 1827. Son of Robert Ogle, of Eglingham, Northumb. *b.* 1817. Barrister. J.P. for Northumberland. Eglingham Hall, Alnwick.

OGLE, William Pomeroy, 1872. Son of Rev. W. R. Ogle, Vicar of Bishops Teignton. *b.* 1859. Ch. Ch. Oxf.

O'GRADY,* Hon. Frederick Standish, 1858-65. Son of the 2nd Visct. Guillamore. *b.* 1847. Wanganui, New Zealand.

O'GRADY, Hon. Reginald Grimston Standish, 1852-55. Brother of the above. *b.* 1839. Inland Revenue Office, Somerset House; died 1874.

O'GRADY, Standish Thomas, 1827, *b.* 1811. Trin. Coll. Cam.

OKEDEN, Uvedale Parry, 1823. Son of the late David Okenden Parry Okeden, of More Crichel, Dorset. *b.* 1808; died 1826.

OKEDEN, William Henry Parry, 1874. Son of the late William Parry Okeden, of Turnworth, Dorset. *b.* 1860. Bengal Civil Service.

OKEDEN, William Parry, 1809-10. Son of David Okeden Parry, who assumed the name of Okeden. Bengal Civil Service; *d.* 1868.

OLDFIELD,* Edmund Prescot, 1873. Son of Henry A. Oldfield, M.D., of Torquay. *b.* 1862.

OLDFIELD, George, 1867, *b.* 1854.

OLDHAM, Charles Furley, 1871. Son of Clement Jackson Oldham, late of Ealing. *b.* 1858. Wine Merchant.

OLDHAM, Clement Hugh, 1866-67. Brother of the above. *b.* 1853. Secretary of the Hospital for Diseases of the Throat and Chest.

OLIVER, William, 1810-12, *b.* 1795. Solicitor.

OLIVER, William James, 1874. Son of R. Oliver, of Lockside House, Kelso.

ONLEY, Onley Harvey Savill- 1806. (See Savill-Onley).

ONSLOW, Denzil Hughes- 1877. (See Hughes-Onslow).

ONSLOW (Sir) Henry (Bart.), 1821. Son of Sir Henry Onslow, 2nd Bart. *b.* 1809. Capt. 10th Regt. *d.* 1870.

ONSLOW, Henry Cope, 1821, *b.* 1809. Demy. and Fellow Magd. Coll. Oxf. deceased.

ONSLOW, William, 1821, *b.* 1810. Emm. Coll. Cam. India Civil Service; deceased.

ORANGE, Charles Burton, 1813-14, *b.* 1799.

ORFORD, Alfred, 1870. Son of John Orford, of Brookes Hall, Ipswich. *b.* 1858. Lieut. Royal Marine Artillery.

ORIEL, Charles George Carpenter, 1812-15, *b.* 1800. Solicitor; died 1874.

ORIEL, Frederick Henry Carpenter, 1817, *b.* 1803. Medical Practitioner; died 1867.

ORIEL, Richard Hicks, 1809-12, *b.* 1797. Solicitor; *d.* 1854.

ORLEBAR, Alexander Charles, 1826. Son of Richard Orlebar, of Hinwick, Beds. *b.* 1813. Lieut. Royal Engineers; drowned at Bermuda 1833.

ORME,* Frederick Doveton, 1853-60, *b.* 1842. Army; died of fever in India 1861.

ORMSBY,* William Arthur, 1824. Son of the late Major Ormsby. *b.* 1812. Univ. Coll. Oxf. Rector of Smallburgh, and Hon. Canon of Norwich.

ORR, Charles Gathorne Edmund, 1876. Son of Rev. Alexander Orr, Rector of Cheriton, Hants.

OSBORN, Edward Haydon, 1848-52. Son of the late Rev. Edward Osborn. *b.* 1832. Gold Medal. St. John's Coll. Oxf. 1st Class Lit. Hum. Newdigate Prize for English Verse 1855. Inspector of Factories, Rochdale.

OSBORN, William Alexander, 1853-60, *b.* 1843. B.N.C. Oxf.

OSBORNE, Ralph Bernal, 1819. (See Bernal-Osborne).

OSMOND, Thomas Johnson, 1819, *b.* 1809.

OSWALD, Henry Murray, 1846-51. Son of Genl. Sir John Oswald, G.C.B. *b.* 1832. Ch. Ch. Oxf. 1st Class Law and Modern History. Rector of Great Hallingbury, Essex.

OTTER, William Bruére, 1819. Son of William Otter, Bishop of Chichester. *b.* 1805. St. Peter's, Cam. Vicar of Cowfold, Sussex. Archdeacon of Lewes; *d.* 1876.

OTTEY,* Francis Ferrand, 1805-11. Son of Philip Egerton Ottey. *b.* 1795. Treasury.

OTTLEY, Herbert Taylor, 1872. Son of Rev. L. Ottley, Canon of Ripon and Rector of Richmond, Yorks. *b.* 1861. Scholar of Keble Coll. Oxf.

OTTLEY,* John Bickersteth, 1858-64. Brother of the above. *b.* 1845. Emm. Coll. Cam.

OTWAY, Loftus. (See Hughes, William J. Marjoribanks).

OVEREND, James, 1863. Left same year. *b.* 1849.

OVEREND, William Heysham, 1863. Left same year. *b.* 1851.

OWEN, Francis, 1818, *b.* 1802.

OWEN, Frederick Charles, 1818, *b.* 1803.

OWEN, John Ord, 1820, *b.* 1806.

OWEN, Langer, 1877. Son of William Owen, of Sydney, New South Wales. *b.* 1862.

OWTRAM, Cuthbert Ellidge, 1878. Son of R. H. Owtram, 37, Warrington Crescent, London. *b.* 1864.

OXLEY, John Stewart, 1875. Son of J. Stewart Oxley, of Fen Place, Turner's Hill, Sussex. *b.* 1863.

OXLEY, Reginald Stewart, 1877. Brother of the above.

P.

PAGAN, Robert Morison, 1872.

PAGE, Arthur, 1810-17, *b.* 1801. Clare Hall, Cam. deceased.

PAGE, Charles Russell, 1806-12, *b.* 1796. Merchant.

PAGE, Edward, 1804-12, *b.* 1791. Clare Hall, Cam. deceased.

PAGE, Harry Marmaduke, 1872, *b.* 1860.

PAGE, John, 1812, *b.* 1803.

PAGE, William, 1806-12, *b.* 1797. Merchant.

PAGE,* William Robert, 1869. Son of T. E. Page, of Winchfield. *b.* 1858.

PAGET, Arthur Coyte, 1822. Son of the late Samuel Paget, of Great Yarmouth. *b.* 1808. Caius Coll. Cam. Barrister; died 1833.

PAGET* (Sir) Augustus Berkeley (K.C.B.), 1834-39. Son of Rt. Hon. Sir Arthur Paget, G.C.B. *b.* 1823. Foreign Office. Ambassador at Rome since 1876.

PAGET,* Cecil George, 1864. Son of Col. Leopold Grimstone Paget, of Wimborne, Dorset. *b.* 1853. Student of Ch. Ch. Oxf. 2nd Class Mods. Curate of St. John's, Mansfield.

PAGET, Charles Edward, 1874. Son of Dr. George Edward Paget (below). *b.* 1858.

PAGET, Frederick, 1819. Brother of Arthur Coyte Paget (above). *b.* 1805 ; died 1866.

PAGET, George Edward, 1824. Brother of the above. *b.* 1809. Fellow of Caius Coll. Cam. 8th Wrangler. M.D. Regius Professor of Physic. F.R.S. President of the Medical Council of the United Kingdom.

PALGRAVE, Francis Turner, 1838-43. Son of the late Sir Francis Palgrave. *b.* 1824. Scholar of Ball. Coll. and Fellow of Ex. Coll. Oxf. 1st Class Lit. Hum. Assist. Secretary Education Department, Privy Council Office.

PALGRAVE, Reginald Francis Douce, 1841-45. Brother of the above. *b.* 1829. Clerk in the House of Commons.

PALGRAVE, Robert Harry Inglis, 1838-43. Brother of the above. *b.* 1827. Banker at Gt. Yarmouth. Editor of *The Economist.*

PALGRAVE, William Gifford, 1838-44. Brother of the above. *b.* 1826. Gold Medal. Scholar of Trin. Coll. Oxf. 1st Class Lit. Hum. 2nd Class Math. Bombay Army. Consul-General for Siam.

PALLISER, Henry St. Leger, 1849-50, *b.* 1839. Royal Navy.

PALLISER, John Augustin, 1849-50, *b.* 1834. 76th Regt.; deceased.

PALMER, Archdale Stuart, 1873. Son of Richard Stuart Palmer, of Calcutta. *b.* 1860. Scholar of King's Coll. Cambridge.

PALMER, Archdale Villiers, 1847-50. Son of Col. George Palmer, of Nazing Park, Essex. *b.* 1832. India Civil Service.

PALMER,* Charles Frederick, 1840-42, *b.* 1828. Royal Navy.

PALMER, Charles James, 1817, *b.* 1807.

PALMER, Edward Howley, 1823. Son of John Horsley Palmer, Merchant, of London. *b.* 1811. Of Canon Hill, Maidenhead. Governor of the Bank of England 1877-79.

PALMER,* Edwin, 1836-42. Son of Rev. W. J. Palmer, B.D., Rector of Mixbury, Oxon, and brother of Lord Selborne. *b.* 1824. Gold Medal. Scholar and Fellow Ball. Coll. Oxf. Hertford and Ireland Scholar, &c. 1st Class Lit. Hum. Corpus Professor of Latin 1870-78. Archdeacon of Oxford, and Canon of Ch. Ch.

PALMER, Francis, 1822, *b.* 1810. Ch. Ch. Oxf. Barrister. 8, Old Burlington Street.

PALMER, George, 1843-45. Son of Col. Palmer, of Nazing Park. *b.* 1828. India Civil Service. Received a Medal and Clasp and the thanks of Her Majesty for distinguished Service in the Indian Mutiny.

PALMER, George Horsley, 1837-38. Brother of Edwin Palmer (above). *b.* 1822. Ex. Coll. Oxf. Rector of Mixbury, Oxon.

PALMER, George Thomas, 1815, *b.* 1802. B.N.C. Oxf. Barrister. Afterwards in Holy Orders.

PALMER, Herbert, 1867. Left the same year. *b.* 1853.

PALMER, William Henry, 1815-16, *b.* 1800; deceased.

PARIS,* John R., 1834-42. Son of the late Dr. Paris, M.D. *b.* 1824. Caius Coll. Cam. Admiralty.

PARISH,* Charles Wellesley, 1869. Son of Capt. Alfred Parish, of the Peninsular and Oriental Co's. Service. *b.* 1857. Royal Marines.

PARISH, William Douglas, 1848-53. Son of Sir Woodbine Parish, K.C.H. *b.* 1833. Trin. Coll. Oxf. Vicar of Selmeston, Sussex. Chancellor of Chichester.

PARK, Lionel Chester, 1871. Son of Alexr. Atherton Park, Senior Master in the Court of Common Pleas. *b.* 1857. Emigrated to Colorado.

PARKE, Samuel, 1807-8, *b.* 1791.

PARKER, Charles Lewes, 1823. Son of the late Joseph Parker. *b.* 1810. Wadh. Coll. Oxf.; deceased.

PARKER, Charles Lewes Edward, 1875.

PARKER, Charles Oxley, 1825. Son of late Charles George Parker, of Springfield, Essex. *b.* 1815. Student of Law. Died of cholera in London 1833.

PARKER, Edward, 1820. Brother of Charles Lewes Parker (above). *b.* 1808. Oriel Coll. Oxf. Rector of Oxendon, Northants, and Hon. Canon of Peterborough.

PARKER, Edward, 1820, *b.* 1808.

PARKER, George, 1818, *b.* 1804.

PARKER, George Hargreave, 1823, *b.* 1813. Holy Orders.

PARKER, John Robert Theophilus Hastings, 1835-39. Son of Capt. Parker, R.N. and grandson of the Earl of Huntingdon. *b.* 1823. Trin. Coll. Dublin. J.P. for Norfolk. Swannington Hall, Norwich.

PARKER, Joseph, 1827, *b.* 1812.

PARKER, Lewis Charles, 1820, *b.* 1810.

PARKER, William George, 1823, *b.* 1810. Scholar of St. John's Coll. Cam. Vicar of Bulkington, Warwick.

PARKER, Wilmot, 1818, *b.* 1804.

PARKES, Francis, 1878. Son of William Parkes, of 8, Grove Road, Surbiton. *b.* 1864.

PARKES, William Jardine, 1875. Brother of the above. Clerk in the British India Steamship Office.

PARMINTER, William George, 1824, *b.* 1809. Chaplain at Stuttgardt.

PARNELL, Charles, 1843-47, *b.* 1828. St. John's Coll. Cam. Incumbent of St. Margaret's, Liverpool.

PARNELL, Charles Jocelyn, 1851-55. Son of Charles Octavius Parnell, Architect. *b.* 1839. Architect; deceased.

PARNELL,* Frank, 1849-56. Brother of the above. *b.* 1838. Student of Ch. Ch. 3rd Class Lit. Hum. Rector of Oxted, Surrey.

PARNELL, Gerald Crecy, 1862. Brother of the above. *b.* 1849. Surgeon. Forest Hill.

PARNELL, Walter George, 1857-61. Brother of the above. *b.* 1846. Banker in Australia; died at Sydney.

PARR, John Hamilton, 1802-4. Son of Edward Parr, of Liverpool.

PARROTT, Joseph, 1822, b. 1808. Solicitor at Buckingham; died 1835.

PARROTT, Richard, 1841-48. Son of John Parrott, of Clapham Common. b. 1830. Wadh. Coll. Oxf. Vicar of Gt. Amwell, Herts.

PARROTT, Septimus, 1841-45. Brother of the above. b. 1829. Of the Stock Exchange.

PARRY, Arthur Jephson Collis, 1872. Son of Rev. E. St. John Parry, of Stoke, Bucks, and grandson of late Bp. Parry, of Barbados. b. 1859.

PARRY,* Edward Hagarty, 1868. Brother of the above. b. 1855. Ex. Coll. Oxf. 2nd Class Mods. Master at Felstead School.

PARRY, George William, 1826, b. 1811.

PARRY, James Bacchus, 1878. Brother of Edward Hagarty Parry (above). b. 1865.

PARRY, Reginald St. John, 1870. Brother of the above. b. 1858. Schol. of Trin. Coll. Cam.

PARSONS, Daniel, 1825, b. 1810. Oriel Coll. Oxf.

PARTRIDGE, Charles Francis, 1826. Son of Henry Samuel Partridge, of Hockham Hall, Norfolk. b. 1811. Trin. Coll. Cam. Holy Orders; died 1860.

PARTRIDGE, Frederick Robert, 1828. Brother of the above. b. 1815. Solicitor at Lynn, Norfolk; died 1878.

PASSLEY,   , 1804-5.

PASSLEY, John, 1804-6.

PATERNOSTER,* John, 1807-12, b. 1797. India Civil Service.

PATERSON, Arthur Bourne, 1874.

PATERSON, Francis, 1841-49, b. 1830. Trin. Coll. Oxf. Holy Orders; died 1854.

PATERSON, James Clement, 1837-42, b. 1826. 2nd European Regiment, Bengal.

PATERSON, William Vautier, 1874.

PATTESON, John Henry, 1876. Son of John Henry Patteson, of Coln St. Aldwyn, Fairford, Gloucestershire.

PATMORE, William Smith, 1816, b. 1802.

PATTINSON, John Henry, 1864-70, b. 1852.

PATTISON, Josiah, 1830, b. 1817.

PAUL, Charles, 1815-18, b. 1802. Cauis Coll. Cam. Vicar of Willow, Somerset.

PAULSON,* Frederick George, 1860, b. 1850. Prize Scholar 1864.

PAULSON,* William Henry, 1860, b. 1847. Gold Medal 1865.

PAYNE (Sir) Charles Gillies (Bart.), 1806-9. Son of the late Sir Peter Payne, Bart. b. 1793. Of Burnham House, Beds.; died 1870.

PAYNE, Charles Herbert, 1870. Son of Wyndham Payne, of Highbury House, Wandsworth. b. 1858. Lieut. 75th Regt.

PAYNE (Sir) Coventry (Bart.), 1806-11, b. 1794. Trin. Hall, Cam. LL.B. Vicar of Hatfield Peverel, Essex; deceased.

PAYNE, David Richard, 1830, b. 1816; deceased.

PAYNE, Henry Towndrow, 1826, b. 1810.

PAYNE, Percy Wyndham, 1870. Brother of Charles Herbert Payne (above). b. 1857.

PAYNTER, Camborne Haweis, 1877. Son of Reginald H. Paynter, of Boskenna, Penzance. b. 1864.

PAYNTER, John, 1824, b. 1812.

PEAKE, Malcolm, 1877. Son of Frederick Peake, of 6, Bedford Row. b. 1865.

PEAKE, Ronald, 1874. Brother of the above. b. 1861. Articled to a Solicitor.

PEARCE, Alfred, 1878. Son of John Swayne Pearce, 13, Craven Hill, Bayswater. b. 1865. Studying in Germany

PEARCE, Edward Charles, 1875. Brother of the above. b. 1862.

PEARCE, Stephen Spencer, 1874. Son of Stephen Pearce, 54, Queen Anne Street.

PEARSE, David William, 1846. Left the same year. b. 1831.

PEARSON,* Charles, 1841-50. Son of Rev. George Pearson (below). b. 1831. Orator. Scholar of St. John's Coll. Cam. 2nd Class Classical Tripos. Assistant Master 1855. Government Inspector of Education in Punjaub.

PEARSON, David Chambers, 1871, *b.* 1859.

PEARSON, Edward Lynch, 1857-64. Brother of Charles Pearson (above). *b.* 1845. Talbot Scholar. St. John's Coll. Cam. 2nd Class Classics. Rector of Castle Camps, Cambridgeshire.

PEARSON,* George, 1801-10, *b.* 1791. Orator. Fellow of St. John's Coll. Cam. Senior Op. Christian Advocate 1834. Rector of Castle Camps; died 1860.

PEARSON, George Charles, 1826. Son of the late William Pearson, of Hopebourne House, Canterbury. *b.* 1814. Ch. Ch. Oxf. 2nd Class Lit. Hum. Rector of St. Margaret's, and Hon. Canon of Canterbury.

PEARSON, George Falconer, 1841-45. Son of George Pearson (above). *b.* 1826. 23rd Madras N. Infantry. Colonel. Conservator of Forests in India 1860-70.

PEARSON,* James Falconer, 1847. Brother of the above. *b.* 1836. Drowned 1854.

PEARSON,* John Batteridge, 1842-51. Brother of the above. *b.* 1832. St. John's Coll. and Fellow and Tutor of Emman. Coll. Cam. 4th Classic. Bell Scholar.

PEARSON, Philip Pennant, 1845-53. (See P. P. Pennant). Brother of the above. *b.* 1834. St. John's Coll. Cam. Senior Opt. and 1st Class Nat. Science. Changed his name to Pennant 1860. J.P. and D.L. of Flintshire.

PEARSON, Thomas Hall, 1852. Brother of the above. *d.* 1853.

PEARSON, William, 1828. Brother of George Charles Pearson (above). *b.* 1816. Ex. Coll. Oxf. Vicar of Granborough, Warwickshire; died 1866.

PEASE, Frederick, 1821, *b.* 1807.

PECK, Kenrick, 1852-53. Son of Rev. Jasper Peck, of Bath. *b.* 1836. Solicitor, 56, Lincoln's Inn Fields.

PEDDER, John Lewis, 1802-10, *b.* 1793. Trin Hall, Cam. LL.B. A Judge in N. S. Wales.

PEDDER, William, 1803-11, *b.* 1796. Army.

PEEL, Alfred Henry, 1878. Son of the Rev. Fredk. Peel, of Malvern. *b.* 1864.

PEEL, Charles Steers, 1836-38. Son of William Peel. *b.* 1821. Worc. Coll. Oxf. Rector of Syresham, Northants, and Rousham, Oxon.

PEEL, Spencer, 1836. Brother of the above. Left the same year. *b.* 1820. Capt. 1st Foot.

PEETE, William Willox, 1813-16. Son of William Peete, of Dartford. *b.* 1798. Wadh. Coll. Oxf. Holy Orders.

PEILE, Horatio Renaud, 1851-56, *b.* 1839.

PEILE,* Percival Bringhurst Babington, 1849-56. Brother of the above. *b.* 1838. Science and Art Department, South Kensington.

PELLY, Justinian, 1878. Son of Justinian Pelly, of Elmsley, Yoxford. *b.* 1864.

PEMBER, Edward Henry, 1847-50. Son of R. Pember, of Streatham. *b.* 1832. Ch. Ch. Oxf. 1st Class Lit. Hum. Barrister. Q.C.

PEMBER, Frederick, 1850-55. Brother of the above. *b.* 1837. Ch. Ch. Oxf.

PEMBERTON, Joseph, 1803.

PEMBERTON,* Stanley, 1822-30. Son of Christopher Robert Pemberton, M.D. *b.* 1811. Ch. Ch. Oxf. Rector of Little Hallingbury, Essex.

PENKIVIL, John, 1816, *b.* 1803.

PENLEAZE, Robert, 1805. Left the same year. *b.* 1792. Magd. Coll. Oxf.

PENNANT, Philip Pennant, 1845. (See P. P. Pearson).

PENNELL,* John Croker, 1835-43. Son of William Pennell, late of East Molesey, Surrey. *b.* 1825. Queens Coll. Cam. Foreign Office; died 1865.

PENNINGTON, John, 1806-7. Of Liverpool; deceased.

PENNINGTON, Sparrow Thomas, 1826, *b.* 1817. Trin. Coll. Oxf.

PENNY, Arthur Edmund, 1832-38. Son of the following. *b.* 1823; deceased.

PENNY,* Edmund Henry, 1807-15, *b.* 1797. B.N.C. Oxf. Reader and Assist. Master. Rector of Great Stambridge, Essex; died 1879.

PENTON, Henry, 1803-5, *b.* 1791.

PEPPER, John, 1802. Left the same year. Vicar of Alfreton.

PERCEVAL, Augustus George, 1844-47. Son of Hon. and Rev. A. P. Perceval, Rector of E. Horsley. *b.* 1829. Oriel Coll. Oxf. New Zealand.

PERCEVAL, Charles John, 1844-47. Brother of the above. *b.* 1831. 27th Regt. New Zealand.

PERCEVAL, Henry Legge, 1845-47. Brother of the above. *b.* 1836. Commander R.N.; deceased.

PERCEVAL, Spencer Arthur, 1844-47. Brother of the above. *b.* 1832. Emigrated to New Zealand.

PERCIVAL,* Thomas Cozens, 1808-15 *b.* 1797. Student of Ch. Ch. Oxf. Rector of Horseheath, Cambs.

PERCY, Edmund, 1824, *b.* 1810. Of Beeston, Notts.

PERKIN, Charles Thornton, 1874. Son of Robert Blakemore Perkin, of Ditton Hill, Surrey. *b.* 1860. Solicitor.

PERKIN, John Arthur, 1876. Brother of the above. *b.* 1862.

PERKIN, Robert Knowles, 1873. Brother of the above. *b.* 1859. Merchant.

PERKINS, Augustus Samuel, 1823. *b.* 1809. Brewer.

PERKS, James, 1873. Son of John B. Perks, of Staneway House, Ewell, Surrey.

PERRINS, Charles William Dyson, 1878. Son of James Dyson Perrins, of Davenham Bank, Malvern. *b.* 1864.

PERRY, Alfred, 1837-40, *b.* 1824.

PERRY, Alfred William, 1877. Son of William J. Perry, J.P. of Ardlin, Blackrock, Dublin. *b.* 1862. Entered Trin. Coll. Dublin.

PERRY, Richard George Davis, 1857-61, *b.* 1844.

PERRY* (Sir) Thomas Erskine, 1816. Son of James Perry, Proprietor of *The Morning Chronicle*. *b.* 1806. Trin. Coll. Cam. Barrister. Chief Justice of Bombay. Member of the India Council. M.P. for Devonport 1854-9 *died 1882.*

PERRY (Sir) William, 1811-18, *b.* 1801. Caius Coll. Cam. Consul General at Venice; died 1874.

PERRY, William Martin John, 1813, *b.* 1803.

PETLEY, Charles Robert Carter, 1822. Son of Charles Carter Petley, of Riverhead, Kent. *b.* 1807. St. John's Coll. Oxf. J.P. for Kent. Riverhead, Sevenoaks.

PETLEY,* Henry, 1825. Brother of the above. *b.* 1815. Wadh. Coll. Oxf. Formerly Missionary in Newfoundland, and Curate of Glynde, Sussex. Now Curate of Gislingham, Suffolk.

PETLEY, John A. Carter, 1833. Brother of the above. Late 58th Regt. Of Auckland, New Zealand; *d.* 1871.

PHELPS,* Lancelot Ridley, 1866-72. Son of Rev. Thomas P. Phelps, Rector of Ridley, Kent. *b.* 1853. Prize Scholar. Scholar and Fellow of Oriel Coll. Oxf. 2nd Class Lit. Hum. and Math. Holy Orders.

PHILETAS, Christopher, 1820. A native of Joannina in Epirus.

PHILLIMORE, Greville, 1832-38. Son of the late Joseph Phillimore, D.C.L. *b.* 1821. Student of Ch. Ch. Oxf. Vicar of Henley-on-Thames.

PHILLIMORE, William Thornton, 1836-38. [Son of William Phillimore, of Deacons Hill, Herts.] Capt. 10th Bengal Native Infantry. Killed in the Mutiny 1857.

PHILLIPPS, Henry Cranmer, 1805-6. *b.* 1793. Royal Navy.

PHILLIPPS, William March, 1803-7. Son of Thomas March Phillipps, of Garendon Park, Leicestershire. *b.* 1790. St. John's Coll. Cam. Holy Orders; *d.* 1818.

PHILLIPS, Arthur Lowndes, 1866-70. Son of Charles Palmer Phillips, of Aldenham, Herts. *b.* 1853; *d.* 1879.

PHILLIPS, Elwin George Wilson, 1876. Son of John South Phillips, of Barton Lodge, Bury St. Edmunds. *b.* 1862.

PHILLIPS, George Richard Turner, 1850-54. Son of Richard Phillips, F.R.C.S. *b.* 1841. King's Coll. London. Surgeon, Leinster Square, Bayswater.

PHILLIPS,* Henry George, 1803-10. Son of John Phillips, Surgeon to the Royal Household. *b.* 1791. Scholar of Emm. Coll. Cam. Rector of Gt. Weltham, Suffolk; died 1874.

PHILLIPS, Mandeville Blackwood, 1857-64, *b.* 1848.

PHILLOTT, George Henry, 1864-68. Son of H. W. Phillott (below). *b.* 1852. Architect at Cheltenham.

PHILLOTT,* Henry Wright, 1827-33. Son of Johnson Phillott, of Bath. *b.* 1816. Orator. Student of Ch. Ch. 2nd Class Lit. Hum. Formerly Assist. Master. Rector of Staunton on the Wye.

PHILLPOTTS,* John Scott, 1832-38. Son of the Bishop of Exeter. *b.* 1820. Ex. Coll. Oxf. Indian Army.

PHILLPOTTS, William, 1819, *b.* 1807.

PICKTHALL, Arthur Christie, 1874. Son of Rev. Charles Grayson Pickthall, Rector of Chillesford, Suffolk.

PICKTHORN, Russell Hay, 1876. Son of Thomas Russell Pickthorn, R.N., late Inspector of Hospitals. *b.* 1862.

PIERSON, Alfred Græme, 1875. Son of Rev. William Frederic Pierson, Vicar of Settle, Yorks. *b.* 1862.

PIGGOT,   , 1805-7.

PIGOT, George, 1820, *b.* 1805. Chaplain in Bombay; deceased.

PIKE, Arthur Leonard, 1875. Son of John Bilton Pike, of Sydenham. *b.* 1861. Entered at New Coll. Oxf.

PILKINGTON, Henry, 1800-5, *b.* 1787. Went to Bury St. Edmunds School. Oriel Coll. Oxf.

PILKINGTON (Sir) Lionel M. Swinnerton (Bart.), 1849. Second son of Sir William Pilkington, 8th Bart. *b.* 1835. Of Chevet Hall, Wakefield.

PILKINGTON, Redmond William, 1800-5, *b.* 1789.

PILKINGTON (Sir) Thomas Edward (Bart.), 1844-47. Eldest son of Sir Wm. Pilkington, 8th Bart. *b.* 1830. Univ. Coll. Oxf.; died 1854.

PINCHING, Archibald Edward, 1862. Son of Charles John Pinching, of Gravesend, M.R.C.S. Left the same year. *b.* 1853. Mining Engineer.

PINCHING, Charles John William, 1862-63. Brother of the above. *b.* 1849. Surgeon at Gravesend.

PINCHING, William Wyatt, 1862-63. Brother of the above. *b.* 1851. Surgeon. Lost at sea 16 Aug., 1878.

PINCKNEY, Erlysman Charles, 1819. Son of Rev. Dr. John Hearne Pinckney, of East Sheen. *b.* 1808. Of Berwick, St. James', Wilts.

PINCKNEY, Herbert, 1878. Son of William Pinckney, of Milford Hill, Salisbury. *b.* 1864.

PINDER, Francis Ford, 1818. Son of Francis Ford Pinder, of Barbados. *b.* 1803. Trin. Coll. Cam. Rector of Gosforth; deceased.

PINDER, George, 1818. Brother of the above. *b.* 1809. 15th Regt. Lieut.-Colonel, retired.

PINDER, Humphrey Senhouse, 1819. Brother of the above. *b.* 1805. Fellow of Caius Coll. Cam. 18th Wrangler. Formerly Rector of Bratton-Fleming, Devon.

PINDER, John Hethersall, 1807-12. Brother of the above. *b.* 1794. Caius Coll. Cam. Canon of Wells. Principal of the Theological College, Wells; deceased.

PINDER, William Maynard, 1807-11. Brother of the above. *b.* 1792. Pemb. Coll. Cam. Barrister; *d.* 1869.

PINHEY, Arthur Francis, 1877. Son of the Hon. Mr. Justice Pinhey, of Bombay. *b.* 1863.

PINNIGER, Henry Herbert, 1854-56. Son of Rev. R. B. Pinniger, Rector of Whichford. *b.* 1841. Pemb. Coll. Oxf. Curate of S. Hincksey; *d.* 1878.

PIPON, James Kennard, 1820, *b.* 1807. 85th Regt.

PIPON, Nathaniel Hodges, 1820, *b.* 1808.

PLUES,* Mark, 1827, *b.* 1816.

PLUES,* Samuel Swire, 1826, *b.* 1815.

PLUMER, Thomas Hall, 1874. [Son of C. Hall Plumer, E. I. C. S.]. R.M. Coll. Sandhurst.

PLUMMER, John, 1809-12, *b.* 1797.

PLUMMER, Stephen, 1806-8, *b.* 1793.

PLUNKETT,* George, 1853-58, *b.* 1842. Capt. Royal Artillery. Adjutant Shropshire Militia.

PLUNKETT, John, 1829, *b.* 1816.

PLUNKETT, William, 1822. Son of Mr. Plunkett, Chairman of The Board of Customs, Dublin. *b.* 1807. Caius Coll. Cam. Barrister of Lincoln's Inn; deceased.

POCKLINGTON, Harry Evelyn Stracey, 1872. Son of Lieut.-Col. George Henry Pocklington. *b.* 1858. Lieut. 15th Hussars.

POCOCK, Charles Ashwell Bowler, 1841-43, *b.* 1829. Commander Royal Navy. Retired.

POLEHAMPTON, John, 1874. Son of Rev. J. Polehampton, Rector of Ightham, Kent. *b.* 1860.

POLLARD, Henry Smith, 1824, *b.* 1810. Linc. Coll. Oxf. Rector of Everdon, Northants; deceased.

POLLARD, Nathaniel Weeks, 1826, *b.* 1814.

POLLARD, Thomas Sydney, 1873. Son of William Pollard, F.R.C.S. Southlands, Torquay. *b.* 1859. Student of Civil Engineering.

POLLOCK,* Arthur Julius, 1876. Son of Arthur Julius Pollock, M.D. *b.* 1863.

POLLOCK,* Bertram, 1876. Son of George Frederick Pollock, of Hanworth, Middlesex. *b.* 1861.

POLLOCK, Charles Stewart, 1877. Son of Sir Charles Edward Pollock, Baron of the Court of Exchequer. *b.* 1864.

POLLOCK,* Ernest Murray, 1875. Brother of Bertram Pollock (above). *b.* 1861.

POLLOCK, Frank, 1872. Son of J. E. Pollock, M.D.

POLLOCK,* Henry Edward, 1878. Son of Arthur Julius Pollock, M.D. *b.* 1864.

POLLOCK, Henry William, 1872. Brother of Frank Pollock (above).

POLLOCK, John George Napier, *b.* 1874. Son of John Osborne G. Pollock, of Mountainstown, Co. Meath. *b.* 1861. Trin. Coll. Dublin.

PONSONBY, Hon. John George Brabazon (Earl of Bessborough), 1822. Son of the 4th Earl. *b.* 1809. Formerly M.P. for Derby and Master of H.M Staghounds.

PONSONBY, Hugh Spencer, 1878. Son of Hon. Spencer Ponsonby-Fane, C.B., Comptroller Lord Chamberlain's Department, &c. *b.* 1865.

PONSONBY, Sydney Alexander, 1875. Brother of the above. *b.* 1863.

PONSONBY, Walter Gerald, 1872. Son of Hon. and Rev. Walter Ponsonby, Rector of Marston Bigot, Somerset. *b.* 1859.

POORE, Herbert, 1875. Son of Sir Edward Poore, Bart. *b.* 1863.

POPHAM, Hugh Francis Arthur Leyborne, 1878. Son of Francis Leyborne Popham, of 23, Park Lane. *b.* 1864.

POPHAM, Strachan Irving, 1821, *b.* 1809. J.P. and D.L. for Co. Argyle; died 1861.

PORCH, Thomas Porch, 1820. (See Reeves).

PORTER, Robert Tindal, 1819, *b.* 1805. E. I. Civil Service. Retired.

PORTEUS,* Beilby, 1816-27. Son of the Bishop of London. *b.* 1807. Ch. Coll. Cam. Formerly Vicar of Edenhall, and Hon. Canon of Carlisle.

PORTMAN,* Henry Fitzhardinge Berkeley, 1851. Son of the Hon. H. W. B. Portman and nephew of Visct. Portman. *b.* 1838. Magd. Coll. Oxf. Rector of Pylle, Somerset.

POSTLE, Edward, 1824, *b.* 1810. Trin. Coll. Cam. Rector of Colney, Norwich; deceased.

POUNSETT, William Felix, 1837-38. Army. 13th Regt. Infantry.

POVAH,* Francis Kohler, 1859. Son of Rev. J. V. Povah, Minor Canon of St. Paul's. *b.* 1849. Ch. Ch. Oxf. Curate of Alton, Hants.

POVAH,* John Richard, 1857-66. Brother of the above. *b.* 1847. Lieut. 1st (Royal) Infantry.

POWELL, Ernest Ormsby, 1875. Son of Rev. Isaac Ormsby Powell, Vicar of Whaddon, Herts. *b.* 1861.

POWELL, John James, 1821, *b.* 1809.

POWELL, Stratford Harley La Barte, 1864, *b.* 1849.

POWELL, Walter, 1819, *b.* 1806. Holy Orders.

POWER, Edward Henry, 1842-43, *b.* 1827. Lieut.-Col. Madras Staff Corps. Barrister-at-Law. Deputy Judge Advocate, Hyderabad district.

POWER,* Robert George, 1836-40, *b.* 1826. Tasmania.

POWLES, John Richard, 1826. Son of the late J. D. Powles, Governor of the Bank of England. *b.* 1812. Merchant in London; deceased.

POWYS,* Thomas Arthur, 1812. Son of Rev. Thomas Powys, Rector of Fawley. *b.* 1801. St. John's Coll. Oxf. Vicar of Medmenham, Bucks; deceased.

POYNDER, Charles Eliot, 1870. Son of Rev. Leopold Poynder, of Southsea. *b.* 1856. Adjutant 5th Madras Native Infantry.

POYNDER, Edmund Samuel, 1829. Son of Thomas Poynder, of Christ's Hospital. *b.* 1817. B.N.C. Oxf. Resided at Trench, near Tunbridge; died 1877.

POYNDER, Frederick, 1828. Son of John Poynder, of South Lambeth. *b.* 1816. Wadh. Coll. Oxf. Denyer Theol. Prizeman. Holy Orders. Master in the School 1838-72. Resides at Cheltenham.

POYNDER, George Frederick, 1863-70. Brother of Charles Eliot Poynder (above). *b.* 1851. Surgeon.

POYNDER, Thomas Henry Allen, 1825. Brother of Edmund Samuel Poynder (above). *b.* 1814. B.N.C. Oxf. Barrister. Resided at Hartham Park, Wilts; died 1873.

POYNDER, William, 1800-7. Son of Thomas Poynder, of Clapham Common. *b.* 1789. Trin. Coll. Oxf. Incumbent of Horne, Surrey; deceased.

PRANCE, William Connell, 1873. [Son of Courtenay Prance, of The Elms, Evesham]. St. John's Coll. Cam.

PRENDERGAST, William Grant, 1828, *b.* 1815. Trin. Coll. Cam. Lieut.-Col. 8th Bengal Cavalry. Died of cholera 1858.

PRESCOTT, Charles, 1813. Son of William Willoughby Prescott, Banker, of London. *b.* 1803. Died in India 1839.

PRESCOTT, Henry James, 1813. (Left the same year). Brother of the above. *b.* 1802. Went to Harrow School. Merchant. Governor of the Bank of England.

PRESCOTT, Richard, 1819. Brother of the above. *b.* 1807; died in India.

PRESCOTT, Thomas William Tottenham, 1815-18, *b.* 1805.

PRESSICK, John Robert Eden, 1823, *b.* 1812.

PRESTON, Henry Edmund, 1818, *b.* 1804. Queens Coll. Cam. Rector of Tasburgh, Norfolk.

PRESTON, James, 1817, *b.* 1804.

PRESTON, James Simons, 1814-16, *b.* 1800. Solicitor.

PRETYMAN, Henry George Middleton, 1828-35, *b.* 1817. Oriel Coll. Oxf. Holy Orders.

PRETYMAN, John Radcliffe, 1825, *b.* 1815. Trin. Coll. Cam. Vicar of Aylesbury.

PREVOST, William, 1807-13, *b.* 1796.

PRICE, John, 1809-11.

PRICE, John, 1821, *b.* 1808. Went to India.

PRICE, Stafford, 1817, *b.* 1805.

PRICE, William, 1808-9, *b.* 1797. Navy.

PRICHARD, Albert Hermann, 1846-49, *b.* 1831. Merton Coll. Oxf. Curate of Sevenoaks 1875-78.

PRIESTLEY, John Richard, 1811. Left the same year. *b.* 1801.

PRINSEP, Douglas Gordon, 1874. [Son of C. C. Prinsep, Assistant Secretary India Council]. R.M. Academy, Woolwich.

PRINSEP, Henry Stewart, 1877. Son of the late Lieut.-Col. Henry Auriol Prinsep, Bengal Staff Corps. *b.* 1863.

PRINSEP, James Frederick McLeod, 1874. Brother of the above. *b.* 1861.

PRINSEP, Reginald Seymour, 1875. Brother of the above.

PRIOR, Richard Chandler Alexander, 1822. (See Alexander).

PRITCHARD, Edward William, 1847-49, *b.* 1833.

PRITCHARD, Frederick, 1826, *b.* 1814; died 1837.

PRITCHARD, Walter, 1826, *b.* 1818. Emigrated to Australia.

PRITCHARD, William Amon Gee, 1826. Son of the late Rev. William Pritchard. *b.* 1812. St. John's Coll. Cam. Senr. Opt. Rector of Brignall, Yorks.

PRITCHETT, Charles, 1821. Son of Rev. Charles Richard Pritchett, formerly Reader at Charterhouse. *b.* 1811 ; died 1827.

PRITCHETT, George Edward, 1834-35. Brother of the above. *b.* 1824. Architect. F.S.A. Oak Hall, Bishop's Stortford.

PRITCHETT, Richard, 1824. Brother of the above. *b.* 1815 ; died 1831.

PRITCHETT, William Delabere, 1834. Brother of the above. *b.* 1822. Cath. Hall, Cam. Missionary in Syria.

PRITT,* Lonsdale, 1832-40, *b.* 1812. Trin. Coll. Cam. Archdeacon of Waikato, New Zealand.

PROBY, Charles, 1811-17, *b.* 1801.

PROBYN, Leslie, 1876. Son of Edmund Probyn, of Huntley Manor, Gloucester. *b.* 1862.

PROCTER, Robert, 1834-35.

PROTHERO, Thomas, 1823. Son of Thomas Prothero, Malpas Court, Monmouthsh. *b.* 1811. B.N.C. Oxf. Domestic Chaplain to the Prince Consort. Of Malpas Court. J.P. and D.L.; died 1870.

PROTHEROE, Mark Davis, 1827, *b.* 1813.

PROWER, John Elton Mervin, 1823-30. Son of Rev. J. M. Prower, Vicar of Purton. *b.* 1811. Wadh. Coll. Oxf. 67th Regt. Major Wilts Militia. Purton House, Wooton Bassett.

PUGET,* Peter, 1810-16, *b.* 1798. Pemb. Coll. Oxf.

PUGH, Brathwaite Sackville, 1866-69, *b.* 1850. St. John's Coll. Cam.

PURNELL, John James, 1829, *b.* 1815. Senior Surgeon of the Royal General Dispensary.

PURVIS, Arthur, 1826. Son of Col. Charles Purvis, of Darsham Hall, Suffolk. *b.* 1813. India Civil Service. Late of Darsham ; died 1877.

PURVIS, Charles Alexander, 1835-37. Brother of the above. *b.* 1819. Col. Madras Artillery.

PURVIS, George John, 1830-37. Brother of the above. *b.* 1816. Indian Army. Lieut. 39th Regt. Madras Native Infantry; deceased.

PYE,* Henry Anthony, 1810-17. Son of Rev. H. A. Pye, Vicar of Cirencester. *b.* 1799. Fellow of Magd. Coll. Oxf.; deceased.

PYM, Charles, 1809-11. Son of Francis Pym, M.P., of The Hasells, Beds. *b.* 1797. Trin. Coll. Cam. Of Hove, Sussex. Assumed the name of Reading; *d.* 1836.

PYM, Francis, 1802-6. Brother of the above. *b.* 1790. Trin. Coll. Cam. Of The Hasells, Beds. J.P. Killed in a railway accident 1860.

PYM, Robert, 1805-9. Brother of the above. *b.* 1793. Rector of Elmley, Yorks.; died 1861.

PYM, William Wollaston, 1804. Brother of the above. *b.* 1792. St. John's Coll. Cam. Vicar of Willian, Herts.

PYMAN, Arthur George, 1864. Left the same year. *b.* 1850; deceased.

PYMAN, Henry Samuel, 1864, *b.* 1848. Solicitor in London.

Q.

QUANTON, , 1803. Son of Mr. Quanton, of Hatton Garden.

QUARTLEY, William Bowdon, 1810-12, *b.* 1796.

R.

RADCLIFFE, Edmund Ford, 1826. Son of Rev. Edmund S. Radcliffe, of Watton le dale, near Preston. *b.* 1812. Indian Civil Service; died 1864.

RADCLIFFE, Robert Edmund Lowndes, 1878. Son of Major-General Robert Parker Radcliffe, R.A., Charlton, Kent. *b.* 1865.

RADFORD, Alexander William, 1830, *b.* 1816.

RAE, Amelius Isaac, 1848. Left the same year. *b.* 1834.

RAIKES, Henry St. John Digby, 1877. Son of Henry Cecil Raikes, of Llwynegrin Hall, Flintshire, M.P. for Chester. *b.* 1863.

RAIKES, Thomas Henry, 1821. Son of Thomas Raikes, of Sudbrook Park, Richmond. *b.* 1807. E. I. Civil Service. Judge. Retired. Resides at Clifton.

RAINE, David, 1806-12, *b.* 1797. Solicitor.

RAINE, Matthew, 1803-4, *b.* 1791.

RAINEY, Arthur Henry, 1873.

RAINEY, Robert Maximilian, 1873.

RAINIER, George, 1825. Son of Daniel Rainier, of Highbury, Middlesex. *b.* 1813. B.N.C. Oxf. Vicar of Ninfield, Sussex; died 1872.

RAINIER, John, 1825. Brother of the above. *b.* 1810. Capt. 98th Regt. H.M. Civil Commissioner at the Cape of Good Hope; died 1869.

RALPH, James, 1836-38, *b.* 1821. India.

RAM,* Stephen Adye Scott, 1878. Son of Stephen Adye Ram. 32, Oakley Square, N.W.

RAMSAY, Edward Plomar, 1818, *b.* 1804.

RAMSAY, James, 1826. Son of Andrew Ramsay. *b.* 1814. Lieut.-Col.; died 1878.

RAMSBOTHAM, Henry Lindsay, 1851-53, *b.* 1837. Indian Army; died 1861.

RAMSDEN, John George, 1828, *b.* 1814. M.A. of St. John's Coll. Cam.; deceased.

RAMSDEN, Richard, 1817, *b.* 1804.

RAMSDEN, Thomas, 1819, *b.* 1804. Holy Orders.

RAMSDEN, William, 1811, *b.* 1801. Ch. Coll. Cam. Rector of Linwood, Lincoln.

List of Carthusians.   193

RANDALL, William Ellis, 1842-45, b. 1828. Emigrated to Natal.

RANDALL, Francis Henry, 1872. Keble Coll. Oxf.

RANDOLPH, Algernon Forbes, 1877. Son of Rev. Edward John Randolph, Rector of Dunnington Yorks. b. 1865.

RANDOLPH,* Bernard Montgomery, 1844-52. Son of Rev. Thomas Randolph, Rector of Much Hadham, Herts. b. 1834. Orator. Ch. Ch. Oxf.; deceased.

RANDOLPH, Charles James, 1873. Brother of Algernon F. Randolph (above). Manor House, Newton Valence, Alton, Hants.

RANDOLPH, William Frederick Herbert, 1875. Brother of Algernon F. Randolph (above). b. 1862.

RANKEN, John Grant, 1801-8.

RAPER, Henry, 1810. Son of John Raper. Left the same year. b. 1799; died 1866.

RASHLEIGH, Carleton, 1865-69. Son of Rev. Henry Burvill Rashleigh, Vicar of Horton Kirby, Kent. b. 1851. Curate of Lighthorne, Warwickshire.

RASHLEIGH, Charles Edward, 1870. Son of Charles E. Rashleigh, of Farningham, Kent. b. 1856; died 1873.

RASHLEIGH,* George Burvill, 1861. Brother of Carleton Rashleigh (above). b. 1848. Ex. Coll. Oxf. 1st Class Math. Barrister. Principal Secretary to the Master of the Rolls.

RASHLEIGH, Henry George, 1873. Brother of Charles E. Rashleigh (above). b. 1858.

RAVENSHAW,* Edward Vincent, 1866-72. Son of G. V. Ravenshaw, of Mortlake. b. 1854. Tea Planter in India.

RAWLINS, Christopher, 1822, b. 1809. Oriel Coll. Oxf. Vicar of Allerthorpe, Yorks; deceased.

RAWLINSON (Sir) Christopher (Knt.), 1819. Son of John Rawlinson, of Alresford, Hants. b. 1806. Trin. Coll. Cam. Barrister. Chief Justice of Madras; resigned 1859.

RAWLINSON,* Edward Creswicke Scott, 1870. Son of Rev. George Rawlinson, Camden Professor of Ancient History at Oxford. b. 1859. Keble Coll. Oxf.

O

RAWLINSON, Henry, 1828. Brother of Sir Christopher Rawlinson (above). *b.* 1813. St. John's Coll. Oxf. Rector of Symondsbury, Dorset.

RAWLINSON, William Edward, 1819. Brother of the above. *b.* 1808. Indian Army. Capt. 2nd European Regt. Dep. Judge Advocate Genl. of Bombay Army; died 1850.

RAWSON, Cecil Frank, 1876. Son of J. Rawson, of Godalming.

RAWSON, Sidney George, 1876. Brother of the above.

RAYMOND, William Forbes, 1800-3. Sid. Suss. Coll. Cam. Archdeacon of Northumberland.

RAYNER, Arthur, 1876. Son of Roderick Rayner, of Hill Side, Wavertree, Liverpool. *b.* 1863.

RAYNER, Charles Joseph Lee, 1877. Son of Robert Lee Rayner, of Mirfield, Yorks. *b.* 1863.

RAYNER, Wilfred, 1878. Brother of the above. *b.* 1864.

READ, Henry, 1853-54, *b.* 1838.

READ, Henry George, 1871. Son of H. B. Read, Finsbury Square. *b.* 1860.

READ, Reginald Bligh, 1852-54, *b.* 1837.

READE, Alfred, 1823, *b.* 1812.

READE, Frederick, 1818, *b.* 1808. St. John's Coll. Cam. Incumbent of St. John the Baptist, Hove, Brighton.

READE, Frederick, 1850-53. Son of the above. *b.* 1834. 57th Regt. Bengal N.I.; died 1855.

READE,* Henry Jonathan, 1811-18. Son of John Reade, of Ipsden. *b.* 1801. Indian Cavalry. Killed in Action at Kolah 1821.

READE, Lewin, 1822, *b.* 1810. Sailor. H. E. I. C. Service.

REECE, Henry, 1874. 10, Ladbroke Square, W.

REES-MOGG. (See Mogg).

REEVE,* Charles Arthur, 1871. Son of Rev. J. W. Reeve, Canon of Bristol, &c. *b.* 1857. Trin. Coll. Cam.

REEVE, D'Arcy Wentworth, 1873. Son of J. Reeve, of Fernside, Wimbledon.

REEVE, Neville Henry, 1853-57. Son of Ellis Reeve. *b.* 1839. Oriel Coll. Oxf. Capt. 45th Regt. Abyssinian Medal.

REEVES, Edgar Lee, 1876. Son of H. W. Reeves, of Richmond.

REEVES, John Frederick, 1824. Son of John Fry Reeves, of Edgarley, Somerset. *b.* 1810.

REEVES, Thomas Porch, 1820. Brother of the above. *b.* 1808. Trin. Coll. Cam. Of Edgarley, Somerset. J.P. Assumed the name of Porch in 1830; died 1877.

REID, Andrew Gildart, 1826, *b.* 1814. Capt. 47th Bengal N.I.; *d.* 1876.

REID, David, 1818, *b.* 1807. Univ. Coll. Oxf. *[illegible]*

REID, George Alexander, 1805-10, *b.* 1794. Life Guards.

REID, Henry, 1818. Brother of David Reid (above). *b.* 1806. Trin. Coll. Cam. Holy Orders.

REID, Henry Solomon, 1803-5, *b.* 1792.

REID, Percy Frith, 1874. Son of L. R. Reid.

REID, Rawson Hart Boddam, 1826. Brother of A. G. Reid (above). Merchant in China; *d.* 1876.

RENAUD, Godfrey Marshall, 1869, *b.* 1858.

RENDALL, John, 1833-34, *b.* 1818. Ball. Coll. and Fellow of Ex. Coll. Oxf. Holy Orders; *d.*

RENNY, William, 1827, *b.* 1814. Queens Coll. Cam. Emigrated to Canada.

REYNARDSON, Charles Thomas Samuel Birch, 1823. Eldest son of General Thomas Birch-Reynardson, of Holywell Hall, Lincolnshire. *b.* 1810. Went to Eton. Trin. Coll. Cam. High Sheriff of Lincolnshire 1859.

REYNARDSON,* John Birch, 1827. Brother of the above. *b.* 1816. C. C. Coll. Cam. Rector of Careby, Lincolnshire.

REYNOLDS, Richard Anthony, 1820, *b.* 1807. 11th Hussars; deceased.

REYNOLDS,* Thomas, 1811-15, *b.* 1798.

RHODES, Abraham, 1845-47, *b.* 1831.

RICARDO, David, 1812-15. Son of David Ricardo, M.P. for Portarlington. *b.* 1803. Trin. Coll. Cam. M.P. 1832-3. Gatcombe Park, Gloucester; died 1864.

RICARDO, Mortimer, 1815. Brother of the above. *b.* 1807. Went to Eton. Life Guards; deceased.

RICARDO, Osman, 1805. Brother of the above. *b.* 1795. Trin. Coll. Cam. M.P. for Worcester 1847-65. Bromesberrow Place, Worcestershire.

RICE, Howard, 1815-18. Son of Rev. Edward John Howard Rice, D.C.L., Rector of St. Luke's, Old Street, London. *b.* 1803. Royal Navy. Afterwards in the 44th Bengal Native Infantry; died 1859.

RICHARDS, Alfred Bates, 1829, *b.* 1820. Capt. in the Army. Editor of *The Morning Advertiser;* deceased.

RICHARDS, Edward Harrison, 1860-63, *b.* 1850.

RICHARDS, Fowell Charles Buxton, 1864, *b.* 1853.

RICHARDS, George, 1821, *b.* 1811.

RICHARDS, Henry, 1820, *b.* 1808.

RICHARDS, Lewis Matthew, 1875. Son of Richard Richards, of Swansea. *b.* 1861.

RICHARDSON, Charles George, 1820. 2nd son of Sir John Richardson. *b.* 1810. Barrister; died about 1843.

RICHARDSON, John, 1823, *b.* 1812.

RICHARDSON, Marmaduke Nelson, 1843-45. Son of William Richardson, Solicitor, of York. *b.* 1829. Late of the 83rd Regt. Now in Australia.

RICHARDSON, William, 1824, *b.* 1810. *b/th of C.G.R. dead*

RICHARDSON, William Benson, 1841-45. Brother of Marmaduke Nelson Richardson (above). *b.* 1827. Univ. Coll. Oxf. Hon. 4th Class. Solicitor at York.

RICHMOND, Harry Inglis, 1862-8. Son of George Richmond, R.A. *b.* 1849. Ball. Coll. Oxf. Barrister.

RICHMOND, John, 1867. Brother of the above. *b.* 1854. Medical Student.

RICHMOND, Thomas Knyvett, 1845-52. Brother of the above. *b.* 1833. Ex. Coll. Oxf. Vicar of Crosthwaite, Keswick. Chaplain to the Bishop of Carlisle.

RICHMOND,* Walter Coleridge, 1865. Brother of the above. *b.* 1852. Cirencester College. Agent to Lord de Tabley.

RICKARDS, Arthur Benjamin, 1871. Son of William Henry Rickards, of Whalley Grange, Manchester. *b.* 1856. Solicitor.

RICKETTS,* Dashwood Poyntz, 1870. Son of D. W. Ricketts (below). *b.* 1859.

RICKETTS, Dashwood Watts, 1815, *b.* 1804. Secretary of Council, Mauritius. Resides at Leamington.

RICKETTS, Poyntz, 1815-18. Brother of the above. *b.* 1803. E. I. Civil Service, Bombay; died 1825.

RIDGEWAY, William Henry, 1851-55. Son of Rev. J. Ridgeway, Vicar of Tunbridge Wells. *b.* 1836. Hertford Coll. Oxf. Hon. 4th Class Lit. Hum. Rector of Sternfield, Saxmundham.

RIDLEY, Frank Colborne, 1878. Son of Rev. Oliver Matthew Ridley, Rector of Bishopstone, Hereford. *b.* 1864.

RIDSDALE,* George John, 1839-44. Son of Rev. Robert Ridsdale, of Tillington. *b.* 1827. Clare Hall, Cam. Vicar of South Raynham, Norfolk.

RIGGE, Henry Fletcher, 1823. Son of Gray Rigge, of Wood Broughton. *b.* 1809. C. C. C. Cam. Formerly Capt. 2nd Lancashire Militia. Of Wood Broughton, Lancashire. J.P. and D.L. High Sheriff 1870.

RILEY, Henry Thomas, 1832-34. Trin. Coll. Cam. Barrister. Author of a " Dictionary of Latin Quotations."

RITCHIE, Arthur Sydney McDonald, 1868, *b.* 1858.

RIVINGTON, Horace Mylne, 1862-63. Son of the late Charles Rivington, of Kensington Park Gardens. *b.* 1848; died 1870.

ROBARTS, Nathaniel, 1828, *b.* 1816.

ROBERTS,* Alfred Temple, 1870. Son of Josiah Roberts, of Cheltenham. *b.* 1857. Demy of Magd. Coll. Oxf. 1st Class Mods. Gaisford Prizeman.

ROBERTS, Charles Henry, 1808-12, *b.* 1797.   Merchant.

ROBERTS, Edward Stokes, 1854-55.   Son of the late Edward Stokes Roberts. *b.* 1838 ; deceased.

ROBERTS, Henniker Peregrine, 1816, *b.* 1803.   Magd. Coll. Cambridge.

ROBERTS, Rowland Bennett, 1853-59, *b.* 1840.   Oriel Coll. Oxford.

ROBERTS, Walter, 1875.   Son of J. Roberts, of Clapham Common.

ROBERTS, William Prowding, 1820, *b.* 1805.

ROBERTSON, Ebenezer, 1809-11, *b.* 1794.   Trin. Coll. Cam. Vicar of Mottiston, Isle of Wight.

ROBERTSON, Edmund Murray, 1876.   Son of the late Edmund R. Robertson, of Hook House, Winchfield. *b.* 1862.

ROBERTSON, John, 1807-11, *b.* 1797.

ROBERTSON, Robert Dunbar, 1811-15, *b.* 1800.

ROBINS, Sanderson, 1816, *b.* 1801.   Ex. Coll. Oxf.   2nd Class Lit. Hum.   Rector of Shaftesbury.

ROBINSON,   , 1803.

ROBINSON, Arthur Hildyard, 1875.   Son of J. H. Robinson, Clerk in the House of Lords.

ROBINSON, Charles James, 1836.   (See Robinson-Dawson).

ROBINSON,* Edward, 1818, *b.* 1807.

ROBINSON, George Augustus, 1841-48, *b.* 1830 ; died 1851.

ROBINSON, Henry Marks, 1875.   Brother of Arthur Hildyard Robinson (above).

ROBINSON, John, 1812, *b.* 1803.

ROBINSON, John Travers, 1820, *b.* 1807.   Jes. Coll. Cam. Rector of St. Andrew's, Holborn ; *d.* 1851.

ROBINSON, John William, 1844-46.   Son of the late Rev. John T. Robinson, Rector of S. Andrew's, Holborn. *b.* 1832. Trin. Coll. Dublin.   Vicar of North Petherton, Somerset.

ROBINSON, William, 1812, *b.* 1801.   Ball. Coll. Oxf.   D.C.L. Doctors' Commons.

ROBINSON, William, 1813-17, *b.* 1802.

ROBINSON,* William Le Fleming, 1843-48. Son of Rev. William Scott Robinson, Rector of Dyrham, Gloucestershire. *b.* 1830. E. I. Civil Service, Bengal, where he held high executive office. Retired 1878.

ROBINSON-DAWSON, Charles James, 1836-42, *b.* 1824. Scholar of Queens Coll. Oxf. Barrister, Melbourne, Australia; died 1870.

RODEWALD,* Alfred Edward, 1875. Son of C. Ferdinand Rodewald, 57, Onslow Square, Brompton. *b.* 1862.

RODGERS, Alfred, 1825, *b.* 1812. Solicitor.

RODGERS, Charles Eboral, 1819, *b.* 1808. Trin. Coll. Cam. Vicar of Harworth, Notts; died 1868.

RODICK, Septimus, 1820. Of Northampton, *b.* 1808. Surgeon at Halstead.

RODWELL, Benjamin Bridges Hunter, 1827-31. Son of late William Rodwell, of Woodlands, Ipswich. *b.* 1815. Trin. Coll. Cam. Barrister. Q.C. Bencher of the Middle Temple. M.P. for Cambridgeshire 1874.

RODWELL, Edgar Kedington, 1837-39. Brother of the above. *b.* 1823. Solicitor at Ipswich.

RODWELL, Hasell, 1841-42. Brother of the above. *b.* 1826. Banker at Ipswich.

RODWELL, John Bramston, 1874. Son of the following. *b.* 1861.

RODWELL, Robert Mandeville, 1837. Son of William Rodwell, of Woodlands, Ipswich. *b.* 1821. Ex. Coll. Oxf. Rector of High Laver, Essex.

RODWELL, William, 1853-58. *b.* 1845.

ROE, Charles, 1822, *b.* 1809. Trin. Coll. Cam. Rector of Little Welnetham, Suffolk.

ROE, William, 1822, *b.* 1811.

ROE, William Gason Hamilton John, 1842-46. Son of George Hamilton Roe, M.D. *b.* 1827. Pemb. Coll. Oxf. M.B.

ROKEBY, Henry Langham, 1875. Son of Rev. H. R. Rokeby, of Arthingworth, Northants. *b.* 1861. R.M. Coll. Sandhurst.

ROKEBY, Ralph Thomas, 1876. Brother of the above. *b.* 1863.

ROLFE, George Crabb, 1824. Son of Thomas Rolfe, of Rayne, Braintree, Essex. *b.* 1811. Scholar of St. John's Coll. Cam. Wrangler. Vicar of Hailey, Oxon.

ROMAINE, William Colin Campbell, 1874. Son of William Govett Romaine, C.B., of Old Windsor. *b.* 1861.

ROOKE,* George, 1807-12, *b.* 1796. Mert. Coll. Oxf. Vicar of Embleton, Northumberland.

ROOKE, Leonard, 1806-8, *b.* 1794. Navy.

ROOPER, John, 1821. Son of the late Rev. Thomas Richard Rooper, of Wick Hill, Brighton, Rector of Abbots Ripton, Hunts. *b.* 1809. Captain Rifle Brigade. Retired. Resides at Leamington.

ROOPER, William Henry, 1820. Brother of the above. *b.* 1808. Univ. Coll. Oxf. Of Hockliffe Pastures, Beds. Formerly Rector of Abbots Ripton, Hunts. Resides at Ouseley Lodge, Old Windsor.

ROPER, Charles, 1826, *b.* 1814.

ROPER, William, 1826, *b.* 1811.

ROPER, William John Duff, 1843-46, *b.* 1830. Linc. Coll. Oxf. Author of Chronicles of Charterhouse.

ROSE,* Conway Lucas, 1828. Son of the late William Rose Rose, of Wolston Heath, near Rugby. *b.* 1817. Trin. Coll. Cam. Furnham House, Chard, Somerset.

ROSE, Herbert, 1875. Son of the above. *b.* 1862.

ROSE, William, 1820, *b.* 1810. Indian Army; deceased.

ROSE, William George, 1821. Brother of Conway Lucas Rose (above). *b.* 1813. Ch. Ch. Oxf. 60th Rifles.

ROSS, Edward George William, 1818, *b.* 1803.

ROTHERHAM, Kenneth, 1875. Son of Alexander Rotherham, of Coventry. *b.* 1863.

ROTHERHAM, Richard Alexander, 1878. Brother of the above. *b.* 1865.

ROUND, Edward John, 1820. Son of George Round, of Colchester. *b.* 1806. Resides at Geneva.

List of Carthusians. 201

ROUND, Henry Lewis, 1844-45. Son of the late Rev. Joseph Green Round, Rector of Woodham Mortimer, Essex. *b.* 1830. Capt. Royal Navy. Assumed the name of Turner in addition to that of Round in 1871.

ROUNDELL, Henry, 1836-42. Son of the following. *b.* 1824. Ch. Ch. Oxf. Vicar of Buckingham; deceased.

ROUNDELL, Henry Dawson, 1801-4. Son of Rev. Richard Roundell, of Gledstone. *b.* 1785. B.N.C. and Fellow of Magd. Coll. Oxf. Rector of Fringford, Oxon; deceased.

ROUNDELL, Savile Richardson, 1801-7. Brother of the above. *b.* 1789. Manager of the Branch Bank of England at Manchester; deceased.

ROUPELL, John Stuart, 1822, *b.* 1807. Fellow of Trin. Hall, Cam. B.C.L. Conveyancer.

ROUQUETTE, Louis, 1870-71. Son of Henry Philip Rouquette, of Walthamstow, Essex. *b.* 1857. Merchant in New Orleans.

ROUS, Hon. Thomas Manners, 1823. Son of the 6th Earl of Stradbroke. *b.* 1810. Ball. Coll. Oxf. Holy Orders; died 1841.

ROUTH, Edward, 1822, *b.* 1810.

ROUTH, James, 1826, *b.* 1816.

ROUTH, Randolph Henry Felix, 1876. Son of C. H. F. Routh, M.D. *b.* 1862.

ROUTH, William de Hague, 1822, *b.* 1811. E. India Co's. Service, Bengal.

ROWLATT, John Henry, 1815. Son of the late William Henry Rowlatt. *b.* 1803. St. John's Coll. Cam. Formerly Librarian and Assistant Reader of the Middle Temple.

ROWLATT, William, 1818. Brother of the above. *b.* 1808. Captain Royal Navy; deceased.

ROWSELL, Philip, 1862-64, *b.* 1850. Merchant Service.

ROXBURGH, Bruce, 1811-12, *b.* 1797. India.

ROXBURGH, Robert, 1811. Left the same year. *b.* 1796. India.

RUCKER, Henry, 1826. Son of S. Rucker, of West Hill, Wandsworth. *b.* 1812. Colonial Brother.

RUCKER, Sigismond, 1823. Brother of the above. *b.* 1810. Merchant; died 1875.

RUDDLE, Francis, 1819, *b.* 1806.

RUGG, Charles, 1844-46, *b.* 1831.

RUMBOLD (Sir) Cavendish Stuart (Bart.), 1826. Son of Sir William Rumbold, Bart. *b.* 1815; died 1853.

RUSH,* Henry, 1824, *b.* 1813. Solicitor; drowned 1839.

RUSHBROOKE, Robert Frederick Brownlow, 1825. Eldest son of Col. Robert Rushbrooke, M.P., of Rushbrooke Hall, Suffolk. *b.* 1814. Major Scots Fusilier Guards; died 1870.

RUSHBROOKE, William Henry, 1825. Brother of the above. *b.* 1815. Commander R.N.

RUSSELL, Alfred Francis, 1865. Son of Francis Russell, of Wateringbury (below). *b.* 1851. Univ. Coll. Oxf. Rector of Chingford, Essex.

RUSSELL, Francis, 1803. Holy Orders.

RUSSELL, Francis, 1824. Son of the late Rev. Dr. Russell, Head Master of Charterhouse. *b.* 1815. Trin. Coll. Cam. 2nd Class Math. Barrister. Recorder of Tenterden. Resides at Wateringbury, Kent.

RUSSELL, Frank, 1863. Left the same year. *b.* 1848.

RUSSELL,* John, 1823-30. Eldest son of Rev. Dr. Russell, the Head Master. *b.* 1814. Orator. Ch. Ch. Oxf.; died 1836.

RUSSELL, John Montague, 1864, *b.* 1849. Lieut. 17th Lancers.

RUSSELL, Sydenham Francis, 1835-39. St. John's Coll. Cam. Rector of Isfield, Sussex.

RUSSELL, Walter, 1872. Son of Francis Russell, of Wateringbury (above). *b.* 1859. Lieut. Royal Engineers.

RUSSELL, William, 1802-4. Son of Rev. John Russell, Rector of Helmdon, Northants. *b.* 1787. Fellow of Magd. Coll. Oxf. Double 2nd Class. B.D.; deceased.

RUSSELL, William, 1824. Son of Rev. Dr. Russell, the Head Master. *b.* 1817. Ch. Ch. Oxf. Rector of Aber Edw, and Llanvareth, Wales.

RUTTER, Hugh Campbell, 1875. Son of Isaac Campbell Rutter, of Hazlewood, Surrey.

RUTTER, Leonard Campbell, 1876. Brother of the above. *b.* 1863.

RUTTON, Henry Loftie, 1811-18, *b.* 1800. Solicitor.

RYDER, Arthur Dudley, 1821. Son of Hon. Henry Ryder, M.A., Bishop of Lichfield. *b.* 1811.

RYDER,* Charles Frederick, 1841-45. Son of Rev. Henry Dudley Ryder, Canon of Lichfield. *b.* 1851. Royal Navy.

RYDER, Hon. Frederick Dudley, 1821. Son of 2nd Earl of Harrowby. *b.* 1806. Trin. Coll. Cam. Foreign Office.

RYDER, Henry Dudley, 1845-52. Brother of C. F. Ryder (above). *b.* 1833. Scholar of Wadh. Coll. Oxf.

RYDER,* Spencer Charles Dudley, 1837-43. Brother of A. D. Ryder (above). *b.* 1825. 14th Bengal N. Infantry.

RYDER,* Thomas Richard, 1805-12, *b.* 1794. Pemb. Coll. Oxf. Vicar of Ecclesfield, Yorks.; died 1839.

RYLANDS, Louis Gordon, 1876. Son of Peter Rylands, M.P. for Burnley, of Massey Hall, Chester. *b.* 1862.

S.

SADLER, Ashton Christopher William, 1846-49. Son of William Stebbing Sadler, of Great Horkesley. *b.* 1833.

SADLER, Robert Stebbing, 1848-50. Brother of the above. *b.* 1839. Old House, Great Horkesley, Essex.

SAINTSBURY, Francis Edward, 1822. Son of John Saintsbury, Merchant of London. *b.* 1811. Royal Navy; died in 1829, after gallant service in H.M.S. Glasgow, off the coast of Africa.

SAINTSBURY,* George, 1810. Brother of the above. *b.* 1796. Assisted Dr. Valpy in editing the Delphin Classics. Afterwards Secretary to the Southampton Docks; died 1860.

SALISBURY, Nicholas Richard, 1811, *b.* 1797. Merchant of Liverpool.

SALMON, Charles Edward, 1878. Son of Capt. Salmon, late 60th Rifles. *b.* 1864.

SALMON, William Henry, 1875. Brother of the above. *b.* 1862.

SALMOND, Charles Francis, 1821. Son of Francis Salmond, Master-Attendant, Fort Marlbro', Sumatra. *b.* 1809. Indian Service ; died 1827.

SALMOND, James William, 1821. Brother of the above. *b.* 1807; died 1847.

SALTMARSHE, Ernest, 1874. Son of Philip Saltmarshe, of Saltmarshe, Yorks. *b.* 1859.

SALTWELL, Charles Herbert Caley, 1875. Son of William Henry Saltwell, of Lincoln's Inn. *b.* 1860. Articled to a Solicitor.

SAMLER, Frederick, 1822. Son of William Samler, of Blackheath. *b.* 1810. Major in the Indian Army ; deceased.

SAMLER, John Harman, 1822. Son of Richard Samler, of Wandsworth. *b.* 1809. Pemb. Coll. Oxf. For 32 years Vicar of Swallowcliffe, near Salisbury ; died 1877.

SAMS, Charles Hamilton, 1851-55. Son of Charles Hewit Sams, of Blackheath. *b.* 1839. Major 64th Regt.

SAMS, John Sutton, 1850-54. Brother of the above. *b.* 1836. Medical Practitioner at Lee, Kent.

SAMSON, Frederick Charles, 1828. Of Tooting, Surrey. *b.* 1819.

SAMSON, George Wood, 1844-48, *b.* 1830. Caius Coll. Cam. ; died 1856.

SANDARS, George Edward, 1875. Son of J. E. Sandars, of Gainsborough.

SANDERS, Arthur Andrew, 1876. Son of Rev. Lloyd Sanders, Rector of Whimple, Devon. *b.* 1863.

SANDERS, Evelyn Francis, 1877. Son of Thomas Sanders, LL.D., of Sanders Park, Charleville, Co. Cork. *b.* 1864.

SANDHAM, Henry, 1847-49. Son of the late Lt.-Genl. Henry Sandham, R.E. *b.* 1832. Keeper of the Civil Engineering Collection, Science and Art Department, South Kensington Museum.

SANDWITH, Fleming Mant, 1866, *b.* 1853. Surgeon. Served in the Russo-Turkish War 1877-78. Medal and Order of the Medjidié, and Gold Cross of Servia.

SANDYS, Henry Jervis, 1877. Son of H. Sandys, of Enniskerry, Co. Wicklow. *b.* 1863.

SANSOM,* John, 1823, *b.* 1812. Queens Coll. Oxf. Rector of Bushingworth and Faldingworth, Lincoln.

SANT, James William, 1876. Son of James William Sant, R.A., Principal Painter in Ordinary to the Queen. *b.* 1862.

SAPTE, Harry Gifford, 1874. Son of Rev. Canon Sapte, Rector of Cranleigh, Surrey. *b.* 1862.

SARGEAUNT, Charles, 1815. Son of John Sargeaunt, of Coleshill, Herts. *b.* 1806. B.N.C. Oxf. No Profession.

SARGEAUNT, Edward Woodbine, 1873. Son of William Charles Sargeaunt (below). *b.* 1860. In the Office of the Crown Agents for the Colonies.

SARGEAUNT, James, 1815. Brother of Charles Sargeaunt (above). *b.* 1805. Capt. 13th Dragoons; died 1852.

SARGEAUNT, James Primatt, 1840-44. Son of Rev. John Sargeaunt (below). *b.* 1831. Jesus Coll. Cam. Of Tewkesbury Park, Gloucester. Formerly Inspector of Military Schools.

SARGEAUNT, John, 1812-17. Brother of James Sargeaunt (above). *b.* 1799. Ch. Ch. Oxf. Rector of Stanwick, Northants; *d.*

SARGEAUNT, John Barmby, 1837-41. Eldest son of the above. *b.* 1823. St. John's Coll. Cam. Barrister. Resides at Bedford.

SARGEAUNT,* Richard Arthur, 1851-58. Son of Rev. John Sargeaunt (above). *b.* 1840. Capt. Royal Engineers.

SARGEAUNT, William Charles (C.M.G.), 1840-47. Brother of the above. *b.* 1829. Colonial Secretary at Natal. Crown Agent for the British Colonies.

SARGEAUNT, William John, 1858-59. Son of Charles Sargeaunt (above). *b.* 1843. Clerk in the Admiralty Office.

SAUNDERS, Alexander Octavius, 1818. Son of the late Robert Saunders. *b.* 1807. Commissariat; died in Mauritius 1836.

SAUNDERS, Alexander William Fleck, 1847-53. Son of the above. *b.* 1837. Emigrated to Australia.

SAUNDERS, Alfred Robert Henry, 1867-71. Son of Augustus Page Saunders, D.D. (below). *b.* 1853. Univ. Coll. Oxf. Solicitor.

SAUNDERS,* Arthur Morrell, 1850-57. Son of the late Charles Alexander Saunders, Secretary to the Great Western Railway. *b.* 1839. Agent of the Madras Railway Company.

SAUNDERS, Arthur William, 1847-53. Son of the late Robert John Saunders, of Eltham, Kent. *b.* 1835. Scholar of B.N.C. Oxf.; died 1854.

SAUNDERS, Augustus Nicholson, 1837. Brother of the above. *b.* 1826. Died at Charterhouse 1838.

SAUNDERS, Augustus Page, 1817. Son of the late Robert Saunders. *b.* 1801. Student of Ch. Ch. Oxf. Double 1st Class. Head Master of Charterhouse. Dean of Peterborough 1833; died 1878.

SAUNDERS,* Cecil Ernest Brassey Pigou, 1869. Son of the late James Fergusson Saunders. *b.* 1859. Now in Madras.

SAUNDERS, Edward Augustus, 1837-41. Brother of the above. *b.* 1825. Madras N. Infantry. Major-General retired. Served in the Indian Mutiny.

SAUNDERS, Edward William, 1847-49. Son of the late John James Saunders (below). *b.* 1836. Major 14th Regiment. Crimean Medal and Clasp. Maori Medal.

SAUNDERS, Frederick William, 1859-62. Son of the late William Septimus Saunders (below). *b.* 1844. Late Capt. 7th Fusiliers; retired.

SAUNDERS, George Nicholson, 1843-52. Brother of Arthur William Saunders (above). *b.* 1833. Major 3rd Punjab N. Infantry; died at Mooltan 1876.

SAUNDERS, George Robert, 1847-48. Son of the late Capt. William Saunders, R.A. *b.* 1836. Capt. Rifle Brigade; deceased.

SAUNDERS, Harry Cecil, 1839-47. Son of the late Charles Alexander Saunders. *b.* 1829. E. I. Civil Service; died in Ceylon 1854.

SAUNDERS, Henry George, 1848-50. Brother of Edward William Saunders (above). *b.* 1830. Major Bengal Staff Corps. Served in the Indian Mutiny Campaign. Medal.

SAUNDERS, Henry Robe, 1839-43. Son of the late Robert John Saunders. *b.* 1829. Capt. Royal Artillery; died 1857.

SAUNDERS,* Herbert Clifford, 1844-52. Son of the late Charles Alexander Saunders, Sec. Gt. Western Railway. *b.* 1834. Ch. Ch. Oxf. 2nd Class Moderations and Lit. Hum. Barrister.

SAUNDERS, Hugh Ward, 1842-45. Son of the late Robert Saunders. *b.* 1828. Captain 7th Bengal Light Cavalry; deceased.

SAUNDERS, James, 1832-33. Son of the late James Fergusson Saunders. *b.* 1818. Natal.

SAUNDERS, John Boyd, 1842-47. Son of the late John James Saunders (below). *b.* 1830. Lieut.-Col. 9th Bengal Cavalry.

SAUNDERS, John James, 1806-9. Son of the late William Saunders, M.D. *b.* 1794. Merchant at Leghorn; deceased.

SAUNDERS,* Leslie Seymour, 1847-53. Brother of Herbert Clifford Saunders (above). *b.* 1837. E. I. Civil Service. Commissioner at Ajmeer.

SAUNDERS,* Montague Stuart, 1851-58. Brother of the above. *b.* 1840. Late Capt. 20th Hussars. Madras.

SAUNDERS, Oliver Augustus, 1857-62. Son of Augustus Page Saunders, D.D. (above). *b.* 1844. Trin. Coll. Cam. Wrangler 1866. Barrister.

SAUNDERS, Reginald Floyer, 1842-48. Son of the late Charles Alexander Saunders. *b.* 1831. E. I. Civil Service. Judge.

SAUNDERS, Robert, 1806-7. Son of the late William Saunders, M.D. *b.* 1792. E. I. Civil Service, Bengal; deceased.

SAUNDERS, Robert Power, 1851-54. Son of the following. *b.* 1839. Capt. Royal Artillery; died 1871.

SAUNDERS, William Septimus, 1818. Brother of Augustus Page Saunders, D.D. (above). *b.* 1803. Merchant in Mauritius; died 1850.

SAVILL-ONLEY, Onley Harvey, 1806-13. Son of Charles Harvey, who assumed the names of Savill-Onley. *b.* 1795. Caius Coll. and Pemb. Hall, Cam. Senr. Opt. Barrister of the Middle Temple. Recorder of Norwich. Stisted Hall, Essex.

SAYER, Edward Lane, 1814. Son of Henry Jenkinson Sayer, Solicitor. *b.* 1806. St. John's Coll. Cam. Vicar of Pulloxhill, Beds. Died at Thames Ditton 1868.

SCHMITZ,* Charles Alfred, 1871. Son of Leonard Schmitz, LL.D. *b.* 1856. Died 1878.

SCHNELL, Frank Macdonald, 1822, *b.* 1811.

SCHRODER, Edward, 1825, *b.* 1811. Special Pleader, Ohio, U.S.A.

SCHRODER, George, 1825, *b.* 1813. Architect at Adelaide, South Australia.

SCHRODER, Herman, 1811-15, *b.* 1800.

SCHRODER, James Peacock, 1814-15, *b.* 1802.

SCOTT, Charles, 1819, *b.* 1803. St. John's Coll. Cam. A.B. 1825.

SCOTT,* Charles Perry, 1857. Son of Rev. J. Scott, of Hull. *b.* 1847. Jesus Coll. Cam. Missionary in China.

SCOTT, George, 1821, *b.* 1807. India.

SCOTT, Herbert Thomas, 1855-60, *b.* 1844.

SCOTT, John, 1813-14, *b.* 1799.

SCOTT, John, 1826, *b.* 1812.

SCOTT, John Anthony, 1828, *b.* 1816; died 1864.

SCOTT, Patrick, 1821, *b.* 1803. E. I. Civil Service.

SCOTT, Patrick William Evelyn, 1874.

SCOTT, Richard Curtis Folliott, 1874. Son of Rev. R. F. Scott, Vicar of Arlesey, Beds. *b.* 1860. Trin. Coll. Cam.

SCOTT, Septimus, 1822. *b.* 1810. India.

SCOTT, Stanley Herbert, 1878. Son of John Thomas Scott. *b.* 1866.

SCOTT, Thomas, 1821, *b.* 1809. Of Tunbridge Wells.

SCOTT,* Thomas Brand Graham, 1818, *b.* 1808. Wine Merchant and Consul at Bordeaux.

SCOVELL, Charles, 1827, *b.* 1812 ; died 1831.

SCRATCHLEY, Charles James, 1824, *b.* 1814. Gold Medal. Scholar of Queens Coll. Cam. and B.N.C. Oxf. 3rd Class Lit. Hum. Rector of Lydeard, St. Lawrence, near Taunton.

SCRATTON, Alfred, 1876. Son of John Scratton, of Cobham, Kent. *b.* 1856.

SCRATTON, John, 1870. Brother of the above. *b.* 1863. Practical Engineer.

SCRIVEN, Alexander, 1815, *b.* 1804.

SCRIVEN, John, 1816-18, *b.* 1808. Lieut.-Col. of the 4th Royal Middlesex Militia ; died 1878.

SEARLE, Frederick Charles, 1872. Son of F. A. Searle. *b.* 1859. Scholar of Pemb. Coll. Cam.

SEARLE, George William Von Uslar, 1873. Son of the late James Searle. *b.* 1860. Exhibitioner and Scholar of King's Coll. Cam.

SECHIARI, George Parasqueva, 1878. Son of Parasqueva George Sechiari, of the Poplars, Edgeware. *b.* 1864.

SECKHAM, Bassett Thorne, 1876. Son of Samuel Lipscomb Seckham, of Hanch Hall, Lichfield. *b.* 1863.

SELWYN,* Henry Charles, 1801, *b.* 1789. Royal Artillery.

SENIOR, , 1803.

SENIOR, , 1803.

SENIOR, William, 1819, *b.* 1805.

SENTANCE, William Valentine, 1868-72.

SERLE, William Ambrose, 1825, *b.* 1812.

SEWELL, Ernest Brooke, 1878. Son of F. N. Sewell, Elmhurst, Upton, Essex. *b.* 1864.

SEWELL, John Brodie, 1848-53. Son of John Sewell, of Fortis Green, Finsbury. *b.* 1839. Partner in the firm of Sewell and Son, Builders and Contractors ; *d.* 1878.

P

SEYMOUR* (Lord) Albert Charles, 1857-65. Son of the Marquess of Hertford. *b.* 1847. Ch. Ch. Oxf. Capt. Scots Fusilier Guards.

SEYMOUR,* Albert Eden, 1853-60. Son of Richard Seymour (below). *b.* 1841. Prize Scholar. Orator. Univ. Coll. Oxf. Vicar of Barnstaple.

SEYMOUR, John Le Marchant, 1858-62. Brother of the above. *b.* 1845. Army. Killed in India 1866.

SEYMOUR,* Richard, 1817. Son of Admiral Sir Michael Seymour, K.C.B. *b.* 1806. Student of Ch. Ch. Oxf. Canon Res. of Worcester. Formerly Rector of Kinwarton.

SEYMOUR, Richard Arthur, 1855-61. Son of the above. *b.* 1843. Univ. Coll. Oxf.

SEYMOUR, Thos. Conway Waith, 1806-8. Emm. Coll. Cam.

SEYMOUR, Walter Richard, 1853-58. Brother of A. E. Seymour (above). *b.* 1838. Ch. Ch. Oxf. Admiralty.

SHACKELL, Francis Bayley, 1849-53, *b.* 1834. Scholar of Oriel Coll. Oxf. 1st Class Mods. 2nd Class Lit. Hum. Holy Orders; *d.* 1861.

SHACKELL, Henry William, 1848-52, *b.* 1832. Scholar and Fellow Pemb. Coll. Cam. 10th Wrangler, 2nd Class. Classical Tripos. Missionary in India.

SHAKESPEAR, John Arthur, 1835-38. Son of Rev. J. M. Shakespear, Vicar of Frodsham, Cheshire. *b.* 1820. Trin. Coll. Cam. No Profession.

SHAKESPEAR (Sir) Richmond Campbell, 1823. Son of John Talbot Shakespear, of the Bengal Civil Service. *b.* 1811. General, Bengal Artillery; *d.* 1861 at Indore.

SHAKESPEARE, George Trant, 1823, *b.* 1809. Indian Artillery.

SHARP, Alban Henry, 1874. Son of Martin Sharp, 3, North Grove, Highgate.

SHARP, Charles, 1873. Son of Samuel Sharp, of Chilworth, Surrey. *b.* 1860. Architect.

SHARP, Henry, 1837-38. Provost-Marshall, Granada, W. Indies.

SHARPLES, Edward, 1838-40, *b.* 1825.

SHAW, Henry, 1802-4.

SHAW, JAMES, 1802-5.

SHAW, John Wyburgh, 1802-4.

SHAW, Robert, 1827, *b.* 1814.

SHEARS, Edmund Augustus, 1871. Son of Wm. Shears, of The Limes, Clapham Common.

SHEARS, James Charles, 1871. Brother of the above.

SHEARS, William, 1869-71, *b.* 1855.

SHEE, Benjamin Basil, 1812-14, *b.* 1803.

SHELLEY, Edward Adolphus, 1820. Son of Sir John Shelley, Bart. *b.* 1812; died 1854.

SHELLEY (Sir) John Villiers (Bart.), 1819. Brother of the above. *b.* 1808. M.P. for Westminster 1852-55; died 1867. Of Maresfield Park, Sussex.

SHEPHERD, Charles William, 1853-56, *b.* 1838. Trin. Coll. Cam. Rector of Trotterscliffe, Kent.

SHEPPARD, Shearman, 1836-40, *b.* 1825. Solicitor.

SHEPPARD,* William Fleetwood, 1875. Son of Edmund Sheppard, Judge in Queensland, Australia. *b.* 1863.

SHERARD, Philip Castell (Lord Sherard), 1815-16. Son of Rev. P. C. Castell Sherard. *b.* 1804. Glatton Hall, Hunts.

SHERIDAN, Francis Cynric, 1823. Son of Thomas Sheridan, and grandson of Rt. Hon. Richard Brinsley Sheridan. *b.* 1811. Colonial Sec. at Barbados. Treasurer of Mauritius, where he died 1843.

SHERIDAN,* Thomas Berkeley, 1821. Brother of the above. *b.* 1811. Royal Navy. Killed accidentally on board H.M.S. Diamond 1826.

SHERWOOD, Richard William, 1821. Son of Edward Sherwood, of Purley, Berks. *b.* 1811. Solicitor. Wellingborough, Northampton.

SHETTON, Arthur, 1841-43, *b.* 1830. Went to Helston School.

SHIPDEN, John, 1825, *b.* 1810.

SHIRLEY, Henry James, 1831, *b.* 1819.

SHOPPEE, Conrad Joseph, 1870, b. 1856.

SHOPPEE, Eustace Cyril, 1873.

SHORE-SMITH, Samuel, 1875. [Son of William Shore-Smith, of 30, York Place, Portman Square]. King's Coll. Cam.

SHORT,* Anthony Holbeche, 1876. Son of Rev. J. H. Short, Temple Balsall, Warwickshire. b. 1862.

SHORT,* Edward Morrison de Courcy, 1870, b. 1857.

SHORT, John Hassard, 1823. Son of Richard Samuel Short, of Edlington, Linc. b. 1810. Trin. Coll. Cam. J.P. and D.L. for Lincoln.

SHORTT, William, 1850-53. Son of the late Colonel Shortt, and nephew of Rev. C. R. Dicken. b. 1836. Lieut.-Col. Late 57th Regiment. Served in the Crimean and New Zealand Wars. Four Medals. Resides at St. Helens, Chesterfield.

SHUTTLEWORTH, Edward, 1817. Son of T. Starkie Shuttleworth, of Ashton Lodge, Preston, Lanc. b. 1806. St. John's Coll. Cam. Vicar of Egloshayle, Cornwall. Hon. Canon of Truro.

SHUTTLEWORTH, John, 1817. Brother of the above. b. 1804. Lawyer at Preston.

SHUTTLEWORTH, William, 1819. Brother of the above. b. 1808. Lawyer and Town Clerk at Liverpool; deceased.

SIBLEY, Arthur Fullerton, 1875. Son of Col. Thomas Harmer Sibley. b. 1862.

SILLEM, Herman Walter, 1873. Son of A. Sillem, of Laurie Park, Sydenham.

SILVER, Henry, 1839-44, b. 1824. Solicitor. One of the writers in *Punch*.

SIMMONS, Francis Carlyon, 1875. Son of G. E. Carlyon Simmons, of Southsea. b. 1861.

SIMONS, Nicholas, 1800-6, b. 1788. St. John's Coll. Cam. Vicar of Bramfield.

SIMPSON, Arthur Bridgeman, 1820, b. 1812.

SIMPSON, Edward, 1825. Son of Edward Simpson, of Lichfield. b. 1815. C. C. C. Oxf. Inner Temple. Assumed the name of Hicks. M.P. for Co. Cambridge 1878. Wilbraham Temple, Cam.

SIMPSON, Howard Robert, 1872, *b.* 1861.

SIMPSON, James Macgregor, 1871-77. Son of Rev. J. H. Simpson, of St. Mark's, Bexhill, Sussex. *b.* 1859. Emigrated to Australia.

SIMPSON, William Bridgeman, 1826. Third son of late Hon. John Bridgeman Simpson, of Babworth Hall. *b.* 1813. Trin. Coll. Cam. Rector of Babworth, Notts.

SIMS, Charles, 1812-16. Son of E. T. Sims, of Hubbard's Hall, Harlow, Essex. *b.* 1803. East India Civil Service.

SIMS, Edward Sidney, 1817. Brother of the above. *b.* 1806. died 1822.

SIMS, Frederick, 1819. Brother of the above. *b.* 1810. East India Merchant Service; deceased.

SIMS, Henry Belmont, 1810-16. Brother of the above. *b.* 1800. Rector of Great Parndon, Essex; deceased.

SIMS, William Unwin, 1808. Brother of the above. *b* 1797. Merchant in London. Chairman of the Gt. Western Railway; died 1839.

SINCLAIR, Charles Albert, 1877. Son of Charles Sinclair.

SINCLAIR, Robert, 1827, *b.* 1817. Civil Engineer.

SISMEY, George Herbert, 1875. Son of T. Sismey, of Hadley Green, Barnet.

SISMEY, Thomas Boulton, 1877. Brother of the above.

SKEY, Francis Wakefield, 1842-45. Son of the late Frederic Carpenter Skey, C.B., F.R.S. *b.* 1831. Surgeon; *d.* 1863.

SKEY, Frederic Charles, 1842-51. Brother of the above. *b.* 1832. Worc. Coll. Oxf. Vicar of Weare, Weston-Super-Mare. Late Precentor of Bristol.

SKIRROW, Arthur George Walker, 1875. Son of Walter Skirrow, 2, Queensberry Place, S.W.

SLADDEN, Arthur, 1870-71, *b.* 1856.

SLADE, Arthur John, 1875. Son of Rev. James Slade, Little Lever, Bolton. *b.* 1862.

SLADE, Felix, 1802-4. Son of Robert Slade, Proctor in Doctors' Commons. *b.* 1792. Proctor in Doctors' Commons; *d.* 1868.

SLADE, George Penkivil, 1848-50, b. 1832.

SLADE,* Montague Maule, 1861-5. Son of Lieut.-General Marcus John Slade, twin brother of Sir Fredk. Slade, Bart. b. 1849. Capt. 10th Hussars.

SLATER, James, 1825, b. 1812.

SLATER, Thomas, 1824, b. 1810.

SLEEMAN, Richard, 1824, b. 1812. Ball. Coll. Oxf. Vicar of Whitchurch, Devon ; deceased.

SMALLWOOD, Henry, 1809-11, b. 1794.

SMELT, Cornelius Robert, 1814-15. Of Northallerton, Yorks. b. 1803.

SMITH, Alexander Fitzwalter, 1877. Son of Colonel Clement James Smith, R.A. b. 1864.

SMITH, Alfred, 1827. b. 1815. Banker at Derby.

SMITH, Algernon Jason, 1877. Son of Jason Smith, of 60, St. James-street, London. b. 1864.

SMITH, Bertram Metcalf, 1877. Son of the late Metcalf-Smith. (Bournemouth).

SMITH, Charles Aubrey, 1875. Son of Charles John Smith, Medical Practitioner of Brighton. b. 1863.

SMITH, Charles Swainson, 1878. Son of Rev. Henry Robert Smith, Rector of Grange - over - Sands, Canforth, Lanc. b. 1865.

SMITH, Edmund, 1823, b. 1809. E. I. Civil Service.

SMITH, Edward Cleaver, 1823, b. 1809.

SMITH, Edward Langdale, 1825. Son of Rev. Edward Smith, of Folkingham, Lincolnshire. b. 1811. St. John's Coll. Cam. Vicar of Chetwode, Bucks.

SMITH, Elijah, 1810. Left the same year. b. 1800.

SMITH, Frederick Evan Cowper, 1874. (See Cowper-Smith.)

SMITH, Frederick Sherard. Son of Col. Clement J. Smith. b. 1860. Of Surbiton, Surrey.

SMITH, George Samuel Fereday, 1821. Son of Richard Smith, of Shenstone Hall, Staffs. b. 1812. Queens Coll. Oxf. Barrister of the Inner Temple. Grovehurst, Kent.

List of Carthusians. 215

SMITH, George Spencer, 1846-48, *b.* 1831.

SMITH, Graham, 1823, *b.* 1812. Trin. Coll. Cam.

SMITH, Henry, 1841-43, *b.* 1832.

SMITH,* Henry Eden, 1878. Brother of Charles Swainson Smith (above). *b.* 1864.

SMITH, Henry Robert, 1876. Son of Robert Smith, of Chesham House, Croydon. *b.* 1862.

SMITH, Henry Sandford, 1877. Son of Henry Maberly Smith, 2, Uxbridge-road, Surbiton, Surrey. *b.* 1864.

SMITH,* Henry Venn Brandram, 1861-70. Son of the Bishop of Victoria (Hong Kong). *b.* 1851. Prize Scholar.

SMITH, Henry William, 1820, *b.* 1806.

SMITH, Herbert Henry, 1862, *b.* 1851.

SMITH, Hugh Wallis, 1823, *b.* 1811. St. John's Coll. Cam. Barrister. Wine Merchant.

SMITH, John, 1804-8.

SMITH, John Charles, 1839-41, *b.* 1824. Queens Coll. Oxf. Vicar of King-Sterndale, Buxton.

SMITH,* John Spencer, 1814-18, *b.* 1803.

SMITH, Mosley, 1823, *b.* 1810. E. I. Civil Service.

SMITH, Poynder, 1826, *b.* 1814.

SMITH, Raynes Waite, 1829, *b.* 1818.

SMITH, Rennell Percy, 1875. [Son of Rev. H. Percy Smith, Vicar of Barton, Suffolk]. R.M. Academy, Woolwich.

SMITH, Richard, 1823, *b.* 1809. Formerly in the Rifle Brigade. Holy Orders.

SMITH, Robert Willan, 1826. Son of Ashby Smith, M.D. *b.* 1814. Scholar of Jesus and Post-Master of Mert. Coll. Oxf. Formerly Incumbent of Stow in Upland, Suffolk. Now residing at Richmond, Surrey.

SMITH, Samuel, 1841-43, *b.* 1831.

SMITH, Samuel Shore. (See Shore-Smith).

SMITH, Samuel Lee, 1869. Son of Alfred Smith. *b.* 1856. Merchant. The Gleanings, Rochester.

SMITH, Sherard Frederick, 1875. 2, Surbiton Terrace, Surbiton.

SMITH, Somers Percy, 1875.

SMITH, Stuart Alfred, 1877. Brother of Samuel Lee Smith (above). *b.* 1864.

SMITH, Thomas Bennett, 1827, *b.* 1816.

SMITH, Walter Joseph, 1873. Son of Timothy Smith, of Boston, Lincolnshire. *b.* 1859. Planter in Ceylon.

SMITH,* William, 1876. Son of the late William Edward Smith. *b.* 1864.

SMITH, William Peters, 1827, *b.* 1813; died 1830.

SMITH,* Windham, 1825. Son of Rev. Sydney Smith, Canon of St. Paul's. *b.* 1813. Trin. and Caius Coll. Cam. Civil Service.

SMYTH,* Charles, 1827. Born in India. *b.* 1815. Captain in the Army; deceased.

SMYTH, Charles Montaubon Carmichael (C.B.), 1801-5. Son of James Carmichael-Smyth, M.D., F.R.S., of Aithernie. *b.* 1790. General. Served in 20th Hussars and 8th Bengal Light Cavalry during the Indian Mutiny; died 1870.

SMYTH (Sir) James Robert Carmichael- (Bart.), 1829. Son of Maj.-Genl. Sir Jas. Carmichael Smyth, Bart. *b.* 1817. (Resumed the name of Carmichael only). See Carmichael.

SMYTH, Mark Wood Carmichael- 1814-15. Brother of the above. *b.* 1801. Capt. 6th Madras Light Cavalry; deceased. (Resumed the name of Carmichael only).

SMYTH, Robert Stewart Carmichael- 1812-14. Brother of the above. *b.* 1799. Late Major 93rd Highlanders. Resides at Frome.

SMYTH, Robert Maclein, 1823, *b.* 1811.

SMYTHE, George Edward, 1860-65. Son of Rev. Patrick Murray Smythe, Rector of Solihull, Warwickshire. *b.* 1846. Ch. Ch. Oxf. Barrister.

SMYTHE, Patrick Murray, 1873. Brother of the above. *b.* 1860.

SMYTHE, William Frederick, 1872. Son of William Smythe, of Methven Castle, Perth. *b.* 1859.

SNOWDEN, Northing, 1823. Son of George Snowden, of Ramsgate. *b.* 1809; died 1826.

SOAMES, Edgar, .1874. [Son of E. Soames, of Bromley]. Went to Westminster School.

SOAMES, Joseph, 1820, *b.* 1806; deceased.

SOLLY, Francis Drake, 1850-54. Son of the late Samuel Solly, F.R.C.S. *b.* 1840.

SOLLY, William Hammond, 1825. Son of the late Samuel Reynolds Solly, F.R.S. *b.* 1814. Went to Harrow School. Trin. Coll. Cam. Of Serge Hill, Hemel Hempstead.

SOLLY, William Herbert, 1848-52. Brother of Francis Drake Solly (above). *b.* 1835. Bengal Cavalry; died in India.

SOLTAU, James Pillans, 1825, *b.* 1812; died at Charterhouse 1836.

SOMERS-COCKS, Arthur Percy, 1878. Son of Arthur Herbert Cocks, C.B. *b.* 1864. Late Bengal Civil Service.

SOMERS-COCKS, Charles Richard, 1826. Son of Lieut.-Col. the Hon. Philip James Cocks, of Stepple Hall, Salop. *b.* 1814. Ch. Ch. Oxf. Vicar of Wolverley, Worcester, and Neen Savage, Salop; died 1875.

SOMERS-COCKS, Herbert Haldane, 1873. Brother of Arthur Percy Somers-Cocks (above). *b.* 1861. R.M. Coll. Sandhurst.

SOMERS-COCKS, Henry Lawrence, 1875. Brother of the above. *b.* 1862.

SOMERSET,* A. Plantagenet Fredk. Charles, 1843-44. Son of Col. the Hon. John Thos. H. Somerset. *b.* 1829. 13th Regt. Lieut.-Col.

SOMERSET,* Charles Bruce Henry, 1852-57. Son of Col. Somerset. *b.* 1841. 3rd Regt.

SOMERSET, Edward, 1878. Son of Francis Flower Somerset, Greenham House, Newbury, Berks. *b.* 1864.

SOMERSET, Fitzroy William Henry, 1856-62. Son of Rev. William George Henry Somerset. *b.* 1845. Brisbane, Australia.

SOMERSET, Henry George Edward, 1841. Son of Lieut.-Genl. Sir Henry Somerset, K.C.B. *b.* 1829. Capt. 3rd Regt. Cape Mounted Rifles. Caffre War 1850-52. Fort Major at Jersey.

SOMERVILLE, Henry, 1817, *b.* 1806.

SOTHEBY, Hans William, 1839-46. Son of Hans Sotheby, East India Company's Service. *b.* 1827. Gold Medal. Fellow of Ex. Coll. Oxf. 1st Class Lit. Hum. Barrister; died 1875.

SOUTH,* Henry Erskine, 1876. Son of the late Mr. South, Paymaster-in-Chief Royal Navy. *b.* 1862. Kingston Crescent, Portsmouth.

SOUTHWELL, Charles Leslie, 1875. Son of T. Martin Southwell, of The Woodlands, Bridgenorth.

SOUTHWELL, Edmund Martin, 1868. Brother of the above. *b.* 1853. Lieut. Salop Rifles. St. Leonards, Bridgenorth.

SOUTHWELL, Frank Marvan, 1870. Brother of the above. *b.* 1859. West Cromwell Road, London.

SOUTHWELL, Harry Kemble, 1871. Brother of the above. *b.* 1860. Magd. Coll. Oxf.

SOUTHWELL, Herbert B., 1869. Son of Charles T. Southwell, of Stoke Newington. *b.* 1856. Pemb. Coll. Oxf. 2nd Class Mods.

SOUTHWELL, William Lascelles, 1868, *b.* 1855.

SPARLING, Charles, 1824. Son of William Sparling, of Petton, Salop. *b.* 1813. Captain 15th Hussars; died 1876.

SPARLING, William, 1824. Twin brother of the above. *b.* 1813. St. John's Coll. Cam. J.P. Petton Park, Salop.

SPARROW, Basil James Harold, 1868-71. Son of Basil Sparrow, of Gosfield Place, Essex. *b.* 1853. Ch. Coll. Cam. Curate of Chacely.

SPARROW, Herbert Edward, 1870. Brother of the above. *b.* 1857. Emm. Coll. Cam. Banker.

SPENCE, Edward Fordham, 1874. Son of James Spence, of 67, Queensborough Terrace.

SPENCER,* George John Trevor, 1812-17. Son of William Robert Spencer, who was a grandson of the Duke of Marlborough. *b.* 1799. Univ. Coll. Oxf. Bishop of Madras. Chancellor of St. Paul's; died 1866.

SPENCER, John, 1803. Left the same year.

SPENCER, John, 1825, *b.* 1811. Jes. Coll. Cam.

SPENCER, John Trevor, 1873. Son of William Cavendish Spencer, of the Bengal Civil Service. *b.* 1859.

SPENCER-STANHOPE, Walter, 1875. (See Stanhope).

SPICER, Stephen Ralph, 1821, *b.* 1806. Worc. Coll. Oxf. Curate of Woodnesborough, Kent.

SPILLER,* Edward Frederick, 1842-48, *b.* 1831. Emigrated to Australia.

SPOONER, Charles Herbert, 1871. Son of Isaac Spooner, of Wightwick Staffs. *b.* 1855.

SPOONER, George Cecil Frederick, 1873.

SPRANGER, Richard Walter, 1839-40. Nephew of the following. *b.* 1823.

SPRANGER, Robert Jefferies, 1824. Son of Rev. R. Spranger, Rector of Low Toynton, Linc. *b.* 1812. Fellow and Tutor Ex. Coll. Oxf. 1st Class Lit. Hum. Holy Orders.

SPRANGER, Stephen, 1826. Brother of the above. *b.* 1813. Trin. Coll. Cam. M.D., F.R.C.S.; *d.*

SPRINGETT, William Leaver, 1823, *b.* 1814.

SPRING-RICE, Gerald, 1877. Son of the late Hon. C. W. T. Spring-Rice. *b.* 1864.

SPRY, Arthur Brown, 1826. Son of James Hume Spry (below). *b.* 1812. Trin. Coll. Cam. Chaplain in India; died 1870.

SPRY, Edmund Hume, 1823. Brother of the above. *b.* 1805.

SPRY, Edmund Trant, 1814. Brother of the above. *b.* 1806.

SPRY, James Hume, 1813. Son of Rev. J. H. Spry, Rector of Marylebone. *b.* 1805. Medical Officer to Charterhouse.

SPRY, Philip Lane, 1825. Son of the above. *b.* 1810. Indian Army. 35th N. Infantry.

SPURRIER, Thomas Henry, 1822, *b.* 1810. Solicitor at Birmingham.

SPURWAY, Edward Popham, 1876. Son of Rev. E. B. Spurway, Rector of Heathfield, Taunton. *b.* 1863.

SPYERS, Thomas Charles, 1852-54. Son of Rev. Dr. Spyers, of Weybridge. *b.* 1837. Surgeon; deceased.

STAINFORTH, Frederick, 1823, *b.* 1810.

STANHOPE, Walter Spencer, 1875. Son of Walter Thos. Wm. Spencer-Stanhope, of Cannon Hall, Yorks. *b.* 1860.

STANLEY, Edward, 1874. Son of William Stanley, of Ponsonby Hall, Cumberland. *b.* 1859.

STANLEY, Owen, 1821. Son of Sir John Thomas Stanley, of Alderley, Bart. *b.* 1811. Commander R.N.; *d.* 1850.

STANLEY, William, 1874. Brother of Edward Stanley (above). *b.* 1861.

STANNETT, George Radcliffe, 1813-16, *b.* 1803.

STANTIAL, Arthur Evered, 1874. Son of Rev. T. Stantial, Vicar of St. John's, Clapham Rise.

STANTON, John Harrison, 1876. Son of John Harrison, Stanton, of Stubb House, Whiston, near Darlington. *b.* 1861.

STAPLES, Samuel, 1808-10. Son of Samuel Staples, of Cumberwell House, Wilts. *b.* 1796.

STARKIE, Thomas Whitaker, 1828, *b.* 1816. St. John's Coll. Cam.; died 1843.

STARLING, John Little, 1875.

STARR, John, 1817. Son of John Starr, Solicitor and Auditor to the Dean and Chapter of Canterbury. *b.* 1804. New Inn Hall, Oxf. Solicitor. Partner with his father. Retired 1840. The Precincts, Canterbury.

STARR, Powys, 1821. Brother of the above. *b.* 1808. Died at Charterhouse 1824.

STARR, Thomas, 1809-12. Brother of the above. *b.* 1794. Trin. Coll. Cam. Barrister. Died at Canterbury 1858.

STARR, William Arthur, 1825, *b.* 1808.

STATHAM, Richard Jervis, 1815, *b.* 1805. C. C. C. Oxf. Rector of Tarporley, Cheshire ; *d.*

ST. AUBYN, Hugh Molesworth, 1878. Son of Rev. A. H. M. St. Aubyn, of Clowlance, Camborne, Cornwall. *b.* 1865.

STAVELEY, George Edmund, 1870-72, *b.* 1856.

STAVERT, Herbert John Brownell, 1875. Son of Archibald, Stavert, of Hoscote, Selkirkshire.

STAVERT, Thomas Hope, 1873-6. Brother of the above. *b.* 1859. R.M. Coll. Sandhurst.

STAVERT, William James, 1873. Brother of the above. New Coll. Oxf.

STEDMAN, Robert Frost, 1827, *b.* 1812. Solicitor at Sudbury.

STEELE, William, 1818, *b.* 1804.

STEER, William Frederick, 1803-5, *b.* 1789.

STEERS, John Reay, 1818, *b.* 1806.

STENHOUSE, Thomas, 1868. Son of Thomas Stenhouse, of 14, Lyndhurst Road, Hampstead. *b.* 1856. King's College, Aberdeen.

STEPHENS, David Evan, 1877, *b.* 1862. Of 10, Quay Street, Carmarthen.

STEPHENS,* Henry, 1827, *b.* 1815.

STEPHENSON,* Benjamin Charles, 1849-55, *b.* 1839. Treasury. Secretary to Lloyd's.

STEPHENSON, Henry, 1818, *b.* 1804.

STEVENS, Percy Wansborough, 1871, *b.* 1861.

STEVENS, Robert, 1844-49, *b.* 1832.

STEVENS, Robert Champion, 1877. Son of John Robert Stevens, 15, Prince's Square, Bayswater.

STEVENSON, Leader Henry, 1861-64, *b.* 1848.

STEWARD, Alfred, 1818-21. Son of William Steward, of Great Yarmouth. *b.* 1803. Wine Merchant in London ; died 1835.

STEWARD, Francis, 1818-22. Brother of the above. *b.* 1806. Trin. Hall, Cam. Rector of Barking, Suffolk. J.P.

STEWARD, Henry Allan Holden, 1878. Son of Rev. Walter Holden Steward, Rector of Whilton, Daventry. *b.* 1865.

STEWARD, Walter John Wyndham, 1878.

STEWART, Donald Charles, 1874.

STEWART, Edward Hamilton, 1876. Son of the Ven. Henry Stewart, D.D., Archdeacon of Dromore. *b.* 1864.

STEWART, Keith, 1821, *b.* 1809.

STEWART, Lewis Maxey, 1872.

STEWART, Montgomerie James, 1874. Son of Rev. James Stewart, Rector of Little Stukeley, Huntingdon.

ST. GEORGE, Charles Hervey, 1877. Son of William Whitmore St. George, of Clifton Park, Birkenhead. *b.* 1863.

ST. GEORGE, Howard, 1872. Brother of the above. *b.* 1858.

STIRLING, Norman William, 1875.

ST. LEGER, Henry Berners, 1874. Son of Colonel John St. Leger, of Park Hill, Rotherham, Yorks. *b.* 1861.

STOCK, John, 1856-58. Son of Edward Stock, J.P. of Poplar, Middlesex. *b.* 1841. King's Coll. London. Formerly a Solicitor. Now in Holy Orders.

STOCKDALE, Joseph Walter, 1823, *b.* 1810. Trin. Coll. Cam. Holy Orders.

STODDART, Henry Moncreiff, 1817, *b.* 1808.

STODDART, William Wellwood, 1817, *b.* 1809. Fellow of St. John's Coll. Oxf. 2nd Class Lit. Hum. Denyer's Prize. Holy Orders.

STOKES, Arthur Romney, 1872.

STONE, Andrew, 1802-5; deceased

STONE, Charles, 1846-48, *b.* 1831.

STONE, George, 1820, *b.* 1808. Banker.

STONE, James Henry, 1810-13, *b.* 1803. Went to St. Paul's School. Trin. Coll. Cam.

STONE, John Urry, 1824, *b.* 1812.

STONE, Samuel John, 1853-58. Son of the late Rev. William Stone, Vicar of Alfriston, Sussex. *b.* 1839. Pemb. Coll. Oxf. Vicar of St. Paul's, Haggerston. Author of Various Hymns and Poems.

STONE, Thomas Arthur, 1810-13, *b.* 1797. Accoucheur.

STONE, William Henry, 1843-49. Son of Rev. William Stone, Canon of Canterbury. *b.* 1830. Gold Medal. Scholar of Ball. Coll. Oxf. 1st Class Lit. Hum. M.B. Physician and Lecturer at St. Thomas's Hospital, &c.

STOPFORD,* Algernon Edward, 1868. Son of Rev. F. M. Stopford (below). *b.* 1858.

STOPFORD,* Frederick Manners, 1841-50. Son of Lieut.-Col. the Hon. Edward Stopford. *b.* 1831. Orator. Ch. Ch. Oxf. Vicar of Tichmarsh, Northants.

STOPFORD,* Montagu Charles Henry, 1848-54. Son of Admiral the Hon. Sir Montagu Stopford, K.C.B. *b.* 1837. Land Agent in Australia.

STOPFORD, Walter James, 1843-46. Brother of F. M. Stopford (above). *b.* 1833. Late Capt. 52nd Regiment. Commissioner of Prisons.

STORKS (Sir) Henry Knight (K.C.B.), 1825. Son of Mr. Sergeant Storks. *b.* 1811. Capt. 38th Regiment. Lord High Commissioner of the Ionian Islands. Governor of Malta. Under Secretary for War, &c. M.P. for Ripon ; died 1874.

STORKS, Trundle Thomas, 1826, *b.* 1812. Jes. Coll. Cam. Holy Orders; deceased.

STORY, Anthony Browne, 1822, *b.* 1810. Solicitor at St. Albans; *d.* 1874.

STORY, Edmund, 1826, *b.* 1811.

STORY, Frederick, 1837-45. Son of Anthony Browne Story (above). *b.* 1827. Solicitor at St. Albans.

STORY, Frederick, 1877. Son of Henry John Story, 83, Alexander Road, London. *b.* 1863.

STORY, Henry James, 1826, *b.* 1814. Solicitor at St. Albans.

STORY, Samuel John, 1828, *b.* 1812. Army.

STORY, Thomas Kemp, 1826, *b.* 1814. 1, Edinburgh Mansions, Victoria Street.

STORY,* William Henry, 1875. Brother of Fredk. Story, Junior (above). *b.* 1861.

STOVIN, Cornelius Frederick, 1874. Son of Dr. Stovin, of Wheatley, Oxon.

STRACHEY, Arthur, 1872. Son of Sir John Strachey, G.C.S.I. *b.* 1858. Trin. Hall, Cam.

STREATFEILD, Alexander McNeill, 1876. Son of Alexander Edward Champion Streatfeild, of Charts Edge, Kent. *b.* 1863.

STREATFEILD, Henry Bertram, 1867-70. Son of the Rev. William Streatfeild, Vicar of East Ham, Essex. *b.* 1852. Ex. Coll. Oxf. Curate of Holy Trinity, Louth, Lincolnshire.

STREATFEILD, Sidney Richard, 1852-53. Son of the following. *b.* 1841. Royal Navy.

STREATFEILD, Sidney Robert, 1820. Son of Richard Thomas Streatfeild, of the Rocks, Uckfield, Sussex. *b.* 1808. Formerly Major 52nd Regt.; deceased.

STRETTELL, Dashwood, 1821. Son of Edward Strettell, Advocate-General at Calcutta. *b.* 1806. Major 20th Madras Native Infantry. Retired 1852. Died at Hillenboro', Kent, 1854.

STRETTELL, John Wynne, 1821. Brother of the above. *b.* 1809. Major Madras Cavalry. Died at Ootacamund.

STRICKLAND, Henry Eustatius, 1876. Son of Sir George Strickland.

STRIDE,* William John Francis Keatley, 1878. Son of W. Stride, of Redbridge, Southampton. *b.* 1865.

STRONGE, Walter Cecil, 1874.

STUART, Alexander, 1874. Son of William Stuart, of Feddal, Perthshire. *b.* 1859. Trin. Coll. Cam. Melville House, Portobello.

STUART, Charles, 1821, *b.* 1808.

STUART, Constantine Wentworth, 1815, b. 1805; deceased.

STUART, Henry, 1821. Son of Rear Admiral Lord George Stuart. b. 1808.

STUBBS, Charles John, 1874.

STUBBS, Stanley John, 1874. Brother of the above.

STURGEON, Charles Wentworth Dillon, 1853-55. Son of Charles Sturgeon, Barrister-at-law. b. 1843. Barrister. F.R.G.S.

SUGDEN, Henry Richard, 1876. Son of Hon. and Rev. Frank Sugden, of Thames Ditton, Surrey. b. 1862.

SULLIVAN,* (Sir) Francis William (K.C.B.), 1844-48. Son of Rev. Frederick Sullivan, Vicar of Kimpton, Herts. b. 1834. Rear Admiral. A.D.C. to the Queen.

SULLIVAN, Henry Eden, 1845-51. Brother of the above. b. 1835. B.N.C. Oxf. Solicitor.

SUMNER,* Charles Almon, 1857-63. Son of Charles Sumner, of Hempsted Court, Gloucestershire. b. 1846. Merchant in San Francisco.

SURRIDGE, Edward North, 1874. Son of North Surridge, of Romford Hall, Essex. b. 1859. Articled to a Solicitor; died 1877.

SURRIDGE, William North, 1874. Brother of the above. b. 1858. Trin. Coll. Cam.

SURTEES,* Henry Ratcliffe, 1825. Son of William Villiers, Surtees, of Rotherfield, Sussex. b. 1814. Worc. Coll. Oxf. Vicar of Stockland, Devon; died 1876.

SURTEES,* John Oliver, 1834-40. Brother of the above. b 1823. Barrister. Emigrated to Australia; deceased.

SURTEES, Robert Lambton, 1824. Son of Robert Surtees, of Redworth Hall, Darlington. b. 1812. Trin. Coll. Cam. J.P. and D.L. Late of Redworth and The Grove, Durham; deceased.

SURTEES * (Sir) Stephenson Villiers, 1815-16. Son of John Surtees, of Dinan, France. b. 1803. Univ. Coll. Oxf. 2nd Class Lit. Hum. B.C.L. Chief Justice at Mauritius; died 1867.

SURTEES,* William Aubone, 1821. Son of Aubone Surtees, of Hedley and Pigdon, Northumberland. *b.* 1810. 52nd Regt.; died 1839.

SUTHERLAND, George Mowbray, 1842-48. Son of Dr. Sutherland, *b.* 1830. Barrister.

SUTHERLAND, Stanley Sutherland, 1846-53. Son of J. W. Sutherland, of Coombe, Croydon. *b.* 1836. Capt. Indian Army; retired.

SUTTON, Gilbert, 1873. Son of Rev. R. Sutton, Rector of Pevensey and Prebendary of Chichester.

SWAINE, George William, 1874. Son of the late George William Swaine. *b.* 1859. 2nd Lieut. 14th (Prince of Wales' Own) Regiment.

SWAN, Edward Daniel, 1860-62, *b.* 1843.

SWAN,* Frederick Thesiger, 1870. Son of Rev. Charles Trollope Swan, of Sausthorpe Hall, Lincolnshire. *b.* 1858. Magd. Coll. Oxf.

SWEET, Thomas Shardalow, 1862. Left the same year. *b.* 1851. Emigrated to New Zealand.

SWIRE, William, 1876. Son of William Hudson Swire, 3, Holland Park, Bayswater. *b.* 1862.

SYKES, Edward, 1848-50, *b.* 1833. Drowned.

SYKES, Godfrey Milnes, 1829, *b.* 1814. Gold Medal. Schol. of Trin. Coll. and Fellow of Downing Coll. Cam. Wrangler. Vicar of Tadlow, Beds; died 1877.

SYM, William Lyter, 1818. Left the same year. *b.* 1806.

SYMONDS, Frederick John, 1864. Son of Rev. A. R. Symonds, Vicar of Walmer, Kent. *b.* 1849. Solicitor in India.

SYMONDS, Sydney Vere, 1864. Brother of the above. *b.* 1853. Died at Madras 1876.

SYNGE,* Francis Julian, 1868. Son of W. W. F. Synge, British Consul at Havana. *b.* 1856.

SYNGE,* Robert Follett, 1865. Brother of the above. *b.* 1853.

T.

TABOR, Samuel James, 1819, *b.* 1806.

TALBOT, Edward Stuart, 1856-58. Son of the Hon. John Chetwynd Talbot (below). *b.* 1844. Slade Exhibitioner. Ch. Ch. Oxf. 1st Class Lit. Hum. 1st Class Law, &c. Holy Orders. Warden of Keble Coll. Oxf.

TALBOT, Hon. George Gustavus Chetwynd, 1820. Son of the second Earl Talbot, K.G. and brother to the 18th Earl of Shrewsbury. *b.* 1810. Ch. Ch.Oxf. Rector of Whithington, Gloucestershire.

TALBOT, Hon. Gerald Chetwynd, 1833-35. Brother of the above. *b.* 1819. Late Director-Genl. of the Military Store Department of the India Office.

TALBOT, Hon. John Chetwynd, 1817. Brother of the above. *b.* 1806. Ch. Ch. Oxf. 1st Class Lit. Hum. Barrister. Q.C.; *d.* 1852.

TALBOT, John Gilbert, 1847-53. Son of the above. *b.* 1835. Ch. Ch. Oxf. Slade Exhibitioner. 2nd Class Mods. Hon. 4th Lit. Hum. M.P. for West Kent 1868-78. Elected M.P. for the University of Oxford 1878.

TALBOT, Hervey, 1849-55. Son of Hon. and Rev. A. C. Talbot. *b* 1838. 18th (Royal Irish) Regt. Lieut.-Col. King's Own Staffordshire Militia. Rhysnant Hall, Montgomeryshire.

TALBOT, Thomas, 1818, *b.* 1804.

TALBOT, Hon. William Whitworth Chetwynd, 1823. Brother of the Hon. John C. Talbot (above). *b.* 1814. Ch. Ch. Oxf. Rector of Bishop's Hatfield.

TALLENTS, Godfrey, 1824, *b.* 1812. Solicitor at Newark-on-Trent.

TALLEY, William, 1844. Left the same year. *b.* 1827.

TAMPLIN, Henry Mitchell Richard, 1853-54. Son of Henry Pagden Tamplin, of Brighton. *b.* 1843; *d.* 1869.

TANIERE, James, 1822, b. 1807.

TANNER, John Lyneham, 1815-17, b. 1799.   St. John's Coll. Cam.

TANNER, Thomas, 1837-38. Surgeon.

TANNER, Thomas Slingsby, 1873.

TANNER, William, 1844-50, b. 1834. Army Surgeon. Serving with Royal Artillery in Afghanistan (1879).

TARBUTT, Edward Octavius, 1826, b. 1813. Died at Charterhouse.

TASKER, John Campbell Wheatley, 1839-42. Son of John Tasker, of Dartford. b. 1824. Pemb. Coll. Cam. Holy Orders. Late of Bath.

TATE,* Charles Maitland, 1823. Son of Rev. J. Tate, Head Master of the Grammar School, Richmond, Yorks. b. 1813. Civil Engineer. Emigrated to America. Returned.

TATE, James, 1816-18. Brother of the above. b. 1801. Head Master of Richmond School, Yorks; d.

TATE,* John Samuel, 1853-57. Son of the above. b. 1839. Orator. Trin. Coll. Cam. Somerset House.

TAUNTON, Hugh Grosvenor, 1877. Son of Ernest Hippisley Taunton, of Freeland Lodge, Eynsham, Oxon.

TAYLER,* Charles, 1808-11, b. 1796. Ch. Ch. Oxf.

TAYLER, William Churchill, 1865, b. 1854. Solicitor in London.

TAYLOR,   , 1803.

TAYLOR, Adam, 1819, b. 1805.

TAYLOR, Alexander, 1804-10, b. 1795.

TAYLOR, Alexander John, 1878. Son of the late Dr. James Taylor, of Burghfield, Berks. b. 1864.

TAYLOR, Arthur Cole Pellew, 1821, b. 1808.

TAYLOR, Clarence Comyn, 1848-50. Son of the late General Sir Henry Taylor, K.C.B. b. 1830. 60th Bengal N. Infantry. Lieut.-Col. retired.

TAYLOR, Edward, 1816, *b.* 1806; died 1816.

TAYLOR, George Henry, 1816, *b.* 1807. Solicitor in London.

TAYLOR, George John, 1821, *b.* 1808.

TAYLOR, George Peter, 1838-42, *b.* 1825.

TAYLOR, Guthrie John Corbet, 1877.

TAYLOR, Guy Noble, 1875.

TAYLOR, Henry, 1822, *b.* 1810.

TAYLOR, Henry Stuart, 1807. Left the same year. *b.* 1791. Caius Coll. Cam.

TAYLOR, James, 1804-5, *b.* 1793.

TAYLOR, John, 1804-10, *b.* 1795.

TAYLOR, John, 1820, *b.* 1808. Civil Engineer.

TAYLOR, John Bladen Metcalfe, 1861-63, *b.* 1846. Lieut. 76th Regt.

TAYLOR, John Henry, 1810-17, *b.* 1800. Surgeon.

TAYLOR, John Tindale, 1865. Son of John Hirst Taylor, of Broadoak, Twickenham, late of Windermere. *b.* 1851.

TAYLOR, Richard, 1820, *b.* 1810.

TAYLOR, Thomas Litton, 1874. Brother of John Tindale Taylor (above). *b.* 1859. Trin. Hall, Cam.

TAYLOR, Thomas Rumbold, 1853-57, *b.* 1841.

TAYLOR, William, 1819, *b.* 1808. Went to India.

TAYLOR, William Addington, 1854-57. Son of Rev. William Addington Taylor, Rector of Litchborough, Northants. *b.* 1840. St. Mary Hall, Oxf. Rector of Syston, Bristol.

TAYLOR, William Allen, 1812-13, *b.* 1797.

TEAGUE, James Alexander, 1826, *b.* 1811. Solicitor in London. Magistrate's Clerk at Guildhall.

TEMPLER, George Denis O'Kelly, 1829. Son of James Templer, of Bridport, Dorset. *b.* 1815. Solicitor at Lyme Regis; died 1872.

TEMPLER, Henry Augustus, 1825. Brother of the above. *b.* 1813. Solicitor at Bridport. Brigade Major Dorset Volunteers; died 1874.

TEMPLER, James Lethbridge, 1822. Brother of the above. *b.* 1811. Capt. in the East India Merchant Service; died 1845.

TEMPLER, Robert Shawe, 1878. Son of Robert B. Templer, J.P. for Co. Armagh. *b.* 1864.

TEMPLER, Walter Francis, 1878. Brother of the above. *b.* 1865.

TENNANT, Claude Cambridge, 1874.

TENNANT, Jocelyn Harvey, 1876.

TENNYSON-D'EYNCOURT. (See D'Eyncourt).

TERREWEST, George, 1815-16, *b.* 1804.

TERREWEST, Reuben, 1815-18, *b.* 1803. Solicitor in London and Lincoln; died 1876.

TERRY, Claude Alexander Imbert- 1871. Son of Henry Imbert-Terry. *b.* 1857. Theological Coll. Lichfield.

TERRY, Henry Machu Imbert- 1866-71. Brother of the above. *b.* 1854. 10, Park Village, West, Regent's Park.

TEULON, George Alexander, 1853-61. Son of Samuel Sanders Teulon, of London, Architect. *b.* 1843. Emigrated. Now living at Mortlake.

TEULON, Greville Newenham, 1852-59. Brother of the above. *b.* 1842. Emigrated to Australia.

TEULON, Howard Maxwell, 1857. Brother of the above. *b.* 1849; died 1859.

TEULON, Josiah Sanders, 1849-57. Brother of the above. *b.* 1838. Scholar of Linc. Coll. Oxf. 3rd Class Lit. Hum. Vice-Principal of Chichester Theological College.

THACKERAY, William Makepeace, 1822. Son of Richmond Thackeray, of the East India Civil Service. *b.* 1811. Trin. Coll. Cam. The Author of *Vanity Fair*, *The Newcomes*, and other works; died 1863.

THARPE, Augustus James, 1820, *b.* 1805. Ch. Coll. Cam. Rector of Snailwell cum Cippenham, Cambs.; died 1877.

THIRLWALL, Connop, 1810-13. Son of Rev. T. Thirlwall, Rector of Bowers Gifford, Essex. *b.* 1797. Fellow of Trin. Coll. Cam. Bishop of St. David's 1841. The Historian of Greece; died 1875.

THOMAS, Alexander, 1817-18, *b.* 1803. Went to Eton.

THOMAS, George John, 1807-10, *b.* 1794. St. Mary's Hall, Oxf. Holy Orders.

THOMAS, Henry, 1813. Left the same year. *b.* 1799.

THOMAS, Robert Mosely Bryce, 1855-58, *b.* 1840. Captain Bengal Staff Corps.

THOMPSON, Albert, 1852-55, *b.* 1840.

THOMPSON, Arthur Peile, 1873.

THOMPSON, Cyril Powney, 1878. Son of Fendall Thompson, Bengal Civil Service. *b.* 1864.

THOMPSON,* Edward Stopford, 1856-61, *b.* 1842. Univ. Coll. Oxford.

THOMPSON, Frank Wolfe, 1872.

THOMPSON, Henry, 1814-16, *b.* 1801. Dublin University.

THOMPSON, John, 1806-11.

THOMPSON, John Chetwood, 1823, *b.* 1810.

THOMPSON, John Henry, 1868, *b.* 1856.

THOMPSON, Robert John Arthur Rolle Rainburgh, 1820. *b.* 1810. War Office. Took the name of Gwyn.

THOMPSON,* Walter Hume, 1867-72, *b.* 1855. Merchant Service.

THOMPSON, William, 1825, *b.* 1813.

THOMSON, Thomas Ellman, 1814-15, *b.* 1799. B.N.C. Oxf.

THOMSON,* William, 1806-11, *b.* 1795. Medical Practitioner.

THOMSON, William, 1814-16, *b.* 1803.

THORNEYCROFT, John Mytton, 1821, *b.* 1809. B.N.C. Oxf. Holy Orders.

THORNEYCROFT, Wallace, 1878. Son of Lieut.-Col. T. Thorneycroft, of Tettenhall, Wolverhampton. *b.* 1864.

THORNHILL, John Bensley, 1820, *b.* 1808. Bengal Civil Service.

THORNHILL, William, 1819, *b.* 1806.

THORNTON, Edward (C.B.), 1824-28. Son of John Thornton, of Clapham. *b.* 1811. East India Civil Service. Chief Commissioner of Punjab. Retired.

THORNTON, George Smith, 1821, *b.* 1808. Went to Harrow School. Merchant. Director of the Sun Insurance Office.

THORNTON, John, 1821. Brother of Edward Thornton (above). *b.* 1809. Bengal Civil Service. Retired.

THORP, Robert, 1853-56, *b.* 1838. 98th Regt.; deceased.

THORPE, Ralph, 1809-14, *b.* 1800. Went to Merchant Taylor's School.

THURLOW (Hon.) John Edmund Hovell- 1830. Son of the 2nd Baron Thurlow. *b.* 1817. Served in 60th Rifles, and 85th Regt. Capt. retired 1854; died 1871.

THURLOW (Hon.) Thomas Hugh Hovell- 1830. Brother of the above. *b.* 1816. Capt. 7th Fusiliers. Retired 1844.

THYNNE (Lord) Edward, 1820. Son of the 2nd Marquess of Bath. *b.* 1807. Oriel Coll. Oxf. Was M.P. for Frome from 1859 to 1865.

TICKELL, Richard Samuel, 1823. Son of Lieut.-Genl. Tickell, E. I. Co. Service (Engineers). *b.* 1810. Went to Eton. Major Indian Army; deceased.

TILDEN, John, 1852-56. Son of John Tilden, of Ifield Court, Northfleet, Kent. *b.* 1839.

TILL,* William, 1801-6. Son of Mr. Till, of the London Waterworks. *b.* 1791.

TILLY, Tobias Harry, 1823. Son of Captain John Tilly, R.M. Packet Service, of Tremough, Cornwall. *b.* 1808. Solicitor at Falmouth. Took an active part in promoting the Falmouth Docks; died 1866.

TIMMINS, William Raikes, 1821, *b.* 1808. Bengal Civil Service.

TINDAL, Acton, 1822-28. Son of Thomas Tindal, of Aylesbury. *b.* 1811. Solicitor at Aylesbury. Clerk of the Peace for Buckinghamshire.

List of Carthusians. 233

TISDALL, Alfred Oliver, 1873.

TOBIN, John James, 1820, b. 1808. M.D.

TOBIN, Thomas Frederick, 1820, b. 1810.

TOD,* Alexander Hay, 1869, b. 1857. Prize Scholar. Trin. Coll. Oxf.

TODD, William, 1874. Of Beverley, Yorks.

TOMBS, William Thomas Symonds, 1877. Son of Rev. Joseph Tombs, Rector of Burton, So. Wales. b. 1863.

TOMKIN, Henry Brickwood Frederick, 1878. Of Buckland, Dover. b. 1866.

TOMKINS, Henry Alfred Colthurst, 1868-72. Son of Rev. Henry George Tomkins, Vicar of Branscombe. b. 1855. Trin. Coll. Cam. Curate of Nailsworth, Gloucestershire.

TONKS, Thomas Anthony, 1859-61, b. 1844.

TORKINGTON, James, 1824. Son of James Torkington, of Great Stukeley Hall, Hunts. b. 1811. Of Stukeley Hall; died 1852.

TORKINGTON, Laurence John, 1821. Brother of the above. b. 1809. Clare Hall, Cam. Lieut. 4th Light Dragoons. Retired 1837; died 1874.

TORRENS, Henry, 1819. Son of Sir Henry Torrens, G.C.B. b. 1806. Bengal Civil Service. Agent to the Court of the Nawab of Moorshedabad; died 1852.

TOTTENHAM, Charles John, 1821. Son of Rt. Rev. Lord R. P. Tottenham, D.D., Bishop of Clogher. b. 1808. Ball. Coll. Oxf. Capt. 2nd Life Guards. Lieut.-Col. Denbighshire Yeomanry Cavalry; died 1878.

TOWER, Charles, 1827. Son of Rev. Charles Tower, of Brentwood. b. 1815. Scholar of St. John's Coll. Cam. Prebendary of Sarum. Rector of Chilmark, Wilts.

TOWER, Thomas, 1824. Son of Christopher Thomas Tower, M.P., of Weald Hall, Brentwood. b. 1809. St. John's Coll. Cam. Barrister.

TOWNSHEND, Thomas William, 1818. b. 1802.

TRAFFORD, Clement, 1807-11, b. 1793. Jesus Coll. Cam.

TRAFFORD, Edward William, 1821, *b.* 1809.

TRAPMANN, Louis Alexander Stuart, 1875. Son of W. H. Trapmann, 8, Roland Gardens, So. Kensington.

TREACHER, Robert, 1833-37, *b.* 1822. Civil Engineer.

TREDELL, Thomas Arthur, 1803-6, *b.* 1794.

TREVELYAN, Alfred Wilson, 1820. Son of Sir John Trevelyan, Bart. *b.* 1807. Lieut. 32nd Regt.; died 1831.

TREVELYAN (Sir) Charles Edward (Bart.), 1820. Son of the Venl. Archdeacon George Trevelyan. *b.* 1807. Assistant Sec. to the Treasury. Governor of Madras, &c. Created a Baronet 1874.

TREVELYAN, Edward Otto, 1823. Brother of the above. *b.* 1810. C. C. C. Oxf. Holy Orders. Of Rockfield, Monmouth.

TREVELYAN, Willoughby, 1817. Son of Rev. Walter Trevelyan, Vicar of Henbury and Rector of Nettlecombe. *b.* 1805. East India Service.

TRISTRAM, Francis Thomas, 1877. Son of Thomas Hutchinson Tristram, D.C.L., of 22, Manchester Square. *b.* 1864.

TRISTRAM,* Henry Baker, 1806-13. Son of Rev. Thomas Tristram, Prebendary of Salisbury, Rector of Barkstone, Lincolnshire. *b.* 1795. Student of Ch. Ch. Oxf. 2nd Class Lit. Hum. Vicar of Eglingham, Northumb.; *d.* 1837.

TRISTRAM, John Christopher, 1878. Son of the late William Barrington Tristram. *b.* 1864.

TRITTON, Henry, 1828, *b.* 1815. Banker in London.

TRITTON, Joseph, 1831, *b.* 1819. Banker in London.

TROLLOPE, Andrew Harvey, 1873. Son of G. F. Trollope, of Streatham, Surrey. *b.* 1860.

TROTTER, Lionel James, 1841-45, *b.* 1827. Post-Master Mert. Coll. Oxf. Indian Army. 1st European Regt.

TROTTER, William Thomas, 1823. Son of William Trotter, of Ballindean, Perthshire. *b.* 1809. E. I. Civil Service.

TROUGHTON, Francis Thomas, 1878. Son of T. Troughton, of Northfleet, Kent.

TROWARD, Albany, 1814-15, *b.* 1799. Col. Indian Army. Military Governor of the Invalid Establishment at Poonah; died 1865.

TROWER, Edward Spencer, 1823, *b.* 1809.

TUCK, Edgar Needham, 1850-54, *b.* 1836; deceased.

TUCKER,* Charles Benjamin, 1878. Son of Walter James Tucker, of Chard, Somerset. *b.* 1865.

TUCKER, Frederick Henry, 1841-42, *b.* 1826. St. John's Coll. Cam. Vicar of Horrabridge, Devon.

TUCKER,* John, 1803-7, *b.* 1790. Vicar of West Hendred, Wantage.

TUCKER, Stephen, 1803-4, *b.* 1788.

TUCKER, William Edwin Pitts, 1875. Son of T. John Pitts Tucker, Solicitor, of Barnstaple, Devon. *b.* 1861.

TUCKER, William Raffles Arthur Gordon, 1877.

TUDOR, Frederick Sidney Scripps, 1849-53. Son of Samuel Tudor, of Gidea Hall, Romford. *b.* 1839. Merchant. Wyton, Yorks.

TUDOR, Owen Scripps, 1849-52. Brother of the above. *b.* 1836. Merchant. Upper Tooting.

TUDOR, William Scripps, 1849-53. Brother of the above. *b.* 1838. Merchant. Queensbury, Buckhurst Hill, Essex.

TUNBRIDGE, Thomas T., 1871. Left after a few days. *b.* 1855.

TUPPER, Arthur Chilver, 1825. Son of Martin Tupper, Surgeon, of Guernsey. *b.* 1816; died 1876.

TUPPER, Charles William, 1833-34. Brother of the above. *b.* 1821. 69th Regt. Now in business in the City.

TUPPER, Daniel, 1822. Brother of the above. *b.* 1812. B.N.C. Oxf. Lord Chamberlain's Office; died 1869.

TUPPER, Heathfield, 1823, *b.* 1808; died 1850.

TUPPER, Martin Farquhar, 1822. Brother of Daniel Tupper (above). *b.* 1810. Ch. Ch. Oxf. D.C.L. F.R.S. Called to the Bar 1835. Author of "Proverbial Philosophy," &c.

TURNER, Adolphus, 1818, *b.* 1805. Foreign Office. Chargé D'Affaires in Uruguay.

TURNER, Edmond Robert, 1838-43, *b.* 1826. Scholar of Caius Coll. Cam. Wrangler. Chancery Barrister.

TURNER (Sir) George James, 1813-15, *b.* 1798. Fellow of Pemb. Coll. Cam. 9th Wrangler. Q.C. 1840. Lord Justice of Appeal in the Court of Chancery. Governor of Charterhouse; died 1867.

TURNER, George Richard, 1838-42. Son of the above. *b.* 1825. Caius Coll. Cam. Rector of Kebshall, Herts; deceased.

TURNER, Henry Blois, 1819. Son of Thomas Turner, M.D., of London. *b.* 1808. General Royal Engineers.

TURNER, James Francis, 1838-44. Son of Sir G. J. Turner (above). *b.* 1827. Univ. Coll. Durham. Formerly Rector of Tidworth, Wilts. Bishop of Grafton and Armidale.

TURNER, John, 1810-11, *b.* 1794.

TURNER,* John Fisher, 1828. Cousin of Richard Bawtree Turner (below). *b.* 1805. Worc. Coll. Oxf. Rector of St. Mary, Major, Exeter; deceased.

TURNER, John Hayward, 1804-5. Son of Samuel Turner, of 21, Upper Wimpole Street. *b.* 1789. Merchant; deceased.

TURNER, Richard Bawtree, 1836-41. Son of Richd. Turner, and nephew of Sir G. J. Turner. *b.* 1822. Ex. Coll: Oxf. Barrister. Died in South Africa.

TURNER, Salmon, 1819, *b.* 1806. Pemb. Coll. Cam.

TURNER, Samuel Blois, 1814. Brother of Henry Blois Turner (above). *b.* 1805. Pemb. Coll. Cam. Rector of All Saints, South Elmham, Suffolk.

TURNER, Thomas, 1828. Son of John Turner, of Thames Ditton. *b.* 1811. Ex. Coll. Oxf. Vicar of Marden, Wilts.

TURNER, Thomas, 1840-44, *b.* 1827. Solicitor.

TURNER, Thomas Hawkins, 1846-49. Son of General H. B. Turner, R.E. *b.* 1834. Lieut.-Col. Bombay Staff Corps; died 1878.

TURNER, Thomas Metcalfe Blois, 1821. Brother of Samuel Blois Turner (above). *b.* 1809. Capt. Bombay Engineers ; died in India 1847.

TURNER, Thomas Peregine, 1819. Brother of John Fisher Turner (above). *b.* 1803. Solicitor at Exeter.

TURNER, William Stephen Turner Mellish, 1823. (See Meryweather).

TURNOR, Henry Martin, 1825. Son of Edmund Turnor, of Stoke Rochford, Lincolnshire. *b.* 1812.

TWEED, Henry Earle, 1843-46. Son of late Rev. James Tweed, of Rayne, near Braintree. *b.* 1827. Gold Medal. Scholar of Trinity and Fellow of Oriel Coll. Oxf. 1st Class Lit. Hum. Latin Essay, &c. Vicar of Coleby, Lincolnshire.

TWELLS, Philip, 1823. Son of John Twells, of Darby House, Sunbury. *b.* 1808. Worc. Coll. Oxf. Called to the Bar. Banker in London. M.P. for London 1874.

TWENTYMAN, Percy, 1876. Son of Lawrence B. Twentyman, of Wimbledon. *b.* 1862.

TWIST, Charles, 1875. Of Wavertree, Liverpool.

TYACKE, Francis Yonge, 1876. Son of N. Tyacke, M.D., of Chichester. *b.* 1861. Articled to a Solicitor in London.

TYRRELL, William, 1818, *b.* 1807. St. John's Coll. Cam. 4th Senr. Opt. Bishop of Newcastle, New South Wales, where he died 1879.

TYRWHITT-DRAKE, Algernon Frederick, 1872, *b.* 1860.

TYRWHITT-DRAKE, John D'Urban, 1877. Son of Capt. John Charles Tyrwhitt-Drake, of Aylesbury. *b.* 1864.

TYRWHITT-DRAKE,* Frederick Edward, 1840-47, *b.* 1828. Pemb. Coll. Oxf. Rector of Pulham, Dorset.

U.

UNWIN, Charles, 1825. Son of John Unwin, of the Treasury. *b.* 1815. Indian Army. Engineers. E. India Board of Control; deceased.

UNWIN, Henry, 1819. Brother of the above. *b.* 1810. East India Civil Service (Bengal); deceased.

UNWIN, William, 1819. Brother of the above. *b.* 1806. Scholar of C. C. Coll. Oxf. Colonial Office; deceased.

UPTON, Archer, 1845-48. Son of the late Archer Thomas Upton. *b.* 1830. Wadh. Coll. Oxf. Rector of Stowting, Kent.

URLING, Richard, 1841. Left the same year. *b.* 1830.

URWICK, William Francis, 1873. Son of William Henry Urwick, of Clapham. *b.* 1859. Wine Merchant.

USHER,* William Henry, 1830-6, *b.* 1820. Royal Navy.

V.

VACHELL, Horatio, 1810-16, *b.* 1798. Pemb. Coll. Cam.

VADE, George Ashton, 1816. Son of Rev. Ashton Vade, Chaplain to H.R.H. the Prince of Wales. *b.* 1802. Ex. Coll. Oxf.

VAIZEY, Joseph, 1825. Son of John Vaizey, of Halstead, Essex. *b.* 1813. Farmer; deceased.

VALENTINE, Richard J. Scobell, 1836-44. Son of Rev. Thomas Valentine, Chaplain of the London Hospital. *b.* 1825. Scholar of St. John's Coll. Cam. Holy Orders. died 1854.

VAN-ATWOOD, Thomas Hasting, 1844-47, *b.* 1829. Ch. Coll. Cam. Drowned at Tenby 1850.

VANCE, Richard Lucas, 1826, *b.* 1815.

List of Carthusians.   239

VANDERZEE, George, 1812, *b.* 1799. Solicitor.

VANDERZEE, George Yorke, 1863, *b.* 1851.

VANDERZEE, Henry, 1813. Brother of George Vanderzee (above). *b.* 1801.

VANE, Francis Patrick, 1873. Son of Frederick Henry Vane, formerly of the 12th Lancers. *b.* 1861. Lieut. Worcestershire Militia.

VANE, Frederick, 1809-11. Son of Col. William Walter Vane, of Canfield Hall, Essex. *b.* 1793. Queens Coll. Oxf. Rector of Bletchingdon, Oxon ; died 1865.

VANE, Walter, 1808-9. Son of Sir Fredk. Fletcher Vane, 2nd Bart. *b.* 1795 ; died 1814 of wounds received in the sortie from Bayonne.

VANE, William Lyonel, 1873-77. Son of Henry Morgan Vane. *b.* 1859. Clare Hall, Cam. R.M. Coll. Sandhurst.

VAUGHAN, Henry Bathurst, 1871, *b.* 1858.

VAUGHAN,* James Barrington, 1862-65, *b.* 1850.

VAUTIER, Augustus, 1806-9.

VENABLES,* Cavendish, 1844 49. Son of Mr. Venables, Sec. to Sir Robert Peel. *b.* 1833. Capt. 57th Regt. Served in the Crimea. Drowned in British Columbia.

VENABLES, Charles John, 1877. Of Avon House, Fordingbridge. *b.* 1865.

VENABLES, Cuthbert Edward, 1877.

VENABLES,* Edmund Ernest, 1861, *b.* 1849.

VENABLES, George Stovin, 1822-28. Son of the Ven. Richard Venables, Archdeacon of Carmarthen. *b.* 1810. Fellow and Tutor of Jesus Coll. Cam. 1st Class Lit. Hum. Prize for English Verse. Barrister. Q.C.

VENABLES, Joseph Henry, 1825-34. Brother of the above. *b.* 1813. Jesus Coll. Cam. Barrister. J.P. for Breconshire and Radnorshire ; died 1866.

VENABLES, Richard Lister, 1822-27. Brother of the above. *b.* 1809. Emm. Coll. Cam. Chairman of the Radnor Quarter Sessions. Of Lysdinam, Brecon. Late Vicar of Clyro.

VENABLES, Thomas Evelyn, 1849-52. Brother of Cavendish Venables (above). *b.* 1835. Merchant.

VENABLES, William, 1824, *b.* 1815. Ex. Coll. Oxf. Medical Practitioner; died 1845.

VENN, John, 1817-18. Son of Rev. John Venn, Rector of Clapham. *b.* 1802. Fellow of Queens Coll. Cam. Bell's Scholar. 12th Wrangler. For many years Incumbent of St. Peter's, and subsequently Rector of St. Owens, Hereford. Prebendary of Hereford.

VERELST, Courtenay Lee, 1871. Son of Charles Verelst, of Aston Hall, Rotherham. *b.* 1855. Coffee Planter in Ceylon.

VERELST, Horace Devereux, 1871. Brother of the above. *b.* 1857. Coffee Planter in Ceylon.

VERNON, Edward, 1839. Left the same year. *b.* 1823.

VERSTURME, Henry Palairet, 1876. Son of Major Versturme, of Clifton. Late 59th Regt. *b.* 1864.

VIAN, Alsager Richard, 1876. Son of William John Vian, of Beckenham, Kent. *b.* 1863.

VICKERS, James William, 1873. Son of J. W. Vickers, of St. Winifreds, Reigate.

VIGNE, Augustus, 1822. Son of Thomas Vigne, of Woodford, Essex. *b.* 1808. Of Bayswater; deceased.

VIGNE, Robert, 1820. Son of Henry Vigne, of Church Hill, Walthamstow. *b.* 1807; deceased.

VIGNE, Thomas Aislabie, 1848-53. Son of Augustus Vigne (above). *b.* 1837. Worc. Coll. Oxf. Now of Cheltenham.

VILLIERS. Edward Ernest, 1817. Son of the Hon. George Villiers. *b.* 1806. Fellow of Mert. Coll. Oxf.; died 1843.

VINER, John Robert, 1819, *b.* 1809.

VINTCENT, Alwyn Ignatius, 1877. Son of L. A. Vintcent, of Cape Town.

VINTCENT, Joseph, 1877. Brother of the above.

VORES, Charles Henry Stiverd, 1875. Son of Stiverd Vores, of Hastings.

VYVYAN,* Wilmot Lushington, 1874. Son of Rev. Sir V. D. Vyvyan, Bart., Rector of Withiel, Bodmin. *b.* 1861.

W.

WADDELL, George, 1824, *b.* 1812.

WADDELL, James, 1852-56, *b.* 1838. Walford and Talbot Prizeman. Actuary.

WADDINGTON, Charles Willoughby, 1878. Son of Col. Thomas Waddington, Bombay Staff Corps. *b.* 1865.

WADDINGTON, Evelyn, 1820. Son of the late William Waddington, of Chatham Place, London. *b.* 1806. Trin. Coll. Cam. 1st Class Classical Tripos.

WADDINGTON, George, 1808-11. Son of Rev. George Waddington, Vicar of Tuxford, Notts. *b.* 1793. Fellow of Trin. Coll. Cam. University Scholar and Chancellor's Medallist. Vicar of Masham, Yorks. Dean of Durham 1840; died 1869.

WADDINGTON, Horatio (Rt. Hon.), 1812-15. Brother of the above. *b.* 1799. Fellow of Trin. Coll. Cam. University Scholar. Chancellor's Medallist. Wrangler. Under Secretary of State, Home Department. Privy Councillor; died 1867.

WADDINGTON, Valentine, 1823. Brother of Evelyn Waddington (above). *b.* 1810. Died at Charterhouse 1823.

WADDINGTON, William Pendrell, 1806-8. Brother of the above. *b.* 1791. Trin. Coll. Cam. Died at Rome 1821.

WADE, Arthur Fenwick Stevenson, 1848-50, *b.* 1837. St. Columba's Coll. New Coll. Oxford.

WADE,* Charles Herbert, 1860-67, *b.* 1849,

WADE, Frederic Gore, 1803-5.

WADE, George Edward, 1863, *b.* 1853.

WADHAM, Arthur Edward Montague, 1877. Son of Edward Wadham, of Millwood, Lancashire. *b.* 1863.

WADHAM, Walter Francis Ainslie, 1877. Brother of the above. *b.* 1865.

WADMORE, Alban Henry Thomas, 1865. Son of Rev. H. R. Wadmore, Incumbent of All Souls', St. John's Wood. *b.* 1851. Solicitor.

WAGGETT, Ernest Blechynden, 1878. Son of John Waggett, M.D., of London. *b.* 1866.

WAGGETT, Philip Napier, 1875. Brother of the above. *b.* 1862.

WAINHOUSE, Robert, 1829, *b.* 1815.

WAINEWRIGHT, John, 1815, *b.* 1805. Taxing Master in Chancery. Belmont, Lee, Kent.

WAINEWRIGHT, Robert Arnold, 1816, *b.* 1807. Solicitor.

WAITE, Charles D., 1819. Son of John Waite, of Willesden House, Middlesex. *b.* 1807. St. Peters Coll. Cam. M.B. Physician. Formerly apprentice to Sir Charles Bell, F.R.S.

WAITHMAN, Henry, 1813, *b.* 1800.

WAKE,* Archibald James, 1869. Son of Sir William Wake, Bart., of Courteen Hall, Northants. *b.* 1856. Trin. Coll. Oxf. Pitsford, Northampton.

WAKE,* Charles Baldwin, 1873. Brother of the above. *b.* 1858. Studying in Hanover to qualify as a Civil Engineer.

WAKE,* Edward St. Aubyn, 1876. Son of Rear-Admiral Charles Wake, *b.* 1862.

WAKE,* Thomas Herbert Drury, 1875. Brother of Archibald J. Wake (above). *b.* 1861.

WAKEFIELD,* Gilbert, 1802-6, *b.* 1790. Army.

WAKEFIELD, Jacob, 1874. Son of William Henry Wakefield, of Sedgwick House, Kendal.

WAKEFIELD, William Steer, 1820, *b.* 1806.

WALFORD, Alfred, 1820. Son of William Walford, of High Beech, Essex. *b.* 1809. Merchant at Liverpool. Of Bebington, Cheshire.

WALFORD, Alfred Saunders, 1853-55. Son of the above. *b.* 1843. Merchant. Bromborough, Cheshire.

WALFORD, Desborough, 1810-12, *b.* 1796. Solicitor at Ipswich ; died 1873.

List of Carthusians. 243

WALFORD, Edward, 1834-41. Son of the Rev. Wm. Walford, of Hatfield Peverel, Essex. *b.* 1823. Gold Medal. Scholar of Ball. Coll. Oxf. Latin Verse, and Denyer Theol. Prize. Editor of the *Gentleman's Magazine*, Author of " Old and New London," " County Families," &c.

WALFORD, Frederick, 1821-28. Son of Joseph Green Walford, Q.C. *b.* 1810. Scholar of Trin. Coll. Cam. Barrister. Recorder of Saffron Walden and Malden; deceased.

WALFORD, Frederick, 1848-49. Brother of Edward Walford (above). *b.* 1835. Went to Durham School. Architect.

WALFORD, John Desborough, 1817. Brother of Alfred Walford (above). *b.* 1805. Gold Medal. Trin. Coll. Cam. Assistant Master at Winchester. Afterwards Bursar; died 1879.

WALFORD, Oliver, 1827-31. Brother of the above. *b.* 1814. Scholar of Trin. Coll. Cam. 1st Class Classical Tripos. Holy Orders. Master in the School 1836. Usher 1838; died 1855.

WALFORD,* Oliver Sutton, 1860-67. Son of the above. *b.* 1848. Trin. Coll. Cam. 3rd Class Classical Tripos. Vicar of Oldland, Bristol.

WALFORD, William Luke, 1851-54. Brother of Alfred Saunders Walford (above). *b.* 1841. Went to the College, Winchester. Trin. Coll. Cam. 2nd Class Classical Tripos. Curate of Fulham; died 1868.

WALFORD, William Sworder, 1864. Son of Rev. Oliver Walford (above). *b.* 1851. Lieut. Royal Artillery.

WALKER, Allen Edward, 1819, *b.* 1806.

WALKER, Andrew, 1810-13, *b.* 1799.

WALKER, Charles, 1819, *b.* 1806.

WALKER, Edward, 1817, *b.* 1804.

WALKER, Francis, 1819, *b.* 1808. Solicitor. Lived in Delamere Terrace, Hyde Park; deceased.

WALKER, Francis, 1845-48, *b.* 1831. Solicitor.

WALKER, Henry James Warren, 1864, *b.* 1850.

WALKER, Isaac John, 1829, *b.* 1816. Ball. Coll. Oxford.

WALKER, James Edward Anderton, 1867, *b.* 1853. Coffee Planter in Ceylon.

WALKER, John, 1817, *b.* 1802. Indian Civil Service.

WALKER, John Cockburn, 1874. Son of Edmund William Walker, of Esher.

WALKER, Reginald Field, 1877. Brother of the above. *b.* 1864.

WALLACE, Alexander John, 1843-49, *b.* 1830. Gold Medal. Post-Master Mert. Coll. Oxf. Prize for Latin Verse.

WALLACE, George, 1823, *b.* 1808. Trin. Coll. Cam. Head Master of the King's School, Canterbury. Rector of Burghclere, Hants.

WALLACE, George Archdale, 1856-59. Son of the above. *b.* 1843. Merchant's Office.

WALLACE, Park, 1878. Son of George Wallace, of Eardiston, Worcester. *b.* 1864.

WALLACE, William, 1862-68, *b.* 1850.

WALLER, William Burton, 1810-11, *b.* 1798.

WALLINGTON, Benjamin, 1827, *b.* 1811. Solicitor in London.

WALLINGTON, Septimus, 1830, *b.* 1816. Surveyor.

WALLIS, Preston, 1821. Son of John Wallis, Vice-Warden of the Stannaries of Devon and Cornwall. *b.* 1807. Solicitor at Bodmin. District Registrar of the Probate Court; died 1858.

WALLS, Joseph, 1821, *b.* 1810. Formerly Vicar of East Kirby, Lincolnshire.

WALMSLEY, Edward John, 1839-42, *b.* 1826. St. John's Coll. Cam. Went to India; died 1849.

WALPOLE, Arthur, 1806-8. Son of the Hon. Robert Walpole. *b.* 1793. Capt. Royal Engineers. Died at Galway 1842.

WALPOLE, Francis, 1806-10. Brother of the above. *b.* 1795. The Home Office; died 1861.

WALSH, Percival Lewis, 1852-55. Son of Percival Walsh, of Appleton. *b.* 1839. Solicitor at Oxford.

WALTER,   , 1803.

WALTER,   , 1803.

WALTER, Norman Ashley, 1877.

WALTERS, Arthur Melmoth, 1878. Son of William Melmoth Walters, Solicitor. *b.* 1865.

WALTERS, Frederico Delano, 1877.

WALTERS, Percy Melmoth, 1876.

WALTON, Herbert Fitzgerald Reed Haynes, 1875. Son of H. Haynes Walton, of London, F.R.C.S. *b.* 1861.

WARBURTON, Henry, 1838-39. Son of Rev. H. Warburton, J.P., Rector of Sible Hedingham. *b.* 1823. Ex. Coll. Oxf. Rector of Sible Hedingham, Essex.

WARBURTON, Henry Pigot Ireland, 1868-70. Son of the above. *b.* 1853. Trin. Coll. Cam. Clerk in the Court of Probate.

WARD, Frank Cavendish, 1839-43, *b.* 1826. Solicitor at Prescot, Lancashire.

WARD, James Duff, 1846-52. Son of Henry B. Ward, of Brocklands, Havant. *b.* 1834. E. I. Civil Service. Retired.

WARD, James Moore, 1877. Son of John Ward, of Lenoxvale, Belfast. *b.* 1862.

WARD, Richard, 1800-4. Son of Rev. Richard Ward, Rector of Somerby, Linc. *b.* 1786. Fellow of Trin. Coll. Cam. Senr. Opt. Chancellor's Medallist. Craven Scholar. Holy Orders; died 1869.

WARD,* Samuel Hawkins, 1803-7, *b.* 1790; deceased.

WARDE, George Lloyd, 1853. Son of Charles Thomas Warde, of Clopton House, Warwick. *b.* 1840; died 1853.

WARDON, Thomas, 1810-13, *b.* 1801. Went to Westminster School.

WARING, Edward Loxley, 1877. Son of William Waring, J.P., of Woodlands, Chelsfield, Kent. *b.* 1863.

WARING, Edward Stokes, 1820, *b.* 1809.

WARING, John Edward, 1820, *b.* 1807.

WARINGTON, William Richard, 1822, *b.* 1809. Died at Charterhouse 1824.

WARNE, Harold Edmund, 1874.

WARNER, John, 1855-57, *b.* 1841.

WARRE, Annesley Tyndale, 1874. Son of C. Bampfylde Warre, of Townlands, Lindfield, Sussex. *b.* 1861. R.M. Academy, Woolwich.

WARRE, Bampfylde Drought, 1873. Brother of the above. *b.* 1859. Merton Coll. Oxf.

WARRE, George, 1802-4. Merchant at Lisbon; deceased.

WARRE, John Whitehead, 1802-4. Drowned in the Wye near Ross.

WARRE, Thomas, 1800-2.

WARREN, Edward Malthus, 1873. Son of Reginald Augustus Warren, of Preston Place, Sussex. *b.* 1859.

WARREN, William Pennefather, 1874.

WASEY, George William Leigh, 1821. Son of Rev. George Wasey, Rector of Ulcombe, Kent. *b.* 1811. Ch. Ch. Oxf. Incumbent of Morville, Shropshire; died 1877.

WATERFIELD, Charles Russell, 1876. Son of O. C. Waterfield, of Temple Grove, East Sheen. *b.* 1862.

WATERWORTH, Charles Albert, 1853-55, *b.* 1840.

WATSON, Edward Dayot, 1828, *b.* 1816. Linc. Coll. Oxf. Went to India; deceased.

WATSON, George William, 1813-18, *b.* 1802. Vicar of Milford, Surrey.

WATSON, Henry Piercy, 1868-71, *b.* 1853. Jesus Coll. Cam.

WATSON,* Henry Robert, 1800-7, *b.* 1789. Army (Guards).

WATSON, Herbert Nicol, 1876. Son of Robert Brown Watson, of New Brighton, Cheshire. *b.* 1863.

WATSON, William Arthur, 1874.

WATTS, , 1803.

WATTS, Robert Rowley, 1844-48. Son of Rev. John Watts, Rector of Tarrant Gunville, and Prebendary of Salisbury. *b.* 1829. Univ. Coll. Oxf. 2nd Class Math. 3rd Class Lit. Hum. Assistant Master in the School. Vicar of Stourpaine, Dorset.

WATTS, William, 1820. Son of Robert Watts, of Hampstead. *b.* 1807. Scholar of Univ. Coll. Oxf. 2nd Class Math. Incumbent of Christ Church, Endell Street, London; died 1847.

WAY, Holroyd Fitz William, 1823. Son of Col. Benjamin Way, of Denham Place, Uxbridge. *b.* 1809. Lieut. 88th Regt.; died 1866.

WAY, William Robert, 1861-64. Son of Rev. C. J. Way, Vicar of Boreham, Essex. *b.* 1849. Brewer. Romford.

WAYET, John, 1822. Son of Rev. John Wayet, Vicar of Pinchbeck, Spalding. *b.* 1808. Silver Medal for English Verse; died 1825.

WAYET, West, 1822. Brother of the above. *b.* 1809. Queens Coll. Oxf. Vicar of Pinchbeck, Lincolnshire. Hon. Canon of Lincoln.

WAYMOUTH, Charles, 1829, *b.* 1806. Trin. Coll. Cam. Holy Orders.

WAYMOUTH, William Francis, 1874.

WEARE, Frank, 1878.

WEATHERHEAD, Alexander, 1867, *b.* 1853.

WEBB, Edward Henry, 1848-50, *b.* 1833. 88th Regt. Killed in the attack on the Quarry, Sebastopol, 7th June, 1855.

WEBB, George Price, 1818, *b.* 1807.

WEBBER, Howard, 1877. Son of Robert Pullen Webber, late of Elmstead, Chiselhurst. *b.* 1863.

WEBBER, William, 1824, *b.* 1812.

WEBB-WARE, Charles Edward, 1878. Son of T. Webb-Ware, of Cheltenham. *b.* 1863.

WEBER, Frederic Parkes, 1877. Son of Hermann David Weber, M.D. *b.* 1863.

WEBSTER, Francis Joseph, 1874.

WEBSTER, George Arthur, 1874. Son of Rev. G. Webster, D.D., Rector of S. Nicholas and Chancellor of Cork. *b.* 1861. Queens Coll. Cork.

WEBSTER, Reginald Godfrey Michael, 1874. Brother of the above. *b.* 1860. Trin. Coll. Dublin.

WEBSTER, Richard Everard, 1859-61, *b.* 1842. Talbot Scholar. Scholar of Trin. Coll. Cam. Wrangler. Barrister. Q.C.

WEBSTER, Thomas, 1823, *b.* 1811. Scholar of Trin. Coll. Cam. Wrangler. Barrister. Q.C.

WEBSTER, Thomas Calthrop, 1856-59. Son of Thomas Webster, Q.C., F.R.S. *b.* 1840. Trin. Coll. Cam. Vicar of St. Mark's, Old Street, London.

WEBSTER, William, 1823, *b.* 1811. Fellow of Queen's Coll. Cam. Holy Orders. Master of the City of London School.

WEDDERBURN,* Charles Francis Webster, 1831. Son of Sir James and Lady Frances Webster-Wedderburn. *b.* 1820. Late Capt. 52nd Regt. Served in India (Medal); also in the Franco-German War. Bronze Cross, &c.

WEDGEWOOD, Robert, 1820, *b.* 1806. Trin. Coll. Cam. Holy Orders.

WEEKES, Augustus Frederick, 1837. Wadham Coll. Oxf. Holy Orders.

WEGUELIN, James Crawford, 1837-39, *b.* 1824. Trin. Coll. Cambridge.

WEIGALL,* Gilbert, 1870. Son of Alfred Weigall, of the Close, Salisbury. *b.* 1858. Keble Coll. Oxford.

WEIL, Basil Manhali, 1861-62, *b.* 1848.

WEIR, John Campbell, 1878. Son of Archibald Weir, M.D., St. Mungho's, Great Malvern. *b.* 1863.

WELBANK, Richard, 1809-13, *b.* 1797. Medical Practitioner.

WELCH, Henry Edward Parker, 1874. Son of Henry Thomas Welch, of Leck Hall, Lancashire. *b.* 1860. Trin. Coll. Cambridge.

WELCH,* John Davenport, 1853-54. Son of James Davenport Welch, of Snaresbrook, Essex. *b.* 1837. War Office, Medical Department.

WELCH, Thomas Stanley, 1875.

WELCH, Walter Barrows, 1875.

WELCH,* William Davis, 1854-55. Brother of J. D. Welch (above). *b.* 1839. Major Royal Marine Artillery.

WELDON, Anthony Arthur, 1877. Eldest son of Sir Anthony Crosdill Weldon, Bart., of Rahenderry, Co. Kildare. *b.* 1863.

WELDON, Thomas Hamilton, 1877. Brother of the above. *b.* 1864.

WELLS,* Francis Ballard, 1821-31. Son of Rev. George Wells, Rector of Wiston, Sussex. *b.* 1811. Orator. Silver Medal. Demy of Magd. Coll. Oxf. Private Sec. to Archbishop of Canterbury 1837-42. Rector of Woodchurch, Kent.

WELLS, Thomas Pratt, 1807-9, *b.* 1793.

WEST, Charles Edward, 1824, *b.* 1815.

WEST, Edward Stamp, 1822. Son of Gilbert H. West, of Willesden, Middlesex. *b.* 1808. Indian Secretary; deceased.

WEST, George, 1805-7. Royal Artillery.

WEST, Gilbert Henry, 1821. Brother of Edward S. West (above). *b.* 1807. Jesus Coll. Cam. Incumbent of Corfe, Somerset; deceased.

WEST, Henry Jorin, 1845-49, *b.* 1829. B.N.C. Oxf. Holy Orders. Master at Radley; died 1859.

WEST, Horace, 1875. Son of the late Frederick West, of The Waldrons, Croydon. *b.* 1861.

WEST, Horace Charles George, 1873. Son of Algernon West, Deputy Chairman Inland Revenue. *b.* 1859.

WEST, James Bankes, 1820, *b.* 1807. Royal Navy.

WEST, Lewis Borrett, 1849-51, *b.* 1834. Merchant.

WEST, Reginald Jervoise, 1872. Brother of Horace Charles West (above). *b.* 1857.

WEST, Temple, 1828. Brother of Gilbert H. West (above). *b.* 1813. Magd. Hall, Oxf. Rector of Tetcott, Devon.

WESTMACOTT, Arthur, 1827, *b.* 1814. Emigrated to Australia.

WESTON, John, 1810-13, *b.* 1797. Medical Practitioner.

WESTON, Spicer James, 1866-70. Son of Edward Weston, of St. Leonards-on-Sea. *b.* 1852. Teacher of Music.

WESTROP, Edward John, 1866-68, *b.* 1852.

WETHERALL,* Charles Augustus, 1840-48. Son of Col. Charles Wetherall. *b.* 1825. Trin. Coll. Toronto. Chaplain to the Forces.

WETHERALL,* Robert Alexander, 1863-66. Son of Lt.-Col. Frederick Augustus Wetherall. *b.* 1852. Coffee Planter in Ceylon.

WETHERED, Edmund Peel, 1876. Son of the Rev. Florence Thomas Wethered, of Hurley, Berks. *b.* 1863.

WETHERELL, Thomas May, 1821, *b.* 1807. Holy Orders. Incumbent of Flaxley.

WETHERMAN, George Arthur, 1856-58, *b.* 1846; deceased.

WHALLEY, Daniel Constable, 1819, *b.* 1806. Pemb. Coll. Cam. Holy Orders. Hemley, near Woodbridge.

WHARTON, Charles Bygrave, 1862-63, *b.* 1849.

WHARTON,* Edward Ross, 1859-63, *b.* 1844. Gold Medal. Talbot Scholar. Scholar of Trinity and Fellow of Jesus Coll. Oxf. Ireland Scholar 1865.

WHARTON, George Henry Lawrence, 1878. Son of Rev. J. C. Wharton, Vicar of Gilling, Yorks. *b.* 1865.

WHARTON, Henry Thornton, 1862-63, *b.* 1846.

WHARTON, John Thomas, 1822. Son of Rev. William Wharton, Vicar of Gilling, Yorks, and grandson of the 1st Lord Dundas. *b.* 1809. Trin. Coll. Cam. J.P. D.L. Skelton Castle, Yorks.

List of Carthusians. 251

WHARTON,* John Warburton, 1851-56. Son of Rev. George Wharton, Vicar of Kinver. *b.* 1837. St. John's Coll. Cam. 3rd Class Classical Tripos. Holy Orders. Assistant Master of the Proprietary School, Bath ; died 1872.

WHATELEY, Francis John, 1873.

WHATELY,* Arthur Pepys,' 1839-47, *b.* 1829. Ch. Ch. Oxf. Barrister.

WHATMORE,* Edward Newman, 1830, *b.* 1818.

WHEELER, William, 1820, *b.* 1807.

WHINNEY, Charles Thomas, 1872. Son of Frederick Whinney, of 90, Regent's Park Road, London. *b.* 1858. Articled to a Solicitor.

WHINNEY, Thomas Bostock, 1872. Brother of the above. *b.* 1860. Student at the Royal Academy.

WHISH,* George Thomas, 1840-44. Son of Rev. R. P. Whish, Vicar of Monkton, Kent. *b.* 1826. 49, Brompton Crescent, London.

WHISH, Henry Fulham, 1837-42. Brother of the above. *b.* 1824. C. C. C. Cam. Curate of St. Michael and All Angels, Brighton.

WHITAKER, Thomas Hordern, 1826. Son of the Rev. Thomas Thoresby Whitaker, Vicar of Whalley, Lancashire. *b.* 1814. Ex. Coll. Oxf. F.S.A. D.L. The Holme, Burnley.

WHITBREAD, Gordon, 1826-31, *b.* 1814. Gold Medal. B.N.C. Oxf. 2nd Class Lit. Hum. Barrister. Governor of Charterhouse.

WHITE, Andrew Douglass, 1806-8, *b.* 1793.

WHITE, Edwin Francis, 1872.

WHITE, Ely Emlyn, 1869, *b.* 1854.

WHITE, Henry John, 1825, *b.* 1814.

WHITE, Herbert, 1858-60, *b.* 1846.

WHITE, John, 1878. Son of John White, of Lee, Kent. *b.* 1865.

WHITE, Reginald James Neville, 1876. Son of James Sewell White, of the Indian Civil Service. *b.* 1863.

WHITE, Richard Hamond, 1809-13, *b.* 1799. Navy.

WHITE, William Frederick, 1825, *b.* 1811. Trin. Coll. Oxf. D.C.L.

WHITE, William Thomas, 1869, *b.* 1852.

WHITE-COOPER, William, 1874. Son of W. White-Cooper, F.R.C.S., of 19, Berkeley Square. *b.* 1861.

WHITEHEAD, Gervase Frederick, 1874.

WHITEHEAD, John, 1848-51, *b.* 1839.

WHITEHEAD,* William Henry, 1808-13, *b.* 1797. Solicitor, of Gray's Inn.

WHITELEY, Thomas Henry, 1876. Son of Rev. J. H. Whiteley, Rector of Pedmore, Stourbridge.

WHITESIDE, Frederick Richard Alexander, 1872. Son of Mr. Whiteside, of the Madras Civil Service.

WHITHAM, Francis James, 1878. Son of James Whitham, of Gledhow, Leeds. *b.* 1865.

WHITING, Algernon Oswald, 1874.

WHITMORE, Charles, 1821, *b.* 1808.

WHITTAKER, George, 1827, *b.* 1811. Fellow of Queens Coll. Cam. 1st Class Class Tripos. Vicar of Oakington, Cambs.

WHITTAKER, Henry, 1822. Son of John Whittaker, of Newcastle Court, Co. Radnor. *b.* 1808. Of Lyston Hall, Herefordshire.

WICKHAM, William Cecil, 1875. Son of Rev. H. J. Wickham, The College, Winchester. *b.* 1861.

WICHE, Charles George, 1834-36, *b.* 1819. M.D.

WIGAN, Alfred Lewis, 1872. Son of Rev. Alfred Wigan, Rector of Luddersdown, Kent. *b.* 1857. Keble Coll. Oxf.

WIGG, John Stone, 1839-43. Eldest son of John Wigg, of Stoneleigh, Kent. *b.* 1827. Solicitor in London. Hungershall Park, Tunbridge Wells.

WIGG, Joseph, 1840-47, *b.* 1830. Merchant's Office. Indian Army; died 1879.

List of Carthusians. 253

WIGGINS, Douglas Robert, 1818, *b.* 1807.

WIGGINS, Matthew, 1820, *b.* 1809.

WIGGINS, Richard Jones, 1820, *b.* 1807. Paper Manufacturer. Rickmansworth.

WIGHT, Thomas, 1808-14, *b.* 1797. Solicitor in London.

WIGHTWICK, Henry, 1825, *b.* 1809. Scholar and Fellow of Pemb. Coll. Oxf. Rector of Codford, St. Peter, Wilts.

WILD, Charles James, 1878. Son of Charles Kemp Wild, Thornlea, Hampstead. *b.* 1865.

WILDE, Charles Robert Claude (Lord Truro), 1827. Eldest son of the 1st Baron Truro. *b.* 1816. Trin. Coll. Cam. Clerk of Assize, Oxford Circuit. Col. Commandant Middlesex Artillery Volunteers. Succeeded his father as 2nd Baron Truro 1855.

WILDE,* Ernest James, 1858. Son of Charles Norris Wilde, 19, Cornwall Terrace, Regent's Park. *b.* 1848. Solicitor.

WILDE (Hon.) Thomas Montague Carrington, 1827. Brother of 2nd Lord Truro (above). *b.* 1818. Trin. Coll. Cam. Registrar of the Court of Bankruptcy at Bristol.

WILKINS, George Dashwood, 1825, *b.* 1813. Bengal Civil Service (retired). 38, Leinster Sq.

WILKINS, William Bushby, 1826, *b.* 1813. Caius Coll. Cam. Barrister.

WILKINSON, Arthur Oats, 1825, *b.* 1815. Stock Exchange. Linkfield House, Red Hill, Surrey.

WILKINSON, George Alexander Eason, 1875. Summerfield House, Putney.

WILKINSON, Herbert Rokeby, 1869-70, *b.* 1855.

WILKINSON, Josiah, 1823, *b.* 1812. Solicitor.

WILKINSON, Thomas, 1876. Son of George Goodley Wilkinson, of Putney. *b.* 1863.

WILLES, Charles Thomas, 1819. Son of Rev. William Shippen Willes, Rector of Preston Bissett, Bucks. *b.* 1808. Of Kingsutton, Oxon. J.P. for Northampton; died 1877.

WILLIAMS, Alfred, 1868. Son of Wellington Williams, of Park House, Leyton, Essex. *b.* 1853.

WILLIAMS, Alfred Frank, 1807-8, *b.* 1793. Fellow of St. John's Coll. Cambridge.

WILLIAMS, Edward Matcham, 1872. Son of Rev. H. Blackstone Williams (above). *b.* 1860. R.M. Coll. Sandhurst.

WILLIAMS, Edwin, 1869-74. Brother of Alfred Williams (above). *b.* 1856. Pemb. Coll. Cam. Law Tripos 1877.

WILLIAMS, Frederick Sims, 1824, *b.* 1812. Scholar of Trin. Coll. Cam. Barrister.

WILLIAMS, Harry, 1871. Brother of Edwin Williams (above). *b.* 1859.

WILLIAMS, James, 1825, *b.* 1816.

WILLAMS, John, 1809-11.

WILLIAMS, John Michael, 1827. Eldest son of Michael Williams, M.P., of Caerhays, Cornwall. *b.* 1813. D.L. for Cornwall, Deputy Warden of the Stannaries. Caerhays Castle, and Gnaton Hall, Devon.

WILLIAMS, Reginald, 1870, *b.* 1859.

WILLIAMS, Sidney, 1867, *b.* 1855.

WILLIAMS, Stephen Frederick, 1840-45. Son of Stephen Williams, Solicitor, of Clapham Common. *b.* 1826. Scholar of St. John's Coll. Cam. Wrangler. Holy Orders. Mathematical Master in the School. Vice-Principal of the Liverpool Collegiate School. Rector of Cold Norton, Essex.

WILLIAMS, Theobald Wolfe I. 1862. Left the same year. *b.* 1850.

WILLIAMS,* Thomas John, 1842-50. Son of John Williams, of Abbey Foregate, Shrewsbury. *b.* 1831. Univ. Coll. Oxf. Rector of Waddesdon, Bucks.

WILLIAMS, William Cowell, 1869-73. Brother of Harry Williams (above). *b.* 1854. Pemb. Coll. Cam. Mathematical Tripos 1876.

WILLIAMS, William Smith Gittinge, 1877. Son of J. H. Williams, of Baltimore, U.S.A. *b.* 1863.

WILLIAMS, Wynn William, 1836-42, *b.* 1823. Emm. Coll. Cam. Capt. 3rd Dragoons.

WILLIAMS-WYNN, Henry Cunliffe, 1876. Son of C. W. Williams-Wynn, M.P. of Coed-y-Maen, Montgomeryshire. *b.* 1863.

WILLIS, Edward, 1817. Son of Richard Willis, of Halsnead Park, Lancs. *b.* 1805. Capt. 37th Regt. retired.

WILLIS, Frederick 1815. Brother of the above. *b.* 1804. Capt. 9th Lancers. Master of the Ceremonies at Dublin Castle.

WILLIS,* John Walpole, 1806-9. Son of Capt. William Willis, 13th Light Dragoons. *b.* 1793. Barrister. Colonial Judge. J.P. and D.L. of Wick House, Worcester; died 1877.

WILLIS, Thomas, 1815-18. Brother of Frederick Willis (above). *b.* 1803.

WILLOCK,* Robert Peel, 1833-39. Son of Robert Peel Willock. Postmaster at Manchester, and cousin of Sir Robert Peel. *b.* 1821. Wine Merchant in Manchester.

WILMER, John, 1822. Son of Bradford Wilmer, M.D. *b.* 1812.

WILMER, William, 1822, *b.* 1811. Lieut.-Col. 8th Royal Irish Hussars. Served with great distinction in India; died at Bombay 1848.

WILMOT, Edmund, 1821. Son of Sir Robert Wilmot, Bart. *b.* 1809. To India. J.P. and D.L. Yorks; died 1869.

WILMOT,* Edward Parry Eardley- 1855-62. Son of Sir John E. Eardley-Wilmot, Bart., M.P. *b.* 1843. St. John's Coll. Oxf. Privy Council Office.

WILMOT, Ernest Augustus Eardley- 1862. Son of Rev. E. R. Eardley-Wilmot, Canon of Worcester. *b.* 1848. Clare Coll. Cam. 1st Class Theological Tripos. Vicar of Windrush, Oxon.

WILMOT, Hugh Eden Eardley- 1862. Son of Sir John E. Eardley Wilmot, Bart., M.P. *b.* 1850. Barrister. Midland Circuit.

WILMOT, William Assheton Eardley- 1853-59. Eldest brother of the above. *b.* 1840. Ball. Coll. Oxf. Capt. 5th Regt.

WILMOT, Woollett Edward, 1821. Son of Sir Thomas Wilmot, Bart., and brother of Edmund Wilmot (above). *b.* 1808. To India; died 1864.

WILSON,* Albany Howard, 1803-6, *b.* 1793.

WILSON, Aubrey William Freeman, 1871. Son of Rev. Freeman Wilson, Rector of East Horsley, Surrey. *b.* 1858.

WILSON,* Charles Grey, 1813-16, *b.* 1801.

WILSON, Ernest James, 1876. Son of Edward S. Wilson, of Melton, Brough, E. Yorks. *b.* 1861. Trin. Coll. Cam.

WILSON, Gilbert, 1878. Brother of the above. *b.* 1864.

WILSON, Herbert Howard, 1876.

WILSON, Hugh Francis, 1853-54. Of Durham. *b.* 1836. Trin. Coll. Oxf. Civil Engineer, South America.

WILSON, John Peter, 1801-6, *b.* 1791.

WILSON, Thomas Harrocks, 1875. Son of T. Wilson, Cooper's Hill, Preston, Lancashire.

WILSON, William Wilson, 1878. Son of W. H. Wilson, of Windbourne, Liverpool. *b.* 1864.

WILTSHIRE, Frederick, 1802-7, *b.* 1792.

WILTSHIRE, George Charles, 1800-5, *b.* 1789.

WINKWORTH, Harry Gordon, 1872-74. Son of L. H. Winkworth, of Rochester.

WINDSOR, Edward, 1831, *b.* 1816.

WINDSOR, William Richard, 1831, *b.* 1821.

WING, John William, 1826-31. Son of Rev. John Wing, Rector of Thornhaugh, Northants. *b.* 1813. Fellow of Univ. Coll. Oxf. 2nd Class Lit. Hum. Barrister. County Court Judge; died 1855.

WINGFIELD, Roland Penrhyn, 1874. Son of Major Walter Wingfield. Rhysnant Hall, Montgomeryshire.

WINGFIELD, William Wriothesley, 1822. Son of William Wingfield Baker, Master in Chancery. *b.* 1814. Ch. Ch. Oxf. Vicar of Gulval, Cornwall.

WINN, John Ashton, 1852-58, b. 1844.

WINSCOM, George Vivian, 1838-41. Son of the late G. Winscom, of Alnwick, Northumberland. b. 1826. Indian Army. Engineers.

WINTHROP, Benjamin Eveleigh, 1825, b. 1812. Wadh. Coll. Oxf. 1st Class Math. Barrister.

WINTHROP, Edward Gamaliel, 1822, b. 1809. St. John's Coll. Cambridge.

WISDOM, Henry John William Cridland, 1877. Son of Henry Constable Wisdom, of Tunbridge Wells. b. 1864.

WISE, Charles Dacres, 1878. Son of Henry Wise, of Charlton Court, Steyning, Sussex. b. 1864.

WITHERBY, John, 1810-11. Solicitor.

WITT, James Beadon, 1848. Left the same year. Eldest son of James Witt, of Swaffham Prior, Cambs. b. 1832; died 1873.

WITT, Sheridan, 1849-51. Son of Charles Witt, Physician, of London. b. 1834. Emigrated to Australia.

WIX,* Hubert Hector John, 1874. Son of Rev. Joseph Wix, Rector of Littlebury, Essex. b. 1861. Exhibitioner and Senior Scholar.

WIX, Louis Arthur, 1864. Brother of the above. b. 1850. Clare Coll. Cam. Solicitor.

WODEHOUSE, Algernon, 1828. Son of the Hon. and Rev. William Wodehouse, of Hingham, Norfolk. b. 1814. Trin. Coll. Cam. Rector of Easton, Winchester. Domestic Chaplain to the Duke of Northumberland.

WODEHOUSE, Campbell, 1837-44. Son of Edmond Wodehouse, M.P., of Sennow Lodge, Norfolk. b. 1826. Ch. Ch. Oxf. Rector of Alderford, Norfolk; died 1868.

WODEHOUSE,* Edmond, 1829-36. Brother of the above. b. 1818. 24th Regt. Major-General.

WOLLASTON,* Edward, 1804-11, b. 1793. Medical Practitioner; deceased.

WOLLASTON, Francis Hayles, 1814-15. Son of Ven. Francis John Hyde Wollaston, Archdeacon of Essex and Vicar of South Weald. b. 1803. Pemb. Coll. Cam. Rector of Dereham. Resigned his Orders; deceased.

WOLLASTON,* John Ramsden, 1802-8, *b.* 1791. Ch. Coll. Cam. Holy Orders. Emigrated to Australia.

WOOD, Alexander, 1802-3; deceased.

WOOD, Alfred Richard, 1872.

WOOD,* Charles, 1801-7. Son of Thomas Wood, of Littleton, Middlesex. *b.* 1790. Served in 52nd Regt. and 10th Hussars in the Peninsula and at Waterloo. Colonel.

WOOD,* Charles Watkins Arthur Harcourt, 1830-38. Son of the late Col. Thomas Wood, M.P. *b.* 1820. 43rd Regt. Retired.

WOOD, Edward, 1826, *b.* 1810.

WOOD, Ernest Reuss, 1865. Son of John Wood, of Liverpool. *b.* 1851. Merchant at Liverpool.

WOOD, Herbert Kennedy, 1873.

WOOD, James, 1816. Son of John Wood, of Seale Lodge, Farnham. *b.* 1804. Ch. Ch. Oxf. Vicar of Warnham, Sussex. Now residing at Worthing.

WOOD, Reginald, 1874. Brother of Ernest Reuss Wood (above). *b.* 1860. Merchant. Liverpool.

WOOD, Richard Warner Kendal, 1822, *b.* 1807. Trin. Hall, Cam. Holy Orders. Husbands Bosworth, Leicester; died 1853.

WOOD, Robert Scorell, 1823.

WOOD, Western, 1843-46. Son of the late Western Wood, M.P. for the City of London. *b.* 1830. Pemb. Coll. Oxf. Emigrated to Australia. Formerly a Member of Council, Queensland.

WOODGATE, Alfred Henry Augustin, 1870. Son of Rev. Canon Woodgate. *b.* 1856.

WOODGATE,* Charles Henry, 1826. Son of Rev. Stephen Woodgate, Vicar of Pembury, Kent. *b.* 1812. Indian Civil Service. Judge; deceased.

WOODGATE, Decimus, 1825. Son of the late F. Woodgate, of Somerhill, Kent. *b.* 1812.

WOODGATE, George Hardinge, 1875. Son of the following.

WOODGATE,* George Stephen, 1820. Son of Rev. Stephen Woodgate, Vicar of Pembury. *b.* 1810. Univ. Coll. Oxf. Vicar of Pembury, Kent; died 1871.

WOODHOUSE, Campbell Hilary, 1873. Son of Henry Woodhouse, of Wyndham Place, London. 107th Regt.

WOODHOUSE, Henry Alderson, 1817, *b.* 1804. Barrister. Attorney-General for Bombay.

WOODINGTON, Henry, 1809-12, *b.* 1794.

WOODLAND, Henry, 1825. From Newton St. Cyril, Devon. *b.* 1812.

WOODRUFF, Thomas, 1818. Son of George Woodruff. *b.* 1805. St. John's Coll. Oxf. Vicar of Wistow, Hunts. J.P.

WOODTHORPE, Charles, 1826. Son of Henry Woodthorpe, LL.D., Town Clerk of London. *b.* 1816. Civil Engineer; deceased.

WOODTHORPE, Frederick, 1825. Brother of the above. *b.* 1815. King's Coll. London. Barrister. Town Clerk of London; deceased.

WOODWARD, John, 1820. Son of John Woodward, of Street, Framfield, Sussex. *b.* 1810. Captain in the Army. Now residing at Folkestone.

WOODWARD, William, 1819. Brother of the above. *b.* 1807. Trin. Coll. Cam. Rector of Plumpton, Sussex; died 1874.

WOODYEARE, John Fountain, 1822. Eldest son of John Elwin Fountain, who took the name of Woodyeare. *b.* 1809. Ch. Coll. Cam. Holy Orders. Crookhill, Rotherham, Yorks.

WOODYEARE, Richard Peter, 1824. Brother of the above. *b.* 1811. Lieut. 67th Regt; died 1835.

WOOLLWRIGHT, Henry Harriott, 1873.

WORDSWORTH, William, 1820-22. Youngest son of William Wordsworth, of Rydal Mount (Poet Laureate). *b.* 1810. Of the Hacket, Westmoreland. J.P. and D.L. for Cumberland. Willow Brook, Eton.

WRANGHAM, Digby Strangeways, 1842-48. Son of the late Digby Cayley Wrangham, M.P., Q.C., of the Rocks, Gloucester. *b.* 1831. St. John's Coll. Oxf. Vicar of Darrington, Yorks.

WRAY, Robert William, 1818, *b*. 1805.

WREFORD, Samuel, 1829. Son of John Wreford, of Broughton House, Kent. *b*. 1814. J.P. for Kent. Lord of the Manor of Broughton.

WRENCH, Alfred Julius Stilwell, 1862. Son of Rev. T. W. Wrench, Rector of St. Michael's, Cornhill. *b*. 1851; deceased.

WRENCH, Henry Sykes Thornton, 1862, *b*. 1853; deceased.

WRENCH, John Mervyn, 1862, *b*. 1849. Civil Engineer; now employed on the Punjaub Railway at Lahore.

WRIGHT, Arthur Franklin, 1876. Son of Rev. Arthur Wright, Rector of Coningsby and Canon of Lincoln. *b*. 1861.

WRIGHT, Charles William, 1876. Son of William Wright, of Woolaton, Nottingham. *b*. 1863.

WRIGHT, Dennis Batson Stewart, 1849-55. Son of D. Wright. Army Surgeon (Guards). *b*. 1837. Ordnance Department.

WRIGHT, Herbert Edwin, 1877. Son of Herbert Wright, Solicitor, of Hornsey. *b*. 1864.

WRIGHT, James Dennis, 1814.

WRIGHT, John, 1837-39. Eldest son of John Wright, of Wickham Place, Essex. *b*. 1821. J.P. and D.L. for Essex. Of Hatfield Priory, Chelmsford. Formerly Capt. Essex Militia.

WRIGHT, John, 1826, *b*. 1814.

WRIGHT, John Peter, 1823, *b*. 1808.

WRIGHT, Lyttleton Maynard, 1876.

WRIGHT, Peter Charles, 1837. Second son of John Wright, of Wickham Place, Essex, and brother of John Wright (above). *b*. 1825. Addiscombe. Died on his way to India 1851.

WRIGHT, Richard Plumley, 1876.

WRIGHT, William, 1813-14, *b*. 1798. Medical Practitioner.

List of Carthusians. 261

WRIGHT,* William George, 1811-17, *b.* 1800; died 1817.

WRIGHT,* William Queneborough, 1834-42. Son of the late W. Wright, of Midhurst. *b.* 1824. Worc. Coll. Oxf.

WRIGHTSON, Thomas Barnardiston, 1819. Son of William Wrightson, of Cusworth, Yorks. *b.* 1806. B.N.C. Oxf.

WYBERGH, Thomas Lawson, 1803-7. Son of Thomas Wybergh, of Clifton Hall. *b.* 1788. Cambridge; died 1812.

WYBERGH, William, 1858-60, *b.* 1843; died 1871.

WYBERGH, William, 1803-6. Brother of Thomas Lawson Wybergh (above). *b.* 1787. Of Clifton Hall, Westmoreland, and Isell Hall, Cumberland.

WYLDE,* Charles, 1842-50. Son of Major-Gen. William Wylde. *b.* 1832. Emm. Coll. Cam. War Office.

WYNNE, Campbell Montague Edward, 1873. Son of the late Llewelyn Wynne. *b.* 1859.

WYNTER,* Lionel Robert, 1857-64. Son of Rev. Philip Wynter, President of St. John's Coll. Oxf. *b.* 1846. St. John's Coll. Oxf.

WYNYARD, Edward George, 1874. Son of William Wynyard, of Hursley, Winchester. *b.* 1861. 2nd Lieut. Warwick Militia.

WYNYARD,* Henry Robert, 1833-40. Son of Major-General Edward Buckley Wynyard. *b.* 1825. St. Mary's Hall, Oxf.; died 1846.

WYNYARD, Montague George Lascelles, 1816. Son of the late Montague John Wynyard, Capt. Coldstream Guards. *b.* 1802. Ch. Coll. Cam. Holy Orders; died 1840.

Y.

YARD, Edward, 1819. Of Barbados. *b.* 1805; deceased.

YARDLEY, Henry Edward, 1872. Son of the late Sir William Yardley, Knt. *b.* 1857. Hadlow Park, Tunbridge.

YATES, Richard, 1800-1.

YATES, Edmund Telfer, 1821. Son of Rev. Richard Yates, D.D., Chaplain to Chelsea Hospital. *b.* 1811. Of Burgh Hall, Norfolk. Oriel Coll. Oxf. Rector of Burgh next Aylsham, Norfolk. J.P. for Norfolk.

YATES, Frederick, 1810-11, *b.* 1794. Actor. The friend, pupil and partner of Charles Matthews, with whom he was co-proprietor of the Adelphi Theatre; died 1842.

YATES, Henry Thomas, 1827. Son of Joseph Yates, of Peel Hall, Lancashire. *b.* 1813. Royal Navy. Afterwards in E. India Company's Service. Drowned at Whampoa.

YATES, Joseph St. John, 1824-27. Eldest brother of the above. *b.* 1808. Gold Medal. Ch. Ch. Oxf. Barrister, Judge of County Courts.

YATES, Robert Charles, 1876.

YELLOLY, John, 1823. Son of John Yelloly, M.D., F.R.S., of Cavendish Hall, Suffolk. *b.* 1809. Trin. Coll. Cam. Formerly Vicar of Tring, Herts. Grove House, Sible Headingham.

YENN, John, 1801-4; deceased.

YORKE (Hon.) Grantham Munton, 1820. Brother of the 4th Earl of Hardwicke. *b.* 1809. 52nd Regt. Afterwards ordained. Formerly Rector of S. Philip's, Birmingham. Prebend of Lichfield. Dean of Worcester; died 1879.

YORKE, Henry Galgacus, 1811. Left the same year. Went to Eton. Ch. Coll. Cam. M.P. for York 1841-8; died 1848.

YORKE, Horatio Arthur, 1863-65. Son of the Hon. and Rev. Henry Reginald Yorke, Canon of Ely. *b.* 1848. Lieut. Royal Engineers.

YORKE,* Reginald Beauchamp, 1856-62. Brother of the above. *b.* 1845. Admiralty Office. Emigrated to Australia.

YORKE, Thomas Henry, 1800-4, *b.* 1785. Univ. Coll. Oxf. Vicar of Bishop Middleham, Durham.

YOUNG, Alfred Horace, 1875.

YOUNG, Archibald, 1829, *b.* 1814.

YOUNG, Charles Allen, 1814-16. Son of Rev. John Young. *b.* 1800. 1st Regt. Served in the Kaffre War 1835. Major. Retired 1843.

YOUNG (Sir) Charles George (Knt.), 1807-11 Eldest son of Jonathan Young, of Lambeth, Surgeon. *b.* 1795. Herald's College. Garter King of Arms 1842. D.C.L.; died 1869.

YOUNG, Charles James, 1865. Son of Rev. James Reynolds Young, Rector of Whitnash (below). *b.* 1851. Emigrated to Queensland, Australia.

YOUNG, Edward, 1821, *b.* 1806. Trin. Coll. Cam. Holy Orders.

YOUNG, Edward Newton, 1810-14. Son of Rev. John Young. *b.* 1795. Ch. Ch. Oxf. 2nd Class Lit. Hum. Assistant Master. Rector of Quainton, Bucks. Chaplain to the Duke of Buckingham.

YOUNG, Francis, 1843-47. Brother of the following. *b.* 1829. Trin. Coll. Cam. 3rd Senr. Opt. Barrister.

YOUNG, Frederick, 1843-49. Son of the following. *b.* 1830. Ball. Coll. Oxf. Rector of Pett, Sussex.

YOUNG, Henry, 1807-12. Brother of Sir Charles George Young (above). *b.* 1797. Solicitor to the Governors of Harrow School; died 1869.

YOUNG, Henry, 1821, *b.* 1810.

YOUNG, James Forbes, 1807-12. Brother of Sir Charles G. Young (above). *b.* 1796. Surgeon. M.D. A distinguished naturalist; died 1860.

YOUNG, James Reynolds, 1823. Son of William Young, of Highbury Grange. *b.* 1807. Scholar of Caius Coll. Cam. Rector of Whitnash, Leamington. Hon. Canon of Worcester.

YOUNG, John, 1805-6, *b.* 1792.

YOUNG, Walter Kershaw, 1869-71. Son of Rev. James Reynolds Young (above). *b.* 1854.

YOUNG, William, 1819, *b.* 1807.

YOUNG, William Douglas, 1873.

YOUNG, William Edward Allen, 1844-52. Son of Rev. Edward Newton Young (above). *b.* 1833. Worc. Coll. Oxf. Hon. 4th Class Law and History. Rector of Pyecombe, Sussex.

YOUNG, William Laurence, 1878. Son of Sir Charles Laurence Young, Bart. *b.* 1864.

YOUNG (Sir) William Norris (Bart.), 1846-48. Son of Sir William Laurence Young, M.P. *b.* 1833. 23rd Regt. Killed at Alma 1854.

YOUNG, William Oliver, 1821, *b.* 1808.

YOUNGE, Charles, 1824, *b.* 1813.

LIST

OF

CARTHUSIANS,

ACCORDING TO DATE OF ENTRY,

1800 to 1879.

N.B.—The List of Day Boys in the Register is imperfect to 1811.

1800.	ALDERSON.	1801.
SIMONS.	PILKINGTON.	HAMLIN.
RAYMOND.	PILKINGTON.	FONBLANQUE.
CREWE.	FORMAN.	CLOGSTOWN.
HEWETT.	FORMAN.	COLES.
POYNDER.	WARRE.	NORRIS.
YORKE.	WARD.	WILSON.
BELL.	BLANE.	BAYLEY.
FREELING.	BLANE.	BATES.
HARTWELL.	YATES.	COLLINS.
O'CONNOR.	EAGLE.	ACKLAND.
EAGLE.	EAGLE.	WOOD.
MACNAGHTEN.	GRANT.	AUSTIN.
MONINS.	LANE.	CURRIE.
MONINS.	WATSON.	RANKEN.
WILTSHIRE.	GRANT.	ROUNDELL.

ROUNDELL.	DALZELL.	EWEN.
SELWYN.	WOOD.	GREGSON.
SMYTH.	SHAW.	GREGSON.
SMYTH.	SHAW.	LENNARD.
HINDS.	SHAW.	BRADBURNE.
JORDAN.	MATTHEWS.	MCKRAITH.
MONINS.	WARRE.	NUGENT.
TILL.	WARRE.	WYBERGH.
FANE.	PEDDER.	WYBERGH.
PEARSON.	PEPPER.	PHILLIPPS.
HAYNES.	HUNT.	CLEMENS.
GREGG.	BUSHBY.	NORRIS.
CASE.	WOLLASTON.	WARD.
BOURCHIER.	MORTLOCK.	FRANKS.
	HINDS.	PHILLIPS.
1802.	HARVEY.	TUCKER.
YENN.	BEALES.	BLANE.
WAKEFIELD.	PARR.	GRIFFITH.
ADDISON.	PYM.	GRIFFITH.
SLADE.	STONE.	DAVISON.
BENCE.	CASE.	HINDS.
MAXWELL.	AINSLIE.	SPENCER.
EARLE.	AINSLIE.	REID.
EARLE.	HOOD.	RAINE.
CHETWODE.		CLERKE.
BROWN.		ELLIS.
RUSSELL.	**1803.**	PEDDER.
HANDLEY.	TUCKER.	WILSON.
JOHNSON.	MACNAGHTEN.	BABINGTON.
HARVEY.	STEER.	CROMMELIN.
WILTSHIRE.	WADE.	DOBSON.
MANSEL.	PEMBERTON.	ISAACSON.
LANE.	PENTON.	TREDELL.

* *List of Day Boys not complete to* 1811.

List of Carthusians. 267

TAYLOR.
ROBINSON.
COCK.
HAYES.
QUANTON.
GOOD.
BARKER.
RUSSELL.
SENIOR.
SENIOR.
FRY.
FRY.
BELL.
GILLET.
WATTS.
BURCHELL.
WALTER.
WALTER.
BOOTH.
GATTY.
GATTY.

1804.

MORGAN.
TAYLOR.
NORRIS.
PASSLEY.
PASSLEY.
DOBINSON.
MILLIGAN.
HODGES.
GIBBONS.
PAGE.
BENTLEY.

TAYLOR.
TURNER.
MONINS.
BABINGTON.
HEALEY.
PYM.
WOLLASTON.
CHETWODE.
JOHNSTON.
DYSON.
TAYLOR.
CURRIE.
LUSHINGTON.
SMITH.
EMPSON.
EARLE.
GROTE.
HAVELOCK.
HAVELOCK.
DAVIES.
GODFREY.
LAW.

1805.

RICARDO.
REID.
FORMAN.
BARNARD.
GATTY.
ANDREWS.
ADAM.
JULL.
LAMB.
MILLIGAN.

O'BRIEN.
COLTMAN.
WEST.
GILLBEE.
PIGGOT.
HODGSON.
HODGSON.
BAILLIE.
MAINWARING.
FULLER.
PHILLIPPS.
RYDER.
COTTON.
FISHER.
FORTESCUE.
PENLEAZE.
HANDLEY.
BICKNER.
BICKNER.
YOUNG.
HARRISON.
NEWELL.
KEMPE.
KEMPE.
BARKER.
HALL.
PYM.
LLOYD.
BLANCHARD.
HALFORD.
OTTLEY.

1806.

WADDINGTON.

METHOLD.
WALPOLE.
WALPOLE.
PAYNE.
PAYNE.
PAGE.
PAGE.
PAGE.
GILBEE.
SEYMOUR.
GROTE.
CRESSWELL.
MORTIMER.
THOMSON.
IVESON.
ALLEN.
IVESON.
DYKEN.
WHITE.
LORD.
SAUNDERS.
SAUNDERS.
DE CRESPIGNY.
WILLIS.
VAUTIER.
BARNARD.
MILES.
TRISTRAM.
COODE.
ROOKE.
HANDLEY.
THOMPSON.
DALZEL.
COLES.

HARRISON.
PLUMMER.
HARVEY-ONLEY.
RAINE.
HOLROYD.
LENNARD.
DOLLMAN.
HARE.
PENNINGTON.

1807.

ROOKE.
GRIFFITH.
THOMAS.
HALE.
BANKHEAD.
BARNES.
BARNES.
BIRD.
WILLIAMS.
MACKENZIE.
KEIGHTLEY.
DARBY.
WELLS.
BATE.
PREVOST.
ROBERTSON.
PATERNOSTER.
FRECKLETON.
TAYLOR.
BELL.
BELL.
CATER.
COMMELIN.

TRAFFORD.
JONES.
HUTTON.
COOKE.
LENNARD.
GUNNING.
PINDER.
PINDER.
ARMSTRONG.
ARMSTRONG.
HUTTON.
LUARD.
EARLE.
YOUNG.
YOUNG.
YOUNG.
HENRIQUES.
LAING.
LINCOLN.
MORRIS.
HOWE.
PARKE.
HUNT.
PENNY.
HINDS.

1808.

WADDINGTON.
BANNISTER.
TAYLER.
GROTE.
DARBY.
HOLLAND.
PRICE.

EARLE.
HOLLAND.
ROBERTS.
DANCE.
PERCIVAL.
COTTON.
WIGHT.
HUDDLESTONE.
GUNNING.
WHITEHEAD.
HALLWARD.
SIMS.
FANE.
CURRIE.
CLERKE.
APPLEWHAITE.
BADELEY.
HARRISON.
BOULTON.
BOULTON.
STAPLES.
VANE.
BAGNEL.
BEALES.
LE MESURIER.
GODING.
EASTLAKE.
MORRIS.

1809.
MILLWARD.
BURY.
BURY.
STARR.

PLUMMER.
HALL.
PYM.
LESLIE.
LESLIE.
HUMPHRIES.
ORIEL.
JONES.
COLLYER.
HOWLETT.
LOWNDES.
ROBERTSON.
CHILTON.
NICHOLL.
MEDDOWCROFT.
MAUDE.
CLERKE.
LANGDALE.
FISHER.
HAVELOCK.
HORSLEY.
McTAVISH.
WOODINGTON.
FULLER.
LLOYD.
AINSWORTH.
OKEDEN.
EDWARDS.
WELBANK.
BEET.
WILLIAMS.
LLOYD.
MAULE.
MEDDOWCROFT.

SMALLWOOD.
THORPE.
CAPE.
WHITE.
CHAPMAN.
VANE.
LE MESURIER.
PRICE.
APPLEBEE.
FARRE.

1810.
BURY.
HUTSON.
PAGE.
CARTER.
YOUNG.
VACHELL.
WALLER.
AGASSIZ.
OAKLEY.
BOWMAN.
MEYER.
HARVEY.
PUGET.
GRANT.
SIMS.
CHURTON.
HORSLEY.
QUARTLEY.
WALFORD.
BARTLETT.
YOUNG.
HUMPHRYS.

PYE.	GRANT.	COOPER.
RAPER.	AUSTIN.	SAINTSBURY.
HUMPHRIES.	GAUTIER.	HEATHER.
OLIVER.	BURNTHORN.	GRANT.
CHAPMAN.	WARDON.	STONE.
WALKER.	THIRLWALL.	TAYLOR.
SMITH.	COSTER.	COOPER.
CARTER.	STONE.	FORTUNE.
WESTON.	TURNER.	YATES.
GRANT.	LAMBE.	WITHERBY.

Note from the Register.—"No sure date of admission of the Day-Boys. All admitted before this time, and most of them left in the School at the death of Dr. Raine."

1811.	PROBY.	REYNOLDS.
AGASSIZ.	SALISBURY.	BEAUCHAMP.
CRANFORD.	RUTTON.	SCHRODER.
GREENALGH.	LAMBE.	RAMSDEN.
DODD.	WRIGHT.	
KNAPP.	OGLE.	1812.
READE.	ROBERTSON.	CHAPMAN.
KNAPP.	BATTISCOMBE.	SIMS.
READE.	YORKE.	WADDINGTON.
FREDERICK.	MYERS.	ORIEL.
GOODE.	MYERS.	PAGE.
GOODE.	BEST.	ROBINSON.
LAMBE.	HIRTZEL.	ROBINSON.
HILLIARD.	ALLAN.	RICARDO.
MENDHAM.	ALLAN.	FAGG.
MENDHAM.	PRIESTLEY.	FAGG.
APPLEYARD.	HARRIS.	DAWKINS.
PERRY.	NEWDICK.	JONES.
GODWIN.	ROXBURGH.	JOSSELYN.
BICKNELL.	ROXBURGH.	DAWSON.

List of Carthusians.

HANNAM.
VANDERZEE.
BERRY.
HARPER.
BARRINGTON.
BABINGTON.
BABINGTON.
JACKSON.
JACKSON.
JACKSON.
SPENCER.
SMYTH.
POWYS.
SHEE.
BEST.
BOONE.
APPLEWHAITE.
BILL.
MENDHAM.
DAWES.
FFITCH.
COOKE.
HALLOWELL.
SARGEAUNT.
TAYLOR.
HEWETT.
CHAPMAN.

1813.
PRESCOTT.
ROBINSON.
SPRY.
LE MESURIER.
WRIGHT.

LAKE.
CAUTLEY.
FARNALL.
BARLOW.
BOODLE.
COATES.
VANDERZEE.
TURNER.
FARRAR.
EVERSLEY.
FREESE.
MAWHOOD.
STANNETT.
EVERSLEY.
WILSON.
BARKER.
LUCK.
PEETE.
PRESCOTT.
FROST.
JONES.
WATSON.
COATES.
SCOTT.
BOODLE.
CATES.
PERRY.
NICHOLSON.
NICHOLL.
MOORE.
CAZENOVE.
HAMMOND.
ORANGE.
HAIG.

HAWKE.
THOMAS.
GOSSIP.
KELLY.
KELLY.
KAY.
BLACKBURNE.
WAITHMAN.

1814.
HUMPHRYS.
BUDD.
THOMSON.
ATHILL.
MACDOUGALL.
BIGNELL.
GOSS.
WRIGHT.
THOMPSON.
TROWARD.
SPRY.
WOLLASTON.
COLLYER.
GWILLYM.
SAYER.
FARRE.
CONSTABLE.
FITZGERALD.
BUCKLEY.
HARDING.
KERR.
SMELT.
SCHRODER.
LEWIS.

BARNARD.
MONINS.
SMYTH.
FISHER.
ARTHUR.
BLAIR.
MACKENZIE.
PRESTON.
CHESTER.
LATTER.
HINCHLIFFE.
DAVISON.
GROTE.
SMITH.
DICKEN.
CHURTON.
YOUNG.
BOYLE.
THOMSON.
NUNN.
KINLOCH.
LLOYD.
TURNER.
BUNBURY.

1815.

ELLMAN.
FIRTH.
PALMER.
PALMER.
TANNER.
DAVIDSON.
DAVIDSON.
PAUL.

BARNES.
BARNES.
BURY.
SCRIVEN.
HOWELL.
TERREWEST.
TERREWEST.
CLARKE.
COLQUHOUN.
BAKER.
ESTRIDGE.
MESSITER.
SHERARD.
GLASSE.
FURLONGE.
LAFOREST.
RICARDO.
CHESTER.
BURY.
SARGEAUNT.
SARGEAUNT.
ROWLATT.
LEGGE.
RICKETTS.
AWDRY.
SURTEES.
JEPHSON.
BEDFORD.
NUTTALL.
WILLIS.
WILLIS.
GILLIAT.
GILLIAT.
LLOYD.

LUSHINGTON.
AYLES.
BOODLE.
CLARK.
BOVELL.
BOVELL.
BOVELL.
STUART.
BLENCOWE.
BLENCOWE.
BLENCOWE.
HUXLEY.
KING.
FRANCIS.
RICKETTS.
GUNNING.
STATHAM.
WAINEWRIGHT.
BURROUGHES.
RICE.
HARMAN.
PRESCOTT.

1816.

TATE.
VADE.
TAYLOR.
MACKENZIE.
COOKE.
HURLE.
BONNEY.
WOOD.
MOLYNEUX.
HOLLOWAY.

HALL.
BUSFIELD.
MILLS.
ALLEN.
PATMORE.
ADYE.
CONEY.
SCRIVEN.
JAGO.
WYNYARD.
DOCKER.
ESTRIDGE.
PORTEUS.
FRENCH.
CLARKE.
PERRY.
ALDERSON.
ATHERTON.
BROCKMAN.
DOLPHIN.
ROBERTS.
PENKIVIL.
HOLDSHIP.
BOLGER.
WAINEWRIGHT.
CAREY.
ROBINS.

1817.
VENN.
GILLIES.
SIMS.
BIDDULPH.
CHADWICK.

PALMER.
WILLIS.
WALFORD.
COLE.
ALLEN.
BLUNT.
THOMAS.
BLUNT.
CHAPMAN.
CLARKE.
SAUNDERS.
GRIFFITH.
BANNATYNE.
BROOKS.
JONES.
HAMILTON.
HAMILTON.
LECKIE.
EVELEGH.
CLARKE.
WOODHOUSE.
TALBOT.
BOURCHIER.
DE SOYRES.
ADAMS.
WALKER.
VILLIERS.
ALDERSON.
STARR.
HATHORN.
BUSFIELD.
SHUTTLEWORTH.
SHUTTLEWORTH.
LUSHINGTON.

BEDDOES.
BEDDOES.
HALIFAX.
DAWSON.
NISBETT.
ORIEL.
WALKER.
EAMER.
CAMPBELL.
MOORE.
MOORE.
BOODLE.
TREVELYAN.
RAMSDEN.
SEYMOUR.
MAUDE.
PRICE.
PRESTON.
FARQUHAR.
MAITLAND.
HARRIS.
BRIDGE.
MACDONALD.
OGILBY.
NORTON.
ISAACSON.
CROZIER.
MARCH.
MARCH.
KIDD.
HAMILTON.
STODDART.
HAIG.
SOMERVILLE.

T

List of Carthusians.

CAMPBELL.	MADAN.	STEELE.
STODDART.	STEERS.	BORRETT.
	CRANFIELD.	CARTWRIGHT.
1818.	JONES.	CARTWRIGHT.
RAMSAY.	WEBB.	KYNASTON.
BEVAN.	HADFIELD.	FARRE.
CAMPBELL.	BAGOT.	PINDER.
BRACKENBURY.	BARRINGTON.	PINDER.
MANT.	READE.	FARQUHAR.
MANT.	SAUNDERS.	BRIGGS.
TURNER.	PARKER.	TALBOT.
WRAY.	BURROUGHES.	GRANT.
CLARKE.	SAUNDERS.	GRANT.
MAURY.	PARKER.	GRANT.
ESDAILE.	HARDING.	CHILDERS.
ESDAILE.	OAKLEY.	CHILDERS.
COCKER.	LEACH.	STEPHENSON.
GOLDSMID.	BROWNE.	TURNER.
ALSOP.	ATKINSON.	ROSS.
GRANT.	LEAVER.	TOWNSHEND.
GRANT.	LEAVER.	HESKETH.
METHOLD.	BODDAM.	REID.
KITCHINER.	CHAMBERS.	REID.
OWEN.	CARY.	CHILCOTE.
CADDELL.	CARY.	CHILCOTE.
JONES.	WIGGINS.	EVANS.
TYRRELL.	ROBINSON.	SCOTT.
ASKEW.	OWEN.	ROWLATT.
FORSTER.	LLOYD.	WOODRUFF.
DOBSON.	BERRIDGE.	HAWKES.
SYM.	STEWARD.	
COLES.	STEWARD.	1819.
EATON.	PRESTON.	WAITE.
CHESTER.	BUNYON.	FULTON.

List of Carthusians.

GREGORY.	BRUÈRE.	TORRENS.
WALKER.	MATHISON.	YOUNG.
SIMS.	COULSON.	MONTGOMERY.
EDGWORTH.	CLARKE.	RAMSDEN.
PINCKNEY.	LANDON.	CLARK.
PINDER.	LECHE.	DICKSON.
GARSTIN.	GLADSTONE.	SHUTTLEWORTH.
CONDELL.	CARRINGTON.	GIBSON.
CONDELL.	D'ALBIAC.	TURNER.
LEWIS.	D'ALBIAC.	JOHNSTON.
MAUDE.	JACKSON.	THORNHILL.
BROWN.	MORSE.	TABOR.
FURLONGE.	MORSE.	RODGERS.
BARROW.	BEVAN.	KNAPP.
BARROW.	SHELLEY.	OSMOND.
PAGET.	LITCHFIELD.	ANSON.
HAMILTON.	BEVIR.	ELLIS.
MURDOCH.	FORBES.	CHAPMAN.
TAYLOR.	FOWLER.	BERDMORE.
POWELL.	DRUMMOND.	TAYLOR.
WRIGHTSON.	DRUMMOND.	KING.
LE MESURIER.	DRUMMOND.	RUDDLE.
PHILLPOTTS.	LOCKLEY.	HUMFREY.
IRVINE.	ALLISTON.	PORTER.
MORRELL.	BOYMAN.	BROWN.
BRUÈRE.	BARRINGTON.	MIDDLETON.
OTTER.	WHALLEY.	MURRAY.
COLEBROOK.	FELLOWES.	SCOTT.
RAWLINSON.	FITZ-HERBERT.	SENIOR.
RAWLINSON.	FITZ-HERBERT.	WALKER.
LITTLEDALE.	GROTE.	WALKER.
UNWIN.	BOOTHBY.	PRESCOTT.
LEACH.	DEAN.	BABINGTON.
BRUÈRE.	DOUGLAS.	FORBES.

BERNAL.	BADDELEY.	WIGGINS.
WOODWARD.	LOYD.	BROWN.
BAGOT.	PARKER.	BECHER.
LANGHAM.	PARKER.	MARTEN.
LANGHAM.	PARKER.	LEEDS.
MEEKE.	WEST.	MACKINNON.
DUNSMURE.	GILMORE.	GILMORE.
TURNER.	WOODWARD.	CANNAN.
BROCKHURST.	FORBES.	PIGOT.
TURNER.	MARTIN.	SOAMES.
EDWARDS.	MIDDLETON.	THYNNE.
EDWARDS.	MIDDLETON.	RODICK.
WILLES.	CROSS.	THARP.
FRANKLYN.	TAYLOR.	OWEN.
BAYLIFF.	TAYLOR.	MACKINNON.
VINER.	HUGHES.	TREVELYAN.
MALET.	TOBIN.	GEDDES.
DODD.	TOBIN.	DANN.
YARD.	IRVING.	JONES.
CHAPMAN.	BOURNE.	HARPER.
CHAPMAN.	ROOPER.	GEPP.
KENYON.	WALFORD.	CHATFIELD.
CROSS.	YORKE.	ROSS.
UNWIN.	LUCAS.	COLE.
MARTIN.	LEIGH.	MASSEY.
	WATTS.	BARROW.
1820.	HIND.	CAZALET.
ESTEN.	HIND.	BLAKE.
JOHNSTON.	GREIG.	GREY.
WADDINGTON.	BAYNES.	ESTEN.
FAIRLIE.	WEDGEWOOD.	ROUND.
BROWN.	FISHER.	WORDSWORTH.
BROWN.	EDWARDS.	CLARKSON.
LIDDELL.	WIGGINS.	CROFTON.

GROTE.
BARRETT.
FORMAN.
JACKSON.
ROBINSON.
MALTBY.
COOKE.
STONE.
CANNAN.
NARES.
BLENCOWE.
SIMPSON.
CONROY.
CLARE.
HOWARD.
HALLOWELL.
KARSLAKE.
BEAUMONT.
THORNHILL.
REYNOLDS.
HARE.
BAGGE.
BAGGE.
MONCKTON.
MONCKTON.
GRIFFITH.
MOZLEY.
BLOIS.
MILNES.
BAGOT.
BOWES.
DEANE.
FRENCH.
FRENCH.

BURGESS.
FRERE.
FAIRBAIRN.
BURTON.
BLAKE.
STREATFIELD.
SHELLEY.
PHILETAS.
TREVELYAN.
FAGAN.
FAGAN.
ANDERSON.
VIGNE.
BLANE.
THOMPSON.
ROBERTS.
JOHNSTON.
HARDY.
BAUGH.
RICHARDS.
MOODY.
BEADON.
WHEELER.
GRANT.
BONHAM.
BONHAM.
ELWES.
HULTON.
PIPON.
PIPON.
HYSLOP.
MORTLOCK.
HODGSON.
FORBES.

WAYMOUTH.
FOSTER.
SMITH.
GOVETT.
ROSE.
TALBOT.
AINSLIE.
NIND.
REEVES.
GRIFFITH.
EVERETT.
BRADDYLL.
BARRETT.
LUXFORD.
JOLLIFFE.
RICHARDSON.
CAMPBELL.
WAKEFIELD.
WARING.
WARING.
HANDLEY.
WOODGATE.
HEBERDEN.
BOYS.

1821.

BRASSEY.
WETHERELL.
BOX.
THORNTON.
CAYLEY.
GORDON.
STUART.
DENNISON.

List of Carthusians.

WHITMORE.	BODDINGTON.	STANLEY.
SCOTT.	BAILLIE.	BARKER.
MARRIOTT.	BAILLIE.	BARKER.
DAY.	JOHNSON.	JODRELL.
ALLEN.	FRAME.	SURTEES.
ALLEN.	TOTTENHAM.	HOWLETT.
MOGG.	ROOPER.	CROSSE.
COMBE.	COLLYER.	COOKSON.
TORKINGTON.	STUART.	PRICE.
HOBHOUSE.	DARNELL.	WALFORD.
HUDSON.	WALLIS.	ALDRICH.
FULTON.	BECKFORD.	LAWSON.
FULTON.	HAMILTON.	ARUNDEL.
FULTON.	POWELL.	BABINGTON.
FULTON.	MADDOCK.	SALMOND.
SMITH.	MADDOCK.	SALMOND.
NICOLL.	BROWNE.	STARR.
MYERS.	HORNE.	HODGES.
HIGGINSON.	CAREY.	BURR.
SPICER.	FRERE.	HUGHES.
RAIKES.	LESLIE.	CAYLEY.
HUTCHINS.	SHERIDAN.	SCOTT.
GAY.	FRENCH.	LINDE.
CHATFIELD.	TIMMINS.	MAITLAND.
DIXON.	STEWART.	BENNETT.
CHATFIELD.	JAMES.	CAMPBELL.
FOUNTAINE.	HARDING.	SCOTT.
RICHARDS.	THORNEYCROFT.	FELLOWES.
RYDER.	LEBLANC.	WILMOT.
FARRE.	MONEY.	WILMOT.
PEASE.	PRITCHETT.	WASEY.
POPHAM.	TAYLOR.	DUDDING.
TURNER.	FRANCKLIN.	HUSSEY.
HOLLAND.	WELLS.	MCCLINTOCK.

List of Carthusians.

EDWARDS.
WALLS.
DE GREY.
DE GREY.
YOUNG.
YOUNG.
ONSLOW.
GREYSON.
HAHN.
MORRIS.
CLAY.
FOWLER.
CURREY.
CURREY.
RYDER.
STRETTELL.
STRETTELL.
CURZON.
GREENING.
ROSE.
BLUNT.
HORTON.
ONSLOW.
ONSLOW.
TAYLOR.
HUGHES.
BARHAM.
THORNTON.
COLE.
ALEXANDER.
BROOKE.
CLARKE.
HOGARTH.
HARE.

DAWSON.
WEST.
YOUNG.
COLE.
YATES.
BARRETT.
TRAFFORD.
BULWER.
SHERWOOD.
CLIVE.
BERRY.

1822.
HOLBERTON.
WOOD.
FITZROY.
THACKERAY.
DRUMMOND.
GOSSIP.
ROUSSELL.
VIGNE.
PAGET.
WINTHORP.
FOUNTAINE.
BRIGGS.
FULTON.
SAMLER.
SAMLER.
SCOTT.
VENABLES.
VENABLES.
SAINTSBURY.
CARTWRIGHT.
AGASSIZ.

GODDARD.
KINDERLEY.
FRESHFIELD.
WEST.
BRIETZKE.
HANCOCK.
CAREY.
LEARY.
ANDREWS.
ESTLIN.
HODGES.
ROUTH.
MINOT.
CHURTON.
EDGAR.
PEMBERTON.
BARNARD.
TINDAL.
KNIGHTON.
TUPPER.
WILMER.
TUPPER.
NASH.
FAWSSETT.
WILMER.
WHARTON.
BARNES.
HOWARD.
COMPTON.
JOHNSON.
HELPS.
BENNETT.
ELLIS.
PALMER.

LLOYD.	COATES.	SMITH.
MARJORIBANKS.	DOBSON.	LESLIE.
BARING.	FORESTER.	WEBSTER.
PLUNKETT.	DOUGLAS.	WEBSTER.
HORNER.	GRAY.	LE GARD.
WHITTAKER.	BAKER.	CURREY.
DANN.	BAKER.	BESNARD.
ROE.	HEBERT.	LUSHINGTON.
ROE.	WAYET.	LUSHINGTON.
HAVERFIELD.	WAYET.	MILES.
WARINGTON.	IRWIN.	SMITH.
STOREY.	BENETT.	WAY.
GILBERT.	TEMPLER.	BAKER.
TAYLOR.	WOODYEARE.	HUGHES.
MACAULAY.	BERKELEY.	TREVELYAN.
MACAULAY.	PONSONBY.	SMITH.
BARKER.	BELL.	ATKINSON.
BARKER.	LITTLE.	KENYON.
JINKIN.	LITTLE.	ATKINSON.
WINGFIELD.	PETLEY.	WADDINGTON.
SPURRIER.	HORDER.	HAWKINS.
ROUTH.	FAWSSETT.	COOKE.
FARRE.	TANIERE.	GIPPS.
RAWLINS.	BELL.	CURTIS.
CROFT.		BURRELL.
READE.	1823.	BOWYEAR.
PARROTT.	OAKELEY.	EVERETT.
BOURDIEU.	DURHAM.	HERRING.
BLAKISTON.	MORTIMER.	LUKIN.
DEAN.	MORTIMER.	BUCKNOR.
SCHNELL.	MORTIMER.	SANSOM.
BROOKS.	YELLOLY.	MITCHELL.
ALEXANDER.	BALDWIN.	MITCHELL.
LAMB.	TICKELL.	DAY.

BADHAM.	DUNLOP.	LORT.
REYNARDSON.	HANMER.	RICHARDSON.
CONSTABLE.	CURZON.	STAINFORTH.
HOPPER.	TALBOT.	WOOD.
KEAYS.	NEAVE.	MONINS.
NEWTON.	SMITH.	TILLY.
FANE.	HOWELL.	DAINTRY.
HAMILTON.	BEAUFORD.	ALLEN.
TROWER.	LEADER.	BOURDILLON.
READE.	SHORT.	ASHHURST.
RUSSELL.	HOLDSWORTH.	BOURDILLON.
DAY.	ELLIS.	BROOKSBANK.
EDGELL.	BROWN.	JENKIN.
SHERIDAN.	SMITH.	FANE.
BULLOCK.	SMITH.	WALLACE.
BULLOCK.	OKEDEN.	EBDEN.
JOLLIFFE.	MYERS.	SHAKESPEARE.
BLAND.	BROME.	SHAKESPEAR.
JAMES.	SMYTH.	BAKER.
PARKER.	JULIUS.	HOLLOWAY.
PARKER.	PROWER.	PALMER.
WILKINSON.	MORGAN.	LIDDELL.
HAMILTON.	ROUS.	HANNAM.
TUPPER.	KYMER.	ALEXANDER.
FELLOWES.	BRIDGER.	PROTHERO.
WRIGHT.	YOUNG.	SPRINGETT.
RUCKER.	TATE.	FITZJAMES.
PRESSICK.	GRAVES.	HASTINGS.
MERYWEATHER.	JONES.	THOMPSON.
HAINES.	BRANDRETH.	KINDERLEY.
ARUNDEL.	BRANDRETH.	IRVING.
ALLISTON.	NICHOLLS.	EDGEWORTH.
RIGGE.	TWELLS.	PERKINS.
STOCKDALE.	GORDON.	TROTTER.

List of Carthusians.

DUNSFORD.
HOPEGOOD.
SNOWDEN.
MORLEY.
BARTRUM.
DOUGLAS.
KNYVETT.
BRIGHT.

1824.
CLARKE.
FRESHFIELD.
FRESHFIELD.
MORRIS.
LUSHINGTON.
NUGENT.
MARRIOTT.
HOUSTON.
VENABLES.
CURREY.
JONES.
THORNTON.
FANE.
WOODYEARE.
KING.
SCRATCHLEY.
HARNY.
HARKINGS.
BYRON.
POSTLE.
MORSE.
RUSSELL.
BOULTON.
HILL.

NORMAN.
HULTON.
ILDERTON.
BIRKBECK.
BRETON.
YOUNGE.
SLATER.
LEATHLEY.
PERCY.
MCPHERSON.
RUSH.
LOCH.
FRITH.
CLARK.
TALLENTS.
TORKINGTON.
GILES.
STONE.
DOWELL.
WADDELL.
FITZ-HERBERT.
BATES.
FOX.
PAYNTER.
CARNE.
JONES.
BATES.
WEST.
SPRANGER.
GORDON.
REEVES.
PAGET.
MANTON.
DICKENS.

TOWER.
MATHIAS.
BOURCHIER.
HUTSON.
JULIUS.
JULIUS.
WILLIAMS.
DAY.
MONTGOMERY.
BOYLE.
BOOTHBY.
NOAD.
PARMINTER.
COOKE.
YATES.
BURTON.
DUMERGUE.
WEBBER.
HUDSON.
RUSSELL.
SPARLING.
SPARLING.
SLEEMAN.
GORDON.
HUGHES.
CAREW.
MANGIN.
MANGIN.
POLLARD.
ILBERG.
LUTWYCHE.
NORTON.
RICHARDSON.
JONES.

List of Carthusians.

LAMB.
DEVEREUX.
ABBOTT.
JOHNSTON.
PRITCHETT.
LEGREW.
ORMSBY.
FAWSSETT.
HIGGINS.
KING.
CROHAN.
BIRLEY.
ROLFE.
HAMILTON.
SURTEES.
CHAPMAN.
LITTLEPAGE.
DAY.
NIVINS.
NIVINS.

1825.
LUDBY.
SHIPDEN.
EWBANK.
HENRY.
HENRY.
WHITE.
GIPPS.
CORRIE.
MYERS.
LUXFORD.
GRANT.
BAYLEY.

JOHNSTON.
CANN.
HOLLYON.
LIGNE.
WHITE.
GEORGE.
GATTY.
STARR.
HALIBURTON.
SOLTAU.
LEECH.
RAINIER.
RAINIER.
MAITLAND.
SMITH.
MATTHEWS.
WILKIN.
SERLE.
WOODTHORPE.
MATHISON.
PARKER.
WIGHTWICK.
TURNOR.
DUNNAGE.
STORKS.
BROUGHTON.
COTTON.
SPRY.
HULL.
JONES.
HODGKINSON.
HARDING.
DILLON.
WOODGATE.

SPENCER.
HOTHAM.
HOTHAM.
GILSON.
RODGERS.
SOLLY.
SCHRODER.
SCHRODER.
BAILEY.
MEREWETHER.
LEBLANC.
HOWES.
COCKSHOTT.
TUPPER.
LISTER.
GILES.
WOODLAND.
UNWIN.
CARPENTER.
KIMPTON.
ALLSOP.
BATTEN.
PARSONS.
SIMPSON.
CUTHBERT.
KEY.
COCKEY.
PRETYMAN.
FALKNER.
RUSHBROOKE.
RUSHBROOKE.
JONES.
HODGSON.
BERDMORE.

BERDMORE.
VENABLES.
McNISH.
BLAND.
HANSARD.
COVENTRY.
PETLEY.
ELLIOTT.
SURTEES.
MASON.
DARLEY.
TEMPLER.
DODSON.
POYNDER.
WINTHORP.
COTTON.
SMITH.
WILLIAMS.
SLATER.
BIRCH.
COOKSON.
THOMPSON.
MACDOUGALL.
GIFFARD.
CROWDY.
WILKINSON.
MAN.
HOLWORTHY.
LLANOS.
VAIZEY.
BROOKS.
GARDNER.

1826.
GASKELL.
JONES.
LUSHINGTON.
PARTRIDGE.
GIBBARD.
STORY.
DUMERGUE.
RUCKER.
TARBUTT.
HAHN.
REID.
REID.
BARKER.
CARDEN.
CURREY.
CARPENTER.
COOKSON.
GARCIA.
WOOD.
NORTON.
LOVE.
WING.
BATEMAN.
HOWORTH.
TEAGUE.
PRITCHARD.
PRITCHARD.
PRITCHARD.
PLUES.
HOOLE.
MAZZINGLIE.
COCKS.
HEBDEN.

CORBETT.
RUMBOLD.
CHAMBERS.
GOODWIN.
WHITAKER.
ASHHURST.
BENCE.
LEMOS.
HAMMOND.
EVERARD.
LANGSTAFF.
LANGSTAFF.
HAINES.
NEVINSON.
PENNINGTON.
RADCLIFFE.
PURVIS.
PAYNE.
WOODTHORPE.
FRANCIS.
SPRY.
POLLARD.
ARNOULD.
HANMER.
GILES.
SPRANGER.
ROPER.
ROPER.
BAGGE.
HARRISON.
CARRINGTON.
CLEMENTS.
MONTGOMERY.
ROUTH.

DIXON.
FRITH.
HARTLEY.
HODGSON.
BEAUCLERK.
BEAUCLERK.
JENNER.
WOODGATE.
JAMES.
JAMES.
BERNARD.
HAWKINS.
WRIGHT.
STORY.
STORY.
CASE.
RAMSAY.
MOGG.
ORLEBAR.
ELDER.
BIRLEY.
BIRLEY.
EDWARDS.
EDWARDS.
BERNEY.
POWLES.
HOPPER.
BODE.
SMITH.
VANCE.
SIMPSON.
ELLABY.
BACK.
WHITBREAD.

GARDNER.
GARDNER.
STORKS.
ATKINSON.
SCOTT.
PARRY.
MARSHALL.
BAXTER.
DAUGHTREY.
BROME.
CLIFTON.
JONES.
PEARSON.
LOCH.
EDGELL.
SMITH.
WILKINS.

1827.
GRIGNON.
RODWELL.
WALFORD.
CROUGHTON.
CLARK.
CAINES.
LARKINS.
SHAW.
AUBERTIN.
AUBERTIN.
TOWER.
GILES.
WHITTAKER.
KITSON.
HILL.

ARMSTRONG.
BAYLEY.
AUBREY.
MAINWARING.
BROWNE.
ALLEN.
PROTHEROE.
ANDERSON.
HANNAM.
HALL.
ARCHER.
NETHERCOTE.
ATKINSON.
WALLINGTON.
PLUES.
DENDY.
WESTMACOTT.
WILLIAMS.
HANSARD.
WILDE.
WILDE.
O'GRADY.
NEVINSON.
MARJORIBANKS.
MEREWETHER.
REYNARDSON.
ALEXANDER.
HAY.
SMITH.
SCOVELL.
FREESE.
ALLEN.
SMYTH.
MARSHALL.

OGLE.
SMITH.
DENNIS.
HOWARD.
EWBANK.
HEAD.
CURTIS.
RENNY.
MUDGE.
SINCLAIR.
BAINES.
COTTON.
EASTWICK.
CHESTER.
GARROW.
FARRE.
STEPHENS.
PHILLOTT.
SMITH.
STEDMAN.
YATES.
JESSOPP.
BOYS.
PARKER.
CROWDEY.
CODD.
LISTER.
MALTBY.
EVANS.
ANSON.
COOKE.
KINDERSLEY.
EMERSON.
HUMPHREYS.

COBBE.
BELL.
HUNTER.
FARR.
GLYNN.

1828.

ACRET.
GALE.
BOSTOCK.
HAMILTON.
RAWLINSON.
MACDONALD.
STARKIE.
HAY.
FOLLETT.
WEST.
TURNER.
FREELING.
WOODHOUSE.
POYNDER.
HANSARD.
FANSHAWE.
FANSHAWE.
LAWSON.
KNIGHT.
STORY.
DIXON.
DENNIS.
GWILLIM.
KEANE.
RAMSDEN.
FITZ-HERBERT.
NETHERCOTE.

JOYCE.
WATSON.
PARTRIDGE.
CLIFTON.
SAMSOM.
ROBARTS.
PEARSON.
GOOCH.
DARLING.
ROSE.
SCOTT.
CARSON.
PRETYMAN.
TRITTON.
GIFFARD.
HODGKINSON.
PRENDERGAST.
HURST.
COBBE.
HUNT.
BRIGGS.

1829.

YOUNG.
POYNDER.
SMYTH.
WAINHOUSE.
LAWES.
CARTER.
BEWES.
WREFORD.
HADFIELD.
BURDETT.
WALKER.

CHAPMAN.
MARSHALL.
SYKES.
GREEN.
MOGG.
PLUNKETT.
BURDETT.
HOWELL.
WODEHOUSE.
MOORE.
CHESTER.
GOWAN.
COBBE.
RICHARDS.
BERNEY.
PURNELL.
COCKLE.
AUBERTIN.
TEMPLER.
BODE.
SMITH.

1830.
RADFORD.
LARKINS.
GORDON.
PAYNE.
FANE.
FANE.
AYTON.
FISHER.
BELL.
DOWN.
COLES.

WHATMORE.
GARROW.
WOOD.
THURLOW.
THURLOW.
HAMILTON.
MARSHALL.
NICHOLSON.
PURVIS.
PATTISON.
WALLINGTON.
USHER.

1831.
BEAUCLERK.
KING.
MEREWETHER.
JOYNES.
BEWES.
LEECH.
WINDSOR.
JAMES.
GOODE.
BUTTS.
HAWKINS.
MASON.
BINGHAM.
WEDDERBURNE.
LEVINSON.
BOYD.
TRITTON.
FISHER.
GRIMES.
BOOTHBY.

HODSON.
SHIRLEY.
MASTERS.
WINDSOR.
BULLOCK.
CLIFFORD.
ELLIS.

1832.
PHILLIMORE.
GIPPS.
GASKELL.
CHEVALLIER.
BEWES.
PHILLPOTTS.
HASTINGS.
BRACKENBURY.
PENNY.
GOUGH.
PRITT.
FANE.
GARDNER.
DISBROWE.
RILEY.
SAUNDERS.
CHEVALLIER.

1833.
FISHER.
WILLOCK.
BABINGTON.
HENNIKER.
HESSING.
RENDALL.

List of Carthusians.

CHAPMAN.	WICHE.	1836.
TUPPER.	PRITCHETT.	LIDDELL.
PETLEY.	PROCTER.	ROUNDELL.
ANSON.	BABINGTON.	PALMER.
BOWEN.	ANDREWS.	DU CANE.
HAWKER.	MANDERSON.	BOOTHBY.
PRETYMAN.		WILLIAMS.
WYNYARD.	1835.	ROBINSON.
GORDON.	BENCE.	JACOBS.
LLOYD.	DAVIES.	BODE.
TREACHER.	DAVIES.	SHEPPARD.
EDWARDS.	CLIFFORD.	FURZE.
FORMBY.	FANE.	GREATOREX.
HULME.	BRIGGS.	KING.
GOODE.	DOLLMAN.	JESSOP.
	KNOX.	ELWYN.
1834.	BOX.	GRAYDON.
ASHHURST.	BOX.	PEEL.
ALSTON.	BOX.	PEEL.
EDEN.	RUSSELL.	VALENTINE.
TALBOT.	HENNIKER.	PHILLIMORE.
PARIS.	ELLIS.	CURTIS.
ELWYN.	HALE.	CURTIS.
WALFORD.	PENNELL.	JOYNES.
HAWKINS.	GLEIG.	DAVEY.
MCCULLUM.	PURVIS.	TURNER.
BLOMFIELD.	HUMPHREYS.	GRAYDON.
WRIGHT.	PARKER.	GIFFARD.
JACOBS.	MEADE.	RALPH.
MOORE.	BENCE.	HULL.
PAGET.	SHAKESPEAR.	HULL.
SURTEES.	COLDWELL.	POWER.
LAW.	DARLING.	
BURROWS.		

1837.	CHILD.	JACOBS.
GREEN.	CHILD.	HULL.
PALMER.	CHILD.	HULL.
SAUNDERS.	CHILD.	GRIFFINHOOFE.
SAUNDERS.	FORSHALL.	ELLIS.
WRIGHT.	BARRINGTON.	FISHER.
WRIGHT.	PERRY.	HOSKINS.
WEEKES.		PALGRAVE.
NEATE.	1838.	PALGRAVE.
BARTTELOT.	GIBBS.	PALGRAVE.
BAGOT.	CARTER.	GATTY.
MILES.	COOKE.	
HAYTER.	LUCAS.	1839.
HUNT.	LUCAS.	FANE.
HENNIKER.	TURNER.	SOTHEBY.
WODEHOUSE.	BANNISTER.	BELLI.
SARGEAUNT.	BROUGHTON.	FISHER.
SHARPE.	SHARPLES.	ARCHER.
PATERSON.	BOOTHBY.	BRODERICK.
FISHER.	BOOTHBY.	BLACKER.
LECHMERE.	BLAND.	SILVER.
POUNSETT.	BODE.	TASKER.
FORMBY.	ELLIS.	SPRANGER.
RODWELL.	TAYLOR.	JOYNES.
BURGESS.	TURNER.	WIGG.
TANNER.	NEATE.	SMITH.
STORY.	WARBURTON.	GRIFFITH.
BRASSEY.	HILTON.	VERNON.
RYDER.	BATHURST.	BOWEN.
CLUTTERBUCK.	GIBBS.	WHATELY.
LAFONT.	WINSCOM.	SAUNDERS.
RODWELL.	TURNER.	SAUNDERS.
WEGUELIN.	COBBOLD.	INNES.
WHISH.	BOOTHBY.	WARD.

U

List of Carthusians.

GIBBS.
CORNEWALL.
WALMESLEY.
CHEVALLIER.
RIDSDALE.
MILLS.

1840.
BLOMFIELD.
LEGH.
LOCKETT.
FOOTE.
KEIGHTLEY.
WHISH.
WETHERALL.
KEIGHTLEY.
COFFIN.
HORROCKS.
GREY.
BERKELEY.
BOSWORTH.
DRAKE.
GAHAGAN.
DELHOSTE.
HOBART.
WIGG.
PALMER.
WILLIAMS.
LOCKWOOD.
SARGEAUNT.
SARGEAUNT.
TURNER.
IRVING.
DEWAR.

1841.
FISHER.
RODWELL.
COLLINS.
PATERSON.
FAIRLIE.
DEANE.
RICHARDSON.
SHETTON.
BURTON.
FOX.
RYDER.
FORT.
MILLARD.
KEY.
URLING.
POCOCK.
COOPER.
FLOYD.
HAMMOND.
SOMERSET.
PEARSON.
PEARSON.
BLAND.
TROTTER.
PALGRAVE.
DRAKE.
SMITH.
SMITH.
DOUGLAS.
PARROTT.
PARROTT.
ROBINSON.
HAGGARD.

HALE.
HALE.
TUCKER.
MACKENZIE.
BYRON.
LOWDER.
STOPFORD.

1842.
COOPER.
WILLIAMS.
JOHNSTON.
SUTHERLAND.
SAUNDERS.
SAUNDERS.
ESPINASSE.
WYLDE.
LOCKER.
BELSON.
CLOWES.
LE BAS.
MILES.
SKEY.
SKEY.
LLOYD.
IRVINE.
CUPPAGE.
SPILLER.
BATTEN.
HANNAM.
WRANGHAM.
DYNELEY.
DOUGLAS.
RANDALL.

List of Carthusians.

JAMES.
DICKEN.
GREEN.
SAUNDERS.
POWER.
COOPER.
DOBINSON.
JENOUR.
DYNELEY.
NAPIER.
DES VOEUX.
ROWE.
COLES.
COLLIER.
COYLE.
MILES.
MILES.
PEARSON.
BATTEN.

1843.
BOYLE.
BARNARD.
RICHARDSON.
BELSON.
STOPFORD.
CLARKE.
BEDDOME.
DASHWOOD.
LECHE.
CUNYNGHAME.
GARDNER.
FONBLANQUE.
COLERIDGE.

PALMER.
BRISCOE.
SAUNDERS.
MILLS.
TWEED.
BATTISCOMBE.
GRIFFINHOOFE.
HALL.
BARNARD.
YOUNG.
YOUNG.
BARNES.
HANSON.
ROBINSON.
HOPE-VERE.
SOMERSET.
ROPER.
COOPER.
LEGH.
BLOMFIELD.
GIPPS.
HILLS.
LUARD.
WALLACE.
JONES.
JONES.
COBBOLD.
PARNELL.
GILBERT.
STONE.
HATHAWAY.
GRAY.
CAZENOVE.
WOOD.

1844.
CATTLEY.
PERCEVAL.
CROOME.
SAMSON.
ATWOOD.
HAGGARD.
HANNAM.
ROBINSON.
RUGG.
ANDREW.
CLAY.
STEVENS.
FISHER.
TANNER.
VENABLES.
HENNIKER.
TALLEY.
HILLIARD.
RANDOLPH.
PILKINGTON.
CURRIE.
GIBBS.
CHURCH.
CHURCH.
PERCEVAL.
YOUNG.
SULLIVAN.
MASFEN.
LEWIS.
ANDERSON.
BIRCH.
BIRCH.
ROUND.

SAUNDERS.
CONOLLY.
MORGAN.
BEDFORD.
BARNES.
BARNES.
BOYD.
CHAPMAN.
LEGGE.
PERCEVAL.
MILLIGAN.
HANSON.
WATTS.
HILLS.
BELLI.

1845.
CRESSWELL.
CRESSWELL.
CODRINGTON.
BEASLEY.
CLEMENTS.
NOWELL.
LAFOREST.
UPTON.
HUDSON.
SULLIVAN.
BARROW.
MOORE.
CORBETT.
BAYLIFF.
ALLEN.
LEGGE.
DANIEL.

GIBBS.
MORGAN.
PERCEVAL.
RYDER.
WEST.
HALE.
RICHMOND.
NEATE.
BALLANCE.
WALKER.
PEARSON.
COLLINS.
HAWKER.
DUNDAS.
RHODES.
DAMER.
BONNER.
HALCOMBE.
BUTLER.

1846.
BRAMLEY.
BRAMLEY.
BRADFORD.
YOUNG.
HAWKINS.
BAYLIFF.
DAMER.
ESPINASSE.
PEARSE.
STONE.
DES VOEUX.
SMITH.
RICHARD.

SADLER.
NICHOLSON.
JONES.
WARD.
MURRAY.
FLOYD.
GIBBS.
CUPPAGE.
DRUMMOND.
BUTLER.
TURNER.
DOWBIGGIN.
KELLY.
HELME.
BOWEN.
CLARKE.
SUTHERLAND.
FISHER.
OSWALD.
IRVINE.
IRVINE.

1847.
BORTHWICK.
HOPE.
PALMER.
COOK.
HILLS.
FIELDING.
COBBOLD.
BINGLEY.
SAUNDERS.
SAUNDERS.
SAUNDERS.

TALBOT.
JELF.
LACY.
PRITCHARD.
SAUNDERS.
HUNTER.
BOSWORTH.
SANDHAM.
BINGLEY.
BOGER.
JAMES.
KING.
HEATH.
DOWNING.
PEARSON.
BONNEY.
SAUNDERS.
HALL.
BOGER.
LEWIN.
PEMBER.

1848.
WALFORD.
TAYLOR.
KITCHEN.
SEWELL.
CHAPMAN.
HAGGARD.
WITT.
WEBB.
ANDERSON.
FISHER.
KEANE.

SLADE.
LACY.
FORSTER.
CURREY.
BRUTTON.
STOPFORD.
ANDERSON.
SADLER.
COBBOLD.
SHACKELL.
PARISH.
NEWTON.
VIGNE.
SAUNDERS.
BARNES.
SYKES.
BLORE.
RAE.
WHITEHEAD.
WADE.
HUNTER.
FAUSSETT.
AMOS.
MALKIN.
DEANE.
SOLLY.
CLARKE.
OSBORN.

1849.
DICKEN.
VENABLES.
PALLISER.
STEPHENSON.

CLIFTON.
TUDOR.
CLARKE.
TUDOR.
WITT.
HOOPER.
ARMITSTEAD.
PARNELL.
MERRIMAN.
BRADFORD.
PEILE.
HENNIKER.
TUDOR.
SHACKELL.
JOSSELYN.
TEULON.
BRODIE.
GREY.
BRATHWAITE.
NEWMARCH.
WEST.
MARSLAND.
MARSLAND.
HOBART.
TALBOT.
JOHNSTON.
WRIGHT.
NOTT.
PILKINGTON.
EVANS.
GORDON.
HAWORTH.
PALLISER.
INGPEN.

IEVERS.
GORDON.
HUNT.
NUGENT.

1850.
HARVEY.
CHAPMAN.
SAUNDERS.
SAMS.
SOLLY.
BULWER.
BROWNING.
BLOXAM.
BAKER.
CLINCH.
GRIGG.
KANE.
READE.
CEELY.
HODGSON.
PEMBER.
KING.
DOWNES.
FORSTER.
MACNAGHTEN.
MURRAY.
HOBART.
GIRDLESTONE.
TUCK.
BAYLIFF.
FORSTER.
SHORTT.
ESDAILE.

PHILLIPS.
FONBLANQUE.

1851.
PEILE.
SAUNDERS.
BAILEY.
RIDGEWAY.
HARDINGE.
MADDEN.
JACKSON.
CHURTON.
RAMSBOTHAM.
BADCOCK.
EVANS.
HUGHES.
LINDSAY.
NICHOLSON.
WALFORD.
HODGE.
JOHNSTON.
MAINWARING.
SAUNDERS.
SAMS.
CURTIS.
SARGEAUNT.
WHARTON.
CARPENTER.
CARTER.
BERRY.
PARNELL.
BULKELEY.
MANN.
BOVELL.

ESDAILE.
BARKER.
EVANS.
BIRCH.
LARCOM.
CUNINGHAM.
CAMPBELL.
PORTMAN.

1852.
LINDSAY.
READ.
CHAMPNEYS.
LEESON.
O'GRADY.
CARPENTER.
KING.
GIRDLESTONE.
CODDINGTON.
BLACKWOOD.
BABINGTON.
BABINGTON.
KNYVETT.
MAYHEW.
TILDEN.
BARROW.
BABINGTON.
STREATFEILD.
PECK.
BORRETT.
NUGENT.
TEULON.
VAN CORTLANDT.
WINN.

List of Carthusians.

JACKSON.
BURNETT.
THOMPSON.
HAWORTH.
MARRYAT.
BURNETT.
EVANS.
EVANS.
SPYERS.
LENNOX.
COXE.
CLAY.
WALSH.
JACKSON.
SOMERSET.
WADDELL.
PEARSON.
CARTER.
GRAY.

1853.
SHEPHERD.
WELCH.
WALFORD.
TAMPLIN.
LAW.
HAVERS.
STONE.
ORME.
WARDE.
WATERWORTH.
RODWELL.
STURGEON.
COLLYER.

LINDSAY.
TEULON.
SEYMOUR.
DANIELS.
INGE.
INGE.
ROBERTS.
TAYLOR.
WILMOT.
FAUSSETT.
READ.
BUTTER.
MACGREGOR.
PLUNKETT.
HALSEY.
THORP.
REEVE.
KENT.
DONNITHORNE.
GILBERT.
OSBORN.
FOWLE.
ELLIS.
FARROW.
CARTER.
FORSTER.
SEYMOUR.
BOWER.
LAWRELL.
TATE.
BARNARD.
WILSON.

1854.
BRODIE.
ALSTON.
HUNT.
ROBERTS.
BOLTON.
BARTON.
BARTON.
HALLET.
NETTLESHIP.
ATKINSON.
FULLER.
EWART.
MURRAY.
MURRAY.
WELCH.
PINNIGER.
CARDALE.
CLIFTON.
HALL.
COOKSON.
ATKINSON.
ATKINSON.
BULLOCK.
CHAMPNEYS.
CHAMPNEYS.
CARTER.
HALLETT.
GOODEVE.
TAYLOR.

1855.
ISAACSON.
CODDINGTON.

SCOTT.
KING.
JEBB.
COOKSON.
DICKEN.
BORRER.
BARLEE.
INMAN.
SEYMOUR.
WARNER.
ARMSTRONG.
HOPWOOD.
GORDON.
WILMOT.
THOMAS.

1856.
THOMPSON.
DAVIES.
YORKE.
OGDEN.
ISAACSON.
BITTLESTON.
WEBSTER.
HOULTON.
STOCK.
ARCHER.
KNAPP.
BEST.
MADDEN.
DOUGLAS.
BOUWENS.
TALBOT.
GIRDLESTONE.

HALE.
GOLDNEY.
SOMERSET.
DALTON.
ANDERSON.
DRUMMOND.
MAJENDIE.
WALLACE.
MEDHURST.
WETHERMAN.
MAY.
MAY.

1857.
HAWORTH.
HAMILTON.
JACKSON.
JACKSON.
COLE.
SUMNER.
HODGSON.
CARR.
HARTSHORNE.
PERRY.
O'BEIRNE.
O'BEIRNE.
CUNDELL.
MACKENZIE.
ALCOCK.
PARNELL.
POVAH.
CAMERON.
BEST.
SAUNDERS.

HALL.
WYNTER.
MASON.
SCOTT.
SEYMOUR.
HOWARD.
PEARSON.
TEULON.
PHILLIPS.
BOYLE.
OGDEN.

1858.
ARCHER.
LE MARCHANT.
MIDDLETON.
WYBERGH.
BAKER.
HOLME.
GLEN.
MAPLES.
SARGEAUNT.
WHITE.
DICKEN.
BUTTER.
O'GRADY.
CAMPBELL.
JERVIS.
HUTCHINSON.
CARR.
BYNG.
HALL.
MAMMATT.
FOX.

OTTLEY.
BITTLESTON.
ERSKINE.
WILDE.
LUCK.

1859.
MYERS.
HAWKINS.
HAWKINS.
HAWKINS.
WEBSTER.
HALLETT.
FLEET.
FLEET.
GIBSON.
CAMERON.
GILES.
ABRAHAM.
FAIRLES.
CURTIS.
CRESSWELL.
BIRTWHISTLE.
BOREHAM.
BOREHAM.
HANSLIP.
GORDON.
TONKS.
SAUNDERS.
BROWN.
POVAH.
HARRISON.
WHARTON.
BRYDEN.

1860.
DICKEN.
PAULSON.
PAULSON.
NEISH.
COOPER.
CARDALE.
SWAN.
LANT.
DAVENPORT.
WADE.
GROOME.
DICKEN.
IRVINE.
WALFORD.
CLAYTON.
RICHARDS.
HARENC.
ELLIS.
ELLIS.
FORTESCUE.
MACKENZIE.
FOOTE.
KING.
MACKENZIE.
SMYTHE.
BLAKESLEY.

1861.
SMITH.
WAY.
WEIL.
TAYLOR.
STEVENSON.

CLARKE.
HARRISON.
CHERMSIDE.
HAMMICK.
VENABLES.
NEPEAN.
MANN.
RASHLEIGH.
DOUGLAS.
BARNES.
BARNES.
SLADE.
BRYDEN.
FORSTER.
BOYLE.
KENT.
BAROUGH.

1862.
MAMMATT.
WILMOT.
DUNN.
COWIE.
KING.
PARNELL.
SWEET.
WILLIAMS.
MACKENZIE.
PINCHING.
PINCHING.
PINCHING.
VAUGHAN.
DAY.
BITTLESTON.

WRENCH.
RICHMOND.
RIVINGTON.
BLAKESLEY.
GROOME.
FORSTER.
WRENCH.
WRENCH.
GORDON.
WALLACE.
BLOXAM.
WILMOT.
OGDEN.
BROWN.
WHARTON.
WHARTON.
ROWSELL.
COLLINSON.
SMITH.

1863.

YORKE.
HOPKIRK.
MIDDLETON.
LYNE.
HOOMAN.
DAVIES.
DORLING.
ELLIOT.
RUSSELL.
HODSON.
BUCKWELL.
KING.
HARDING.

ILBERT.
LLOYD.
WETHERALL.
CARR.
FLETCHER.
DUNN.
WADE.
KINGSCOTE.
INGRAM.
ALMOND.
ALLAN.
FORSTER.
BORTON.
LAMMIN.
OVEREND.
OVEREND.
JACKSON.
GATTY.
HULTON.
POYNDER.
MOGG.
VANDERZEE.

1864.

MARWOOD.
SYMONDS.
KERR.
HORE.
MAPLES.
WIX.
WALFORD.
HERVEY.
MARCH.
PYMAN.

PYMAN.
CONNELL.
GANDELL.
BUSHNELL.
HILL.
HERTSLET.
BADDELEY.
ANDREWS.
MACLAREN.
BARRY.
BARRY.
LACEY.
PATTINSON.
KERR.
INGLIS.
COURTENAY.
RICHARDS.
PAGET.
PHILLOTT.
WALKER.
MACAN.
MACAN.
RUSSELL.
POWELL.
MATTHEWS.
GORDON.
BEAUCLERK.
JOSEPH.
COXHEAD.
GELL.
DICKSON.
SYMONDS.

1865.
FLOYER.
DOUGLAS.
MAPLES.
YOUNG.
WOOD.
MOGG.
OGDEN.
MATTHEWS.
LAMMIN.
GLEN.
RUSSELL.
HOSE.
SYNGE.
FIRTH.
RASHLEIGH.
HUXLEY.
CARTER.
BYNG.
TAYLOR.
BOREHAM.
CUNNINGHAM.
LAMBE.
RICHMOND.
BRINE.
ACKLOM.
CAMERON.
BLOMFIELD.
BROWN.
CAMERON.
GIBSON.
FITZ PATRICK.
TAYLER.
WADMORE.

MILLS.
FORBES.

1866.
NEISH.
PHELPS.
OLDHAM.
WESTROP.
COOMBS.
EDMONDS.
GRIFFITHS.
PHILLIPS.
BERRYMAN.
CLARK.
RAVENSHAW.
PUGH.
LIVEING.
NICOLL.
HAMMICK.
LEECH.
CLAYTON.
CLAYTON.
KIRKHAM.
SANDWITH.
HAINES.
TERRY.
NICOLL.
ACLAND.
WESTON.
HALL.
DAVIES.
KING.

1867.
HULTON.
WALKER.
DORLING.
STREATFEILD.
JONES.
BUCHANAN.
BUCHANAN.
KEITH.
SAUNDERS.
BERE.
GIPPS.
NORMAN.
PALMER.
MOIR.
CROSSE.
WEATHERHEAD.
BITTLESTON.
BURNSIDE.
THOMPSON.
EMPSON.
INGLIS.
GRIFFITH.
ERSKINE.
FRANCIS.
BARROW.
BLAXLAND.
GIBSON.
OLDFIELD.
GOULD.
HANSON.
CLARKE.
ACOCKS.
KEANE.

WILLIAMS.
KING.
CARTER.

1868.
SPARROW.
WARBURTON.
MOGG.
SENTANCE.
BAKER.
BAKER.
EASTLAKE.
HANSELL.
MINTER.
MAC IVER.
SYNGE.
KEANE.
CURZON.
PARRY.
GORDON.
KIRBY.
TOMKINS.
MERRIMAN.
MOGG.
SOUTHWELL.
SOUTHWELL.
LACEY.
GORDON.
THOMPSON.
FOX.
ABDY.
ABDY.
LILLY.
ATHERTON.

HAINES.
WATSON.
STOPFORD.
STENHOUSE.
RITCHIE.
GARRETT.
WILLIAMS.

1869.
HAINES.
TOD.
ELRINGTON.
BISHOP.
CLARKE.
WHITE.
WHITE.
DREW.
PARISH.
CARTER.
WILKINSON.
SOUTHWELL.
MORGAN.
SHEARS.
COLDWELL.
WAKE.
YOUNG.
ATHERTON.
BROWN.
SMITH.
JEAFFRESON.
BEASLEY.
BOYLE.
SAUNDERS.
BOYCE.

PAGE.
RENAUD.
DALDY.
DAY.
WILLIAMS.
WILLIAMS.

1870.
SLADDEN.
PAYNE.
PAYNE.
PARRY.
FRANCIS.
GLEN.
SHOPPEE.
ROBERTS.
MAYOW.
GOULD.
SPARROW.
ROUQUETTE.
CHATER.
GIBBON.
SWAN.
WEIGALL.
KING.
SHORT.
RASHLEIGH.
BOURKE.
RAWLINSON.
SOUTHWELL.
GIBSON.
GIBSON.
STAVELEY.
NEAL.

FOSTER.
SCRATTON.
WOODGATE.
POYNDER.
DREW.
WILLIAMS.
ORFORD.
RICKETTS.
POWELL.

1871.
KEEN.
NICHOLSON.
BISHOP.
BRINE.
HULTON.
PARKE.
CLARKE.
READ.
CHAPMAN.
REEVE.
HAMPSON.
GUISE.
SIMPSON.
HEWETT.
COLES.
SCHMITZ.
MATHIAS.
SPOONER.
JONES.
RICHARDS.
BENTLEY.
SOUTHWELL.
LE BAS.

ILDERTON.
BOX.
WILSON.
VERELST.
VERELST.
GUILDING.
TUNBRIDGE.
VAUGHAN.
OLDHAM.
DAVIES.
PEARSON.
NEWMAN.
NEWMAN.
SHEARS.
SHEARS.
WILLIAMS.
STEVENS.
TERRY.
BOULTON.
ADDISON.

1872.
MERRIMAN.
EGERTON.
PAGE.
TYRWHITT-DRAKE
KING.
DOBBIE.
BUTLER.
COLES.
GIFFARD.
PONSONBY.
NELSON.
SIMPSON.

DEAKIN.
DEWRANCE.
PARRY.
RUSSELL.
COLE.
BURROWS.
BURROWS.
CORNISH.
JONES.
CHERRY.
KEIGHTLEY.
HERBERT.
LOVELESS.
CHAPMAN.
WHITE.
PAGAN.
OGLE.
WEST.
FREND.
FORDER.
SMYTHE.
MASTERMAN.
CORRIE.
BRINTON.
BROWNE.
YARDLEY.
CAMPBELL.
WHITESIDE.
WOOD.
NALDER.
THOMPSON.
BURROWS.
KENNEDY.
KEIGHTLEY.

POCKLINGTON.
LUCAS.
STEWART.
OTTLEY.
ST. GEORGE.
HAY.
NAPIER.
ANTROBUS.
FISHER.
GUNN.
COX.
WILLIAMS.
FRITH.
WINCKWORTH.
STOKES.
POLLOCK.
POLLOCK.
WIGAN.
SEARLE.
CORY.
HUTCHINSON.
BAKER.
RANDALL.
WHINNEY.
WHINNEY.
BEAVAN.
JOHNS.
CASTLE.
STRACHEY.
GROWSE.
———
1873.
WAKE.
SMITH.

LOVEGROVE.
TISDALL.
BANBURY.
LEY.
NICHOLSON.
KEIGHTLEY.
REEVE.
RAINEY.
POLLARD.
DORLING.
COLEBROOKE.
MAC GEORGE.
STAVERT.
STAVERT.
GRIFFITH.
THOMPSON.
VICKERS.
AMES.
SMYTHE.
WHATELEY.
CARTER.
LLOYD.
VANE.
DAVIES.
OLDFIELD.
LEIGH.
LUCY.
VANE.
MARKBY.
SHARP.
HAVELOCK.
YOUNG.
SUTTON.
DE ZOETE.

FINNIMORE.
BLACKETT.
HANSELL.
BOSCAWEN.
WOODHOUSE.
SILLEM.
RASHLEIGH.
RANDOLPH.
CURREY.
KNOLLEYS.
BIRCH.
RAINEY.
GREENE.
WARRE.
COLLIE.
LEWES.
URWICK.
ACLAND.
WEST.
NORRIS.
MAINGAY.
MORGAN.
WYNNE.
MILLER.
BUTT.
SPOONER.
FRASER.
EASTON.
EDDIS.
BADEN POWELL.
GAGE.
HURRELL.
BURDON.
LA FARGUE.

WARREN.
CONEY.
BOURNE.
MILDMAY.
MACARTNEY.
MARSHALL.
GATTY.
COCKBURN.
HOPKINS.
PRANCE.
BUCKLEY.
GILLHAM.
MAYNE.
SEARLE.
JOWERS.
PERKS.
CARPENTER.
DRUCE.
GALPIN.
BARRINGTON.
GREIG.
WOOLWRIGHT.
TROLLOPE.
HICKMAN.
SARGEAUNT.
PALMER.
COMBE.
CAMPBELL.
CHATAWAY.
CHALMERS.
SOMERS COCKS.
DE MOLEYNS.
BUCKLEY.
GAY.

TANNER.
HAYTER.
LAMB.
DENT.
DENT.
HOWARD.
HOWARD.
CORRANCE.
SHOPPEE.
HANSELL.
FINCH-HATTON.
DICKENSON.
COOPE.
HARDMAN.
PERKIN.
SPENCER.
AINSLIE.
WOOD.
DEVENISH.

———

1874.

BROWN.
SURRIDGE.
SURRIDGE.
PATERSON.
REID.
FURBER.
HAINES.
DAVIDSON.
COWIE.
BORTHWICK.
FORDER.
DORLING.
WARRE.

BOYLE.
HOLMAN.
HARPER.
COBB.
HALLWARD.
STEWART.
COOPER.
BERESFORD.
MORRISON.
MORRISON.
EVAN-THOMAS.
WHITEHEAD.
CATHCART.
WARNE.
ARCHDALE.
BARLOW.
BARNETT.
DE BRISAY.
BONNER.
BYNG.
CLIFTON.
CORRIE.
DYNE.
EDWARDS.
EDWARDS.
GALSWORTHY.
GROVES.
HOBBS.
KERR.
PRINSEP.
REECE.
SCOTT.
SOAMES.
STEWART.

List of Carthusians.

STUBBS.	STANLEY.	GRANT.
STUBBS.	TODD.	HALL.
TENNANT.	EGERTON.	LANGDON-DOWN.
WAKEFIELD.	MARSHALL.	CHATFIELD.
WELCH.	CAPEL-CURE.	LIDDELL.
DRUCE.	HAMPSON.	SAPTE.
DEARE.	JENNER.	DRUCE.
TAYLOR.	HARDMAN.	WHITE-COOPER.
HACON.	BATCHELOR.	BLOMFIELD.
PEARCE.	D'EYNCOURT.	MASTER.
MACKINNON.	VYVYAN.	PATERSON.
ESPINASSE.	AINSLIE.	GUTHRIE.
STOVIN.	CARTER.	GARDNER.
HOLT.	SWAINE.	EVELYN.
DANIELL.	SCOTT.	MAUD.
BISHOP.	JOHNSON.	HOLLWAY.
SMITH.	PRINSEP.	ROMAINE.
MANSEL.	EVAN-THOMAS.	MACKENZIE.
JACQUES.	CHEPMELL.	WOOD.
WEBSTER.	FORBES.	BARKWORTH.
HARWOOD.	STANTIAL.	PEAKE.
OLIVER.	DUNCAN.	ANCRUM.
WARREN.	FORBES.	STUART.
SALTMARSHE.	POLEHAMPTON.	WINGFIELD.
CROSSE.	HEDGES.	HAWORTH.
JACKSON.	BORRADAILE.	MEDLICOTT.
BLUNT.	PLUMER.	HAYTER.
RODWELL.	HULL.	BISHOP.
PICKTHALL.	WYNYARD.	OKEDEN.
WEBSTER.	HANSELL.	HODGKINSON.
WEBSTER.	GILLETT.	FARRAR.
CLEEVE.	DUMERGUE.	HATCHARD.
JELLETT.	SPENCE.	WATSON.
STANLEY.	CLARK.	BARROWS.

WAYMOUTH.
ELLIS.
WIX.
KEMBALL.
GUINNESS.
GINSBURG.
NICHOLSON.
DAMES.
DAMES.
ST. LEGER.
SHARP.
POLLOCK.
WALKER.
JONES.
STRONGE.
PERKIN.
PAGET.

1875.
BLUNT.
PARKER.
POWELL.
WOODGATE.
JACKSON.
EADY.
VORES.
CRASTER.
MASTER.
POLLOCK.
ROBINSON.
HARINGTON.
PONSONBY.
MILLER.
DOUGLAS.

OXLEY.
BENNETT.
SMITH.
SIMMONS.
MAN.
BURTON.
TAYLOR.
MACKNESS.
CHOLMELEY.
JOHNSTON.
WILKINSON.
DEMPSEY.
SMITH.
DOWN.
WILSON.
KENT.
STAVERT.
BOURNE.
PIERSON.
MCNEILL.
ROBINSON.
GLASGOW.
DUNCAN.
COOPER.
GREEN.
NORRIS.
SMITH.
ROBERTS.
TUCKER.
GREY.
IVATT.
DAY.
DEVEY.
GREENWAY.

COLE.
BOWER.
SLADE.
MACKENZIE.
TWIST.
LATHAM.
BAXENDALE.
COLT.
LINZEE.
DAVIS.
AMES.
CASS.
SMITH.
MARSHALL.
ENGLEHEART.
GOVETT.
MAC GEE.
WAGGETT.
STUTFIELD.
STANHOPE.
CAVENDISH.
COCKSHOTT.
STIRLING.
WALTON.
APTHORP.
WAKE.
SKIRROW.
LAST.
PEARCE.
SIBLEY.
MORGAN.
STARLING.
STARLING.
SOUTHWELL.

x

PRINSEP.
BROWN.
NAPIER.
SHEPPARD.
MALDEN.
FOX-STRANGWAYS
GUILLEMARD.
KEITH-FALCONER
KEITH-FALCONER
CAMPION.
CATHCART.
SHORE SMITH.
STORY.
COLVIN.
HULTON.
JAMES.
GUINNESS.
FRERE.
LYON.
PARKES.
SALTWELL.
BACON.
CONGREVE.
GANDELL.
COCKSHOTT.
POORE.
GREENWAY.
PIKE.
MEE.
WICKHAM.
JACKSON.
RUTTER.
WEST.
GONNE.

GIBBONS.
ENGLAND.
RODEWALD.
HOLLAND.
SOMERS COCKS.
HENLEY.
SISMEY.
SALMON.
BURD.
DAVIES.
KIRKPATRICK.
YOUNG.
LOWNDES.
ROKEBY.
RICHARDS.
LEAKE.
MACTAGGART.
SANDARS.
MONCKTON.
BIRCH.
RANDOLPH.
DAVIS.
MARSHALL.
HAYES.
HEAD.
HEAD.
CLAPCOTT.
LEWIS.
CLEVELAND.
MALCOLMSON.
ERSKINE.
WELCH.
BARNETT.
MARSHALL.

CLEEVE.
TRAPMANN.
ROTHERHAM.
FALCON.
DEAS.
DYSON.
HEWETT.
ROSE.
CURREY.
CHATTERTON.
AINGER.

1876.

MITCHELL.
GILLING-LAX.
HARLAND.
TYACKE.
KEATE.
RUSSELL.
REEVES.
GARDNER.
WILSON.
STANTON.
JACKSON.
HUNTER.
ORR.
CLEMENTS.
MONCKTON.
MATCHAM.
PHILLIPS.
SANT.
PROBYN.
MACDONALD.
DU CANE.

List of Carthusians.

MACLAGAN.	STEWART.	FISHER.
TENNANT.	STRICKLAND.	BROOKS.
WHITELEY.	SWIRE.	STREATFEILD.
CONNOP.	WILLIAMS-WYNN	HARRISON.
SCRATTON.	WATERFIELD.	LEA.
DOBBIE.	WRIGHT.	LEACH.
AINGER.	MCCONNEL.	SUGDEN.
WRIGHT.	HAMILTON.	RAWSON.
MUNRO.	DICKINSON.	TWENTYMAN.
HAWKINS.	PATTESON.	ERSKINE.
ABRAHAM.	VIAN.	MORRIS.
BROADWOOD.	BINGLEY.	ROBERTSON.
CLARKE.	HANKEY.	PICKTHORN.
COOPER.	HARRISON.	HUBAND.
FOSTER.	CROWE.	WILKINSON.
GIBSON.	BOMPAS.	MILLER.
HUGHES.	HARRISON.	COOPER.
HOPWOOD.	HULKES.	KOE.
HERIOT.	EDIS.	MACPHERSON.
JONES.	ROKEBY.	RAWSON.
LAWRENCE.	GROOM.	LAST.
MORGAN.	HAYTER.	BARLOW.
MAUD.	RYLANDS.	FOSTER.
NEWILL.	GREEN.	WILSON.
NORRIS.	HEWETT.	CAYLEY.
NICHOLSON.	YATES.	HAMMOND.
NELSON.	WATSON.	MESSENT.
POLLOCK.	MAY.	FOX.
POLLOCK.	CHOLMELEY.	WALTERS.
PERKIN.	CAUTLEY.	MCCONNEL.
ROUTH.	LECKIE.	COOK.
RAYNER.	WHITE.	HALL.
SHORT.	WAKE.	SANDERS.
SPURWAY.	SMITH.	BARWELL.

CAMPBELL.	HAMILTON.	GLEICHEN.
BROWN.	VENABLES.	MILNE.
DU CANE.	BLUNT.	LOCKER.
FRASER.	PERRY.	WEBBER.
HOLLWAY.	KAYESS.	GODFREY.
HEATON.	ESCOMBE.	EMERIS.
HUNT.	JUPP.	MAGNIAC.
KEPPEL.	WELDON.	MALCOLMSON.
LIPSCOMB.	MC NEILL.	MCCONAGHEY.
RUTTER.	FAIRLIE.	COWPER-SMITH.
LISTER.	LANGLEY.	SANDYS.
SOUTH.	DRAKE.	HOW.
HELME.	EDWARDS.	MILNER.
FOSTER.	EVANS.	MURRAY.
BOMPAS.	HOWARD.	SISMEY.
BUCKINGHAM.	MACPHERSON.	SMITH.
MARSHALL.	TOMBS.	WADHAM.
WRIGHT.	WELDON.	WISDOM.
SMITH.	GURDON.	WARING.
INGRAM.	WRIGHT.	SANDERS.
WETHERED.	BLENKIRON.	WEBER.
ALISON.	ENGLAND.	FAIR.
DES VOEUX.	HUGHES.	BENSLEY.
SECKHAM.	SMITH.	DOUGLAS.
VERSTURME.	SPRING RICE.	DYSON.
BIRCH.	GALSWORTHY.	FURBER.
WRIGHT.	GILLETT.	VENABLES.
	BARMBY.	WADHAM.
1877.	TAUNTON.	SMITH.
FRERE.	FRITH.	MATTHEY.
COBBOLD.	LAX.	WALKER.
STEPHENS.	KEELING.	BERESFORD.
GIBSON.	BLAKESLEY.	WALTER.
AMOS.	FINCH.	BALFOUR.

CAMPBELL.
BOWLBY.
GORDON.
OWEN.
PAYNTER.
VINTCENT.
RAIKES.
WARD.
COWIE.
BARMBY.
CROPPER.
EWING.
NORRIS.
RAYNER.
PINHEY.
WADHAM.
VINTCENT.
LEWIS.
DAWSON.
TAYLOR.
ST. GEORGE.
NICHOLSON.
STEVENS.
STORY.
ELLIOT.
MAUDE.
WILLIAMS.
KING-HARMAN.
TUCKER.
HOLMES.
SMITH.
OXLEY.
HARRISON.
MONCKTON.

EWING.
BUTLER.
PRINSEP.
FERGUSON.
SMITH.
POLLOCK.
SINCLAIR.
WALTERS.
EDEN.
RANDOLPH.
CLEAVER.
TRISTRAM.
PEAKE.

———

1878.

WEIR.
LATTER.
ADAMS.
WEBB-WARE.
MILLIKEN.
PARRY.
POPHAM.
LOWTHER.
BOGER.
BARROWS.
YOUNG.
PEEL.
SOMERSET.
ARCHDALE.
MUNRO.
ILES.
BROWN.
THORNEYCROFT.
BEALE.

CHATAWAY.
JENNEY.
WHITE.
RAYNER.
TEMPLER.
KING.
GRABHAM.
DEMPSEY.
WILSON.
PELLY.
LANE.
BENSLEY.
SEWELL.
SCOTT.
HEAD.
MORLAND.
MORLAND.
BOYLE.
CARR.
JENNER.
MERCER.
OWTRAM.
GRIFFITH.
WEARE.
MANTELL.
GONNE.
WALLACE.
EARDLEY.
DINGWALL.
GIRDLESTONE.
GREEN.
DIXON.
HERIOT.
MAINGAY.

List of Carthusians.

PARKES.	MACONOCHIE.	WADDINGTON.
SECHIARI.	WILSON.	LATHAM.
CURWEN.	MCGILDOWNEY.	DICKINSON.
FAULKNER.	DARBY.	BOISRAGON.
HOBBS.	TUCKER.	BARNETT.
MILNER.	MASTERS.	PONSONBY.
PERRINS.	BUSHE-FOX.	TROUGHTON.
WALTERS.	STEWARD.	SOMERS-COCKS.
PINCKNEY.	JACQUES.	WHETHAM.
JOHNSON.	HERON.	MARTEN.
BRAUND.	FAIRLIE.	TRISTRAM.
NEED.	JACKSON.	HUMPHREYS.
KEENE.	CLIFTON.	BORRADAILE.
PEARCE.	BARKER.	BELL.
WAGGETT.	HANBURY.	ANCRUM.
TEMPLER.	GULICH.	SMITH.
WHARTON.	JOHNSTON.	HAYDON.
KNOX.	RIDLEY.	WILD.
NEWSON.	STRIDE.	LEACH.
JOYCE.	CROPPER.	BULLOCK.
SMITH.	THOMPSON.	HORNE.
CANE.	RADCLIFFE.	HAWKS.
POLLOCK.	ELLIS.	GARNETT.
CAPEL.	EDDIS.	HUNTER.
CAUTLEY.	BARTON.	TOMKIN.
COKAYNE.	ST. AUBYN.	LEGGE.
EBDEN.	TAYLOR.	MORSE.
RAM.	WISE.	ROTHERHAM.

Farncombe & Co., Printers, Lewes.

www.ingramcontent.com/pod-product-compliance
Lightning Source LLC
Chambersburg PA
CBHW022043230426
43672CB00008B/1051